Cracker Cavaliers

John R. Poole

The publication of this book

is due in part to a grant from the

John and Mary Franklin Foundation.

Cracker Cavaliers

The 2nd Georgia Cavalry under Wheeler and Forrest

John Randolph Poole

Mercer University Press, 2000

ISBN 0-86554-697-5
MUP/H516

© 2000 Mercer University Press
6316 Peake Road
Macon, Georgia 31210-3960
All rights reserved

First Edition.

∞The paper used in this publication meets the minimum require-
ments of American National Standard for Information Sciences—
Permanence of Paper for Printed Library Materials, ANSI Z39.48-
1984.

Library of Congress Cataloging-in-Publication Data

CIP data are available from the Library of Congress

Preface

In 1861, many young men thought they would find glory in the cavalry. They would soon learn, like warriors in other ages, that glory is not something experienced in battle, but something perceived by others who were not there.

The great battles of the Civil War were fought mostly by infantry. Cavalry usually participated, as they did at Murfreesboro on the last day of 1862, but their numbers were relatively small in comparison with the infantry. The cavalry's role was to provide information to infantry commanders, to carry out raids on enemy communications and supply lines, to protect the flanks of the infantry, and to cover any withdrawal of the infantry. It was a never-ending task. While the infantryman might have long periods of relative inactivity between battles, the cavalryman's work was constant.

If the cavalrymen rarely charged *en masse* into the teeth of enemy artillery and infantry, they nevertheless had important, dangerous work to do, especially in the Western Theater. Without Wheeler's effective cavalry work, Bragg's army might have been destroyed in Kentucky during 1862, or at Tullahoma, Tennessee, in 1863. During 1864, Confederate cavalry were vital to Johnston's defensive tactics above Atlanta. The 2nd Georgia Cavalry was in the thick of all of this action.

The men of the 2nd Georgia, like all Confederate cavalrymen in the Western Theater, were usually poorly armed, poorly fed, poorly clothed, and in the latter stages, poorly mounted. As a general rule, the Federal cavalry that opposed them was far better armed and equipped. Moreover, the Union troopers were as tough and determined as the southerners, and often there were more of them.

Technically, a regiment should have had 1,000 men, but when the 2nd Georgia rode off for its first engagement, there were only 450 men in the ranks. Very likely, there were never that many men in the regiment again. Unfortunately, there is very little surviving information specifically related to the activities of the regiment. However, the regiment's history can be traced through its brigade and division commands. It is a history that parallels the experiences of the Army of Tennessee.

While the purpose of this book is to relate the experiences of the 2nd Georgia Cavalry Regiment, there are several instances where the narrative goes beyond the 2nd Georgia experience. This is done to ensure a proper perspective on the importance of the regiment's contributions and a better understanding of its role. For instance, the regiment's participation in the fighting at Sunshine Church is best understood if one is familiar with all of the action in Stoneman's raid.

Records reveal 1,324 men who served in the 2nd Georgia Cavalry during the course of the war, but those records are undoubtedly incomplete. Information on individual soldiers in the regiment is sketchy. Service records are almost non-existent for 1865, except for the surrender in April. There is enough information, however, to glimpse the hardships and suffering of these men, who fought on long after they realized they could not win.

> *In the last decade of the twentieth century, when Buddy Strickland was approaching middle age, he had an unforgettable dream. He dreamt that, across a room, he saw a man who looked exactly like him. He walked over and extended his hand, saying, "Hello, I'm William Perry Strickland." The familiar stranger replied, "I know. I'm Henry Perry Strickland, and I am you and you are me."*

Gen. Nathan Bedford Forrest, first brigade commander over the 2nd Georgia Cavalry.

Photo courtesy of Hargrett Rare Book and Manuscript Library, University of Georgia Libraries.

Gen. Joseph Wheeler, Chief of Cavalry for the Army of Tennessee.

Photo courtesy of Hargrett Rare Book and Manuscript Library, University of Georgia Libraries.

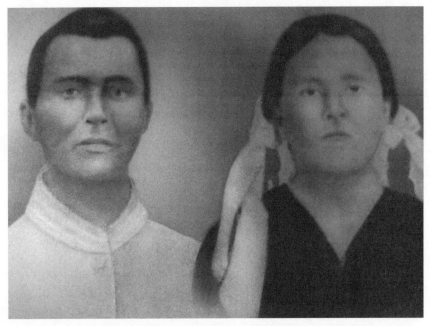

Cpl. Henry Perry Strickland and Mary Mundy on their wedding day, Nov. 21, 1864.

Courtesty of A. H. Hurd.

Col. Charles Constantine Crews of Cuthbert, commander of the 2nd Georgia Cavalry Regiment, and later the Georgia Cavalry Brigade.

Photo courtesy of A. H. Hurd.

Lee & Gordon's Mill, scene of heavy fighting during the Battle of Chickamauga, including a conflict involving the 2nd Georgia Cavalry.

Parson's Battery, 4th U.S. Artillery, H Company and M Company near the Union center at the Battle of Stones River. This battery of four 3" Ordinance rifles and four 12-pounder howitzers helped the Union center stand firm after the right had been driven back, December 31, 1862.

Monument on the Farmington battle site.

Fair Garden, Tennessee near Sevierville, where the 2nd Georgia suffered numerous casualties during the Knoxville Campaign in the winter of 1864.

ROBERT McAFEE HOUSE

After the seizure of Big Shanty (Kennesaw), by Sherman's forces, June 9, 1864, Brig. Gen. Kenner Garrard's cav. div. ☰ was posted on the left flank during operations on the Kennesaw Mountain front.

Garrard's cav. guarded Noonday Creek valley from Woodstock to the left of the 17th A. C. (in the rugged Brushy Mtn. area), with patrols on the Canton, Bell's Ferry & Alabama roads. Daily conflict with his opponent - Maj. Gen. Joseph Wheeler's Cavalry ☰ - marked the period from June 11 to July 3.

The Robert McAfee house was Garrard's h'dq'rs. during a portion of this period.

The Robert McAfee House on Bells' Ferry Road in Cobb County was headquarters for General Kenner Garrard's Union Cavalry for a time, and the surrounding area was the site of several cavalry conflicts involving the 2nd Georgia. McAfee House historical marker.

A re-enactment of the Brown's Mill battle, near the actual site of the July 1864 battle. Although it was a conflict between opposing cavalry forces, much of the fighting was done on foot.

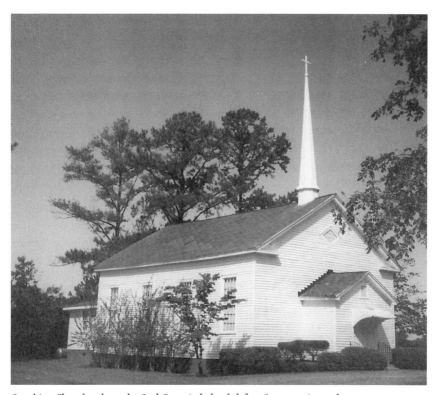

Sunshine Church, where the 2nd Georgia helped defeat Stoneman's cavalry.

Postwar photograph of Joseph D. Story,
pvt., G Company.

*Photo courtesy of Francis J. O'Neal
Collection at USAMHI*

Postwar photograph of William H. Morgan, cpl., I Company.

Photo courtesy of Della M. Martin Collection at USAMHI.

Postwar photograph of William H. Morgan, cpl., I Company, on right. On left is John T. Morgan, Pvt., K Company, 30th Georgia Infantry.

Photo courtesy of Della M. Martin Collection at USAMHI.

Pvt. Garrett L. Wesley, E Company.

Photo courtesy of Mary Ellen Lowery Collection at USAMHI.

Moses Mills

Photo courtesy of John William Worsham and Gail Pitt

Pvt. John H. Adams, bugler for Company K, was a 26-year old native of Decatur County when he joined the 2nd Georgia Cavalry.

Photo courtesy of Ida K. Boyce

Cracker Cavaliers

The tensions gripping Georgia in 1860 extended all the way down to Cainey Strickland's farm on the Flint River in Clayton County. His young neighbor, Moses Mills, was also troubled by the talk of secession and war.

Moderate leaders Robert Toombs of the Georgia Whigs and Howell Cobb of the Democratic Party had come over to side with the fire-eaters, and public sentiment for secession was high. Cainey Strickland and Moses Mills were part of a minority who questioned the conventional wisdom. With four grown sons and no slaves, Strickland had little to gain and much to lose if war came.[1] Mills had four slaves, but he "saw the hand of God" in the abolition movement.[2]

On 19 January 1861, Georgia seceded from the Union, and on 12 April, the first shots of the Civil War were fired at Fort Sumter in Charleston. In July came news of a great Confederate victory at Manassas, Virginia, and some observers thought the fighting might be over. It soon became apparent, however, that a longer conflict was coming.

After the crops came in that fall, local cavalry companies emerged in several Georgia counties. In Clayton County, recently partitioned from Fayette County, Capt. Francis Thompson Gayden formed the Clayton Dragoons, and the young men began to come in from the farms. One of those who joined the company was Moses Mills. Although he thought freeing the slaves would be a "blessing to whites as well" [as blacks], Mills felt strongly about Georgia's right to choose its own destiny. He thought, too, that there was "…much of envy and jealousy over the prosperity of the South…." [3]

Also joining the Clayton Dragoons on the last day of October were three of Cainey Strickland's sons. The two youngest, Cary and Henry, were still living on the family farm. Milsey Strickland came up from Pike County to join his brothers in the company, which now also included Henry's close friend, Reuben Mundy. (The eldest of the Strickland brothers, Charles, would join the 44th Georgia Infantry the following summer.)

For the most part, the men in these new calvary companies were not the "sons of rich lawyers and planters" described by General William Tecumseh Sherman. That may have been an apt description for the aristocratic cavaliers in Virginia's mounted regiments, but the men in the Clayton County company came mostly from modest farms and small towns. And, they were typical of the men in other companies that later formed the 2nd Georgia Cavalry. They ranged in age from sixteen to sixty-three, but most were in their twenties One of the privates, James Henderson Waldrop, had just completed a term as Clayton County's first sheriff.[4] Several of the new troopers were ministers, and at least one, Pvt. John T. Lamar, was a physician. Although Lamar served as assistant regimental surgeon during 1863, he apparently spent most of his service in the ranks.[5]

The piety and patriotism of their families were revealed in their names, as biblical names abounded. Many others were named after heroes of the revolution—Thomas Jefferson, George Washington, Patrick Henry, Benjamin Franklin, and, most popular of all, Francis Marion, the southern guerilla fighter of the Revolution.[6]

In many ways, the Strickland brothers were typical recruits. They were all in their twenties, with Henry, the youngest, having just reached his twentieth birthday the previous spring. They came from modest farms, they were Protestants whose ancestors came from England, and they served alongside their close friends and relatives.

In other ways the Stricklands were not so typical, as they joined the company despite their father's strong objections to the war. Also, they did not fit the physical mold of the wiry cavalryman. Milsey was almost 6'2" tall,[7] and Henry was above average height and sturdily built. Grandchildren and Mundy descendants remember stories of Henry's physical strength and toughness that stretch the imagination.[8]

Although Henry was elected corporal soon after enlisting, the Stricklands, like most of their comrades, endured the next three years with no improvement in rank. A January 1865 report of the Inspector General decried the lack of promotions among cavalry troopers in the Army of Tennessee. "Recommendations have frequently been made for the promotion of men and subalterns upon the ground of conspicuous personal skill and gallantry, under the provisions of the act of Congress, but thus far, as I learn from General Wheeler, they have not met in a single instance with favorable consideration of the War Department. It is a matter of regret that the reward of merit and heroism has thus been withheld."[9]

Another common thread for the Stricklands and their comrades was that they all served alongside their brothers, cousins, friends, and neighbors. Most Civil War companies were formed in counties, and combined with companies from neighboring counties to form regiments. Even a casual look at the rosters in the various cavalry companies shows that the units were full of brothers and cousins. The close knit nature of these units may explain why so many Civil War soldiers, North and South, so often displayed almost unbelievable courage. Not only were they fighting for the friends and relatives who were their comrades, they were fighting for their own reputations and status in the community.

It is unlikely that very many of the men in the company shared Moses Mills' view that the hand of God was in the freeing of the slaves. It is equally unlikely, however, that the slavery question was a significant motivator for very many of the men. Like Cainey Strickland, most had no slaves. It was the universal view of the Rebel soldiers, however, that their State had a right to control its own future. The matter of "states rights" was even more important than the Confederacy. Indeed, most felt they were the true guardians of the independence won by other rebels in the Revolutionary War. In their view, the independence won in 1783 left thirteen independent states. Those sovereign states had "…come together in 1787, as principals, to create a federal government as their agent, giving it specific delegated authority—specified in our Constitution. Principals always retain the right to fire their agent. The South acted on that right when it seceded."[10]

In Georgia, this sentiment was nurtured by Governor Joe Brown who had no more use for the Confederate government than for the U.S. government in Washington. Brown spoke openly of an independent

State of Georgia, and favored his own state militia over the Confederate military.

The Southern cavalrymen shared not only their forefathers' vision of independence, but also their disdain for military discipline. Just as those colonial soldiers of an earlier generation would simply go home without leave to handle personal, family, or business matters, so too would the Rebel cavalryman. Henry and Cary Strickland took such personal time in November of 1864 to get married.

Surviving muster rolls show more than 100 men of the 2nd Georgia Cavalry as "Away Without Leave" at some point in the war. Records show that fully one-third returned to duty, but that number is almost certainly incomplete. It is interesting to note that the regiment's company commanders seemed to know at once which soldiers were merely AWOL and which were deserters. The absence of most would be recorded as AWOL, while a few were listed as deserters on their first day of absence.[11]

The independence of the untested Southern cavalrymen in 1861 was matched only by their naivete. Hadn't the victory at Manassas demonstrated that the war would soon be over? Were the recruits of that October too late to share in the glory?

---

1 Clayton County tax and census records (Atlanta GA: Georgia Department of Archives and History).

2 Mamie Elrod, *Life as I Recall It, or Sunshine and Shadows on a Long Trek,* unpublished memoir, ca. 1941.

3 Ibid.

4 Joseph H. H. Moore, *History of Clayton County, Georgia 1821-1983* (W.H. Wolf Associates, 1983).

5 Personal Papers file, drawer 253, Box 30, (Atlanta GA; Georgia Department of Archives and History).

6 Compiled Service Records, 2nd Georgia Cavalry (Atlanta, GA: Georgia Department of Archives and History).

7 Ibid.

8 Joe Mundy, William E. Strickland, Charles Strickland, Sara Strickland Poole, Doris Strickland Wilcox, recollections.

9 W.C. Dodson, ed. *The Campaigns of Wheeler and His Cavalry* (Jackson TN: The Guild Bindery Press) 417.

10 Walter Williams, *Macon Telegraph* @ 1995 (Macon GA).

11 Compiled Service Records, 2nd Georgia Cavalry.

A Regiment Is Born

In February of 1862, the Clayton Dragoons were one of four cavalry companies that moved to Camp Stephens in Albany, Georgia, joining with Captain Winburn Lawton to form the beginnings of a new regiment. Lawton and his Dougherty Hussars had transferred from the Army of Northern Virginia, where they were D Company of the cavalry battalion in Cobb's Georgia Legion. In addition to the Clayton Dragoons and his own company, it appears that Lawton now had with him Captain Charles Crews' company from Randolph and Calhoun counties, Captain George Looney's Campbell County company, and Captain James Mayo's company of men from Dougherty and neighboring Mitchell, Baker, and Lee counties.[1]

In March or April, the five companies moved to Camp McDonald at Big Shanty, (now Kennesaw) some twenty-five miles north of Atlanta. Camp McDonald was the largest training facility in Georgia, and many other new units were encamped there.[2] One of the new recruits for the regiment during this period was Andrew J. Vickers. Vickers had been authorized by the War Department to raise a regiment, and had done so, assembling the unit at Camp McDonald. When members of the regiment did not elect him colonel, Vickers enlisted as a private in Captain George Looney's I Company of Lawton's new regiment, and served in that capacity throughout the war.[3]

On 9 April, Secretary of war George W. Randolph wrote T. R. R. Cobb that he had spoken with the President and was "…authorized to say that you can increase your infantry and cavalry to eight companies...." Randolph noted that this would leave one cavalry company unattached, which could be "...united with the five raised by Captain W. J. Lawton to assist in forming his regiment." [4] While it appears no additional company was transferred from Cobb's Legion, several officers from that command did move that April to the fledgling regiment. Some time in April or early May, five new companies were added, and by 6 May the 2nd Georgia Volunteer Cavalry Regiment was complete.

The five new companies, which soon became Companies D, E, G, H, and K, had been training since March at Camp Ector, one mile south of Griffin in Spalding County, Georgia.[5]

With the completion of the regiment, Lawton became a colonel. His regimental staff at this point apparently included Lt. Col. Arthur Hood, Adjutant R.F. Lawton, and surgeons James L. D. Perryman and James Shorpshire. Quartermaster Sgt. Isaac Carter and Assistant Quartermaster Sgt. James A. Hill were added later, promoted from the Clayton and Spalding County companies.[6]

Another member of the regimental staff was Lt. Col. J. B. "Bee" Eberhardt, but his role and dates of service are unclear. He is recorded as being present at the surrender, and may have served as regimental commander for the last month of the war.[7]

The ten companies with their counties of origin and their commanders as of 6 May 1862, are shown below, as recorded in the Georgia Department of Archives.[8]

A Company—Randolph and Calhoun Counties —Capt.Charles Constantine Crews—Thirty-one year-old Crews was soon promoted to serve on the regimental staff, and would later command both the regiment and the brigade. His successor as company commander was Capt. Bennett Bridges. Both Bridges and twenty-one year-old 2nd Lt. J. Fleming Crews were wounded at Dover in February of 1863. Although there is no record of who commanded the company immediately after Dover, it very likely was 1st Lt. John Trippe. Trippe was discharged with a disability in October of 1863, and was apparently replaced by young Crews, now recovered from his wound. Fleming Crews was promoted to captain in October of 1864, and served until the end of the war.

B Company—Dougherty County—Capt. Winburn J. Lawton— Ironically, very few records exist on Capt. Lawton's Dougherty Hussars. There is no record of who succeeded Lawton as company commander after he moved on to command the regiment, but it may have been 1st

Lt. G. J. Wright. Only twenty-nine men are identified, either in the Compiled Service Records or by the Georgia Roster Commission, as members of the company. Other officers in the company were 2nd Lt. J. F. Marshall, 2nd Lt. C. H. Canfield, and 3rd Lt. Robert Stith Parham.

C Company—Mitchell, Dougherty, Baker, and Lee Counties—Capt. James W. Mayo—With prior service as a 2nd Lt. in Cobb's Legion, Mayo was promoted to major in April 1863. He commanded the regiment in the summer of 1864 until he was seriously wounded during the Battle of Atlanta. First Lt. Peter Twitty was promoted to Captain and succeeded Mayo as company commander until his capture in January of 1864. Capt. W. C. Hood then took over command of C Company for the remainder of the war.

D Company—Walton and Monroe Counties—Capt. William D. Grant. Grant was later succeeded by Capt. Robert R. Mitchell, formerly a 2nd lieutenant in the Company. Mitchell was wounded and captured in January of 1864, and the former 1st Sgt., Capt. James Shepard apparently took over command of the company.

E Company—Spalding County, the "Ben Milner Dragoons"—Capt. Francis M. Ison. Ison was promoted to major and apparently served as a regimental staff officer before becoming regimental commander as a lieutenant colonel in March of 1863. 1st Lt. Thomas J. Brooks was promoted to captain and succeeded Ison as company commander. Robert Thompson succeeded Brooks and served as company commander briefly until felled by illness. His apparent successors were two former privates who rose from the ranks. James F. Fambro was promoted to captain and probably assumed command of the company in June of 1863. Captain James Ellis was serving at the surrender.

F Company—Clayton County, the Clayton Dragoons—Capt. W. Hardy Chapman—Chapman was elected captain and company commander 6 May 1862, to replace Capt. Gayden who retired. Capt. Chapman served until his resignation with a disability in February of 1865. There is no clear record of his successor. Gayden later became a 1st lieutenant in the cavalry of the Georgia State Guards. Lt. Joseph Franklin Johnson also retired in May due to being "over age." He was replaced by James Elijah DeVaughn, who transferred from another unit. Although a resident of Montezuma in Macon County, DeVaughn was originally from Clayton County where his parents owned a plantation a mile east of Jonesboro on what is now Lake Jodeco Road. DeVaughn was captured at Sugar Creek, Tennessee 9 October 1863, so he could not have taken over the company after Chapman's retirement. It appears, however, that he was promoted to captain and commanded a company prior to his capture. Twenty-four-year-old Benjamin Camp was promoted from 1st sergeant to 2nd lieutenant, and may have replaced Chapman as company commander in the closing weeks of the war, although he was shown as in the hospital with "abcesses" on the roll of December, 1864.

G Company—Baker, Calhoun, Chatham, Dougherty, Henry, Lee, Marion, Muscogee, Randolph, Spalding, Sumter, Talbot, Terrell, Upson, and Webster counties—Capt. Thomas H. Jordan—Jordan was killed on 1 August 1863, and succeeded by Capt. Thomas M. Merritt. One of the privates in Merritt's company was his nephew, R. M. Fletcher of Butts County, who enlisted 1 March 1864. G Company served much of the war as escort for Gen. Benjamin Franklin Cheatham, and therefore had very different experiences from other companies in the Regiment. Twice wounded, Cheatham was regarded as a capable, hard-fighting officer. He commanded infantry at the brigade, division, and corps level at various times. Service as his escort was not particularly "safe" or easy duty, as evidenced by Jordan's death.

H Company—Fulton and DeKalb counties, the Magruder Dragoons—Capt. Caleb Arthur Whaley—Whaley was promoted to major with the rank dated to 6 May 1862, implying a later date for the actual promotion. Whaley may have replaced a regimental staff officer wounded at Murfreesboro 13 July. When the Regiment was split after Lawton's resignation during the Kentucky campaign, Whaley commanded four of the companies in a "battalion" under Joe Wheeler. It appears likely that, for a brief period before his death, he commanded the Regiment when it was reunited. He was succeeded as commander of H Company first by Capt. Oliver Winningham and then by L. S. Mead and Francis M. Allen, both of whom were promoted to captain after serving as 1st lieutenants.

I Company —Campbell County—Capt. George C. Looney—Campbell County, which no longer exists, was located in what is now extreme south Fulton County, with the City of Fairburn as county seat. Although he remained a captain, Looney was the last recorded commander of the 2nd Georgia, being assigned to that task in January of 1865 and serving at least into March. It is not clear who replaced him as company commander, but it seems likely that 1st Lt. Thomas P. Dean became commander of I Company without being promoted to captain.

K Company —Decatur County—Capt. James E. Dunlop—1st Lt. James A. Butts was promoted to captain and apparently replaced Dunlop as company commander when the latter took over the Regiment late in 1862. Butts resigned his commission in August of 1863, and it is not clear who replaced him as company commander.

The Regiment apparently mustered into Confederate service on or about 6 May 1862, as that date is given on some records as an enlistment date for many of the original volunteers in the various companies.[9]

While the five companies of the 2nd Georgia were in training at Camp McDonald, a small Federal raiding party, dressed as civilians, stole a locomotive at Big Shanty and struck out to destroy Confederate rail lines. The Anderson Raiders of the "Great Locomotive Chase" were soon captured and imprisoned in Atlanta. Lt. DeVaughn of F Company was assigned responsibility for the Provost detail that hung the raiders on June 27.[10] The detail was apparently drawn from the men of the five companies at Camp McDonald.[11]

Camp life carried special dangers in a war where one of every thirteen soldiers died of disease. Surviving muster roles for the 2nd Georgia show just seven men as dying and six others as being discharged with disabilities in camp before the regiment went into active service. However, there are some 126 names on those muster roles for whom there is no record beyond their enlistment, and very likely some of these succumbed to training camp maladies. While there were undoubtedly some training accidents, most of the recorded deaths were attributed to disease. Throughout the war, disease was predictably the major cause of casualties among these men who lived through oppressive heat, numbing winters, and torrential rains for three years, while rarely sleeping under even a canvas roof. Surviving records show only about fifty men as being sent to the hospital during the war, but that is almost certainly an incomplete count.[12]

None of the training camp deaths are attributed to accidental gunshot wounds, and it appears that training for the Regiment did not involve very much live firing of weapons.[13] In fact, as late as 2 July 1862, the Regiment was described as "unarmed" by Secretary of War Randolph.[14] Although the men likely had a variety of personal weapons, ammunition would probably have been in too short supply to allow any extensive live fire exercises.

Like the weapons, the horses were also brought from home, so horse and rider were well acquainted with each other. In 1862 the value of their horses ranged from $75 to $300, with most set at about $200, and the men were to be compensated for the use and risk of the horse. This dependence on individually-owned horses would later prove to be a serious impediment to the readiness of the Rebel cavalry, but in the early part of the war it generally meant that the Confederate trooper was better mounted than his Union adversary. While the Southerner brought his hand-picked mount to the fight, the Northerner was often dependent on a poor quality horse sold to the government by some unscrupulous agent. A few of the men in the 2nd Georgia were riding borrowed horses. Randolph County provided horses for some of the men in A Company, as did Captain Crews and a few other officers.[15]

Even in the closing months of the war, the Inspector General was "agreeably surprised" to find the mounts of Wheeler's men to be well cared for, if a bit thin. The IG's report did reveal that "not a few" of Wheeler's men had been forced to use mules when replacing their lost horses.[16]

If the southerners had an early advantage in horseflesh, it was more than offset by their appalling lack of effective military weapons. The Union cavalry carried breech-loading Sharps carbines, Colt revolving rifles, and later, seven-shot Spencers, as well as Colt Navy revolvers or the Remington New Army. Spencer repeaters were in common enough supply to become a huge advantage for the Union cavalry in the second half of the war. The popularity of these weapons among the blue troopers is illustrated by the October 1864 reaction of the 14th Illinois upon learning that the promised repeaters would not be issued. When the men of the regiment learned they would have to take the field with Springfield muskets, many smashed the weapons against trees and the regiment mutinied.[17] A surprising number of the Southern cavalrymen, on the other hand, had no weapons at all. A great many carried shotguns, practically useless except at very close quarters.

As the war progressed, some Rebel horsemen were able to replace their shotguns with captured Yankee carbines. By late 1864 there were "...a great many fair Spencer rifles, and other breech-loading weapons of a superior character..." in use among Wheeler's troopers. Unfortunately for their new owners, however, the steel cartridges for these weapons were so hard to come by that they were often useless. The January 1865 inspector general's report on Wheeler's Cavalry by Col. C. C. Jones, Jr. noted that "The principal weapons in the hands of the men are the long and short Enfield rifle, the Springfield musket, the Austrian rifle, a variety of breech-loading rifles, viz.: the Spencer, the Burnside, Sharp, Maynard…and various kinds of pistols.[18] The short Enfields were perhaps the most common weapon among Wheeler's men.[19] These were effective weapons, but like all muzzle loaders, not particularly well suited for mounted actions. Col. Jones urged that the cavalrymen be equipped uniformly with Spencers and supplied with ammunition from the Richmond arsenal.[20] Even if the War Department had acted on this recommendation, it came too late.

Nathan Bedford Forrest told his enlisted men early in the war to forego the saber and, if possible, arm themselves with two pistols. But, until 1863, most of the men in the 2nd Georgia had no pistol, a weapon that was almost essential for mounted operations.[21] The lack of sidearms is probably the reason that members of the 2nd Georgia clung to sabers longer than the men who remained under Forrest. The Colt Navy .36 and the Remington New Army—or Confederate-made copies—eventually became the most common sidearms,[22] though a bewildering variety of pistols were in use right up to the end of the war.[23]

By 1864, most of Wheeler's men had abandoned their sabers, finding them to be of little value and a hindrance when operating out of trenches like infantry, as they frequently did in the Atlanta campaign. Col. Jones' report urged that "At least one regiment in each brigade should be armed with pistols and sabers" and used as a reserve for mounted charges.[24]

Like other cavalrymen North and South, the men of the 2nd Georgia traveled light. Their saddles were mostly the lightweight McClellan Model 1859, although a few may have had the "Mexian" or Texas model favored by their Lone Star comrades. Even most of the officers rejected martingales, breast straps, double reins, and other fancy accouterments.[25] Rolled blanket and poncho were usually carried on the saddle, as cavalrymen often did not see their brigade wagons for days at a time.

The 2nd Georgia trooper carried his rifle or shotgun not in a saddle boot, but slung over his back on a leather strap, usually barrel down. By 1863, most carried a handgun or two, more likely stuck in a belt than carried in a holster. On his belt the cavalryman hoped to have a cartridge box and a pouch for percussion caps. Some of the men were never issued these items, however, and many others lost them to wear and incessant soakings with rainwater. Replacements were hard to come by, and many of the troopers had to carry their ammunition in pockets, haversacks, and saddlebags. There the ammunition would mingle with a tin mess kit, two spare horseshoes, a few nails and a small hammer, along with spare shirt, socks and underwear. A wooden or metal canteen and perhaps a pair of field glasses would hang from the saddle.[26]

Cavalry or infantry, southerners in the Western Theater usually wore brimmed hats rather than kepis. A photograph of Pvt. William Harrison Morrow of F Company shows him wearing a kepi and with a Navy Colt in his belt. However, Pvt. Morrow served later in the Georgia Militia, and the gray uniform and other accouterments shown in the photograph may be from that service.[27]

In winter, the trooper hoped to augment his shirt, shell jacket, and wool trousers with a heavy coat. Many "suffered greatly" however for lack of jackets, pants, overcoats, shoes, and blankets.[28] Replacements for worn out gauntlets and riding boots were also often unavailable. Records show clothing was issued to at least some of the men of the 2nd Georgia in March and June of 1864.[29] Henry Strickland's 1864 wedding day photograph shows him in a simple gray tunic, but that garment may have been made by his mother or sisters especially for the occasion. Most of the men depended on their families to send them homemade clothing.

Food was a constant problem for the wide-ranging cavalry, and the men often shared their meals with their horses. The cavalryman's ramrod served double duty as a spit for broiling his meat, and corn shucks served as dish rags and wrapping paper. One veteran related how the troopers' mess was managed. "Our rule was," he said, "that each member of the mess should cook a week, provided nobody growled about the cooking; in which event the growler was to take the cook's place. As may be imagined, this rule was not very conducive to good cooking, and some of the revolting messes were uncomplainingly swallowed would have destroyed the digestion of any animal on earth except that of a rebel cavalryman.

"Once the cook, finding that he was about to serve out his week in spite of his efforts to the contrary (consisting of sweetening the coffee with salt, salting the soup with sugar, etc.) grew desperate, and proceeded to boil with the beef a whole string of red pepper. Of course it made a mixture hot enough to blister the nose even to smell it. John____ got the first mouthful, and it fairly took his breath away. As soon as he could speak, he blurted out, "Great Caesar, boys, this meat is as hot as hell —

but (suddenly remembering the penalty for complaining) it's good, though!" [30]

Camp life was sometimes more difficult for the cavalry due to the constant presence of flies and the added duty of caring for the animals. But cavalrymen spent relatively little time in camp, as their duties usually called for them to be "out and about" even during long lulls in the fighting.

Not even their generals knew it in 1862, but the Confederate Cavalry, especially in the Western Theater, would re-write the book on cavalry operations, even as the era of the mounted warrior drew to a close. The sweeping mounted charges of European conflicts were rarely feasible in the deep South, where woods, thickets, mountains, and river bottoms dominated the landscape. Often the horse became just a mode of transportation for Rebel cavalrymen who would fight on foot when the enemy was engaged.[31]

During its three-year existence, the 2nd Georgia Cavalry would participate in more than 175 different engagements in Kentucky, Tennessee, Alabama, Georgia, South Carolina, and North Carolina. Elements of the Regiment also served for short periods of time in Virginia. The inspection report of January 1865 showed one company on detached service in Virginia.[32] This may have been F company, as Henry Strickland told his son Will years later that he had served for a time in Virginia.[33] The 2nd Georgia was involved in practically innumerable skirmishes, and participated in most of the major campaigns of the Western Theater, from the invasion of Kentucky to the siege of Knoxville to the Atlanta and Carolinas campaigns.

According to various records, the 2nd Georgia may have had as many as eleven different commanders during the course of the war, including:[34]

Winburn J. Lawton	Charles C. Crews	J. B. Eberhardt
Arthur Hood	James W. Mayo	Francis M. Ison
Caleb Arthur Whaley	George.C. Looney	W. H. Chapman
James E. Dunlop	Benjamin M. Camp	

It appears, however, that some of these officers commanded the regiment only on an interim basis, if at all. Lt. Col. Arthur Hood, second in command under Winburn Lawton, was relieved of his duties and resigned at Lawton's request, for failures during the Kentucky campaign.[35] Hood, however, may have taken over for Lawton during brief periods in 1862. Caleb Whaley commanded a "battalion" derived from the Regiment during the Kentucky campaign, and may have commanded the Regiment for a few days or hours before his death in 1862. Benjamin Camp is not shown as rising above lieutenant, and Hardy Chapman resigned due to disability on 10 February 1865, while still a captain and commander of F Company.[36] Eberhardt is not shown as commanding the regiment, but he is the highest ranking officer recorded with the regiment at the surrender in April of 1865.[37]

Like Lawton, C. A. Whaley had been a captain in Cobb's Legion early in the war. While with the Army of Northern Virginia, he was wounded and sent to a Richmond hospital. Based on his quick rise to major, Whaley was the early standout among the company commanders.

Charles Constantine Crews was the most enduring of the regiment's commanders. He began his career as a captain commanding the 2nd Georgia's A Company. By November of 1862 he was a lt. colonel, apparently on the regimental or brigade staff, as Dunlop was commanding the regiment and Wharton was commanding the brigade at this time. Later, at various times, Crews commanded both the regiment and the brigade under Wharton's, Martin's, Morgan's and Allen's divisions. Records show he was wounded during the Carolinas campaign, and was disabled at the surrender. It has been claimed that he was promoted to brigadier general during the last two weeks of the war, but there are no records of the promotion.[38]

---

[1] Joseph H. Crute Jr., *Units of the Confederate States Armies* (Gaithersburg MD: Old Soldier Books, reprinted 1987) 82.

[2] William Smedlund, *Campfires of Georgia Troops 1861—1865* (Sharpsburg GA, 1994) 118.

[3] Hugh M. Longino, Letter to Miss Lillian Henderson, 10 April 1926, (Atlanta GA: Georgia Department of Archives and History) Georgia Roster Commission file.

[4] *War of the Rebellion, Official Records of the Union and Confederate Armies,* Series IV Vol. 1 (Washington DC: U. S. Government Printing Office) 43.

[5] Smedlund, *Campfires of Georgia Troops.*

[6] Compiled Service Records, (Atlanta GA: Georgia Department of Archives and History).

[7] Ibid.

[8] Ibid.

[9] Ibid.

[10] James E. DeVaughn, *Reminiscences of Confederate Soldiers, Vol. XIII* (Atlanta GA: Georgia Department of Archives and History) unpublished compilation.

[11] Robert Bridgers, ed. *Confederate Military History, Vol. III* (Georgia Confederate Publishing Co. 1897).

[12] Compiled Service Records, 2nd Georgia Cavalry.

[13] Kenneth A. Hafendorfer, *They Died by Twos and Tens, the Confederate Cavalry in the Kentucky Campaign of 1862* (Louisville KY: KH Press, 1995) 121.

[14] *War of the Rebellion, Official Records* Vol. 16 Part III, 717.

[15] Compiled Service Records, 2nd Georgia Cavalry.

[16] W. C. Dodson, ed. *Campaigns of Wheeler and His Cavalry* (Jackson TN: The Guild Bindery Press) 408.

[17] Stephen Z. Starr, *The Union Cavalry in the Civil War,* Vol. III (Baton Rouge LA: Louisiana State University Press, 1985) 595.

[18] Dodson, ed. *Campaigns of Wheeler and His Cavalry,* 408.

[19] Albert Castel, *Decision in the West—The Atlanta Campaign of 1864* (Lawrence KS: University Press of Kansas, 1992) 380.

[20] Dodson, ed. *Campaigns of Wheeler and His Cavalry,* 408.

[21] *War of the Rebellion, Official Records* Vol. 20 968, 969.

[22] Louella H. Bales, *Confederate Cavalry* (Jacksonville FL: 1989) 285.

[23] Dodson, ed., *Campaigns of Wheeler and His Cavalry,* 410.

[24] Ibid.

[25] Theo F. Rodenbaugh, *The Photographic History of the Civil War, Vol. 2 The Cavalry* (Secaucus NJ: The Blue and Gray Press, 1987) 316.

[26] William C. Davis, *The Fighting Men of the Civil War* (New York NY: Gallery Books, 1989) 67—75.

[27] *Historical Bulletin #1* (Clayton County Historical Society, May 1963)

[28] Dodson, *Campaigns of Wheeler and His Cavalry,* 412.

[29] Compiled Service Records, 2nd Georgia Cavalry.

[30] Dodson, *Campaigns of Wheeler and His Cavalry,* 30.

[31] Davis, *The Fighting Men of the Civil War,* 89.

[32] Dodson, *Campaigns of Wheeler and His Cavalry,* 412.

[33] William E. Strickland, recollections.

[34] Bridgers, ed. *Confederate Military History,* 145.

[35] Hafendorfer, *They Died by Twos and Tens,* 490.

[36] Georgia Roster Commission of 1903 (Atlanta GA: Georgia Department of Archives and History)

[37] Compiled Service Records, 2nd Georgia Cavalry.

[38] Stewart Sifikis, *Who Was Who in the Confederacy* (New York NY: Facts on File, 1988)

Henry Sees the Elephant

When Henry Strickland and his brothers joined the Clayton Dragoons in the fall of 1861, Southerners had reason to be optimistic. True, the early successes had come primarily in the East, but a Confederate victory at Belmont, Missouri, early that November seemed to confirm that Southern arms could dominate the West as well. The situation soon changed.

On 24 November, General Felix Zollicoffer was killed and his army routed at Mill Springs, Kentucky. In quick succession, Union forces captured Forts Henry and Donelson, opening the way to Tennessee. In Albert Sidney Johnston, the South had perhaps the most widely respected military leader on the continent, but he assumed command of the Western Department of the Confederate States of America with barely 20,000 men under his command. With that force, he was expected to defend a front that stretched from the mountains of Kentucky and East Tennessee across the Mississippi to the Kansas border. Even as Johnston doubled the size of his army, his days grew shorter. He was killed in the standoff at Shiloh, 4 April 1862.

By the time Henry Strickland and his comrades had completed their training, the military situation in the Western Theater had changed from positive to grim. The 2nd Georgia was ordered to Chattanooga on 29 June 1862, still "unarmed." On 4 July, orders came down to hold the regiment at Dalton to await further orders. Those "further orders" came through on 6 July, to "push preparations" in the 2nd Georgia and 8th

Texas Cavalry. They were to be the first regiments in Col. Nathan Bedford Forrest's new brigade under Gen. Kirby Smith's command in the Department of East Tennessee.[1] Lawton's company commanders at this time were:[2]

A Company	Capt. Charles Crews
B Company	unknown, but may have been 1st Lt. G. J. Wright
C Company	Capt. James Mayo
D Company	Capt. William Grant
E Company	Capt. Francis Ison
F Company	Capt. Hardy Chapman
G Company	Capt. Thomas Jordan
H Company	Capt. C. A. Whaley, Capt. Samuel Mead or Capt. Oliver Winningham
I Company	Capt. George Looney
K Company	Capt. James Dunlop[3]

The men of the 8th Texas, Terry's "Texan Rangers," were veterans of several conflicts, had "seen the elephant," in the popular expression of the time, and had seen Col. Terry and his successor killed.[4] Now under the command of Col. John Austin Wharton, these Texans were "men who knew how to fight," and already were among the most respected cavalry units of the war.[5] Most of the Georgians, however, were fresh off the farm, and they apparently did not make a good first impression on Forrest. According to one source, some of these new troopers were unhorsed in mounted firing drills, causing Forrest to curse loudly. Forrest's curses won over the Texas Rangers, who had not been eager for a new commander since the death of Col. Terry.[6] (Forrest had gained some notoriety for his escape from Fort Donelson and for his personal courage at Fallen Timbers after the Battle of Shiloh the previous April, but he was not yet the larger-than-life figure that he would become.)

If Forrest was worried about their performance in battle, he never-theless soon had his still incomplete brigade in action. Less than a week later, Forrest was ordered to move into middle Tennessee and attempt to slow Maj. Gen. Don Carlos Buell's offensive against Chattanooga. Forrest biographer Robert Selph Henry wrote:

> *On July ninth, the little column consisting of only the Texans and Lawton's Georgians, hardly more than 1,000 men, crossed the Tennessee River, climbed steep Walden's Ridge, dropped down into the long, narrow trough of Sequatchie Valley well to the north of the*

Federal forces in the same valley of Battle Creek, and climbed again to the plateau of Cumberland Mountain, where, on the night of the tenth, the troopers bivouacked around the little mountain courthouse at Altamont.

On the eleventh, they marched on past the long columned portico of the summer hotel at Beersheba Springs, where they turned down the mountain and, after a thirty-mile march, halted at the county-seat town of McMinnville. There they were joined by Morrison's 1st Georgia Cavalry...by two companies of Tennessee cavalry...and two Kentucky companies—bringing the total force up to about 1,400 men.

The march was made with no halt, except for a short time to feed and water the horses at the village of Woodbury. There, at eleven o'clock on Saturday night, the people turned out to welcome Forrest's troopers with hospitable attention for man and beast— including the cakes and pies and other delicacies which the Woodbury housewives had prepared for their own Sunday dinners. That afternoon, Forrest was told, a Federal patrolling party had raided the village and carried off many of its men to the jail at Murfreesboro, under vague charges of giving aid and comfort to the Confederacy.

The garrison at Murfreesboro, the largest and most important along the railroad, consisted of two regiments of infantry, a cavalry detachment and a four-gun battery—the whole force being about equal in number to that which Forrest was bringing against it.[7]

After the fall of Fort Donelson on 16 February 1862, Murfreesboro, Tennessee, was occupied by the 9th Michigan Infantry under Col. William Duffield and three companies from the 7th Pennsylvania Cavalry under Maj. James Seibert, encamped at the Maney estate. The 3rd Minnesota Infantry under Col. Henry Lester was nearby just north of Stone's River with a battery of artillery.[8] Various sources put the number of Union soldiers present at 1,400 to 1,750.[9] "Murfreesboro was under martial law, with Capt. Oliver Cromwell Rounds as provost marshal." Brig. Gen. Thomas Turpin Crittenden had just arrived on 12 July to assume overall command.[10]

To the citizens of Murfreesboro, Rounds was "the tyrant, the usurper, the threatener, the cruel avenger, the arrogant insulter of ladies— under whose iron mandates innocent citizens were sent to northern prisons." Now the citizenry were in a state of near panic, as Gen. Crittenden had promised to execute the twelve civilians held in the Courthouse, for the 7 July "murder" of five members of the 7th Pennsylvania. In fact, the Yankee cavalrymen had been killed in a skirmish with a Capt. Bond of Wilson County and his newly raised company of volunteers. Bond had taken steps to ensure that the Federal commander at Murfreesboro knew who had attacked the cavalry patrol, but Crittenden was determined to institute an "iron rule" that would make Capt. Rounds' governance seem like "good times." Crittenden warned the citizens that in the future, for every union soldier killed, he would execute 100 civilians in the community where it occurred.[11]

Apparently, the civilian captives were unlikely bushwackers. One, Dr. Lunsford Black, was a local physician. Another was Charley Ridley, a youth of fifteen or sixteen, and another was W. R. Owen, a Primitive Baptist Preacher. Also among the twelve were local citizens Jim Manor, J. C. Carnahan, Newton Carnahan, Albert McGill, Bart Ring, and Simp Harris.[12] These captives, Forrest vowed to the citizens of Woodbury, would be freed on the morrow, 13 July, Forrest's fortieth birthday.

About one o'clock that Sunday morning, Forrest and his men left the hospitality of Woodbury and headed for Murfreesboro, some eighteen miles distant. Before daybreak, H Company of the 8th Texas surprised and captured the eighteen Federal pickets guarding approaches to the town. According to the chaplain of the 8th Texas, shots were exchanged during this capture, alerting the Federal garrison and bringing the rest of the Texas Rangers at a gallop.[13] Forrest, however, reported that the pickets were captured without a shot being fired, and indeed, the Federal garrison did seem surprised when the gray cavalry galloped into town a short time later.[14]

According to one account, Forrest then gave orders for a three-pronged attack, with the Texans peeling off against the 9th Michigan and the Pennsylvania cavalry, the 2nd Georgia moving against the provost guard and those elements of the Michigan infantry guarding the Courthouse in the center of town, while Baxter Smith's Tennessee Battalion moved to cut off any retreat attempts on the Lebanon and Nashville pikes. The 1st Georgia was to follow and provide a reserve that could be sent wherever needed. Once the initial objectives were achieved, the brigade would be reunited to attack the Minnesota infantry and their artillery.[15]

Another account[16] says that the 2nd Georgia was assigned to join the 8th Texas in their attack on the Michigan and Pennsylvania troops, while other accounts have put the 2nd Georgia in action immediately against Lester's Minnesota infantry and its four cannons.[17] It seems logical that Forrest would not have left Lester unattended while he attacked the other Union positions. However, Forrest's own report indicates that Col. J. J. Morrison of the 1st Georgia Cavalry, "with a portion of the 2nd Georgia, was ordered to storm the courthouse," and that "Lt. Col. Arthur Hood, of the 2nd Georgia, with a portion of his force was ordered to storm the jail, which he did, releasing many prisoners confined for political offenses; he also took the telegraph office, capturing the operator."[18] Several civilian witnesses also put the 2nd Georgia around the Courthouse.[19]

The official record does raise some questions. If Hood was leading the attack on the jail and telegraph office, and the 2nd Georgians before the courthouse were temporarily under the command of Morrison, where was Col. Lawton? According to Forrest's report, Lawton was "…with the 1st Georgia, the Tennesseans and Kentuckians" confronting Lester's Minnesotans.[20] Why would Lawton have been with the 1st Georgia instead of his own regiment? Is it possible that Forrest confused Lawton with Morrison? After all, he had met the two men just a few days before.

Whatever the assignment of the 2nd Georgia, it is evident that at about 5 A.M., they began a charge with Forrest and the rest of the brigade in column at "a fast gallop." As the column entered the town, four of the ten "Texan Ranger" companies followed Forrest and the 2nd Georgia instead of peeling off with Wharton. This left Wharton with only a fraction of his command to attack the Michigan and Pennsylvania camps. One source puts the number of men with Wharton at 240,[21] but Wharton's chaplain wrote that only 120 men followed Wharton on the charge.[22] Whatever the number, Wharton was apparently unaware that he had, at best, little more than half of his regiment as he charged through the teamsters and cavalry camps and into the Michigan infantry. The attack caught the sleepy Federals by surprise and forced them to fall back to a defensive position on the fringe of the camp. Wrote one of the Federals later, "We were all in a huddle and the Rebels came on yelling like Indians, their horses on a gallop." Bitter, hand-to-hand fighting followed, and Col. William Duffield, commander of the

9th Michigan, was wounded. Lt. Col. John Parkhurst then assumed command of the regiment.[23]

After the initial surprise, the advantage shifted to Parkhurst. Armed mostly with shotguns and Navy Colt revolvers, the Texans were outnumbered and outgunned. Some twenty-four of the Rangers were killed or wounded in the charge, and Wharton himself was seriously wounded in the arm.[24] As Wharton realized that much of his command was absent, the two sides settled into an exchange of "punishing fire" from their respective positions.[25]

Meanwhile, part of the 2nd Georgia and the four errant companies of Texas Rangers had met heavy resistance from some 200 Federals of the 9th Michigan barricaded in the Courthouse and surrounding buildings. Another part of the 2nd Georgia under Lt. Col. Hood soon captured the jail, the telegraph office and some of the other houses on the square shielding Federal troops. Men of the 2nd Georgia also captured Gen. Crittenden in the Spence Hotel, along with his entire staff and other Federals in nearby buildings. At some point during this fighting, Forrest became aware of the Texans' presence, and he sent them to rejoin their regiment.[26]

The arrival of the gray horsemen in the town square brought unrestrained joy to local citizens, many of whom ran into the streets even as the firing continued." The glad cry of 'our boys have come' rang from one end of the town to the other, and staid elderly citizens clapped their hands in delight…that day when the rebels burst so suddenly upon us was the happiest day experienced by the citizens of Murfreesborough during the war."[27]

But men from B Company of the 9th Michigan were still pouring heavy fire from the Courthouse. Two mounted charges by the 2nd Georgia failed. According to a civilian witness, "The major of the 2nd Georgia Cavalry had eleven bullet wounds and fell off his horse near the Methodist Church…."[28] No record has been found regarding the identity of this officer, and it may have been not a major of the 2nd Georgia, but Forrest's aide Lt. Col. James Saunders, whom the civilian saw fall.[29]

Four men from F Company fell. Privates Robert Payne and David Morris were wounded and F.M. Farris and Still Henderson were killed. Henderson's son, Robert Still Henderson, Jr. was born six months later, on 28 December 1862. Also among those killed were Sgt. Thomas Duke of I Company, Sgt. Francis Preston of D Company, and Pvt. William Thompson of A Company.[30] Most of the 2nd Georgia casualties incurred at Murfreesboro this day apparently came here at the Courthouse.

Finally, the Rebel cavalrymen dismounted and a detachment from E Company moved on the courthouse under a covering fire. Seven troopers reached the gate to the courthouse yard, where three of them were shot down. Among those who fell here likely were privates Gus Darden and James Hicks.[31] One of the fallen men had the ax which was to be used to batter the door down.[32] "A lieutenant of the 2nd Georgia Cavalry, standing near the first window on the east side of the court house, north of the balcony, was shot in the head, the blood spattering on the brick wall by a window; and the blood stain is on the wall to this day. He was shot by Federals concealed in a house on the northeast side of the square."[33] This was probably 2nd Lt. Robert Thompson of E Company. The only 2nd Georgia lieutenant known to be a casualty this day, Lt. Thompson survived his wound.[34] (It is also possible that the wounded officer was not from the 2nd Georgia, but was either Lt. William Hutchins or Lt. Jesse Crabbe of the 1st Georgia.)

One of the men braved heavy fire to retrieve the lost ax, and the door was broken open. Pvt. Henry Clay Burr of E Company was one of the four 2nd Georgia troopers who entered the courthouse and started a fire on the brick floor.[35] Eventually, the rising smoke forced the Federals to surrender. When the Yankee captives were herded into the streets, Capt. O. C. Rounds was not among them. "Frantic and furious," the ladies of Murfreesboro, still in their "night attire," rushed into the streets to point out the quarters of the hated provost marshal. The first search of the building yielded nothing, but the women urged Forrest's men to look again. Finally they found Rounds "hiding under a fat feather bed in his thin summer underwear."[36]

After the capture of the courthouse, Forrest took the 2nd Georgia, the 1st Georgia, and the Tennessee battalion against the 3rd Minnesota Infantry, which had moved into a defensive position northwest of town. There were almost 1,000 men riding with Forrest at this point. One source numbers the Minnesota regiment at 575 men[37] while another[38] puts the number at closer to 900. Whatever the actual number, the Federals had a strong position and they were well armed infantry, supported by four artillery pieces. Their opponents were mere cavalry, armed mostly with shotguns, a few revolvers, and no artillery.

At the sound of battle, Lester had been attempting to hook up with Duffield when he saw the gray cavalry in the woods in his front and on his left flank. He immediately put his men in line of battle on the crest of a hill, and in short order began shelling the Confederates.[39] Forrest reported that "The Georgians under Captain Dunlop and Major Harper, made a gallant charge almost to the mouths of the cannon." [40] This report implies that K Company, commanded by Dunlop, was the only 2nd Georgia Company employed in the frontal assault. However, the postwar writings of a G Company veteran indicate that other elements of the regiment were also engaged. Cpl. Littleton Marion Spinks of G Company wrote, "On Forrests' raid at Murfreesboro, we captured one regiment and their general and then went one mile north of town and charged a regiment and four cannons and were repulsed." [41] It was probably in this action that K Company Pvt. Francis Adams had his horse shot from under him, and privates William Chester and John Shales were seriously wounded. Chester would die four days later.[42] Regarding this action, Lester reported only that "A charge was made upon our left from the woods, but was easily repulsed, with some loss to the enemy."[43]

After two hours of unsuccessful fighting, Forrest took the 1st Georgia and the Tennessee battalion on a flanking movement. Striking the camp in the rear of the 3rd Minnesota, after a "sharp fight," he killed or captured all of the 100 infantrymen left behind to guard the camp and defend Lester's rear.[44] When the Union artillery turned to meet this challenge, the 2nd Georgia charged and broke the Union line. The Federals reformed in another defensive position, however, still with artillery support.

Forrest now apparently realized that further assault against the artillery would cause great loss. Indeed, some of his officers suggested that enough had been accomplished. Forrest replied, "I didn't come here to make half a job of it." Leaving the 1st Georgia in place, he then took the 2nd Georgia out past the Lebanon Pike and joined the Texas Rangers who were still faced off against the 9th Michigan at the Maney Estate. With Lawton's whereabouts still not clear, Lt. Col. Arthur Hood was ordered to take the 2nd Georgia to a position on the enemy's left. The arrival of this new threat on his flank led Lt. Col. Parkhurst to surrender. It was now around noon, and the fighting had been almost continuous since 5:00 A.M.[45]

Forrest then turned his attention again to the 3rd Minnesota and its menacing artillery. Forrest sent word to Col. Lester that the 9th Michigan had surrendered, and gave him the same offer given

Parkhurst—surrender or there will be no quarter. Lester asked to see Col. Duffield, and he was escorted through the town to visit the wounded officer. As he rode through the town, Forrest's men moved quickly between intersections to give the impression of a much larger force. Lester reported that, after conferring with Duffield, he "agreed to refer the matter of surrender to my officers. Accordingly the matter was represented to them as derived from Colonel Duffield, and the great majority, looking upon further resistance as involving the certainty of an ultimate defeat with great loss, and with no possibility of an escape or assistance, it was decided to surrender, which was done at 3:30 P.M." [46]

In his report, Lester estimated the Confederate strength at 2,600 troops and "some hundreds of citizens…being in all about 3,000 men." [47] Forrest's ruse had obviously worked, as both Lester and Parkhurst greatly overestimated his strength. The Federal officers were wrong on another point—the prospect of being reinforced. Buell had already started reinforcements from Nashville and had put some twelve regiments on the Chattanooga road. Buell had "…at present no remarks to make upon what appears to be a most disgraceful affair…" other than to comment that it may "..embarrass me considerably." He later reported that the Union defeat at Murfreesboro had "…caused serious delay in the means of supplying the army so that it can move on the Decatur route. The difficulty has been increased by damages to bridges by swollen streams. [48]

The artillery captured at Murfreesboro became Capt. White's battery and apparently remained in the same brigade with the 2nd Georgia throughout the war. [49] Many 2nd Georgia cavalrymen served temporary stints with the battery. Men returning from the hospital often had no horse, and would be temporarily attached to the battery.

Forrest reported his losses at Murfreesboro as twenty-five killed and forty to sixty wounded, but conceded that he had not received complete casualty reports and that the estimate might not be accurate. [50] Some historians believe that Confederate casualties probably exceeded 100. [51] Chaplain B. F. Bunting's report of twenty-four casualties among the Texas Rangers, [52] combined with a known eighteen casualties in the 2nd Georgia, indicate that losses were probably somewhat less than 100, and that Forrest's estimate may have been fairly accurate. Among the wounded were Col. Wharton, Col. James Saunders, and at least four lieutenants.

For the 2nd Georgia, their first combat was one of their worst in terms of casualties. The Regiment suffered at least eight killed and ten wounded, including Pvt Green Smith of H Company, whose spine was injured by a runaway team. Known casualties for the 2nd Georgia are shown below.[53]

William J. Thompson, bugler	pvt., A Company	Killed
Francis Preston	sgt., D Company	Killed
Agustus Darden	pvt., E Company	Killed
William Hamil	pvt., E Company	Wounded
James Hicks	pvt., E Company	Killed
John Parrish	pvt., E Company	Wounded
Robert Thompson	2nd lt., E Company	Wounded
F. M. Farris	pvt., F Company	Killed
Robert "Still" Henderson	pvt., F Company	Killed
David P. Morris	pvt., F Company	Wounded
Robert Payne	pvt., F Company	Wounded
Thomas Brooks	pvt., G Company	Wounded
Newton Beauchamp	pvt., H Company	Wounded
Green Smith	pvt., H Company	Injured
Thomas Strickland	pvt., H Company	Killed
Thomas Duke	sgt., I Company	Killed
William Chester	pvt., K Company	Wounded
John Shales	pvt., K Company	Wounded

Forrest reported Union losses at "about 75 killed and 125 wounded," along with 1100 to 1200 captured. Forrest also captured the four pieces of artillery, sixty wagons, about 175 horses, and extensive supplies.[54] The amount of captured small arms was large, but they were primarily long rifles of the infantry, and not well suited to use by cavalry. The arms captured from the 200 or so federal cavalrymen probably allowed some of the men of the 8th Texas to exchange their shotguns for proper carbines, and to add another pistol to their belts. (Most of Siebert's cavalrymen had been captured with the teamsters in the initial attack of the Texans.) The Rangers were known for carrying as many as four pistols, two on the belt and two more on the saddle.[55]

Forrest's victory at Murfreesboro along with Morgan's raid into Kentucky put the Federals on the defensive. It was two weeks before the damage to the Nashville and Chattanooga Railroad was repaired, and subsequent cavalry actions further delayed Buell's planned offensive against Chattanooga.[56] For a time at least, it served to dampen the morale of Union soldiers, especially among cavalry units.[57]

Forrest's action on his 40th birthday made him a hero in the South and a villain in the North. The Rebel victory at Murfreesboro also gave southern cavalrymen reputations as daring and effective fighters. Contemporaries wrote of their "unflinching courage" and their "willingness to kill."[58] From this point on, Federal commanders as well as Confederate regarded Confederate cavalry units as generally superior to their northern counterparts. This impression persisted even after several embarrassing failures by Confederate cavalry in the following months.

U. S. Grant later called Forrest "about the ablest cavalry leader in the South," and Sherman called him "the most remarkable man our Civil War produced on either side." During the war Sherman also called him "that devil Forrest," who must be "hunted down and killed if it costs ten thousand lives and bankrupts the Federal treasury." Biographer Henry wrote of Forrest that "He was not only a commander but himself a trooper in the very midst of combat, wounded four times, with horses shot under him twenty-nine times, and with no fewer than thirty enemy soldiers accounted for in hand-to-hand fighting in the almost innumerable affairs at arms in which he was engaged."[59]

Forrest's ferocity became legend even among his own men, and he apparently expected them to be as fearless as he. Years later, one veteran of the 2nd Georgia's I Company, Hugh Longino, remembered that Forrest could at least try to be reassuring to a young private. Longino wrote, "The first time that I was ever advance guard at the front and advancing on the enemy, General Bedford Forrest rode up to me and asked me had I ever been in that position before, and when I told him that I had not, he told me there was no danger, that when I came up on the enemy to fire and fall back, but did not tell me what to do in case the enemy came out of the brush behind me, and closed in on me, the very thing that I was fearing." [60]

The understandable fears of Longino and his comrades apparently did not show. General Sherman called the southern cavalrymen "youngbloods of the South" who are "splendid riders, first-rate shots, and utterly reckless." They were, he said, "The best cavalry in the world." Sherman's wartime correspondence shows clearly that he admired the southern cavalrymen, but he also included them in a group that he thought might have to be executed or imprisoned after the war. "They are the most dangerous set of men that this war has turned loose upon the world," said Sherman. "War suits them, and the rascals are brave, fine riders,…bold to brashness…They hate Yankees, per se, and don't bother their brains about the past, present, or future…. These men must all be killed or employed by us before we can hope for peace." [61]

It should be noted that practically all of Sherman's experiences with Confederate cavalry were in the Western Theater, far from the more famous cavalry under Jeb Stuart in the Army of Northern Virginia. While the Northern Virginia cavalry has far greater renown in popular history, it was in the Western Theater that Confederate cavalry would do "…far more real damage to the Federal war effort than all of Stuart's bold strokes combined." [62]

When the fighting ended at Murfreesboro, according to Cpl. Spinks, "General Forrest then made us a speech and told us he was going all over Tennessee, and our next raid was on Lebanon which was a long and hard march all night and when we got there the Yankees were all gone." [63]

Stunned by the fall of the Murfreesboro garrison, Buell ordered Gen. William Nelson to move out of Alabama and retake Murfreesboro and McMinnville. As Nelson moved toward Murfreesboro. Forrest then appeared between Nelson and Nashville, destroying rail lines and taking prisoners. On the forced march from McMinnville, described by Cpl. Spinks, Forrest's men reached Lebanon shortly after sunrise on 20 July, hoping to surprise the 700 Federal cavalry who had been sent there from Nashville. "We dashed into the city in fine style," reported Forrest, "but found that the enemy, having notice of my approach, had retired about 12 o'clock, leaving me in the undisturbed possession of that place."[64] Forrest at this point had only about 1100 men, as Morrison's 1st Georgia Cavalry had been sent back to East Tennessee.

Forrest then set his brigade in motion again, toward Nashville. On 21 July the brigade passed the Hermitage, former home of Andrew Jackson, before his men ran into Union pickets near Stones River, capturing several and driving the rest away. At Mill Creek, Forrest attacked a stockade guarding the bridge, taking some twenty prisoners and sending the remainder fleeing southward. After burning the bridge and stockade, the Brigade followed the fleeing Federals, captured another forty, and burned another bridge. Cpl. Spinks of G Company almost drowned when his horse "…fell and went under the water. My lieutenant went about a mile and got me another horse and I went on my way rejoicing but lost my coat."[65]

Moving along the Nashville & Chattanooga Railroad, Forrest then attacked a Union outpost at Antioch Station where he took thirty-five more captives, destroyed a "large amount of stores," as well as freight cars and another bridge. Federal reports put Forrest's losses at twenty killed or wounded, but Forrest claimed not to have lost a single man.[66] Regarding Federal losses, Forrest reported, "In the several skirmishes there were 10 killed and some 15 or 20 wounded, 97 prisoners (94 privates and 3 lieutenants), besides destroying a considerable amount of stores at Antioch Depot." He added that he lost not a single man killed or wounded, and that "…the entire force, officers and men, under my command acquitted themselves with great credit, and bore the fatigue and risk of the expedition in a manner only to be borne by Confederate troops." Added Forrest, "The officers and men of my entire command, flushed with victory and our past success, are anxious and ready to meet the enemy."[67] Records show only one man of the 2nd Georgia, Pvt. James T. Beardin of D Company, whose death on 31 July could have been from wounds suffered during this raid.[68]

With Forrest's troopers carrying out raids within sight of the Federal garrison at Nashville, U.S.—appointed Governor Andrew Johnson became greatly alarmed. The Governor urged that the citizens of Nashville be forced to provide the materials and labor to fortify the city against an attack by Forrest's little band.[69]

It was during this time that Pvt. John Francis Moon of the 2nd Georgia's I Company was captured. One of eight Moon brothers to serve in Confederate armies, Pvt. Moon was sent out to relieve some pickets, apparently on that Sunday morning in Lebanon, but made a wrong turn and was captured about eight miles from Nashville on the LaVergne Pike. A day or so later he was on his way to Nashville, escorted by two soldiers, when the little party stopped by a "fine spring" for a rest. The two escorts lingered at the spring, perhaps reluctant to march out again in the hot Tennessee sun. After a while, the reclining Pvt. Moon began to snore softly. Soon, the two Union soldiers were also snoring, but their sleep was real and Moon's was not.

Moon said later that his greatest difficulty was in resisting the temptation to slay the sleeping Yankees. Expecting that he would likely be recaptured, however, and not wishing to be executed, Moon left the guards asleep as he crept away. His only other difficulty was in deciding to rejoin his company instead of returning to his wife and five children. It must have occurred to Pvt. Moon, however, that his brothers—W. W.

"Lump" Moon in I Company, Madison Moon in D Company, and five others in infantry regiments—might resent his returning home. About the middle of September, Moon caught up to I Company at Woodsonville, Kentucky.[70]

With men and beasts exhausted, Forrest's Brigade arrived back in McMinnville on 24 July, hoping for rest. But the raid around Nashville further alarmed Gen. Buell, who now intensified the pursuit of the little brigade of Georgians, Tennesseans and Texans. Gen. William Nelson had already sent the 4th Kentucky Cavalry under Col. David Haggard in pursuit of Forrest, and on the 22nd Nelson brought ten regiments of infantry to meet Haggard at Antioch Station. Nelson had told Buell, "To chase Morgan and Forrest, they mounted on race horses, with infantry in this weather is a hopeless task."[71] Perhaps in response to this lament, another cavalry and artillery force under Gen. Richard Johnson was on 2 August on the road toward McMinnville by way of Sparta. That same day, Nelson's combined infantry/cavalry force moved through Murfreesboro toward McMinnville. Arriving at McMinnville later that day, Nelson found only the 8th Texas. Forrest had moved to Roddy with the rest of his brigade, including the 2nd Georgia.[72]

Nelson and Haggard chased the 8th Texas to the Galfkiller River, a mile south of Sparta, where the Texans linked up with John Scott's Cavalry Brigade, which now included the 1st Georgia Cavalry Regiment.[73]

While Forrest met with General Braxton Bragg in Chattanooga, Lt. Col. Arthur Hood of the 2nd Georgia took the brigade toward Sparta. Again we find the second in command leading the regiment. Where was Colonel Lawton? Perhaps he remained behind with Forrest, or perhaps he was ill.

It is not clear whether the 2nd Georgia and the rest of Forrest's brigade arrived in time to participate in the fight at Sparta. In any case, the fight apparently amounted to little more than a late afternoon artillery duel, with the Federals withdrawing back to McMinnville.[74]

Indications are that Forrest's entire Brigade remained in Sparta for much of August. Apparently, however, the 2nd Georgia was not simply picketing or sitting idly in camp, as records show them active miles from Sparta northwest of Nashville. On 11 August, Pvt. David D. L. West of A Company and Sgt John B. Hill of C Company were wounded near White Oak .[75]

Surviving muster rolls indicate that something unusual occurred on 15 August. The horses of at least fourteen E Company privates and one C Company officer are shown as being killed at White's Creek this day, but there are no records of a conflict or casualties for the regiment. What could have led to so many horses being killed when there were no other casualties? Perhaps artillery rounds fell among held horses, or perhaps there was some sort of accident. Whatever befell the horses may have also injured Private William Duke of I Company, for he died 19 August in a Chattanooga hospital, little more than a month after brother Thomas' death at Murfreesboro.[76]

According to one account, some time after 17 August, Forrest left the 2nd Georgia at Sparta and took the remainder of the brigade against a large wagon train between Woodbury and Readyville.[77] Attacks on the 26th and 27th at "Round Mountain" failed, with considerable losses to the 8th Texas, as the wagons were defended by infantry, cavalry, and artillery. Other records show that the 2nd Georgia was in a "skirmish" at Readyville, Round Hill, Tennessee on 28 August, the day that Bragg's army shoved off from Chattanooga on its invasion of Kentucky.

On the 29th, Forrest, as ordered by Bragg, began moving back to the Sequatchie Valley, where his cavalry would screen Bragg's movement. Fortunately for the men of the 2nd Georgia, they remained at Sparta while the rest of Forrest's Brigade was "roughly handled" in engagements at Short Mountain Cross Roads and at Little Pond, with some 100 Confederate troopers killed.[78]

---

[1] *War of the Rebellion, Official Records of the Union and Confederate Armies* Vol. 16 Part II (Washington, D.C.: Government Printing Office, 1890) 709, 711, 717, 729.

[2] Compiled Service Records, 2nd Georgia Cavalry, Georgia Department of Archives and History, Atlanta.

[3] Georgia Roster Commission of 1903, (Atlanta GA: Georgia Department of Archives and History).

[4] B.F. Bunting, Chaplain, Terry's Texas Rangers, Wartime manuscript MSS#25-0567 (Galveston TX: Rosenberg Library).

[5] Brian C. Pohanka, *Don Troiani's Civil War* (Mechanicsburg, PA: Stackpole Books, 1995) 23.

[6] Kenneth A. Hafendorfer, *They Died by Two's and Tens-The Confederate Cavalry in the Kentucky Campaign of 1862* (Louisville KY: KH Press, 1992) 121.

[7] Robert Selph Henry, *Nathan Bedford Forrest—First with the Most* (New York NY: Smithmark Publishers, 1994) 85-86.

[8] Hafendorfer, *They Died by Twos and Tens,* 127.

[9] Ibid. See also, Stanley F. Horn, *The Army of Tennessee* (New York NY: Bobbs-Merrill Company, 1941) 161.

[10] Clement Evans, ed. *Confederate Military History Vol. VII* (Wilmington NC: Georgia Confederate Publishing Co., 1897).

[11] William H. King, "Forrest's Attack on Murfreesboro" *Confederate Veteran Magazine* Vol. 32, 430.

[12] Ibid.

[13] Bunting, manuscript MSS#25-0567

[14] *War of the Rebellion, Official Records* Series I Vol. 4, 809.

[15] Hafendorfer, *They Died by Twos and Tens*, 113.

[16] Bunting, manuscript MSS#25-0567.

[17] John Allen Wyeth, *That Devil Forrest* (Baton Rouge LA: Louisiana State University Press, 1959) 73.

[18] *War of the Rebellion, Official Records* Series II Vol. 4, 810-811.

[19] King, "Forrest's Attack on Murfreesboro" *Confederate Veteran Magazine* vol. 32, 430. See also *Confederate Military History* Vol. XII, 531-532.

[20] *War of the Rebellion, Official Records* Series I, Vol. 26 Part I, 810.

[21] Hafendorfer, *They Died by Twos and Tens*, 142.

[22] Bunting, manuscript MSS #25-0567.

[23] Hafendorfer, *They Died by Twos and Tens*, 142.

[24] Bunting, manuscript MSS#25-0567.

[25] Henry, *Nathan Bedford Forrest*, 85-88.

[26] Ibid.

[27] Ibid.

[28] King, "Forrest's Attack on Murfreesboro" *Confederate Veteran Magazine* Vol. 32, 430.

[29] *War of the Rebellion, Official Records* Vol. 26, Part 1, 811.

[30] Compiled Service Records, 2nd Georgia Cavalry.

[31] Ibid.

[32] Evans, ed. *Confederate Military History* Vol. VII, 531.

[33] King, "Forrest's Attack on Murfreesboro" *Confederate Veteran Magazine* Vol. 32, 430.

[34] Compiled Service Records, 2nd Georgia Cavalry.

[35] Evans, ed. *Confederate Military History* Vol. VII, 531.

[36] King, "Forrest's Attack on Murfreesboro" *Confederate Veteran Magazine* Vol. 32, 431.

[37] Hafendorfer, *They Died by Twos and Tens*, 129-130.

[38] King, "Forrest's Attack on Murfreesboro," *Confederate Veteran Magazine* Vol 32, 431.

[39] *War of the Rebellion, Official Records* Series I Vol. 26 Part 1, 807.

[40] Ibid.

[41] Mamie Yeary, *Reminiscences of the Boys in Gray* (Dayton OH: Morningside Press, 1986)

[42] Compiled Service Records, 2nd Georgia Cavalry.

[43] *War of the Rebellion, Official Records* Series I Vol. 26 Part 1, 807.

[44] Ibid.

[45] Hafendorfer, *They Died by Twos and Tens,* 129-130.

[46] *War of the Rebellion, Official Records,* Series I vol. 26 Part 1, 808.

[47] Ibid.

[48] Ibid, 792.

[49] Georgia Soldier Roster Commission of 1903 (Atlanta GA: Georgia Department of Archives and History).

[50] *War of the Rebellion, Official Records* Series I Vol. 26 Part 1, 811.

[51] Hafendorfer, *They Died by Twos and Tens,* 132.

[52] Bunting, manuscript MSS #25-0567.

[53] Compiled Service Records, 2nd Georgia Cavalry.

[54] *War of the Rebellion, Official Records,* series I Vol. 26 Part 1, 811.

[55] Pohanka, *Don Troiani's Civil War,* 23.

[56] Thomas L. Connelly, *Autumn of Glory: The Army of Tennessee 1862–1865* (Baton Rouge LA: Louisiana State University Press, 1971) 202.

[57] Starr, *The Union Cavalry in the Civil War, Vol. III,* 87.

[58] Davis, *The Fighting Men of the Civil War,* 74, 93.

[59] Henry, *Nathan Bedford Forrest,* 16-17.

[60] Longino, Letter to Miss Lillian Henderson, 10 April 1926.

[61] Davis, *Fighting Men of the Civil War,* 74, 89.

[62] Ibid.

[63] Yeary, *Reminiscences of the Boys in Gray.*

[64] *War of the Rebellion, Official Records* Series II Vol. 16 Part 1, 811, 818.

[65] Yeary, *Reminiscences of the Boys in Gray.*

[66] Hafendorfer, *They Died by Twos and Tens,* 144.

[67] *War of the Rebellion, Official Records,* Series II Vol. 16 Part 1, 811, 818.

[68] Compiled Service Records, 2nd Georgia Cavalry.

[69] Stanley F. Horn, *The Army of Tennessee* (New York NY: The Bobbs-Merrill Company, 1941) 161.

[70] John F. Moon, "Cavalry War Service" in *Reminiscences of Confederate Soldiers,* Vol. XIII (Atlanta GA: unpublished compilation, Georgia Department of Archives and History).

[71] Hurst, *Nathan Bedford Forrest,* 105.

[72] Hafendorfer, *They Died by Twos and Tens,* 172.

[73] Ibid, 255.

[74] Ibid.

[75] Compiled Service Records, 2nd Georgia Cavalry.

[76] Ibid.

[77] Hafendorfer, *They Died by Twos and Tens,* 255.

[78] Ibid, 274—275.

The Kentucky Campaign

On 6 September, Forrest's Brigade was ordered to move toward Nashville, providing a screen for Bragg's Army and harassing Buell's Army as it fell back toward the Cumberland River. The Union fall back was not just due to Bragg's movement, but to Gen. Kirby Smith's thrust into Kentucky and his overwhelming victory at Richmond, Kentucky. By the morning of the 7th, the 2nd Georgia, the 8th Texas, Bacot's Squadron, and Baxter Smith's Tennessee Battalion had passed through Lebanon and were on their way to Murfreesboro. Apparently, Forrest had sent scouting parties well ahead, for he reported to Bragg that the enemy was evacuating Nashville.[1]

On 8 September, Forrest's Brigade reached Murfreesboro, and a day later they crossed the Cumberland River at the mouth of Stones River. On the 10th, the Brigade was on the Louisville Turnpike headed toward Tyree Springs when it encountered Union cavalry units and drove them off. On the Gallatin Road north of Tyree Springs the next day, Forrest's men captured the advance guard of the 9th Michigan Infantry, mortally wounding one officer. The Union infantry moved up with two pieces of artillery, and a skirmish of perhaps two hours followed. Apparently out of concern that other Union forces would come up and he would be trapped, Forrest withdrew, and several of his wounded men were captured. Two would later die.[2] Regimental records show no casualties for the 2nd Georgia this day and make no mention of this action. However, Cpl Littleton Spinks of G Company did recall the regiment being involved in several "small engagements" shortly after crossing the river into Kentucky.[3]

As Forrest's cavalry crossed into Kentucky early on the morning of 12 September, Col. Joe Wheeler's cavalry was fighting a delaying action against Gen. T. L. Crittenden's Division nearby at Woodburn. Hearing the sounds of battle, Forrest took his brigade to attack, a move that almost proved disastrous. Mistaking Wheeler's Brigade for the enemy, Forrest sent the 8th Texas forward and took the 2nd Georgia and the Tennessee battalion on a flanking movement. Wheeler's men, who were in hot pursuit of a Union cavalry/infantry force, became alarmed when they saw another large cavalry force before them, and an even larger force on their rear. Wheeler's men began to fall back in disarray before the two sides realized the mistake.[4]

Two days after the incident at Woodburn, General Braxton Bragg reorganized his cavalry forces into two brigades, one under Forrest and another under Wheeler, and assigned each brigade to an infantry wing commander. Forrest's new brigade, much smaller than Wheeler's, now consisted only of the 2nd Georgia, the 4th Tennessee, and Bacot's Squadron. This tiny brigade was charged with protecting the army's right wing under Leonidas Polk as they invaded Kentucky.[5]

The 2nd Georgia crossed the Green River in advance of Polk's infantry, which on 16 September formed in line of battle at Munfordville, Kentucky. When the Confederate infantry began moving up behind the cavalry, the commander of the 4,000 man Federal garrison there surrendered their fort without a shot.

As the gray columns pushed north, Polk ordered Forrest to put a strong force in front of the infantry's wagon train, protect the flanks of the infantry, and at the same time, push ahead and destroy the L&N rail line between Louisville and Elizabethtown. It was an impossible task for so small a force, and it almost led to the destruction of the 2nd Georgia.

Bacot's Squadron and the 4th Tennessee were sent to guard the wagon train, while the 2nd Georgia was divided into two groups to guard the flanks of Polk's infantry and destroy the rail line. Maj. Caleb Whaley took four companies to Polk's right, and Col. Lawton took six companies to the left. Shortly thereafter, according to one account,[6] Lawton sent three companies with Lt. Col. Hood to destroy the railroad at Elizabethtown.

While Hood was in Elizabethtown late on the afternoon of 20 September, he reportedly was surprised by the 2nd Michigan Cavalry and a number of his men captured as he beat a hasty retreat.[7] No reference to this action has been found in the official record, and surviving muster rolls show no members of the 2nd Georgia captured at Elizabethtown this day.[8] If the facts of the Elizabethtown encounter are unclear, the events of the following morning are well documented.

Lawton and Hood met near Hodgenville early on the 21st, and moved northeast to Boston. From Boston, Lawton sent Hood with a small force toward Lebanon Junction to destroy the L&N Railroad. Leaving most of his men near Wilson's Creek, Hood moved forward with a scouting party. Early that afternoon this small party ran into Col. Lawrence Shuler's 4th Indiana Cavalry Battalion at Lebanon Junction. Hood's scouts fled back to Wilson's Creek where the rest of the party joined the hasty retreat. Pvt. W. C. D. Broadnax of D Company had his horse shot out from under him,[9] and according to one Federal source, five Confederate troopers were killed, and seventeen wounded.[10] Pvt. Broadnax managed to escape, but thirty-two others were captured according to Federal reports. Surviving muster rolls identify twenty-three men, mostly from A and E companies, as captured, but no dead and only Pvt. Addison Davis of G Company as wounded.[11] Two of the Union troopers were reportedly wounded and eleven were captured.[12]

Pvt. William Ball of A Company and Pvt. Drewry Bailey of E Company were among the captured, and both were soon dead from prison camp maladies. A number of the captured troopers were exchanged, however, and returned to the Regiment, including A Company 1st Sgt. Jake Little. Another of those exchanged was Pvt. James Fambro of E Company, who would rise to captain later in the war.[13] Also captured was seventeen-year old Pvt. James John McDonald, who later became Col. Crews' aide-de-camp. Young McDonald escaped soon after his capture. He would go on to serve throughout the war without being wounded, although he had five horses killed beneath him.[14]

The back-to-back failures at Elizabethtown and Lebanon Junction led to Col. Lawton preferring charges against Hood, and Hood's subsequent resignation.[15] Apparently, both Lawton and Forrest blamed Hood for the defeats.

After Lebanon Junction, the 2nd Georgia moved to Hodgenville for a rendezvous with Wharton and Wheeler. While the two cavalry brigades resided here, General William Hardee issued orders which assigned four 2nd Georgia companies under Maj. Whaley to Joe

Wheeler's Brigade. Evidence suggests that the companies with Whaley were his own H Company, along with D, I, and K, leaving companies A, B, C, E, F, and G with Lawton.[16] On this same day, however, Col. Lawton informed Forrest of his plans to resign his commission, apparently for personal reasons unrelated to Hood's failures. Lawton gave as reasons his age of "past 45" and the fact that his wife and daughters were alone on his Albany plantation.[17] Lawton may also have had health problems. His apparent absences at critical times during the summer are not explained in the records, but he may have had lingering problems from wounds or illness related to his previous service in Virginia.

Lawton may have been discouraged by the splitting of his regiment, but it is also possible that the regiment was split because of Lawton's plans to retire. With both Lawton and Hood gone and Whaley assigned to Wheeler, the remaining six companies of the 2nd Georgia were widely scattered. Two companies were detached to Colonel L. W. O'Bannon to guard the wagon train, one company was assigned police duty in Bardstown, and another was assigned to the Engineer Corps. In addition, thirteen men were sent to Danville with condemned horses and twenty men were sent to guard the mills at Fairfield and Bloomfield.[18] This left just two companies actually present with Forrest. Based on accounts of veterans after the war, it appears that companies E and F were with Forrest.[19]

Late that evening Forrest sent word to General Polk that his brigade had been reduced to a skeleton, and was incapable of carrying out its assigned missions. On the 25th, Forrest himself was gone, replaced by Col. John Wharton and sent back to Tennessee to raise another cavalry brigade. Very likely, Forrest had requested this reassignment, as his current brigade had been reduced by Bragg to little more than a regiment. As Hafendorfer wrote, Forrest "...had taken the beaten and disheartened remnants of John Adam's Brigade, the disorganized Tennesseans under Baxter Smith, and the inexperienced Georgians under Winburn Lawton, and had forged them into one of the South's most noted cavalry brigades." [20]

Technically, six companies of the 2nd Georgia were now in Wharton's Brigade, but as we have seen, only two companies, probably E and F, joined him at Boston after Forrest's departure. Indeed, in his report of 27 September, Wharton claimed only one company of the 2nd Georgia still available to him.[21] It is not clear how long this condition remained, but it seems likely that Polk or Bragg would have made some moves to return some of the detached 2nd Georgia companies to Wharton's badly depleted force. The assignment with the engineers and the police duty in Bardstown probably did not last long. And, as we will see, there is evidence to suggest that the two portions of the Regiment were reunited sometime before 14 October.

Whether with Wheeler or Wharton, men of the 2nd Georgia were involved in almost daily conflicts throughout the Kentucky campaign. On 1 October, blue infantry struck Wharton's Brigade on Polk's right flank at Wilsonville, Shepherdsville, and in front of Mount Washington at Floyd's Fork. According to one account, "Lieutenant DeVaughn made a handsome fight at Mt. Washington, with twenty men, contending against a Federal regiment."[22] Presumably, DeVaughn's detachment in this fight was from his own F Company.

That evening, Wharton's men checked Shuler's 4th Indiana Cavalry Battalion, the same unit that had surprised Lt. Col. Hood's scouting party at Lebanon Junction. The following morning there was more skirmishing as more Federal units moved up. By noon, Gen. Crittenden was on the scene with his infantry, and sent the Union cavalry against Wharton's position across the stream. The Federals were driven off, but Wharton withdrew back to Mt. Washington, where he paused to throw a few artillery rounds into his former position where the vastly superior Union force was now passing. By nightfall, Wharton had retired a mile further to the Salt River.

Hafendorfer surmised that three companies of the 2nd Georgia were with Wharton by 3 October, and that they began that day watching the road from Taylorsville to Fairfield.[23] Evidence suggests that A Company, E Company, and F Company that evening rejoined Wharton's main force as they fell back toward Bardstown. If the 2nd Georgia troopers on police duty at Bardstown had not previously rejoined Wharton, they almost certainly did so at this point. Polk was planning to evacuate Bardstown and Wharton's Cavalry would screen his movement toward Danville.[24]

Seeing Wharton's vulnerability, Buell on 4 October sent three full divisions of cavalry and infantry to encircle Wharton's cavalry near Bardstown. Wharton reacted to this challenge by putting his brigade in columns of four, and leading them south on the Bardstown Road to meet the enemy in his rear. At the fairgrounds, Wharton took the brigade cross country and struck the 3rd Ohio, 1st Ohio, and 2nd Kentucky cavalry regiments. A member of the 1st Ohio wrote later that the Rebels charged "yelling like demons" and Baxter Smith of the 4th Tennessee wrote that the charge was "stimulated by that wild yell peculiar to the Southerner."[25]

One of the Confederates who charged the front of the 3rd Ohio wrote, "we turned on them, halting in front of this picket fence with our bridle reins thrown over our saddles and with six-shooters in each hand, began to empty saddles. This caused them to break and they ran." Wharton "charged headlong into the well-formed federal cavalry lines, scattering them like chaff," wrote a member of the 8th Texas. Another member of the Texas Ranger regiment wrote that "the federals were panic-stricken and were driven over the open country, interspersed only by rail and rock fences, in detached bodies of 20 or 50, and so on, by only a few Rangers driving them like cattle on the prairies." Wrote Hafendorfer, "It was not only the men of the 8th Texas now pursuing the Federals, but also men of the 4th Tennessee and the 2nd Georgia." A member of the 58th Indiana Infantry wrote "This sudden retrograde movement of the cavalry caused a good deal of excitement and confusion among the infantry," and another Union infantryman, said "we were considerable worsted."[26]

Pvt. Henry Burr, who that past July had braved the Federal fire at the Murfreesboro Courthouse, was a participant in Wharton's breakout at Bardstown, indicating that probably all of the 2nd Georgia's E Company was with involved here.[27] Lt. DeVaughn's action at Mt. Washington on 1 October indicates that Company F was also with Wharton and probably involved in the Bardstown breakout. Pvt. William Murray of A Company was killed in the Bardstown action.

The following day Wharton's command was sent to gather supplies at the Lebanon depot, and to cover the flank near Danville. They were ordered to remain there, for Bragg still did not believe that he was contending with Buell's entire army. For this reason, Wharton did not arrive in Perryville until the 7th, the day before the climactic battle of the Kentucky Campaign.

Meanwhile, Wheeler's Brigade, including the four companies of the 2nd Georgia under Maj. C. A. Whaley, had been stubbornly resisting Gen. C. C. Gilbert's advance. Gilbert wrote after the war, "Our advance was vigorously resisted by Wheeler's cavalry, forming the rear-guard of Hardee's corps, which was retiring before us."[28] About 8 A.M. on 6 October, Gilbert's Corps ran into Wheeler's defensive line just east of Springfield at the city cemetery. After a brief artillery exchange, the 87th

Indiana and the 2nd Minnesota, and perhaps other elements of Steedman's Brigade, tried unsuccessfully to dislodge Wheeler's dismounted men from behind the stone walls and fences at the cemetery. Hardee had ordered Wheeler to hold Springfield until 11 A.M., and it was almost noon before the arrival of fresh brigades from Gilbert's Corps forced Wheeler to withdraw.[29]

Wheeler's withdrawal was only about three miles to Pleasant Run on the road to Perryville. Here his dismounted men formed another defensive line on high ground. By mid-afternoon they were again engaged, first with Ebenezer Gay's cavalry brigade and then with Steedman's infantry. The fighting here lasted about two hours, and, according to Union reports, resulted in about ten Rebel casualties and three or four wounded Federals. Wheeler's only comment on casualties was that, "Our dead we buried, and our wounded we brought off the field...."[30]

Late that afternoon, Wheeler set another defensive line at another stream, Little Beech Fork, less than two miles away. As the Union cavalry advanced, Wheeler grew uneasy with this position and fell back several hundred yards to higher ground. A few of his men were captured before they could reach the new position on Grassy Mound. Gay's cavalry, some 1,300 strong, advanced up the slope but were driven back by heavy fire.[31] The 2nd Georgia troopers with Whaley and the rest of Wheeler's men spent the night of 6 October on Grassy Mound, and awoke to find most of Gilbert's Corps gathering before them.

On the morning of 7 October, Gilbert's Corps was only some seven miles from Perryville. However, the Federals did not reach the small village until late that evening, and when they did arrive, they found Hardee's Corps strongly entrenched on a ridge beyond Doctor's Creek.[32]

Earlier that day on the Springfield Road, Wheeler ambushed Gay's advance cavalry at Brown's Hill. As his brigade came forward, Gay dismounted his men and sent them against the Rebel troopers in position behind haystacks and rail fences. When heavy fire stopped their advance, Gay inexplicably sent 500 troopers of the 9th Kentucky on a charge up Brown's Hill. The men of the 9th Kentucky "...very soon struck for their homes, hatless, and considerably demoralized." Seeing this, Wheeler ordered his mounted reserve to charge, speeding Gay's retreat.[33]

By noon, Union artillery and infantry were on the scene and firing on Wheeler's position. Around 1 P.M. Wheeler fell back to successive positions until he reached Peter's Hill, where he formed another line of battle. Caleb Whaley's 2nd Georgia companies were apparently part of this line, as parts of the 1st and 3rd Alabama and the 1st Kentucky were held in mounted reserve. This time it was Union infantry that advanced, but again heavy fire from the defensive line forced the Federals to halt. As the Union infantry went to ground, Wheeler sent the mounted reserve on a charge in column. The Union line broke and retreated down the Springfield Road. Seven officers and men of the pursuing Rebels were killed farther down the road when ambushed by two infantry regiments hidden in the cornfields. All of the prisoners taken in the countercharge escaped in this ambush, but the Alabamians and Kentuckians were able to return to Wheeler's line in good order. That night, under orders from Hardee, Wheeler fell back to Perryville.[34] The 2nd Georgia men and their comrades had been through two long days of fighting, but it would be a long time yet before they could rest.

The only known casualty for the 2nd Georgia from the fighting of the 7th was Pvt. William A. Ellis of E Company, who was wounded. One of six Ellis men in the company, including an eventual company commander, William had a particularly eventful career. Prior to joining the 2nd Georgia he had served with another unit and was wounded at Shiloh. For some unrecorded reason, court martial proceedings were started against him on 3 May, 1863, but he was back in service just a few days later. His military career apparently ended in the fighting around Atlanta 20 July, 1864, when he was wounded a third time.[35]

On 8 October, the Battle of Perryville began when Wheeler led his brigade on a dawn charge down Lebanon Road, routing McCook's cavalry and a line of infantry supported by artillery, and chasing them more than a mile and a half. Wheeler's men took more than 140 prisoners on this charge, but more importantly, the boldness of the charge led Gen.Thomas Leonidas Crittenden to think that his corps faced a much larger force. Crittenden formed his corps on a hill west of the small village, apparently intending to turn the Confederate left flank. Wheeler's repeated charges kept Crittenden at bay, however, as he stopped his advance and began placing his brigades in line.[36] It was probably in this action that Pvt. William Goodson of the 2nd Georgia's D Company was killed.[37] For the rest of this bloody day, Wheeler's cavalry was only lightly engaged, and guarded the Danville and Lebanon pikes.[38]

When the Confederates that afternoon launched their main attack against the Federal left, their advance was led by Wharton's cavalry. Wharton's Brigade "made a sweeping gallop as if on dress parade" driving the 2nd Kentucky Cavalry and the advance of the 33rd Ohio Infantry back to their main infantry line. Gen. Polk later wrote that "Wharton charged the enemy's extreme left with great fury, passing over stone walls and ravines, driving back the enemy's infantry several hundred yards." Bragg ordered Wharton to clear the surrounding high ground in preparation for Cheatham's attack, and the mission was accomplished. Several members of the brigade were killed or wounded in the charge, however, and Wharton's men fell back when the 19th Indiana Artillery joined the fray.[39]

Later Wharton's Brigade helped place an artillery battery on the far right where it could fire on McCook's flank, manned by Col. John Starkweather's brigade. Acting on orders from Bragg, Wharton moved to Starkweather's left in preparation for a charge. Heavy fire from the 4th Indiana Artillery changed Wharton's mind, however, and he moved his brigade into the woods and out of sight. It is not clear how many casualties were inflicted by this barrage, but a veteran of the 8th Texas reported "…a complete set of fours cut down…" by a single artillery round that passed through four horses and took both legs off one trooper below the knee.[40]

While Wharton was thus engaged on the Union left, Wheeler was busy on the Confederate left around the Lebanon Road. Dismounted troopers from his brigade advanced over half a mile, taking possession of the Williams farm house. As their artillery traded fire, Wheeler's dismounted men and the dismounted men of the 1st Kentucky skirmished in the woods. An attempt by the 1st Kentucky to flank Wheeler was repulsed, as was a charge by one of Wheeler's companies. It is not clear whether Wheeler knew at the time that he faced an entire Union corps, but in the late afternoon he fell back to the Moreman House. At least some historians think that the vigor of Wheeler's action led the Federal command to again overestimate the size of the force in front of them.[41]

The Battle of Perryville was especially bloody on the Federal left, with "close hand-to-hand fighting right up to nightfall."[42] Wharton's Brigade was posted on the Confederate right flank, and was "…frequently hotly engaged with the enemy."[43] Wrote one historian, "At the close of the day, there was no doubt in anybody's mind about the outcome of the immediate engagement. It was a complete victory for the 15,000 Confederates engaged. They had everything their way. The battlefield was in their possession; the Federals had been driven back a mile or more, broken and disorganized."[44] Wheeler later wrote, "At every point of battle the Confederates had been victorious. We had engaged three corps of the Federal army; one of these, A.M. McCooks, to use Buell's language, was 'very much crippled,' one division, again to use his language, 'having in fact almost entirely disappeared as a body.'"[45]

But Bragg had become aware that Buell's main force, some 68,000 strong, was on the field, and that night he ordered a withdrawal toward Harrodsburg and a possible rendezvous with Kirby Smith's army. For the gray cavalry, this meant more rear guard skirmishing, which began early on the next morning before all of Bragg's Army had cleared the town. At Nevada Station, Gay's cavalry brigade was close on Wharton's rear guard threatening the safety of the infantry. Wheeler reported skirmishing throughout the day, but the Union push could not have been great because Wheeler and Wharton had separate camps that night just four miles from Perryville and Buell's army.[46]

It should be noted that at some point during the retreat from Kentucky, the 2nd Georgia's G Company was assigned to drive cattle for the army. The assignment was short-lived, however, as they soon rose from lowly cattle drivers to escort company for Gen. Benjamin Franklin Cheatham, one of the most noted fighters in the Army of Tennessee. They would serve in that capacity through Stones River, Chickamauga, and Missionary Ridge. Accounts of their return to the Regiment vary. One account has G Company rejoining the 2nd Georgia during the winter of 1864, presumably upon their return to Dalton after the Knoxville Campaign. Another account says G Company remained as Cheatham's escort until after the fall of Atlanta.[47]

Early on the morning of 10 October, Wheeler moved out the Danville Road, and ran into McCook's cavalry. The Confederates pushed McCook's men back, but around mid-day encountered the lead division of Crittenden's Corps at Salt River. General William Smith's Division drove Wheeler toward Danville, "killing and capturing some."[48]

On the 11th and 12th, Wheeler made successful attacks upon Union columns, taking sixty prisoners.[49] Wheeler's reports on these movements of Union forces apparently led Bragg to abandon any idea he might have had of giving battle at Harrodsburg. After joining with Smith there, Bragg "was able to present a battle front made up of his greatest available force." Kirby Smith reportedly urged Bragg to attack, but the Commander had apparently lost the resolve that made him invade Kentucky in the first place.[50]

Said Confederate Gen. Basil W. Duke, "Had the battle been joined at Harrodsburg, it would have been the only great field of the war—east or west—on which the Confederate forces were numerically the stronger; and every other conceivable factor was in their favor. Never was the morale of an army better than that of General Bragg's on the eve of that anticipated conflict. The men seemed to realize what was at stake and to fear nothing but retreat, which should carry back war and invasion to their homes and people....General Bragg ought to have fought them then and there, and must have won. But the gloomy and hostile destiny which seemed to visit her banners...smote our commander at Harrodsburg with a consternation which no man in his ardent undaunted ranks shared then or can understand now."[51]

At least one Union general shared this assessment. Gen. Gilbert, whose third corps had been so delayed by Wheeler's men, later wrote, "It was a piece of very good fortune for the Union side that the Confederates did not return to renew the battle, for they would have had such an advantage in numbers and in the character of their troops that the Army of the Ohio would have been placed in great peril. In not returning to Perryville and resuming the battle, he lost for the Confederacy perhaps the only opportunity it ever had of fighting a great battle with a decisive preponderance in numbers and the character of its troops."[52] (While Bragg's contemporaries were extremely critical of his decision to abandon Harrodsburg, some historians have contended that he had little choice but to retreat if he was to avoid being trapped.)[53]

Bragg apparently had little grasp of the magnitude of the Union losses. McCook's brigades had been badly depleted, and Gilbert's and Crittenden's two corps could muster only some 36,000 battleworthy men after the fight. Union casualties were 4,211 compared with 3,405 for the Confederates.[54] Some historians rank this battle along with Gettysburg and Atlanta as pivotal events in the war. The Confederate armies in the Western Theater would never again be so far north, and they were in imminent danger of having their escape routes cut off by Buell.

Bragg's ability to escape was due primarily to the cavalry brigades under Wheeler and Wharton. In charging Wheeler with the responsibility of covering his retreat, Bragg also made him "chief of cavalry," with authority to give orders in the name of the commanding general.[55] It proved to be a timely move, one which very likely saved Bragg's army from destruction.

Like the American infantryman in World War II who regarded as rear echelon "anyone whose foxhole is behind mine," Civil War infantrymen early in the war derided the fighting ability of the cavalry. In the Kentucky campaign, however, the Confederate cavalry probably saved the army from destruction, and the infantrymen knew it. Throughout the withdrawal from Kentucky, it was cavalry alone that retarded the Union pursuit, with practically no help from the Confederate infantry. Conversely, it was almost always Union infantry that the Rebel troopers engaged, as "The enemy's cavalry, so repeatedly beaten by Wheeler's command, was sent to the rear, and infantry alone used by them to fight every step of their march. These Wheeler met at Mount Vernon, Barren Valley, Rocky Hill, Bushy Mound, Wild Cat, Pittman's Crossroads, Little Rock, Castle River, and several other points, inflicting upon them considerable loss."[56]

As Bragg began his retreat from Kentucky on 13 October, the Rebel cavalry not only saved Bragg's army, their success probably led to Buell's dismissal. Before daylight on 14 October, Bragg sent a lengthy message to Wheeler, outlining the retreat plan. The Army of the Mississippi would retreat from Crab Orchard down the Wilderness Road, while Kirby Smith's Army of Kentucky would move out of Lancaster east toward Big Hill. Wheeler's orders were to cover the rear of the retreating armies. It was a daunting challenge, but Wheeler was supremely confident that his thin cavalry lines could keep Buell's columns from striking the rear of the retreating Confederate infantry. In response to letters from infantry commanders urging him to hold back the enemy, Wheeler wrote, "Do not destroy anything. Do not abandon anything. Push on as rapidly as you can, and I will keep back the enemy. General Smith says the safety of his army depends upon my doing so, and I will do so at any cost." Based on Kirby Smith's letter of 15 October to Bragg, Wheeler's confident letter kept Smith from destroying his wagons and artillery.[57]

Buell was determined to trap and destroy the Confederates, especially Bragg's Army of the Mississippi. He ordered Thomas Crittenden's Corps and Alexander McCook's Corps south toward Stanford, with Edward McCook's Cavalry Brigade in advance. Gilbert's Corps he ordered to Lancaster, with the 1st Kentucky and 2nd Indiana cavalry regiments screening the gap between his two main columns. Even as Wheeler received his orders before dawn, the vast blue army was on the move.[58]

Dawn on 14 October found Wharton in a defensive position on the Wilderness Road, just north of Stanford and behind the Hanging Fork River. Wheeler was in position on the Lancaster Road just west of town, with pickets guarding his flanks along Dick's River.[59]

The first action came when the 2nd Indiana Cavalry drove in Wheeler's pickets and crossed Dick's River near the Lexington Pike. They were forced back across the River, however, when Col. Henry Ashby's Tennessee Cavalry moved down from Camp Dick Robinson. The 1st Kentucky bumped into Wheeler's main body and pulled back to wait on the infantry.

At this point Wheeler sent word to Wharton that he must hold out at Stanford as long as possible. Wheeler also asked Wharton if he needed reinforcements. Wharton had been asking for reinforcements since September, in large part because of the breakup of the 2nd Georgia. Subsequently, Gen. William Hardee had ordered Wheeler to send two "battalions" to Wharton. There is no clear record that the reinforcements were ever sent, but there is one significant piece of circumstantial evidence that they were. That evidence is the death of Maj. Caleb Whaley.[60]

As we have seen, Whaley was commanding four companies of the 2nd Georgia under Wheeler after Lawton's resignation and the breakup of the Regiment. On 14 October, however, Whaley was wounded *near* Stanford and died there on 22 October.[61] Since Wharton was at Stanford on the 14th and Wheeler was well north at Lancaster, it seems likely that the two elements of the 2nd Georgia were reunited in Wharton's brigade prior to the 14th. Very likely, Whaley became the regimental commander at this time.

It is not clear how Whaley was wounded, but there were two Federal accounts that a Confederate lieutenant colonel was found mortally wounded in Stanford this day.[62] This officer was almost certainly Maj. Whaley. It is possible that his rank was either misread or misreported. It is also possible, if indeed he had been put in command of the regiment, that Whaley was wearing the insignia of a lieutenant colonel. It should also be noted that, in his report of the campaign, Wheeler reported that the cavalry dead included "…field and company officers of every grade *except that of colonel…,* "lending further evidence that the dead officer at Stanford was not a colonel, but Major Whaley.[63] From the record it is clear that Whaley was wounded outside of Stanford, brought back to the town, and left there when Wharton retreated down the Wilderness

Road. Union or Confederate, commanders usually tried to take their wounded with them when they moved. Whaley may have been left in the hope that the advancing Federals could give him quicker medical attention.

The fighting had commenced about mid-morning when McCook's cavalry struck advance elements of Wharton's cavalry at Hawkins Branch. Since records show that Whaley was wounded *near* but not in Stanford, it was probably here that he fell.[64] The 2nd Georgia held its ground against the Federal cavalry here, but fell back on Wharton's main body when Wood's Infantry Division arrived on the scene. Known casualties for the Regiment in this action were W. H. Lewis of Company B, captured, and Pvt. Holcomb Henry Hall of Company C, wounded.[65]

After an artillery duel, Wood's Division, supported by two other infantry divisions, advanced in line of battle. Wharton fell back to a position on the Wilderness Road, some 3 1/2 miles north of Crab Orchard at Walnut Flat Creek. Here again they fought a delaying action against advance elements of the Federal column. Pvt. Judge Hogan of the 2nd Georgia's D Company was killed in this action.[66]

Wheeler linked up with Wharton near Crab Orchard in the early morning hours of 15 October. If the two elements of the 2nd Georgia had not already been reunited at Stanford, they certainly were now.

During the day, they fought delaying actions at Cedar Creek, Barren Mound, and Bushy Mound. In the latter engagement, the Confederates ambushed the 1st Kentucky Cavalry, pouring a murderous fire into the Federals from point blank range. The surprised Kentuckians immediately fled back down the hill.[67]

Over the next two days, the Confederate cavalrymen fought Federal infantry at Mount Vernon, Valley Woods, Rocky Hill, and Wildcat Mountain. The cavalrymen were almost continuously in the saddle and in harm's way as, according to one source, they "fought no less than 26 separate engagements in five days and nights" during this period.[68] A Texas cavalryman wrote that for a ten-day period there was never an order to unsaddle. Each day brought new dangers but no new rations for the starving cavalrymen. They wrote of digging corn kernels out of the earth where some infantry officer's horse had been fed the previous day, or of trimming scraps of meat from beef bones left by the abandoned campfire of a retreating infantry unit.[69]

The final conflicts of the campaign came on 19—21 October, with skirmishes at Nelson's Crossroads, Bloomfield, and Pitman's Crossroads.

One Texas Ranger's letter reflected an experience shared by the men of the 2nd Georgia. "From the day we entered Kentucky until the day we passed out of the state, 38 days, our regiment in part or as a whole had been under the fire of the enemy's guns 42 times, including Perryville Battle as one of those times. Fighting and skirmishing occurred every day and some days more than once. Except at Perryville our losses were generally light, but coming so frequently they amounted to many in the aggregate."[70]

Bragg wrote to Wheeler, "Your services have been most valuable and brilliant. No cavalry force was ever more handsomely handled and no army better covered." The pursuing Federals were also impressed. Wrote one soldier in Crittendon's Corps, "Provided with a 'Jackass Battery' Bragg's rear guard was skillfully maneuvered."

Another Union soldier, in Hazen's Brigade, wrote, "At every favorable point, they (Wheeler's Cavalry) lay in wait, concealed until the advance was close upon them, then would come shells from two small field pieces and a show of making a stand to compel the deployment of a regiment or two." According to Buell, "General Bragg's rear was covered by cavalry handled with more skill than had ever been known under similar circumstances."[71]

Wheeler was promoted to brigadier general for his success in covering Bragg's withdrawal from Kentucky.[72] It was the kind of work his cavalry would do so well for Gen. Joseph Johnston and the Army of Tennessee in the Atlanta campaign.

---

[1] *War of the Rebellion, Official Records of the Union and Confederate Armies* Series II Vol. 16 (Washington DC: U.S. Government Printing Office, 1890) 799—800.

[2] Kenneth A. Hafendorfer, *They Died by Twos and Tens—The Confederate Cavalry in the Kentucky Campaign of 1862* (Louisville KY: KH Press, 1992) 374.

[3] Mamie Yeary, *Reminiscences of the Boys in Gray, 1861—1865* (Dayton OH: Morningside Press, 1986).

[4] Hafendorfer, *They Died by Twos and Tens,* 380.

[5] Ibid, 467.

[6] Ibid, 470.

[7] Ibid.

[8] Compiled Service Records, 2nd Georgia Cavalry (Atlanta GA: Georgia Department of Archives and History).

[9] Compiled Service Records, 2nd Georgia Cavalry.

[10] Hafendorfer, *They Died by Twos and Tens,* 487.

[11] Compiled Service Records, 2nd Georgia Cavalry.

[12] Hafendorfer, *They Died by Twos and Tens,* 487.

[13] Compiled Service Records, 2nd Georgia Cavalry.

[14] Clement Evans, ed. *Confederate Military History, Vol. VII* (Georgia Confederate Publishing Co., 1897) 814.

[15] Hafendorfer, *They Died by Twos and Tens,* 490.

[16] Evans, ed., *Confederate Military History Vol. VII,* 531, 552, 603, 604, 889.

[17] Hafendorfer, *They Died by Twos and Tens,* 498-499.

[18] *War of the Rebellion, Official Records* Series II Vol. 16 Part 2, 881-882.

[19] Evans, ed. *Confederate Military History,* 531, 552, 603, 889.

[20] Hafendorfer, *They Died by Twos and Tens,* 513.

[21] Ibid, 518.

[22] Evans, ed. *Confederate Military History Vol. VII,* 604.

[23] Hafendorfer, *They Died by Twos and Tens,* 589.

[24] Thomas L. Connelly, *Army of the Heartland—The Army of Tennessee* (Baton Rouge LA: Louisiana State University Press, 1971) 247.

[25] Hafendorfer, *They Died by Twos and Tens,* 646—654.

[26] Ibid.

[27] Evans, ed., *Confederate Military History Vol. VII,* 532.

[28] Charles C. Gilbert, "On the Field of Perryville" In *Battles and Leaders of the Civil War Vol. III* (Edison NJ: Castle Books, 1995) 52.

[29] Hafendorfer, *They Died by Twos and Tens,* 676-677.

[30] Ibid.

[31] Ibid, 681-697.

[32] Stanley Horn, *The Army of Tennessee* (New York NY: The Bobbs-Merrill Company, 1941) 180.

[33] Hafendorfer, *They Died by Twos and Tens,* 681-687.

[34] Ibid.

[35] Compiled Service Records, 2nd Georgia Cavalry.

[36] Joseph Wheeler, "Bragg's Invasion of Kentucky" in *Battles and Leaders of the Civil War, Vol. III* (Edison NJ: Castle Books, 1995) 15-17.

[37] Compiled Service Records, 2nd Georgia Cavalry.

[38] Connelly, *Army of the Heartland,* 266.

[39] Hafendorfer, *They Died by Twos and Tens,* 720-726.

[40] Ibid,722.

[41] Ibid, 724-726.

[42] Horn, *The Army of Tennessee,* 184.

[43] B.F. Bunting, Chaplain, Terry's Texas Rangers, Wartime Manuscript MSS #25-0567 (Galveston TX: Rosenberg Library).

[44] Horn, *The Army of Tennessee*, 185.

[45] Joseph Wheeler, "Bragg's Invasion of Kentucky" In *Battles and Leaders of the Civil War, Vol. III* (Edison NJ: Castle Books, 1995) 17.

[46] Hafendorfer, *They Died by Twos and Tens*, 748-749.

[47] Evans, ed. *Confederate Military History Vol. III*, 655, 889.

[48] Hafendorfer, *They Died by Twos and Tens*, 752.

[49] Dodson, ed., *Campaigns of Wheeler and His Cavalry*, 25.

[50] Horn, *The Army of Tennessee*, 186-187.

[51] Ibid.

[52] Ibid.

[53] Connelly, *Army of the Heartland*, 279.

[54] *Atlanta Constitution*, 4 Sept. 1996.

[55] Dodson, ed. *Campaigns of Wheeler and His Cavalry*, 26-32.

[56] Ibid.

[57] Ibid.

[58] Hafendorfer, *They Died by Twos and Tens*, 779-786.

[59] Ibid.

[60] Ibid.

[61] Georgia Soldier Roster Commission of 1903, Box 79, Location 3297-13 (Atlanta GA: Georgia Department of Archives and History).

[62] Hafendorfer, *They Died by Twos and Tens*, 779—786.

[63] *War of the Rebellion, Official Records* Series I Vol. 26 Part 1, 889.

[64] Georgia Soldier Roster Commission of 1903.

[65] Compiled Service Records, 2nd Georgia Cavalry.

[66] Ibid.

[67] Hafendorfer, *They Died by Twos and Tens*, 798 -799.

[68] N. C. White, "Through the Woods with Joe Wheeler" in *Reminiscences of Confederate Soldiers* Vol. XII (Atlanta GA: Georgia Department of Archives and History) 105-115.

[69] J. K. P. Blackburn, "Reminiscences of the Terry Texas Rangers" in *Terry Texas Ranger Trilogy* (Austin TX: State House Press, 1996) 132.

[70] Ibid, 129.

[71] Hafendorfer, *They Died by Twos and Tens*, 824—834.

[72] John P. Dyer, *From Shiloh to San Juan—the Life of Fightin' Joe Wheeler* (Baton Rouge LA: Louisiana State University Press, 1941) 57.

Return to Murfreesboro

With the reorganization of the Confederate Cavalry under Gen. Wheeler in November of 1862, the 2nd Georgia was once again a unified regiment, now under the command of Lt. Col. James E. Dunlop, and part of Wharton's Brigade. Described in service records as a "steady, well qualified officer," Dunlop suffered from arthritis, which would force his resignation the following March.

In addition to the 2nd Georgia, the brigade consisted of the 3rd Georgia, 8th Texas, 4th Tennessee, 1st Confederate and 3rd Confederate cavalry regiments as well as the 14th Alabama Cavalry Battalion and Davis' Tennessee Battalion. The 2nd Georgia's command structure for the next five months is shown below.[1]

Wheeler's Division
   Wharton's Brigade
      Dunlop's Regiment

A Company	Capt. Bennett Bridges
B Company	unknown
C Company	Capt. James Mayo
D Company	Capt. William Grant
E Company	Capt. Thomas Brooks
F Company	Capt. Hardy Chapman
G Company	Capt. Thomas Jordan
H Company	Capt. Francis Allen
I Company	Capt. George Looney
K Company	Capt. James Butts

As part of Wharton's Brigade, the 2nd Georgia was now in a cavalry division under five-foot six-inch, 26-year old Gen. Wheeler, the "War Child." In addition to commanding the division, Wheeler also had his own brigade. A West Pointer, Wheeler is described by historians as "Fighting Joe," aggressive and possessed of iron nerves and great endurance.[2] After the war, Gen. Sherman said of him, "In the event of war with a foreign country, Joe Wheeler is the man to command the cavalry of our army."[3]

Some historians have questioned Wheeler's fitness for the role of "Chief of Cavalry."
At least one has implied that he achieved this high station because he pandered to Gen. Bragg.[4] Bragg had been his benefactor, and Wheeler supported Bragg when many other officers were abandoning him. It can be argued, however, that he was simply being loyal to his commander, despite that commander's unpopularity. Indeed, he showed similar loyalty to all of his successive commanders, and most of the top infantry generals expressed high regard for Wheeler's competence—a remarkable testimony in an army rife with turmoil and intrigue in its officer corps. Long after the War, General Lafayette McLaws reportedly wrote, "Take him all in all, General Joseph Wheeler was the ablest cavalry officer in the Confederacy. He never made raids to get into the newspapers, nor did he carry a brazen trumpet to announce to the world his coming. He went straight forward, modestly, always in devoted earnestness to do as he was ordered."[5]

Wheeler's detractors offer evidence that he, unlike Forrest, was often ineffective when operating independently.[6] Indeed, it is easy to imagine that such responsibility may have been too much for one so young and inexperienced. Whatever his shortcomings, however, no one has questioned Wheeler's courage or his energy.

Certainly Wheeler was popular with the private soldiers. He shared their camps and their rations, even when better food and accommodation was available to him, and he shared their experience in battle. Wrote one veteran in an 1898 edition of the *Atlanta Journal,* "General Wheeler never asked his men to go where he would not lead, and for this we loved him, and gladly rode with him into places where we knew all could not come out alive....I never met him that he did not seem to try to show by his salutation that he respected the private as much as the private respected the general."[7]

The nicknames given Wheeler by his troopers show their affection for him. They called him "Fightin' Joe," "War Child," and "Little Bee Keeper," the latter connected to his habit while on the march of searching the tree tops for a bee tree.[8]

Based on the diary of a young lieutenant in the 4th Tennessee, Wharton's brigade, after leaving Kentucky, arrived at Knoxville on 1 November in a deep snow. Lt.. W. B. Corbitt wrote that, after a few days rest, the command was ordered to Kingston, where they remained for two weeks. The Brigade then crossed the mountains to Sparta, and a week later moved on to Murfreesboro. Bragg was spreading his Army, now officially the Army of Tennessee, in a wide arch southeast of Nashville. Polk's Corps occupied the center at Murfreesboro along with Wharton's Cavalry Brigade, which included Dunlop's 2nd Georgia.[9]

Apparently, some members of the 2nd Georgia's F Company were not at Murfreesboro with their comrades. A 6 November 1862 notice in the *Atlanta Intelligencer* directed,
"All members belonging to the Clayton Dragoons are hereby required to report to their command immediately, or they will be considered deserters, treated accordingly."

W. C. Chapman
Capt. Commanding
Clayton Dragoons[10]

During November and December of 1862, Wheeler was "engaging the enemy's pickets daily" between Nashville and Murfreesboro. In one of these fights, Wheeler himself was painfully wounded in the foot when a shell exploded under his horse, killing an aide at his side. The horse was one of sixteen to be killed while carrying Wheeler, who also had many staff officers wounded or killed at his side.[11] According to dispatches from the command, the 2nd Georgia and the rest of Wharton's Brigade were apparently not with Wheeler until 27 November.[12] Lt. Corbitt's diary also indicates that Wharton's Brigade was not involved with Wheeler during this time.[13]

On 5 December, Pvt. Henry Burr of E Company, who had come through unscathed at Murfreesboro, Bardstown, and Perryville, suffered a broken arm which disabled him for a time.[14]

On 9 December, Wheeler attacked a brigade of Yankee infantry, "capturing many prisoners."[15] A report of 10 December 1862, showed the 2nd Georgia Cavalry with 342 "effectives" and a total of 399 men.[16] That report also stated that one company (G Company) was providing escort for Gen. Cheatham and another company was on duty in Virginia. The record does not indicate which company was in Virginia at this time, but almost exactly a year later companies B, C, D, and F had men wounded or captured in Craig County near Cassville, Virginia.[17]

The Confederate picket line at this time extended almost thirty miles to within two miles of Yankee-occupied Nashville. Wharton's men constantly patrolled this countryside, and on 23 December, a detachment from the 8th Texas under Lt. M. C. Gordon and the 2nd Georgia under Lt. John F. Trippe captured fourteen men in the advance picket of the enemy on the Nolensville Pike. Several Union soldiers were left dead and wounded on the ground, while the Confederates "sustained no loss," except for Pvt. Perry Gray's horse.[18]

John Trippe of the 2nd Georgia's A Company had been a private in the 5th Georgia Infantry Regiment at the beginning of the War. Discharged with a disability in March 1862, he nevertheless joined the 2nd Georgia where he was elected a lieutenant as the regiment mustered into Confederate service.[19] Trippe did not know it at the time, but the encounter on the Nolensville Pike signaled the beginning of a major Union offensive.

On Christmas Day, Wharton reported fighting with the enemy "from sunrise until dark," near Nolensville, killing six and wounding fourteen. Wharton listed his own losses as three men wounded. Wharton also complained that while other cavalry commanders were drilling, his men had been in combat for ten continuous days. "The service that I am required to perform here is too much for my force, and it will soon be unfit for service," wrote Wharton. He added, "I take great pride in this brigade, and do not intend that it shall be used up without advising you of it."[20] Lt. Corbitt noted in his diary this day, "A general advance of the enemy commenced today hard fighting at Nolensville."[21]

The next day Wharton's scouts found Rosecrans' three corps, some 47,000 men, on the move through a cold mist and fog. Gen. A. M. McCook's corps was headed toward Murfreesboro on the Nolensville Pike, T. L. Crittenden and George H. Thomas were headed for the same destination on the Nashville and Franklin pikes. If not checked, these columns threatened to cut Bragg off from Hardee, and destroy the widely dispersed Confederate forces.

As the Union columns poured through the hilly countryside, Wharton abandoned Nolensville and his outpost at Franklin, and took positions on ridges north of Triune. From these high positions Wharton's batteries opened a lively artillery fight. The sounds of the firing carried to Bragg's headquarters, where the surprised commander was learning from Wheeler that Federal columns were also approaching LaVergne, barely fifteen miles away.[22] Lt. Corbitt's diary simply noted, "Skirmishing all along the front today. Cavalry retiring slowly before the enemy."[23]

Gen. Wheeler promised Bragg that he could delay this three-pronged advance for four days, and with Wharton's brigade, on 27 December, began a "vigorous" resistance which made good on the promise. Bragg that day began a frantic effort to consolidate his scattered forces before they were cut off. Hardee began moving his corps from Eagleville toward Murfreesboro, "leaving Wood's Brigade and Wharton's cavalry to skirmish with the enemy near Triune. This was done boldly and successfully, and they rejoined the command on the 28th at Murfreesboro."[24]

Assisted by the fog and drizzle, Wharton and Wood held out all day on the ridge above the Triune junction against overwhelming numbers. Lt. Col. R. Charlton of the 45th Mississippi reported regarding these skirmishes that "General Wharton's cavalry behaved in the most gallant manner, protecting their flanks while retreating."[25] As the fog lifted in the afternoon, the Union artillery became an overwhelming factor, and Wharton and Wood were driven off the high ground late in the day. Retreating in the fading light, the men of the 2nd Georgia must have taken some satisfaction in their day's work, for they had helped Hardee escape. Wharton's Brigade camped that night on a dirt road leading from the Shelbyville to the Salem Pike.[26]

In his official report of the battle, Gen. Bragg wrote, "To the skillful manner in which the cavalry was handled, and the exceeding gallantry of the officers and men, must be attributed the four days' time consumed by the enemy in reaching the battlefield, a distance of only twenty miles from his encampments, over fine macadamized roads." It was a feat that Generals Polk and Hardee said could not be done.[27]

The following day the 2nd Georgia was involved in a skirmish at Perkins Mill, and on the 29th they were involved in a more substantial action at Wilkinson's Crossroads. In his report of the action on the 29th, Wharton wrote that, "…we were engaged the entire day between the

Franklin dirt road and the Wilkinson pike with a large force of the enemy's cavalry, and that the Texas Rangers acted with even more than their usual gallantry in a dashing charge saving one regiment of the brigade from a complete rout by the enemy's forces." Wharton went on to explain that, "The Rangers, being armed with revolvers, are better prepared to meet the enemy's cavalry than other regiments in the brigade."[28]

It is quite possible that the 2nd Georgia was the "one regiment" saved by the charge of the Texans at Wilkinson's Crossroads. Whichever of Wharton's regiments was struck here, the Union Chief of Cavalry reported that he found them "in strong force" at Wilkinson's Crossroads. Gen. David S. Stanley wrote, "Our cavalry drove them rapidly across Overall's Creek, and within one-half mile of the enemy's line of battle. Unfortunately, their advance proved too reckless…and after a gallant struggle were compelled to retire, with the loss of Major Rosengarten and…the brave Major Ward."[29]

Whether or not they were the rescued regiment, the 2nd Georgia suffered casualties this day. Pvt. Lewis Davis of F Company had his horse shot from beneath him, and in C Company, Pvt. Thomas Brooks and Cpl. William Busbee were wounded. Pvt. A. S. McCollum of C Company and Lt. William Carruthers of K Company were captured.[30]

Based on Lt. Corbitt's diary for 29 December, it appears unlikely that his 4th Tennessee was the "rescued" regiment. The entry reads simply, "The Command moved out on the Wilkinson pike to meet the enemy this morning Heavy skirmishing all day fired on by Gen Cheatham's skirmishers this evening wounding Wood Seat of the Escort & killing two men of Malone's Battalion"[31]

Astoundingly, Wharton's report of the Wilkinson's Crossroads action indicates that most of his troopers still did not have sidearms. Moreover, many still had only shotguns as their long arm.[32]

Despite their inadequate weapons, the cavalrymen so delayed Rosecrans that Bragg was able to assemble his 34,000 infantrymen two miles north of Murfreesboro, near Stones River, before the Union columns arrived on 30 December. Rosecrans found the Confederate flanks covered by Wheeler's Brigade on the right and Wharton's on the left.

Wheeler, however, was not personally present on the right flank that day. Around midnight on the 29th, Wheeler had taken elements of several regiments, about 3,000 men, on a "daring raid completely around the flank and rear of the whole Federal army."[33] Neither Wheeler nor Wharton mentions any detachment of the 2nd Georgia participating in this raid.[34] Lt. Corbitt's diary said only that, "The command formed on Gen Cheathams left A sharp fight came off this evening lasting from 3 oclk until night"[35]

Wheeler's cavalrymen set out at full gallop when it was raining and so dark that "one could not see the trooper by his side." At dawn on the 30th , Wheeler struck Starkweather's Brigade of Rousseau's Division at Jefferson, just as its sixty-four-wagon train was arriving in camp. According to one Union officer, "Wheeler's men, dismounted, advanced gallantly to the charge, when they were just as gallantly met." After about two hours of fighting, Wheeler remounted his troopers and continued on to La Vergne. He left behind twenty destroyed wagons and 122 killed, wounded, and missing Union soldiers.[36]

Arriving at La Vergne about mid-day, Wheeler fell upon the 300-wagon supply train for McCook's Corps. Several hundred Union soldiers were captured and over $1 million worth of army stores were destroyed. Enough arms were captured "to arm a brigade," and Wheeler was able to remount many of his men.[37] An officer in one of Thomas' brigades, passing through LaVergne the next morning, described the scene where Wheeler's men had destoyed the 300 wagons of McCook's Corps. "The turnpike as far as the eye could reach was filled with burning wagons. The country was overspread with disarmed men, broken down horses and mules. The streets were covered with empty valises, trunks, knapsacks, broken guns, and all the indescribable debris of a captured and rifled army train."[38]

Later in the day, Federal trains at Rock Spring and Nolensville suffered the same fate, with another 300 soldiers taken prisoner.[39] In reporting the spoils of the raid later, one of Wheeler's officers added, "We also had an immense deal of fun."[40]

By some accounts, Wheeler showed up on Bragg's right flank at dawn 31 December, in time for the Battle of Stone's River.[41] (The Confederates referred to this as thc Battle of Murfreesboro, but this narrative will use the Stone's River designation to avoid confusion with Forrest's 13 July action.) One account has Wheeler not returning back from his raid until early that afternoon.[42]

The Battle of Stones River began in earnest at first light on the last day of 1862. Confederates in McCown's Division struck McCook's Corps on the Federal right. A thick cedar grove between the two forces

"...was shot down by rifle fire and the trees lay in a tangled mass."[43] The Rebel infantry charged the cedar grove and McCook's men fell back, as brigades from Polk and Cleburne's divisions attacked to McCown's right. At the same time, Wharton's Cavalry Division had swung around the Union right and was "viciously hacking at right and rear."[44] (Note that Wharton's command is now described as a "division" after the addition of several other regiments.)

Wharton's attack has been described as "....a wild, Indian-style open field charge..." where his troopers struck the enemy flank on the Nashville Road.[45] This was probably the greatest mounted charge in which the 2nd Georgia participated. Wharton had divided his brigade into three commands—Texas Rangers, 2nd Georgia, and 3rd Confederate regiments under Col. Harrison; 1st Confederate, Davis Battalion, Malone's Battalion, and Murray's Regiment under Col. Cox; and the remainder serving as a reserve and protecting the battery. The 2nd Georgia this day was commanded by Maj. Francis Marion Ison. Col. Dunlop' s arthritis may have disabled him on this bitterly cold day.[46]

Promptly at daylight, Wharton's men started at a trot around the enemy's right. The trot soon became a full gallop, as the troopers attempted to gain the rear of the Federals fleeing McCown's Infantry. After galloping over two miles, Wharton's Brigade formed up near the Wilkinson Pike, in front of McCook's retreating infantry. Almost immediately, Wharton ordered Cox's command to charge, which they did "in gallant style." Simultaneously, four companies of Texas Rangers charged and captured a four-gun Union battery, complete with horses, drivers, and harnesses. The 2nd Georgia and 3rd Confederate regiments apparently held the ground immediately in front of the enemy.[47]

In addition to the capture of the four-gun battery, this action netted another artillery piece and some 1,500 infantry captives, including the 75th Illinois Infantry. These were sent back behind the Confederate line and into Murfreesboro.[48]

By this time, the Confederate infantry had driven McCook's men well beyond the Wilkinson Pike, and Wharton again started his men around the enemy's right flank. As they approached the Nashville Pike, Wharton's cavalry found a Union wagon train guarded by artillery and a "heavy body of cavalry"...with a considerable body "drawn up nearer to me to give battle." Wharton stationed Harrison's command—the 2nd Georgia, the Texas Rangers, and the 3rd Confederate regiments—on the enemy's right flank, and sent Ashby's regiment and Hardy's company on a frontal charge. "They were met by a counter charge of the enemy, supposed to be the 4th Regulars, with drawn sabers." As Ashby's command became "hard pressed," Harrison's command, including the 2nd Georgia, was ordered to charge, "which they did in the most gallant and handsome manner." This charge completely routed the Union cavalry.[49]

Wharton then took advantage of the confusion caused by this retreat of the advanced cavalry, sending his entire brigade in a mounted charge against the enemy cavalry and infantry force protecting the wagon train. "This order was responded to in the most chivalrous manner, and 2,000 horsemen were hurled on the foe. The ground was exceedingly favorable for cavalry operations, and after a short hand-to-hand conflict, in which the revolver was used with deadly effect, the enemy fled form the field in the wildest confusion and dismay, and were pursued to Overall's Creek, a distance of two miles. After they had crossed Overall's Creek, the enemy reformed out of range of our guns." This action yielded 1,000 union infantry captives in addition to many pieces of artillery and several hundred wagons.[50]

Union Col. Lewis Zahm's report of the engagement gave a forthright description. "…the First and Fourth retired pretty fast, the enemy in close pursuit after them, the 2nd East Tennessee (Federal) having the lead of them all. Matters looked pretty blue now….I was with the three regiments that skedadled and among the last to leave the field. Tried hard to rally them, but the panic was so great that I could not do it. All the officers and men behaved well through all the fighting up to the stampede, which was not very creditable."[51]

As Wharton's men charged the Union position, their battery, which had not been able to keep up with their advance, came under attack from some 300 Federal cavalrymen. Hearing of this threat, Wharton and two of his staff turned back in time to see the twenty men in the battery quickly unlimber their guns and repulse the charging Federals. After fleeing Wharton's artillery, however, this Federal cavalry fell upon the wagon train now in the hands of some of Wharton's men. With most of Wharton's Brigade still in pursuit of the enemy toward Overall Creek, they were able to recapture much of the wagon train and artillery. Still, Wharton was able to "bring off a portion of the wagons, 5 or 6 pieces [sic] of artillery, about 400 prisoners, 327 beef cattle, and a goodly number of mules cut from the wagons."[52] Most importantly, the retreat of Sheridan's infantry this day was due in large part to delays in receipt of ammunition, precipitated by Wharton's attack on the wagon train.[53] For the common soldiers of the 2nd Georgia Cavalry, the greatest significance of this attack was that all of the men who had been armed only with shotguns or other inadequate weapons were able to exchange them for weapons of "a more approved nature."[54]

Wharton was lavish in his praise of the brigade. "When it is borne in mind that the operations of this brigade were entirely in rear of the enemy, and not a mile from his line of battle; when it is likewise borne in mind that it successfully engaged all arms of the service—infantry, artillery, and cavalry—and captured and sent to the rear more prisoners than the command numbered, I think it will be cheerfully conceded that they performed meritorious and important services and are entitled to the commendation due from the commanding general to gallant soldiers."[55] Lt. Corbitt's diary entry was more subdued. "Cavalry did good work today capturing artillery, wagons & cattle together with several hundred prisoners."[56]

In estimating enemy casualties, Wharton commented only that they "...suffered severely, losing many officers and men, both killed and captured." One of the Union casualties was Col. Minor Milliken, "killed by Pvt. John Bowers of Company K, Texas Rangers, in single combat." Wharton put his own loss at about 150 killed, wounded, or missing.[57]

Surviving muster rolls show some sixteen casualties for the 2nd Georgia from 27 December to the 31st. These include five killed, five wounded, and six captured. Two of these were officers; 2nd Lt. John Wimberly of I Company was among the wounded, and 2nd Lt. William Carruthers of K Company was captured.[58]

Meanwhile, Gen. Cheatham's attack on Cleburne's right had also succeeded in driving Union defenders beyond Wilkinson Pike. Cheatham himself was probably in the thick of this action as three of the men in his escort were wounded. Nineteen year-old Pvt. William Caldwell of the 2nd Georgia's G Company died of his wounds a few weeks later, but Pvt. Thomas Brooks and Pvt. Jacob Champion recovered and returned to duty.[59]

By mid-morning McCook's entire corps had been pushed back so that its line was at a right angle to its original position, and the Federal position had taken on the aspect of a "half open jack knife."[60]

As at Perryville, the Confederates were briefly in position to deliver a knockout blow, but this time there were no reserves. The Union center, buttressed by every available artillery piece and every available brigade, held firm against repeated charges by Donelson's Tennessee brigade, which suffered extremely high losses.

New Year's Day was a bitterly cold stalemate with neither commander prepared to renew the battle. While the infantry huddled in their
trenches trying desperately to keep warm, the Rebel cavalry was ordered
to attack the enemy wherever possible on the Nashville Pike. Late that
afternoon, Wheeler's and Wharton's brigades attacked a large wagon
train at La Vergne, capturing about 100 wagons, 150 men, 300 mules,
and a piece of artillery. Most of the wagons could not be moved, and
were burned. A detachment of the 2nd Georgia was also in a skirmish
this day at Stewart's Creek. Most importantly, however, the Cavalry's
scouting informed Bragg that he was mistaken in his belief that the
Federals were retreating after their defeat on the first day of the battle.[61]

After four hours of fighting, Wharton's men headed back through
the cold night to Murfreesboro, some forty miles distant. They arrived
back on the Confederate left at about 1:00 A.M.

On 2 January, Bragg sent Gen. John C. Breckinridge against a ridge
west of the river which the Federals had occupied and fortified with
artillery. Breckinridge considered the assault, an "impossible thing" and
told Bragg so. But Bragg insisted, and Breckinridge led the attack at
about 4:00 in the afternoon. All went well at first, as the Union brigades
retreated toward the river. But as Breckinridge's men crossed the ridge,
they came within range of some fifty-eight Union cannons. The artillery
barrage that greeted the Confederates has been estimated to have been
at a rate of 100 shots per minute, and more than 1,700 Confederates
were killed assaulting this "nest" of artillery. Breckinridge's men retreated from a charge that "deserves to be ranked with Pickett's at
Gettysburg."[62]

Gen. Wharton's horse was killed as he personally took charge of an
artillery battery in an attempt to support Breckinridge. As Breckinridge's
men withdrew, Wharton's dismounted cavalry advanced to meet them
and cover their retreat. All that night the men of the 2nd Georgia were
back in the saddle, now protecting the right rear flank of Bragg's Army.

The Battle of Stones River was over. The Confederates had won the
first day decisively, and on the second day of fighting no ground was
won or lost. "For all practical purposes Bragg won the battle. However
his failure to pursue the victory and his actual retreat from the vicinity
placed the city in Rosecrans' hands, giving him a victory by default."[63]
As they retreated in a cold rain on 3 January, the men of the 2nd Georgia
must have wondered, as did the rest of the Confederates, what they had
to do to win. Cpl. Littleton Spinks of G Company wrote of the battle,

"This was a bloody fight and I thought we were getting the best of it, but Bragg fell back to Shelbyville."[64] Just as at Shiloh and Perryville, they retreated from a battle where they had fought well and won the field. It would not be the last time.

For the men in the 2nd Georgia, the retreat was made more gloomy by the absence of comrades lost in battle. Among the missing in the 2nd Georgia was Alexander S. McCollum of C Company, captured during the skirmishing prior to the main battle at Stones River. This is McCollum's account of his POW experience:

> On the 31st day of December, 1862 and the first day of January, 1863, a great battle was fought on Stone River near Murfreesboro, Tennessee between General Rosecrans on the Federal side, with General Bragg opposing him on the Confederate side.
>
> As the great armies approached the cavalry on both sides were thrown forward, and we experienced a number of minor cavalry encounters, in one of which I fell prisoner to the Third Ohio Cavalry. I was held under guard at an infantry picket post that night, and the next morning there was added quite bunch of other prisoners who had been similarly captured.
>
> We were held in the rear of the army of Gen. Rosecrans and witnessed the two days' battle. The right wing of the Federal Army faced a thick cedar grove, while the Confederates faced the same grove. This grove was shot down by rifle fire and and the trees lay in a tangled mass. The Confederates pushed through the cedar grove, and the Federal Army swung back until the prisoners were almost in a loop between the right wing and center of the Federal Army, and directly under the fire of the Confederate guns, and close beside us was the Federal wagon train. The prisoners were put to a double-quick for safer land, and the wagon train stampeded in the same direction. Just before us lay a railroad, and when the excited mules, four to each wagon, reached the railroad and the wagon wheels struck the iron rails, the wheels skidded, and the mules were thrown into the ditch. The stampede was something worth while, and as I remember it eclipsed my fear of the Confederate bullets as they passed, some of them seeming to whisper while others went screaming through. The wagon whips were poping, every teamster shouting to his mules, and the mules straining every muscle, and when they went into the ditch the teamsters went with them, and unsaddled, lay on the ground. The wagons were quickly righted up by other help and the mules thrown back in place, and no questions asked as to whether they were hurt, and no first aid was given. It was a cyclone time. We were soon halted

on account of the heavy firing, for the Confederate cavalry in the rear of Rosecrans' army were burning his wagon trains, and we had to right about face; and so we were held in full view of the battle until the two days fighting was over. After that we were held on the same ground. We had not seen nor heard of anything to eat since the day we were captured, and when a prisoner mentioned the matter we were told in language never seen in a prayer book nor heard in a Sunday School, that our cavalry had burned everything.

In marching through a sedge field we came upon a place where a sheep had been butchered and the head was still lying there, and we had no way of knowing how long it had lain there. A prisoner picked it up and said he would make a Texas dish of it. Our spirits soon rose when we saw a wagon load of corn in the rear unloading, and was guarded by soldiers with fixed bayonets. We were now in number about twelve hundred prisoners. We were marched by the corn pile and each prisoner was given two ears of corn. Only one prisoner made word of complaint. He told the Yankees they did not know how to feed up; that we ought to have a bundle of fodder to every two men. Anyhow, we parched our corn; and the picture of two aged citizens, held as prisoners pro tem, has never passed from my memory. They could have made the same progress with their eating had they been trying to chew buck shot. The prisoners would place their parched corn on a flat rock and scrub it with another flat rock and then lick the lower rock; thus replenishing the stock of sand we had in our gizzards. We were then placed in a bowling basin where we remained for several days while the rain was greatly falling. When our blankets were wet through, we were given five crackers each and marched to Nashville in the rain. We passed through the section where our cavalry had burned the wagon trains. Dead horses and mules had been rolled out of the road, and many square spots of ashes marked the spot where the wagons had stood. It all looked good to us. It was really refreshing.

We made the march to Nashville in something less than a day, as the distance was only twenty five miles. Some of the prisoners were placed in the penitentiary, some in a college building and some in the State House. I had the honor of being assigned to the State House. The next morning a box of crackers was carried up the stairs and O joy! we were told we were to have five more crackers each, and you never saw "such a gittin" up stairs you never did see. The box was placed upon the floor with a rent in the top which exposed some of the crackers to view. Several prisoners made an effort to secure a cracker; others followed till the men stood helpless and their heads formed a level stage, and on that stage a witty boy was singing a ditty when other boxes were brought. A file of Yankee soldiers with fixed bayonets soon cleared the situation and we received our five crackers and then we were soon locked up in box cars. That night we spent in Bowling Green, Ky. where the accommodation consisted in one floor upon which we could lie down. I had a fever and was suffering from intense thirst and I had no water in my canteen. All the prisoners were strangers to me. A boy said to me, "My canteen is full; drink all you want." He told me his name was Leonidas Boyle Baker, and that he was a member of the Kentucky cavalry. His countenance, his manner and his courtly bearing impressed me that he came of a find (sic) family.

From Bowling Green, Ky. to Alton, Illinois, we were transported on four rivers and rode on four boats. First, on the Barron River we rode on the Hettie Gilmore; on the Green River, the Fannie McBurnie; on the Ohio River, the Courier, and on the Mississippi River, the Hannibal.

On board one of the boats a young man told me there was an order for the prisoners to organize in clubs of twenty and one of the twenty was to be a sergeant to represent his club in the issue of three days' rations, and that there was an overflow of nine men. The young man told me his name was Lee Baker, and that he was the same boy who had given me the drink of water back in Bowling Green and he said he wanted us to stay together. I told him to make me sergeant and I would take care of the situation. I soon presented my application which was promptly honored, and we had three days' rations for nine men, and three days' rations for eleven of my neighbors in Southwest Georgia.

Some of the prisoners discovered a small door on the floor of the lower deck. It looked like it might open into the river below. They were soon in there and found a lower room to the boat called "the Hatch" and it was stacked with barrels of syrup and barrels of whiskey. The door above was surrounded by a wall of prisoners who passed down their canteens and their orders were promptly filled. Our nine canteens went down with an order of five whiskey and four for syrup, and the order was quickly filled in good, businesslike manner.

Our boat touched at Evansville, Indiana where the prisoners were ordered to load the boat with supplies. After a preliminary interview in which we agreed upon a course of action, my men responded to the call. When the job was over I had a large side of bacon and an unbroken box of crackers added to our stock of supplies. On the bow of the boat sat a number of barrels, and a Yankee soldier with a fixed bayonet was on guard there. I went up to him prepared to do business. I told him that history recorded many tragedies that had occurred on this historic river and the men wanted to be assured of a good watchman, and that I would like for him to keep his watch far down the river. He cut me off by saying, 'If you want to steal coffee, you be quick about it." I immediately made a dive for that coffee and lowered the supply in the barrel and got by with it. When the clouds rolled away following the discovery of the opening of business in the hatch, we found ourselves in position to open up a retail grocery and liquor business.

At Cairo, Illinois we were marched up into the central part of the city, in time of a heavy snow, where we stood in line and listened for quite a while to a speaker who dwelt at length on our having been forced into service, and the great opportunity we now had of taking the oath of allegiance to the United States without even the embarrassment of the presence of a commissioned officer, and of enjoying all the privileges of this great country. The citizenry looked on with breathless interest, and the prisoners glanced both ways on the line. When the order was given: 'Now all of you will take advantage of this step six paces to the front; Forward, March!' Not a single prisoner stirred his foot, and we were marched back through the fluffing snow. I chanced to be one of a number placed on the top deck of the boat. It rained and it sleeted. All the wrap I had became so frozen that I rolled it up and chucked it into an open four barrel. We walked the deck all night. My toe nails turned purple, and I rubbed my feet vigorously, and thus escaped serious consequences. Some of the men had to have their feet amputated, and some froze to death.

From Alton, Illinois we were carried by railroad to Chicago and placed in Camp Douglas prison, and were each given an armful of hay for our winter bed.

Soon after our arrival four thousand Confederate prisoners captured at an Arkansas post, were placed in camp Douglas, bringing us up in numbers to five thousand. We were not required to work, and our table fare was scant. Three days' rations were issued at a time. The cooks were our fellow prisoners, elected and controlled by the section of prisoners they served. Our breakfast call was at 9:30 A.M. We had a tin cup full of what was called coffee. I have never known what it was, but I heard others say that it was white oak acorns, beans and sawdust. It was hot, Black and bitter, but it did not kill us. On a tin plate we had little beef, said to be the refuse of the city markets. One narrow loaf of stale light bread was allotted each man for a day. We had just two meals each day. The second meal was at 4:00 o'clock P.M. when our tin cup would contain a part of a cabbage leaf, and sometimes a small Irish potato in lieu of the cabbage. On our tin plate we had a small, scant bit of real bacon, and a few Boston beans. Our cooks would excuse us when our plates were empty. We were a courtly family, and very respectful toward our cooks. Sometimes charges were preferred against our cook who would get a fair trial at a called conference of those he served, and his case passed upon.

We were lined up and searched from head to foot by the Chicago police, and a prisoner was not allowed to have anything of value on his person.

We have never known the personalties of a number of ladies in Illinois who assembled a good stock of clothing and donated it to the Confederate Prisoners in Camp Douglas. There were two ladies who contributed so generously that they were accorded the privilege of naming a state whose prisoners should be first served and have all the clothes they wanted. One lady named Texas, because the prisoners from this state were so far from home. The other lady named Georgia, and gave her reasons for such choice. The Texas and Georgia prisoners of my section held a conference and by unanimous consent passed resolutions that we would not accept a benefit that could not be equally shared by our fellow prisoners. The goods were brought in and opened up. The Georgia and Texas prisoners were then marched in and told of their privileges, and what they took was negligible.

Rough and hardy prisoners of other states were looking upon us, and some were moved to tears as they saw the self denial and magnimity of the men of Texas and Georgia. I have always felt that there was something in that atmosphere that was divine. Georgia and Texas walked away with the short end of the deal and all were satisfied.

The detachment of prisoners, among who I was numbered, left Camp Douglas on the first day of April 1863, and were transferred by rail to Baltimore, Md., thence on a boat called the Long Island, to City Point, Va. on the James River, where they were exchanged on the fourth day of April.

We were told that something over a thousand prisoners had died in Camp Douglas during our confinement of two months there. The dead were hauled away to the Rebel Grave-yard each morning at 8:00 o'clock, varying from twenty five to thirty each day, and many of these, we understood, had been preyed upon by wharf rats during the time they were in the dead house. We never knew in what manner our dead were buried, or where the Rebel Grave Yard was.

There was great rejoicing when we were told to be ready to go south; but my joy was shadowed by a great sorrow of heart, for Lee

Baker had lain by my side for many days with a slow fever, and resent-
ed the suggestion of a hospital, for we felt it would be certain death.
He said his mother lived in Kentucky within the Federal lines, and he
could write to her and she would send him some money; but he had
rather die than for his mother to know how he was fixed; but I knew
that his mother had rather know, so she could have her way. She sent
him twenty five dollars, but he was not allowed to have it when it
reached the prison; but he was given a small sum in checks on the sut-
ler's stores inside the prison, and I would visit these stores and buy oys-
ter soup and such other things as he would suggest. He would sometimes speak of a sister living in Knoxville, Tenn. and would say that if
he could get to her he would be taken care of; but Knoxville was a long
way off in the South, and his liberty to go any where on his own
motion was still further away—And, now our parting day had come.
Poor Lee, he had not had a dose of medicine, his tongue was hard
coated and racked, and his lips were almost black; All the time he
wanted a swallow of fresh water, and I had been his silent nurse. He
looked at at me so pleading and said: 'You are all going South and I
must stay here and die, for I cannot march.' I said to him: 'Lee, pull
yourself together, fold you blanket, throw it over your sholder, get in
line and answer to your name. When we are far enough outside the
prison gate that you will not be thrown back in there, throw yourself
on me.' It was a long march to the car. I went to the limit of my
strength and landed Lee Baker in the car. The guards who attended us
seemed care-free, for no prisoner wanted to escape, and and when the
cars would make a stop the prisoners would jump out and in at the
freight car door and nothing was said about it. At Pittsburg, Pa. I
jumped out of the car door and was pumping some water. I did not
hear the hail, but I heard the clicking of a gun, and I whirled to see a
rifle pointed at me. I sprang back with enough water to give Lee a
swallow.

On being turned over to the Confederate Officers at City Point,
Va. we were soon on freight cars, to be distributed to points we knew
not where. Far in the night I heard the Conductor call 'Knoxville,
Tennessee!" I shouted, 'Knoxville" Lee, Knoxville! Your sister! Your sister! I helped him off the train. The little shadow disappeared from me
in the starlight. Several months afterwards I received a long letter from
him in which he said he was well and strong.

A.S. McCollum
Company C—Second Regiment, Georgia Cavalry [65]

[1] Compiled Service Records, 2nd Georgia Cavalry (Atlanta GA: Georgia Department of Archives and History).

[2] Albert Castel, *Decision in the West, the Atlanta Campaign of 1864* (Lawrence KS: University Press of Kansas, 1992) 111.

[3] Theo F. Rodenbaugh, *The Photographic History of the Civil War, Vol. III, the Decisive Battles of the Cavalry* (Secaucus NJ: The Blue & Grey Press, 1987) 279.

[4] Thomas L. Connelly, *Autumn of Glory: The Army of Tennessee, 1862-65* (Baton Rouge LA: Louisiana State University Press, 1967) 5.

[5] W.C. Dodson, ed. *The Campaigns of Wheeler and His Cavalry* (Jackson TN: The Guild Bindery Press) 59.

[6] Castel, *Decision in the West,* 111.

[7] John P. Dyer, *From Shiloh to San Juan Hill—the Life of Fightin' Joe Wheeler* (Baton Rouge LA: The Louisiana State University Press, 1941) vii.

[8] Ibid, 59.

[9] W.B. Corbitt, Diary (Atlanta GA: The Robert W. Woodruff Library, Emory University).

[10] *Atlanta Intelligencer,* 6 November 1862 (Atlanta GA: Georgia Department of Archives and History).

[11] Dodson, ed., *The Campaigns of Wheeler and His Cavalry,* 42.

[12] Ibid, 44.

[13] Corbitt, diary.

[14] Clement Evans, ed., *Confederate Military History, Vol. VII* (Georgia Confederate Publishing Company, 1897) 532.

[15] Dodson, ed., *The Campaigns of Wheeler and His Cavalry,* 46.

[16] *Official Record, War of the Rebellion.* Series I Vol. 20 Part 2 (Washington DC: U.S. Government Printing Office 1890) 446.

[17] Compiled Service Records, 2nd Georgia Cavalry.

[18] Ibid. See also, *War of the Rebellion, Official Records.* Series I Vol. 20 Part I,159.

[19] Georgia Soldier Roster Commission of 1903 (Atlanta GA: Georgia Department of Archives and History) Box 79, Location 3297-13.

[20] *War of the Rebellion, Official Records.* Series I Vol.20 Part I, 159.

[21] Corbitt, diary.

[22] Thomas L. Connelly, *Autumn of Glory,* 44-45.

[23] Corbitt, diary.

[24] *War of the Rebellion, Official Records* Vol. 20 Part I, 772.

[25] Ibid., 906.

[26] Corbitt, diary.

[27] Dodson, ed., *The Campaigns of Wheeler and His Cavalry,* 50.

[28] *War of the Rebellion, Official Records* Series I Vol. 20, 969.

[29] Ibid.

[30] Compiled Service Records, 2nd Georgia Cavalry.

[31] Corbitt, diary.

[32] *War of the Rebellion, Official Records* Series I Vol. 20, 969.

[33] Stanley Horn, *The Army of Tennessee* (New York NY: The Bobbs-Merrill Co., 1941) 198.

[34] *War of the Rebellion, Official Records* Series I Vol. 20, 959, 956.

[35] Corbitt, diary.

[36] G. C. Kniffin, "The Battle of Stones River" in *Battles and Leaders of the Civil War, Vol. III* (Edison NJ: Castle Books, 1995) 614.

[37] Horn, *The Army of Tennessee,* 198.

[38] Ibid, 199.

[39] Kniffin, "The Battle of Stones River" in *Battles and Leaders of the Civil War, Vol. III,* 614.

[40] Dyer, *From Shiloh to San Juan Hill—the Life of Fightin' Joe Wheeler,* 68.

[41] Ibid. See also, G. C. Kniffin, "The Battle of Stones River" 614.

[42] Connelly, *Autumn of Glory,* 57.

[43] A. S. McCollum "A True Story of the Civil War" in *Reminiscences of Confederate Soldiers, Vol. XIII* unpublished volume (Atlanta GA: Georgia Department of Archives and History) 1.

[44] Horn, *The Army of Tennessee,* 200.

[45] Connelly, *Autumn of Glory,* 57.

[46] *War of the Rebellion, Official Records* Series I Vol. 20, 965-67.

[47] Ibid.

[48] Ibid.

[49] Ibid.

[50] Ibid.

[51] Ibid.

[52] Ibid., 968.

[53] Richard O'Shea, *Battle Maps of the Civil War* (New York NY: SMITHMARK Publishers, 1992) 79.

[54] *War of the Rebellion, Official Records* Series I Vol. 20, 968.

[55] Ibid.

[56] Corbitt, diary.

[57] *War of the Rebellion, Official Records* Series I Vol. 20, 968.

[58] Compiled Service Records, 2nd Georgia Cavalry.

[59] Ibid.

[60] Dyer, *From Shiloh to San Juan—The Life of Fightin' Joe Wheeler,* 69.

[61] Ibid.

[62] Ibid.

[63] Douglas Welsh, *The Complete Military History of the Civil War* (Greenwich CT: Brompton Books Corp. 1990) 59.

[64] Mamie Yeary, *Reminiscences of the Boys in Gray* (Dayton OH: Morningside Press, 1986).

[65] McCollum, "A True Story of the War" *Reminisceces of Confederate Soldiers, Vol. XIII* unpublished compilation (Atlanta GA: Georgia Department of Archives and History).

From Dover to Tullahoma

Following Stones River, the 2nd Georgia and other elements of Wharton's Brigade were again involved in the work of covering a withdrawal. Before daylight Sunday morning, 4 January, Wharton was ordered to move his brigade back into Murfreesboro. Here and on the Shelbyville Pike this day, the 2nd Georgia skirmished with Union forces. This indicates that the 2nd Georgia was one of the three regiments that Wharton left here to burn a bridge and retard any Union pursuit. They later rejoined the Brigade encamped on the Shelbyville Pike, where they remained until 29 January.[1]

On 10 January, a report of unit strength for the 2nd Georgia showed just 283 "effectives" and nineteen officers present for duty, with an aggregate present total of 438 men. While effective strength had declined considerably during December, the aggregate number actually went up by thirty-nine men. One factor that must have contributed to the disparity between effectives and the aggregate number was the availability of horses: only 292 mounts were with the regiment on 10 January 1863.[2]

Wheeler, who had previously commanded a brigade even while serving as chief of cavalry, was promoted to major general and was no longer serving a dual role, but was commanding a cavalry corps that included divisions under Generals Wharton, Martin, Morgan, and Forrest.

Wharton officially assumed command of a cavalry division on 22 January, and at that time the cavalry brigades were reorganized. Probably at this same time, Charles Crews was placed in charge of a brigade. The fact that he remained a colonel may indicate that this appointment was considered temporary—indeed, for the remainder of the war he alternated between command of the regiment and command of a brigade.[3] For about the next eight months, the 2nd Georgia's command structure looked like this:

Wheeler's Corps
Wharton's Division
Crews' Brigade (2nd, 3rd, 4th, Georgia & 7th Alabama)
Ison's Regiment

A Company	Capt. Bennett Bridges
B Company	unknown
C Company	Capt. James Mayo
D Company	Capt. William Grant
E Company	Capt. Thomas Brooks
F Company	Capt. Hardy Chapman
G Company	Capt. Thomas Jordan
H Company	Capt. Francis Allen
I Company	Capt. George Looney
K Company	Capt. James Butts[4]

Born in Tennessee, John Austin Wharton grew up on a plantation in Brazoria County, Texas. From 1846 to 1850 he attended South Carolina College (now the University of South Carolina) where he commanded the cadet corps. While in Columbia, he married Eliza Penelope Johnson, daughter of South Carolina Governor David Johnson. After college he returned to Texas and became a lawyer and a planter. He joined Terry's Texas Rangers in 1861 as a captain, and rose to colonel and regimental commander in 1862 after the deaths of Col. Benjamin Terry and Lt. Col. Thomas Lubbock.[5] Wharton was wounded at Shiloh and again at Murfreesboro. He rose to prominence when he replaced Forrest as brigade commander during the Kentucky Campaign. The professional soldiers in the command structure of the Western Theater were not sure this citizen soldier was fit to command, but he quickly proved his mettle. His breakout at Bardstown against overwhelming odds was especially noteworthy. Wharton was promoted to brigadier general on 18 November 1862, after the retreat from Kentucky.[6]

As Bragg's infantry went into winter camp at Tullahoma and Shelbyville, the cavalry stepped up the pressure on Rosecrans' supply line. The Battle of Stones River "left Rosecrans' Army badly crippled," and Wheeler's raid just prior to the battle greatly depleted Union food supplies, leaving the Union Army in a desperate situation.[7] Wheeler kept up the pressure, attacking supply lines and shipping on the Cumberland River.

Meanwhile, Wharton's division and the 2nd Georgia were left to screen the army at Tullahoma and Shelbyville. It was tough duty in the bitter cold. Sleet covered the troopers with an "icy armor," and icicles dangling from their horse's mane and tail would "rattle like beads."[8] Early on the morning of 29 January 1863, Wharton's Division broke camp and "moved off on the scout."[9] Lt. Corbitt's diary entry indicates that junior officers were unaware that they were embarking on a winter march of more than 100 miles. Wheeler planned with General Bragg to renew his attacks against Union shipping, and ordered Forrest to join him in the effort in the vicinity of Fort Donelson. Along with the rest of Wharton's Division, Crews' Brigade, including the 2nd Georgia, set out with Wheeler to rendezvous with Forrest.

Passing through Shelbyville and Unionville, they reached Eagleville about 4:00 P.M. and camped south of town. The following day they continued north, reaching Triune at mid-day and Franklin about 4:00 o'clock. Lt. Corbitt reported that they camped that night "at Dr. Perkins farm" one mile from town on the Columbia road.[10]

The long march continued northwest past Nashville for four more days until, on 3 February, according to Lt. Corbitt's diary, they arrived before the Union fortifications at Dover and "commenced the attack."[11] Upon linking up with Forrest, Wheeler learned that Union authorities had become aware of their presence and had suspended all shipping on the Cumberland River. Not wishing to remain idle after his long winter march, Wheeler changed his objective from river shipping to the fortified positions at Dover. (Many histories refer to this engagement as a second Fort Donelson, but the battle occurred not at the fort but at fortified positions in the town.) [12]

Forrest was concerned that an attack on the strong Union works at Dover in the bitter cold could not be successful, and had only reluctantly agreed to Wheeler's proposal. Forrest's mood was not improved when his mounted attacks on the east side of the Union position were twice repulsed, and both times the General's mount was killed. A third charge, this one on foot, was successful, with Forrest's men driving Federals from houses on the east side of town. From these houses, the

Rebels opened an effective fire on the Union positions. "At this moment," Wheeler reported, "the enemy commenced running out toward the river, and our men in the houses seeing this, and thinking it to be a movement on our held horses, abandoned their favorable position, and rushed back to protect them. But for this accident the garrison would have surrendered in a very few minutes. Gen. Forrest then withdrew and discontinued the action."[13]

Wheeler's statement that the garrison might have fallen had Forrest's men held their position was not completely unfounded, for Wharton's command had broached Union positions on the south and southwest side of town. The 2nd Georgia, 11th Texas, and 4th Tennessee regiments, charged on foot, "killing and wounding many of the enemy," driving them from their works and capturing a battery and a number of prisoners. Before night fell, they had a strong position on the west-side of town, but ammunition was running desperately low. Then, during the evening, a Union infantry brigade from Fort Henry began attacking the Texas Rangers, who had been posted to guard the rear and approaches from Fort Henry. Wheeler learned also that Union Gen. Granger was moving rapidly up the Cumberland with 5,000 men on transports and a fleet of gunboats.[14] Wheeler then withdrew, having engaged less than half of his force in the attack.[15]

Wheeler's failure at Dover is a major piece of evidence that he was not effective commanding independent operations. The details necessary for independent command—such as ammunition supply—seemed to escape him. After this defeat, Forrest vowed never to serve under Wheeler again, and he never did.[16]

According to Wheeler, the Confederates lost thirty-six killed and 114 wounded out of a total force of about 1100 men engaged. Gen. Wharton was almost killed, a rifle ball just grazing his chest.[17] Surviving muster rolls identify eleven casualties for the 2nd Georgia at Dover, including Capt. Bennett Bridges of A Company, who was severely wounded in the hip and captured. Company A's second in command, 1st Lt. Fleming Crews, was also wounded, but later returned as captain and company commander. Bridges was exchanged almost exactly one year later and resigned his commission, probably due to disability. Also in A Company, Pvt. L. Fountain was killed.[18]

In C Company, Pvts. Blount Sutton and John Norgan were wounded, and in E Company Pvt. Daniel Kerbo and Cpl. John Huckaby were wounded. Huckaby later died of his wounds. Pvt. E. R. Tomlinson of F

Company may have been killed at Dover, but conflicting dates are given for his death. Pvt. Daniel Belcher of K Company was severely wounded in the shoulder, and died on 3 March.[19]

In H Company, Pvt. John Gibson was "severely wounded in the groin" and captured. Although Wheeler was given a detailed account of Gibson's wound,[20] Gibson was a prisoner of the Union forces, indicating that he may have been purposely left for capture in the hope that he would receive more timely medical attention.

For the next four days, Wharton's brigade was headed back south on what can only be called a retreat after a failed attack. They went into camp near Columbia on 8 February and remained there through the 11th. No doubt the men and horses were exhausted after the long ride to Dover and back. On the 13th they arrived at Lewisburg, and from the 15th through the 21st they were camped near Berlin.[21]

Pvt. William Caldwell of G Company died of wounds on 23 February at Murfreesboro.[22] Since G Company, as Cheatham's escort, was not involved in the fighting at Dover, Caldwell's wound probably came from the earlier Battle of Stones River.

During February and March of 1863, Wheeler's cavalry made daily raids on Union communications between Nashville and Tullahoma. In one of those engagements, Gen. Rosecrans lost two trains to Wheeler, along with "several prisoners and $30,000 in greenbacks."[23]

Wharton's report of 4 March included the statement, "I attack them every day," but most of the engagements for the 2nd Georgia this bitter winter were apparently minor. Lt. Corbitt's diary shows the 4th Tennessee mostly in camp during that February and March.[24]

Reporting from his Unionville, Tennessee, headquarters on 24 March, Gen. Wharton noted that, "The 2nd Georgia, under Major [F. M.] Ison, drove them from the forks of the pike yesterday toward Triune."[25] Ison had replaced Col. Dunlop, whose arthritis had forced his retirement.[26]

The same bitter weather that aggravated Col. Dunlop's arthritis took its toll in the ranks. Pvt. Cary Strickland of F Company who was sent to the hospital during this period, was just one of the men sick this winter. On the last day of March, Pvt. William M. Bullard of I Company found his mess mate and brother-in-law "Lump" Moon dead in camp. That same day, Cary Strickland's brother Milsey joined him in the hospital, with a bullet wound in his left hand that led to the amputation of the third finger.[27]

On 4 April, Wheeler issued orders to Wharton for moving and pick-eting with his command. The 11th Texas and the 3rd Confederate Regiment marched off for Liberty, Tennessee, via Fairfield, Woodbury, and Mechanicsville. The following day, Wharton left on the same route with the rest of his command, leaving one unidentified regiment at Beech Grove.

May of 1863 brought some respite to the men of the 2nd Georgia. During this period, some of the men, including Pvt. Morris Dixon of A Company, were detached as foragers. Muster rolls for May and June also show 2nd Georgia troopers as detached to "Wheeler's Elite corps," including Pvt. Robert Powell of A Company, Pvt. James Lawrence of C Company, and Pvt. James Kimsey of H Company. May was not a good month for Lt. James Wilson of K Company, however. He was captured while "on a scout" 22 May near Hoover's Gap. Pvt. John Montique of E Company was also captured that day.[28]

During June, the 2nd Georgia and other regiments of Wharton's division were on picket duty in front of Shelbyville, while Forrest was covering the Spring Hill area. Probably from information provided by these pickets, Wheeler became convinced that Rosecrans was about to begin an offensive. Around 21 June he sent General Martin with 930 men to join Forrest, with the idea that he would take some of the men at Spring Hill on a raid to disrupt Rosecrans' supplies and communica-tions. The raid, with engagements on the 22nd, 23rd, and 24th con-firmed that Rosecrans was advancing out of Murfreesboro toward the Confederate positions at Tullahoma and Shelbyville. Union Brigadier Robert Mitchell, commanding the 1st Cavalry Division, reported that he "...engaged the 2nd Georgia, 4th Georgia, 7th Alabama, and 51st Alabama with four pieces of artillery," on the 23rd and 24th.[29]

The 3rd Georgia Cavalry was also in the actions of the 23rd and 24th, and one of the regiment's troopers wrote in his diary for the 23rd, "Ra! This day was Brilliant & Glorious day for 3rd Ga Cav. We whipped them in every attempt to drive us." Julius Dowda's entry for the follow-ing day began, "We fought them at Rover & drove them down the Nashville Pike...."[30]

At least one 2nd Georgia trooper became a casualty in the fighting at Rover, when Pvt. Thomas Williams of I Company was captured.[31]

Bragg, not wanting to be caught with the Tennessee River at his back, began a retrograde movement to Chattanooga. It once again fell to the 2nd Georgia to help cover the retreat of the Army of Tennessee. The cavalry not only had to cover Bragg's slow movement over a single road, they had to allow time for salvaging the immense quantities of commissary and quartermaster supplies stockpiled at Shelbyville.

Convinced that Rosecrans would try to cut Bragg's line of march to Chattanooga, Wheeler sent Wharton's Division to Wartrace and Guy's Gap to guard the flank.[32] This seems to have put the 2nd Georgia and the rest of Wharton's Division out of the cavalry's heaviest fighting in the Tullahoma Campaign, which came at Shelbyville on 27 June. However, records do show four members of C Company captured on the 27th, indicating that it was not a totally uneventful day for the regiment. Privates Samuel Blaylock, and Daniel Collins later died of smallpox as POWs at Camp Douglas in Chicago. Privates William Parmenter and Joseph Hughes survived.[33]

Wheeler's plan was to rendezvous with Forrest and Martin at Shelbyville on 27 June. Since Morgan's Division had just left for a raid into Kentucky, it appears that Wheeler had only his escort with him this day as he rode toward Shelbyville. Martin's exhausted men and horses arrived at Shelbyville about noon in a "drenching rain," with most of their ammunition damaged and most weapons unserviceable. Wheeler arrived a short time later, just as some 200 of Martin's men on the left flank were overrun by a large enemy force. The Union force included a cavalry division under Gen. David S. Stanley and an infantry corps under Gen. Gordon Granger, a total of 13,613 men. On the right, part of this Union force had cut off another 200 of Martin's troopers, forcing them to retreat.[34]

This left Wheeler with fewer than 600 men and Forrest nowhere in sight. Wheeler and these 600 men were literally all that stood between the attacking Union forces and the rear of Bragg's wagon train, which had just left the area.[35] One must wonder why Wheeler did not immediately send for Wharton's veteran division, only a short distance away at Wartrace. Perhaps he considered their position on the flank too important to abandon. More likely, he simply didn't have the time or opportunity to get a courier out of Shelbyville.

Although outnumbered twenty to one, Wheeler had little choice but to fight and hope for Forrests' arrival. The Federals charged the small band of Confederates three times, and Wheeler attempted a breakout but was driven back into town. The Confederates reformed at the courthouse, where the fighting at times was hand-to-hand. The desperate fighting continued for over two hours as Wheeler tried to hold on until Forrest arrived.[36]

Writing in the 18 June 1898 issue of *Harper's Weekly*, Dr. John A. Wyeth gave a vivid description of this Shelbyville "affair" in which he participated as one of Wheeler's privates.

> The enemy were repulsed in the attack on the center of the Confederate line. Time and again they assaulted the plucky little band, each time to be driven back in confusion. General Wheeler was everywhere, encouraging and animating the men to stand firm. His reputation for ubiquity, for dash, for 'bull-dog obstinacy' and for 'nerves of steel' was never so well earned as on that day, when he saved the wagon trains of Bragg's army and rescued Forrest from disaster. About 5 o'clock in the afternoon, when there was a comparative lull in the attack, General Wheeler—leaving where they were Colonel A. A. Russell's Fourth Alabama cavalry, consisting of about 200 men, with orders to 'stand until they were ridden down, and then for every man to take care of himself'—withdrew the rest of his command to the south bank of the river.
>
> The last wagon had crossed the bridge; the cavalry and artillery were all safely over the river, and the bridge was about to be fired, when Major Rambeau, of General Forrest's staff, rode up and informed General Wheeler that General Forrest with two brigades, was within two miles of Shelbyville, and coming at a rapid rate to cross the river. General Wheeler at once appreciated the danger in which General Forrest was placed. Although the enemy was already in strong force in the outskirts of the town, General Wheeler—calling for volunteers to follow him, with the gallant General Martin and 50 men of his division, and with two pieces of artillery—re-crossed the river to charge the enemy and drive them back and hold the bridge until Forrest could cross.
>
> Although he and Martin charged the enemy with great intrepidity, and for a while drove them back, the odds were too great. The Union cavalry rallied and charged them in turn; riding through and over them. The two pieces of artillery—having nothing but solid shot—were of little use. The enemy sabered the gunners and passing on took possession of the bridge. A regiment of the enemy came down the river in our rear and took possession of a little island in the middle of the river above the bridge. They also formed a line of battle parallel with the river and seemed satisfied that they had Wheeler hemmed in with no possibility of escape.

When the general saw this he gave the word: 'Every man take care of himself the best he can.' With saber drawn, myself by his side, cutting his way through the enemy, he made for the bank of the river. Fortunately the stream was swollen. Shot at with carbines and pistols and cut at with sabers, he put spurs to his horse and plunged down the steep bank into the river, I following him the best I could, the enemy shooting at us from the flank and rear, from island and from river bank. Undaunted, the general swam right on to the opposite bank and rallied his men on the other side. I was less fortunate, getting no further than the island, where I was captured.

General Wheeler, dressed in a blue shirt, sword in hand, hat off, charging through the enemy's line and leaping down the precipitous river bank, presented a picturesque sight rarely witnessed in battle. It is estimated that about fifty men were lost in this daring attempt to escape. This movement of General Wheeler, in re-crossing the river, was not necessary to save General Bragg's wagon train. That had already been accomplished; but it was done on a grand impulse to save from disaster General Forrest, an officer who, with all his magnificent genius and brilliant success when commanding alone, was a little restive under the orders of his superiors. There is in all history no nobler, or more chivalrous, act than was performed by this young cavalry leader on that eventful day.[37]

The Federals had recognized Wheeler, and tried hard to capture him. They later told the people of Shelbyville that they beaten Wheeler that day, but that he was "The bravest man in the world." Wheeler's mounted 15-foot jump into the Duck River had impressed foe and comrade alike.[38] According to one account, only thirteen of the fifty men with Wheeler survived, as most were shot in the water or drowned.[39] The sacrifice was for nothing, as Forrest had already forded the river, keeping his promise never to fight under Wheeler again.

It was the first time that Union cavalry had "whipped" Wheeler, but their hopes that they had broken the effectiveness of the Rebel cavalry were soon dashed. Other engagements followed immediately for Wheeler's men in the Tullahoma Campaign, where they were able to put more men, including the 2nd Georgia, in the field with good ammunition. Cavalry veterans wrote after the war that they "revenged themselves" for Shelbyville with "…successful engagements at Allisonia Bridge, New Church, Elk River Bridge, University Place, and many others during that hazardous but successful retreat."[40] The veterans made a good point. Although historians have been critical of the near disaster at Shelbyville, the fact is that Wheeler on the 27th and subsequent days accomplished his mission, and he did so against seemingly overwhelming odds. He kept the Union forces away from Bragg's army and his wagon train of vital supplies.

At first light on the 28th, Wheeler, now reinforced by the Georgians and Tennesseans under Wharton, counterattacked the pursuing blue coats, forcing them back to the river. Later that day his men checked the progress of a "heavy infantry column" attempting to turn Bragg's right flank near Manchester. The following morning they struck those same columns near Tullahoma, and that evening brought Gen. Thomas' whole corps "to a stand" there. The Confederate cavalry continued fighting the following day as Gen. Thomas later wrote, "The resistance of General Wheeler was so stubborn that General Negley was delayed until the trains of the enemy had crossed Elk River."[41] This fighting was carried out by Martin's, Forrest's, and Wharton's divisions.

On 1 July, Wheeler attacked and "totally defeated" Union Cavalry at New Church, and on the 4th "drove back the enemy at University Place, defeating them so completely as to cause them to discontinue their pursuit, thus enabling Gen. Bragg to cross the Tennessee river without molestation."[42]

Lt. Corbitt's diary entry for this day reads, " The ball opened this morning about 8 oclk by the Yanks driving in the pickets of the 8th Texas & charging the Regt in camps The Rangers counter charged driving the Yanks back on his reserves when they (the Rangers) were compelled to retire before Superior numbers The 4th Ten became warmly engaged at 8 1/2 oclk & drove the enemy back thus ending Bragg's retreat from Tullahoma Camped in Souders Cove tonight Jas Heam wounded today."[43]

Rosecrans' Tullahoma offensive was brilliantly planned and executed, forcing Bragg's Army out of Tennessee. However, his hopes of forcing Bragg to give battle north of the Tennessee River were dashed, primarily due to the work of the Confederate cavalry. According to one source, Rosecrans had only to average five miles a day to achieve this purpose, but the 13,000 men under Wheeler had "fought the leading columns of the enemy at every favorable position," greatly slowing their advance.[44]

[1] W. B. Corbitt, Diary (Atlanta GA: The Robert W. Woodruff Library, Emory University).

[2] *War of the Rebellion, Official Records* Vol. 17 Part 2 (Washington DC: U.S. Government Printing Office, 1890) 835.

[3] Compiled Service Records, 2nd Georgia Cavalry (Atlanta GA: Georgia Department of Archives and History).

[4] Ibid.

[5] Robert Maberry, *Handbook of Texas* (Galveston TX: Rosenberg Library)

[6] Stewart Sifikis, *Who Was Who in the Confederacy* (New York NY: Facts on File, Inc., 1988) 302.

[7] John P. Dyer, *From Shiloh to San Juan: The Life of Fightin' Joe Wheeler* (Baton Rouge LA: Louisiana State University Press, 1941) 70.

[8] W. C. Dodson, ed. *Campaigns of Wheeler and His Cavalry* (Jackson TN: The Guild Bindery Press) 84.

[9] Corbitt, diary.

[10] Ibid.

[11] Ibid.

[12] Dodson, ed. *Campaigns of Wheeler and His Cavalry,* 69.

[13] *War of the Rebellion, Official Records* Series I Vol. 23 Part 1, 40.

[14] Dodson, ed. *Campaigns of Wheeler and His Cavalry, 69—71.*

[15] *War of the Rebellion, Official Records* Series I Vol. 23 Part 1, 40

[16] Dyer, *From Shiloh to San Juan: The Life of Fightin' Joe Wheeler,* 77.

[17] R. F. Bunting, Chaplain, Terry's Texas Rangers, Wartime manuscript MSS #25-0567 (Galveston TX: Rosenberg Library).

[18] Compiled Service Records, 2nd Georgia Cavalry.

[19] Ibid.

[20] Ibid.

[21] Corbitt, manuscript MSS #25-0567.

[22] Compiled Service Records, 2nd Georgia Cavalry.

[23] Dyer, *From Shiloh to San Juan: The Life of Fightin' Joe Wheeler,* 80.

[24] Corbitt, diary.

[25] *War of the Rebellion, Official Records* Series I Vol. 23 Part 2, 725.

[26] Compiled Service Records, 2nd Georgia Cavalry.

[27] Ibid.

[28] Ibid.

[29] *War of the Rebellion, Official Records* Series I Vol. 23 Part 2, 725, 542-546.

[30] Julius Dowda, Diary, (Atlanta GA: Georgia Department of Archives and History).

[31] Compiled Service Records, 2nd Georgia Cavalry.

[32] Dodson, ed. *Campaigns of Wheeler and His Cavalry,* 87.

[33] Compiled Service Records, 2nd Georgia Cavalry.

[34] Dodson, ed. *Campaigns of Wheeler and His Cavalry,* 87.

[35] Ibid. 88.

[36] Dyer, *From Shiloh to San Juan—The Life of Fightin' Joe Wheeler,* 83—84.

[37] T. C. DeLeon, *Joseph Wheeler, the Man, the Statesman, the Soldier* (Atlanta GA: Byrd Printing Company, 1899) 98—102.

[38] Dodson, ed. *Campaigns of Wheeler and His Cavalry,* 90—91.

[39] Dyer, *From Shiloh to San Juan: The Life of Fightin' Joe Wheeler,* 85.

[40] Dodson, *Campaigns of Wheeler and His Cavalry,* 91. See also, Julius Dowda diary, Georgia Department of Archives and History.

[41] Ibid. 94-96.

[42] Ibid.

[43] Corbitt, diary.

[44] Dodson, ed., *Campaigns of Wheeler and His Cavalry,* 98.

"Barren Victory, Sullen Despair"

The 2nd Georgia was camped near Trent on 7 and 8 July when the men received the bad news from Gettysburg and Vicksburg. On 12 July, with the rest of Wharton's division, they headed out for Rome, Georgia, crossing Lookout Mountain and camping that night at McLemore's Cove. They passed through LaFayette the following day and reached Rome about 4:00 P.M. They camped that night two miles from town on the Cave Springs Road.[1]

Records for 31 July 1863, show the 2nd Georgia still commanded by Lt. Col. Francis Marion Ison and part of Col. Charles C. Crews' First Brigade, Wharton's Division. G Company under Capt. Thomas H. Jordan is still shown as detached to serve as Gen. Cheatham's escort.[2] Jordan was killed in this service 1 August 1863. The previous day, Pvt. John Freeman of G Company "died in service." Lt. Thomas Mickleberry Merritt was promoted to captain and succeeded Jordan as company commander.[3]

Wharton's command apparently spent the rest of the summer in the Rome area, moving their camp to the Kingston Road, eight miles from town on 2 August. Here they were probably able to acquire new saddles made in the factory there, as well as replenish other supplies and acquire horses. It was also a time for drills, reviews and inspections.[4] The respite was over soon enough.

Rosecrans' next offensive came on 29 August as his army crossed the Tennessee River south of Bridgeport. Elements of the 2nd Georgia probably were on picket duty this day, as Pvt. Robert Rhodes of C Company was captured.[5]

Marching orders for Wharton's Division came the next day. On the morning of 31 August, the division broke camp and headed north, camping at 8:30 that night near Dirt Town. Another day's march brought them to LaFayette.[6] By 5 September, the 2nd Georgia and Wharton's entire division were stationed at Alpine, Georgia. On that date and for the next ten days, the regiment was involved in skirmishing with Union forces under Maj. Gen. D. S. Stanley, chief of cavalry.[7] Two of the three Fains in K Company were captured on 7 September. Apparently wounded, James Fain died on 19 September, and Edward died of lung inflammation on 23 December as a POW. (A month after Edward's death, the last of the three Fains, William, was mortally wounded at Sevierville, Tennessee, and died 1 February 1864.)[8]

In the face of the Union advance, Bragg began to evacuate Chattanooga on 8 September, the Army of Tennessee falling back to LaFayette.

At Summerville on the 10th, two companies of the 2nd Georgia were apparently surprised by the Union 3rd Brigade, 1st Cavalry Division under Col. Louis Watkins. Several members of the two companies were killed or wounded, and "about half a dozen captured" according to Watkins' report.[9] Surviving muster rolls show only Pvt. Almond Hays of I Company as captured.[10] Corbitt's diary entry for this date reads, "The enemy reported advancing on Rome. The whole command ordered to defend it. Left picket stand at 4 oclk this evening advanced to within 4 miles of Dirttown & went into camps at 11 oclk tonight."[11] From these reports, one might surmise that Wharton's men were widely spread on picket duty, attempting to detect Union movements. The attack on the two 2nd Georgia companies likely prompted Corbitt to write of the "advance on Rome."

For the next two days, Wharton apparently was trying to keep his cavalry division between Rome and the Union infantry. By 12 September, McCook's Corps was at Alpine, Thomas' marching through Steven's Gap at Lookout Mountain, and Crittenden's marching south from Chattanoonga.[12]

On the 13th Wharton formed his dismounted men in a line of battle eight miles from LaFayette, skirmishing with blue-coated soldiers 300 yards in their front. That evening Wharton fell back about two miles. The following day the picketing troopers reported "Yanks all around." The night of the 17th the troopers watched Breckinridge's infantry pass their camp on the Chattanooga Road north of LaFayette. The artillery barrage began early the next morning.[13]

Lt. Corbitt's diary entry for 19 September reads, "Canonading resumed this morning at 8 oclk. E M Smith returned this morning. The great battle just begun. Canonading very heavy."[14] The Battle of Chickamauga was underway, and it would be the bloodiest single day of the entire War.[15]

As the fighting opened, Wheeler's cavalry was in position on the left flank of the Army of Tennessee, with Wharton's Division, including the 2nd Georgia, about two miles behind Breckenridge's Division as it engaged the enemy. Wharton's chaplain wrote that his division "…shared a prominent part in the attacks upon the wagon trains of the enemy & was enabled to inflict very severe damage upon him & captured a considerable number of prisoners."[16] The only known casualty for the 2nd Georgia on the 19th was Pvt. Asmun Shackleford of E Company, who suffered a disabling wound.[17]

A portion of Wheeler's command was apparently mounted when they renewed the attack on the morning of the 20th, the decisive day of the battle. Veterans of Wheeler's Cavalry wrote that they "drove the foe from their works, capturing many prisoners, horses, wagons, and other property, and driving them in confusion to within a few hundred yards of Rosecrans headquarters at Crawfish Spring."

The Union line broke under Longstreet's charge and their retreat soon turned into a rout. McCook, Crittenden, and Rosecrans himself were caught up in the fleeing mob and carried back toward Chattanooga. Only the stand of Gen. Thomas and Bragg's own timidity prevented a worse disaster for the Union forces.

Later on this bloody Sunday, Wheeler's dismounted troopers, following the generally forward and right flow of the attack, encountered fresh bodies of Union infantry, artillery and cavalry at Lee and Gordon's Mill. At first the Federals fell back slowly to successive defensive positions, but eventually it became a "hasty and disorderly retreat, our troops capturing prisoners, wagons, horses, small arms and guns…."[18]

Pvt. Benjamin Harris of H Company, wounded in the action, is the only casualty recorded for the regiment on the 20th.

At dawn the following day, a portion of Wheeler's men re-mounted and moved through a mountain pass into Dry Valley, "…directly in the rear of Rosecrans right flank…close to the enemy's main forces and entirely separated from our troops." The Union command sent a large cavalry force out of Chattanooga to drive away the Rebel cavalry. But Wheeler attacked first, and drove the blue cavalry "in disorder" back toward Chattanooga. Leaving the 8th Texas to watch his rear, Wheeler took the remainder of his force, which probably included the 2nd Georgia, to attack a brigade of cavalry moving up the valley with a large wagon train. Again Wheeler's attack was successful, and developed into a running battle of some seven miles. Veteran troopers remembered that a large number of Union cavalrymen were killed and wounded, and some 450 captured, along with the entire wagon train.[19]

Skirmishing continued for Wheeler's cavalrymen around Chattanooga on the 22nd, with the gray riders driving straggling bands of Union soldiers back to their fortifications near Chattanooga. While skirmishing with Federals in their works in the fading light, Wheeler received orders to press the right flank of Thomas' retreating command. Wheeler immediately disengaged and led his command on a night march of some twenty miles before stopping to rest. Early on the 23rd, he received new orders from Bragg, directing him to sweep the top of Lookout Mountain, still held by Union troops. After another forty miles of marching, much of it up the mountain, the exhausted men and horses began their "sweep" in the dark. Wheeler reported that he began the attack as soon as he reached the top of the mountain with his 300 man escort, and that his men made a successful night assault against enemy fortifications.[20]

At least part of the 2nd Georgia was involved in Wheeler's sweep of Lookout Mountain that night. Post war records show Pvt. George Swindle of C Company and Pvts. Francis Duke and Hugh Longino of I Company participated in this action, suggesting that at least two companies from the Regiment were involved. For Frank Duke it was a fateful day, as he fell mortally wounded. Hugh Longino remembered in later years that he was near his friend Frank when he fell.[21]

Wheeler reported after the battle that his troopers captured 2,000 Federal soldiers, 100 wagons and teams, and eighteen stands of colors. The 2nd Georgia's Col. Crews was among the group of officers he praised for their "...zeal, energy, and gallantry during the engagement."[22] According to Wharton's chaplain, his Division "...shared a prominent part in the attacks upon the wagon trains of the enemy & was enabled to inflict very severe damage upon him & captured a considerable number of prisoners."[23]

Total casualties among Wheeler's Cavalry at Chickamauga have been estimated at 375 killed, wounded, and captured.[24]

After the battle, General Cheatham's escort, G Company, 2nd Georgia Cavalry, commanded by Captain Thomas M. Merritt, was assigned the task of collecting small arms left on the field by the enemy. Cheatham cited their "industrious service," and it may be assumed that the members of G Company finished the task better armed than they started it.[25]

The victory at Chickamauga brought little satisfaction to the men of the 2nd Georgia or the rest of the Army of Tennessee. According to Lt. Gen. D. H. Hill, the men in the ranks knew that Bragg's failure to pursue the fleeing Federals meant that their sacrifices would be for naught. Hill had come down to Georgia from Virginia to command Hardee's Corps at Chickamauga while Hardee was on assignment in Mississippi and Alabama. Wrote Hill of Chickamauga:

> There was never more splendid fighting in '61, when the flower of the Southern youth was in the field, than was displayed in these bloody days of September, '63. But it seems to me the *elan* of the Southern soldier was never seen after Chickamauga—that brilliant dash which had distinguished him was gone forever. He was too intelligent not to know that the cutting in two of Georgia meant death to all his hopes. He knew that Longstreet's absence was imperiling Lee's safety, and that what had to be done must be done quickly. The delay in striking was an exasperation to him; the failure to strike after the success was crushing to all his longings for an independent South. He fought stoutly to the last, but, after Chickamauga, with the sulleness of despair and without the enthusiasm of hope. That 'barren victory' sealed the fate of the Southern Confederacy.[26]

Given Hill's assessment, the performance of those men in battle over the next two years is all the more remarkable.

After Chickamauga, half of Wheeler's command was left to picket for the infantry at Missionary Ridge while the other half, including the 2nd Georgia, moved against Union communications. Wheeler's brigade commanders had protested that the men and horses were too "jaded" for this mission.[27] Given the hard riding of the three days and nights after the battle, their protests are understandable. Nevertheless, early on the last day of September the men found themselves crossing the Tennessee River at Cottonport. Almost immediately they encountered and defeated a large Union force, taking nearly 100 prisoners. Late in the day they were joined by Davidson's and Armstrong's brigades from Forrest's command, bringing their total strength to 3,793 men. Wheeler organized this command into three divisions under Brigadier Generals Martin, Davidson, and Wharton. The 2nd Georgia remained under Wharton.

That night they started in a heavy rain for Walden's Ridge and the Sequatchie Valley, no doubt bringing memories to the men of the 2nd Georgia of the march prior to their first combat, more than a year before. In the darkness there was brief skirmish with a Union cavalry regiment, which fled leaving ten prisoners.[28]

The next day, Wheeler decided to circle behind Rosecrans at Chattanooga and attack his supply trains there. Generals Wharton and Martin, who had opposed the expedition in the first place, expressed their view that such a mission would bring disaster, and urged Wheeler to reconsider. Again not heeding the advice of subordinates, Wheeler took "about 1,300 of the best mounted men," and set out through the valley in the first hours of 2 October. It appears that the 2nd Georgia remained with Wharton's Division, which was ordered to cross the Cumberland Mountains and capture the garrison at McMinnville.[29]

Although the 2nd Georgia was not marching with Wheeler, following Wheeler's movements contributes to a better understanding of the regiment's role in this campaign. It was still dark when Wheeler captured his first prey, thirty-two wagons, 200 mules and horses, and a number of prisoners. The 4th Alabama was detailed to take charge of the prisoners, leaving Wheeler with fewer than 1,000 men as he proceeded down the valley.

Shortly after dawn, Wheeler's cavalry encountered a Union column, which they dislodged from successive defensive positions until they reached Anderson's crossroads near Jasper. There the Rebels found a huge train of 800 six-mule government wagons and some 200 suttler's wagons, guarded by a brigade of cavalry in front, another in the rear, and an infantry brigade on the flanks. The battle that followed lasted nearly two hours, but the stubborn resistance eventually turned into a rout. Wheeler reported taking 1,000 prisoners, more than the number of Confederate cavalry on the field. The wagons were loaded with ammunition, medical supplies, food, and other quartermaster stores. The noise of the exploding ordnance in the burning wagons was clearly audible to Rosecrans and his soldiers in Chattanooga.[30]

As the destruction progressed, Wheeler sent most of his command south with captured livestock and prisoners. Then, as he withdrew with his small rear guard late that evening, Wheeler was struck by an overwhelming Union force, but managed to escape into the darkness, and on the morning of 3 October rejoined Wharton. According to General Wharton's chaplain, it was the 2nd Georgia and the rest of Crews' Georgia Brigade that "...gallantly disputed" the advance of the enemy, giving Wheeler and Wharton time to capture McMinnville by midmorning, 3 October.[31]

While the men of the Georgia Brigade were contending with the enemy, the rest of Wheeler's men were "re-outfitted" at McMinnville. The commander of the Union garrison there, Andrew Johnson's son-in-law, Maj. Michael Patterson, was outraged that the Rebels took clothes, hats, boots, watches, and money from his officers and men. Wheeler reported capturing 587 prisoners there, as well as a locomotive with a large train of cars, 250 horses, and supplies of ammunition and equipment.[32]

Over the next five days, the Union cavalry corps under Gen. Stanley, which included divisions under generals George Crook, Mitchell, and McCook, continued to engage Wheeler's rear guard, "...frequently with considerable loss to themselves."[33] By 6 October, the 4th Tennessee (and probably the entire Tennessee Brigade) had taken over this rear guard action, and the Georgia Brigade was apparently back with Wheeler's main body.[34] Despite the presence of this large, 13,000-man force in his rear, Wheeler methodically continued his path of destruction, primarily on the railroad and railroad bridges over the Duck and Stones rivers.

On 6 October, Wheeler's command camped at White Bridge on Duck River, except for Davidson's Division, which camped near Shelbyville. Wheeler became concerned that Davidson was vulnerable to attack by Stanley, and ordered him to fall back on Martin's Division if approached by Stanley's force. Apparently growing more apprehensive, Wheeler later countermanded that order and told Davidson to join the main body as soon as possible. For some reason, Davidson did not obey the order.[35]

Early on the next morning, Crook's Union cavalry and "mounted infantry", many armed with Spencer repeating carbines,[36] attacked Davidson. Instead of falling back on Martin's Division as previously ordered, Davidson retreated toward Farmington with heavy losses. The Federals vigorously pursued Davidson's panic-stricken troopers for some eight hours, sabering a number of them in the saddle as they fled. Wheeler, apparently with Martin's Division, and Wharton led their men at a gallop toward Farmington to intercept Davidson's fleeing troopers. Wheeler arrived at Sim's Farm about 4:00 P.M. and set a defensive line across the Lewisburg Pike. Davidson's men soon arrived and passed through this line and crossed the river. Soon after, the Federals "...advanced in a bold front, but were met with grape and cannister from our artillery and a destructive fire of small arms, and repulsed in each and every charge which they made."[37] No doubt fatigued from the chase of more than eight hours, and now facing a determined foe, Crook's men retired a short distance and made no further charges as the day waned.

Chaplain Bunting's description of this action was slightly different. In fact, Bunting's description is more in line with Union accounts of driving Wheeler from the Sims Farm line. Bunting wrote, "At Farmington his (Wheeler's) other divisions were completely demoralized. They were speedily falling back before the advancing foe; but just at the opportune time, Gen Wharton's division came up the pike, from the direction of Duck River." Under the cover of a dense cedar brake, the Federals "furiously attacked" Wharton's cavalry, inflicting severe casualties on the Texas Rangers at the head of the column. But the rest of the division, which included the 2nd Georgia, "swung round onto the pike below the town" and checked the Federal advance. Martin's and Wharton's divisions then joined the retreat toward the Tennessee River with the Federals in pursuit.[38] Pvt. Cole Brogdon of the 2nd Georgia's A Company was captured during this action.[39]

Today on Highway 64 at Farmington there is a marker commemorating the Confederates who died there. It reads, "In memory gallant dead of Maj. Gen. Wheeler's Cavalry Corps who fell in an engagement with the Federal forces on this field, Oct. 7, 1863." Twelve names are inscribed on the monument, one of whom—William Smith—may have been a member of the 2nd Georgia's F Company. Lt. Smith is shown on a muster roll as captured at Sugar Creek, 9 October 1863. There is no accompanying POW record of Lt. Smith, however, which could mean that he was not captured, but killed.[40]

The 2nd Georgia apparently was heavily involved in rear guard action during the retreat to Alabama, as the regiment suffered at least thirty-one casualties from six different companies on 8 and 9 October. In H Company alone, eleven men were captured. One member of F

Company was killed and eight were captured, including Lt. DeVaughn, who had led the "handsome fight" at Mount Washington a year before. Known casualties for the regiment are:[41]

Glenn Lunceford	2nd lt., D Company	wounded & captured
James Conner	pvt., D Company	captured
Howard McGuaghey	cpl., D Company	captured
Erasmus Ham	pvt., E Company	captured
William Hamil	pvt., E Company	captured
Thomas Kimble	pvt., E Company	captured
John Wellmaker	pvt., E Company	mortally wounded
James DeVaughn	1st. Lt., F Company	captured
William Smith	1st. Lt. F Company	captured
William David Cates	pvt., F Company	captured
D. D. Denham	pvt., F Company	capturred
W. H. Huie	pvt., Company F	mortally wounded
Presley Morris	pvt., F Company	captured
H. M. Smith	cpl., F Company	captured
Martin Smith	pvt., F Company	captured
George Stinchcomb	pvt., F Company	captured
William Austin	pvt., H Company	captured
J. J. Blunton	pvt., H Company	captured
Samuel Buice	pvt., H Company	captured
V. Chronic	pvt., H Company	captured
J.A.J. Duren	cpl., H Company	captured
James Harris	pvt., H Company	captured
James Kimsey	pvt., H Company	captured
A. R. Owens	pvt., H Company	captured
John Plaster	pvt., H Company	captured
Thomas Plaster	pvt., H Company	captured
Madison Brown	pvt., I Company	captured
E. C. Mobley	pvt., I Company	captured
Thomas Butler	pvt., K Company	captured
W. A. Creamer	pvt., K Company	captured

Wheeler's command escaped across the Tennessee River at Muscle Shoals, Alabama on 10 October. Chaplain Bunting claimed for General Wharton all the credit for the "success" of the raid. No doubt reflecting a rivalry between Wheeler and Wharton, Bunting wrote that Wharton's Division "...saved the entire command from disgrace, if not from capture." He added, "Gen. W. succeeded by his presence of mind, coolness,

& gallantry in saving the fortunes of the day. To him and his Division is attributable the final success of the raid."[42]

Historians have been appropriately critical of Wheeler's conduct of this campaign, which provided more evidence that the young major general was not at his best with an independent command. But if Wheeler's performance was weak, then so was Stanley's. With vastly superior numbers, many of his men armed with repeating carbines, Stanley was not only unable to trap or destroy Wheeler, he could not prevent him from escaping with his booty intact. Despite the near disaster, Wheeler brought out all of the captured wagons and livestock as well as 3,000 Tennessee recruits.[43]

Soon after crossing into Alabama, Gen. Wharton journeyed to Richmond where he asked that he and the Texas Rangers be transferred west of the Mississippi. His request was not fully granted, but he apparently came home a major general.[44] He would not long remain the division commander over the 2nd Georgia.

[1] W. B. Corbitt, Diary (Atlanta GA: The Robert W. Woodruff Library, Emory University).

[2] *War of the Rebellion, Official Records* Vol. 23 Part 2 (Washington DC: U.S. Government Printing Office, 1890) 943.

[3] Compiled Service Records, 2nd Georgia Cavalry (Atlanta GA: Georgia Department of Archives and History).

[4] Corbitt, diary.

[5] Compiled Service Records, 2nd Georgia Cavalry.

[6] Corbitt, diary.

[7] *War of the Rebellion, Official Records* Vol. 30 Part 1, 889.

[8] Compiled Service Records, 2nd Georgia Cavalry.

[9] *War of the Rebellion, Official Records* Vol. 30 Part 1, 913.

[10] Compiled Service Records, 2nd Georgia Cavalry.

[11] Corbitt, diary.

[12] Richard O'Shea, *Battle Maps of the Civil War* (New York NY: SMITHMARK Publishers, 1992) 119.

[13] Corbitt, diary.

[14] Ibid.

[15] Glenn Tucker, *Chickamauga—Bloody Battle in the West* (New York NY: Bobbs Merrill Company, Inc., 1961) 389.

[16] R. F. Bunting, Chaplain, wartime manuscript MSS#25-0567 (Galveston TX: Rosenberg Library).

[17] Compiled Service Records, 2nd Georgia Cavalry.

[18] Ibid.

[19] *Campaigns of Wheeler and His Cavalry*, 106-107.

[20] Ibid. 110.

[21] Hugh Longino, letter to Miss Lillian Henderson, 10 April, 1926 (Atlanta GA: Georgia Department of Archives and History). See also, Compiled Service Records, Second Georgia Cavalry.

[22] Dodson, ed. *Campaigns of Wheeler and His Cavalry*, 111.

[23] Bunting, unpublished manuscript.

[24] Robert Johnson and Clarence Buel, editors, *Battles and Leaders of the Civil War*, Vol. III (Edison NJ: Castle Books, 1995) 675.

[25] *War of the Rebellion, Official Records* Vol. 30 Part 1, 77—80.

[26] Daniel H. Hill, "Chickamauga—The Great Battle of the West" *Battles and Leaders of the Civil War, Vol III*, (Edison NJ: Castle Books, 1995) 662.

[27] Dodson, ed. *Campaigns of Wheeler and His Cavalry*, 17.

[28] Ibid. 118-120.

[29] Ibid. 121

[30] Ibid. 123.

[31] Bunting, unpublished manuscript.

[32] Dodson, ed. *Campaigns of Wheeler and His Cavalry*, 124.

[33] Ibid.

[34] Corbitt, diary.

[35] Dodson, ed. *Campaigns of Wheeler and His Cavalry*, 125-126.

[36] Richard Ruhanen, Jr., "A Fighting Carpenter" *Civil War Times Illustrated* February, 1996.

[37] Dodson, ed., *Campaigns of Wheeler and His Cavalry*, 126-127.

[38] Bunting, unpublished manuscript.

[39] Compiled Service Records, 2nd Georgia Cavalry.

[40] Ibid.

[41] Ibid.

[42] Bunting, unpublished manuscript.

[43] Dodson, ed. *Campaigns of Wheeler and His Cavalry, 128.*

[44] Bunting, unpublished manuscript.

The Knoxville Campaign

On the night of 11 November 1863, the 2nd Georgia Cavalry Regiment under Lt. Col. F. M. Ison was part of a four-brigade cavalry force that united with Gen. Longstreet at Sweetwater, Tennessee. They had been detached to the "Department of East Tennessee" where their mission was to support Longstreet, whose first order of business was to attack Burnside who was moving on Knoxville. The 2nd Georgia was short one company, as Marion County's G Company was still serving as an escort for Gen. Cheatham in Hardee's Corps.

Wheeler was at the head of the cavalry as it rode toward Sweetwater with two brigades under Gen. William T. Martin and two under Gen. Frank C. Armstrong, formerly with Forrest. In late October or early November of 1863, Wheeler's Cavalry had "…re-crossed the river at Courtland, Ala., and from thence through a desolated country marched to Kingston, Ga., and thence to Parker's Ford, on the Little Tennessee River."[1]

As they marched into east Tennessee that fall, with just two days' rations and no wagons, the cavalrymen moved through some of the most spectacular scenery in the country. The beautiful mountain forest, with its bright foliage and running streams, gave no hint that the cavalrymen were headed into a winter of bitter cold and equally bitter fighting.[2] The trip was not just a pleasant excursion, however, as Pvt. Ab Lockett of the 2nd Georgia's A Company drowned crossing the Holston River on 3 November.[3]

Records on the 2nd Georgia's chain of command during this period are confusing. Although some records show that the 2nd Georgia did not become part of Martin's Division until 10 December 1863, correspondence by a veteran of the 6th Georgia shows that Crews' First Brigade, consisting of the 1st, 2nd, 3rd, 4th, and 6th Georgia regiments, was one of the four brigades under Martin as he moved toward Sweetwater that November.[4] Moreover, Wharton's command was ordered to Varnell Station on 4 December, and the 2nd Georgia clearly was not part of his command at that time.[5]

The date of the 2nd Georgia's assignment to Martin's Division may be 6 November 1863. Lt. Corbitt's diary shows that his 4th Tennessee Cavalry was placed in a new brigade that day, apparently made up entirely of Tennessee regiments.[6] It seems likely that the new Georgia Brigade and new divisions were created at the same time.

The veteran of the 6th Georgia also wrote after the war that, on 24 December 1863, Crews' First Brigade, Georgia cavalry, the 1st, 2nd, 3rd, 4th, and 6th regiments, was part of John T. Morgan's division.[7] This is consistent with a Union report in the Official Record which shows Morgan's Division, including Crews' Brigade and the 2nd Georgia, reaching Morristown on December 13.[8] Confederate records in that same volume, however, show the 2nd Georgia as part of the 2nd Brigade under Col. James J. Morrison, Martin's Division, from November through December. Moreover, those records show Crews not as First Brigade commander, but as commander of the 2nd Georgia Regiment from 10 December through April of the following year. Both of these entries cannot be right, and the veteran's recollections seem to confirm the Federal record.

These discrepancies would make it very difficult to determine just how the 2nd Georgia was involved in the Knoxville campaign, had it not been for the letters of the 6th Georgia veteran. Supported by the Federal report in the Official Record, his recollections indicate that the 2nd Georgia moved toward Knoxville as part of Crews' Brigade, Martin's Division. They further indicate that, after Wheeler returned to Bragg's army and Martin took charge of the entire cavalry command at Knoxville, Morgan assumed command of the division which included the Georgia Brigade and the 2nd Georgia Cavalry Regiment. The Official Record for 31 December shows the following command structure for the regiment.[9]

Morgan's Division
Crews' Brigade (1st, 2nd, 3rd, 4th, and 6th Georgia)
Ison's Regiment[10]

A Company	Capt. Fleming Crews
B Company	unknown
C Company	Capt. James Mayo
D Company	Capt. Robert R. Mitchell
E Company	Capt. James Fambro
F Company	Capt. Hardy Chapman
G Company	Capt. Thomas Merritt
	(detached with Cheatham)
H Company	Capt. Francis Allen
I Company	Capt. George Looney
K Company	probably 1st Lt. Jesse Barber

Longstreet faced serious supply problems this winter, operating in an area with strong Union sympathies. Horses were in such short supply that oxen were used to haul artillery pieces. Shoes for man and beast were in short supply. So critical was the shortage of horseshoes, that they were stripped from dead animals, and broken-down animals were killed for their shoes. Later, during the siege at Knoxville, the Confederates watched the river for dead horses and mules floating down, so the carcasses could be pulled out and the shoes removed.[11]

Longstreet gave his men permission to exchange shoes with captured Yankees, but emphasized they must have something to exchange and could not leave the POWs barefooted. General Porter Alexander later wrote, "It was quite an amusing thing (to us) to see a ragged rebel with his feet tied up in a sort of raw beef-hide moccasin, which the men learned to make, come up to a squad of prisoners, inspect their feet, and select the one he would 'swap' with." Alexander noted that the POWs usually took the loss of their shoes with good humored resignation.[12]

Historians have generally agreed that Bragg's detachment of Longstreet's two divisions from the Army of Tennessee was pure folly.[13] Bragg was dividing his army just when the already superior forces of the Army of the Cumberland were being combined with Grant's Army of the Tennessee and two corps under Gen. Joe Hooker from the Army of the Potomac. This gave the Union commander 80,000 men to hurl against Bragg's 36,000 in three days of fighting culminating with the Union victory at Missionary Ridge on 25 November.[14]

The men in Crews' brigade were less attuned to the strategic implications of this splitting of forces, but they had very strong opinions about Longstreet's conduct of the Knoxville Campaign. They felt Longstreet could "walk in and take the place" if he moved before the Yankees had time to improve Knoxville's meager fortifications.[15] But Longstreet did not move rapidly.

Longstreet's infantry crossed the Tennessee River 13 November at Loudon on a pontoon bridge. Wheeler's cavalry crossed that same day at Motley's Ford. Leaving enough of his men to picket the river from Kingston to Loudon, Wheeler that night, with Martin and Armstrong, moved out toward Maryville. It appears that no companies of the 2nd Georgia were left on picket duty, and that the entire regiment was involved in a skirmish that night at Blythe's Ferry.

The following day the regiment was with Wheeler when he attacked the 11th Kentucky Cavalry at Huff's Ferry and then drove them out of Maryville, taking some 300 prisoners. Wolford's brigade of cavalry came to the aid of the 11th Kentucky, and Wheeler then "charged and drove him over the river in confusion, capturing one hundred and ten of his men, besides killing and wounding a large number."[16]

At dawn on Sunday the 15th, Wheeler re-crossed the Little River to seize and hold the high ground overlooking Knoxville on the southeast. Wheeler soon encountered "a superior force" of four Federal cavalry brigades under Sanders, Shackleford, Wolford, and Penderbicker.[17] After a brief fight, the Federals, with an artillery battery to support them, "…fell back behind Stock Creek, destroyed the bridge, and took a strong position on an elevation overlooking the city."[18] Wheeler then dismounted half of his command, crossed the swollen creek under the cover of his artillery, and struck the left wing of the Union line. This action was carried out by Martin's men, including the 2nd Georgia; Armstrong's men were still on the other side of the creek, and a portion of them were engaged in repairing the bridge so the artillery could cross. The *Atlanta Intelligencer* reported, "The brave Alabamians and Georgians of Martin's division dismounted and fought for five miles as infantry, driving the enemy before them."[19] As Armstrong and the artillery began to cross, Martin's men re-mounted and the entire Confederate force charged on horseback. The charge routed the Federals, "…sweeping them pell-mell towards Knoxville. One-hundred and fifty prisoners were captured; a portion of the flying troopers hurled themselves into the river and attempted to gain the other bank, while others went at lightning speed into the city. A portion escaped by scattering in all directions, and the ground for three miles was strewn with their dead and wounded. Gen. Sanders, the Federal commander, was mortally wounded and died two days later."[20]

Shortly after the engagement at Stock Creek, Wheeler received a message from Longstreet requesting that he rejoin the infantry "unless you are doing better service by moving along the enemy's flank...."[21] On the morning of 16 November, the 2nd Georgia and the rest of Wheeler's men "started up the Kingston-Knoxville road at a rapid gait, meeting no opposition until we arrived within sight of the large brick house at Campbell's Station." According to one enlisted man in Crews' Brigade:

> There we found our rapid advance checked by a small cavalry command—probably not more than a regiment, which seemed inclined to contest our further advance. For some time we engaged them with artillery, as the range was too great for rifles to be effective. After a short exchange of pleasantries they disappeared behind a ridge, and we saw no more of them that day. What loss they incurred, if any, I never learned. Why we did not advance farther was a puzzle to us of the ranks just then, but we were shortly enlightened when we saw a mass of blue coats debouch from the woods almost in our rear and deploy in the open field into column of regiments and advance rapidly toward Campbell's Station, but, fortunately they were on the Loudon-Knoxville road, and were some two-hundred yards north by west of the Kingston-Knoxville road, less than half a mile between the roads at that point. They passed on and disappeared as had the cavalry.[22]

Wheeler's Cavalry bivouacked where they were, and moved out the next morning behind Confederate artillery as Longstreet prepared to attack Burnside's force, still arriving at Knoxville. The cavalry took no part in this action, as it was being sent to attack Union forces at Concord Station. To their great delight, the troopers found no Union soldiers at Concord Station, but did find 2,000 loaves of fresh-baked wheat bread abandoned by the retreating foe. One trooper later wrote, that this find was "...something we had not seen or tasted for a month or more, probably more, as our wagons could not keep up with our rapid moves, and more often than not we were dividing rations with our horses."[23]

In less than two hours, the men of the 2nd Georgia and the rest of Wheeler's four brigades, undoubtedly full of bread, were retracing their steps back to Campbell's Station. They arrived in time to join in the pursuit of Burnside's infantry, now in rapid retreat after the engagement with Longstreet's men. The cavalrymen galloped ahead of Longstreet's infantry and pursued the Federals all the way to Knoxville.[24]

Said one enlisted man of Crew's Brigade, "We fully expected Longstreet would move to the assault on the next morning, (18 November) and great was our surprise and chagrin when the day passed so quietly that I cannot recall a single shot being fired, unless it was a few cannon at greater or less intervals and a few rifle shots at long and ineffective range."[25]

If the men in the ranks were "chagrined," at the conduct of the war in the Western Theater, then the men in Richmond were furious. The fighting around Chattanooga had opened with a Federal victory at Orchard Knob on 23 November, the day before Thanksgiving.

On that same day, the men of the 2nd Georgia and their comrades were surprised at Kingston. Wheeler's four brigades were sent there on another night march, at the order of Longstreet, in an attempt to capture two regiments of Union cavalry at Kingston. The cavalrymen arrived tired and hungry near Kingston at three o'clock on the morning of the 23rd. According to Wheeler, many men and animals, too tired to continue, had been left along the road. After an hour's rest, Wheeler had his men in motion, in the hope of surprising the Yankee cavalry regiments at daybreak. Instead of just two cavalry units, however, the Confederates encountered a strong line of infantry, artillery, and cavalry in defensive positions. Wheeler carried on a half-hearted skirmish the whole day with the Union force under a Col. Byrd. Most of the cavalrymen could see nothing to shoot at, and some of them slept through what was primarily an artillery duel.[26]

Already impatient with the slow pace set by Longstreet, the cavalrymen were further irritated by the lack of action at Kingston. While one might wonder if the troopers really wanted to see combat that badly, it is only natural for soldiers to grumble at "hurry up and wait" situations, and that is exactly how they saw the Kingston encounter—a hard overnight ride with a sense of urgency followed by a day of lying around while contending artillery units swapped fire. Said one enlisted man in Crews' Brigade, "As General Wheeler was directing the operations, we expected that a determined effort would be made to drive the enemy out of Kingston, and to hold the place, but nothing of the kind occurred.... "At dusk we withdrew quietly and wended our way back to the intersection of the Loudon road, hungry, thirsty, and disgruntled." The 2nd Georgia and the rest of Crews' Brigade were left at this intersection to guard against any attack on Longstreet's communications. [27]

With the crisis developing outside Chattanooga, Wheeler returned to General Bragg on 24 November, leaving Gen. Martin in charge of the cavalry at Knoxville. It was probably at this point that the 2nd Georgia became, for a time, part of Morgan's Division.

Wheeler reached Bragg in time to see the forty-three Union regiments break the Confederate center at Missionary Ridge on 25 November. Pvt. Moses McGarrah of G Company, one of the 2nd Georgia's men serving as Cheatham's escort, was killed in this battle.[28] Another G Company trooper, Cpl. Littleton Spinks, wrote of Missionary Ridge, "On November 24th the Yankees came out with seven lines of battle and drove us back to Dalton, Ga. It was the worst stampeded army I ever saw."[29] Bragg resigned that day, and was subsequently replaced by Joseph E. Johnston.

Success also eluded the Confederates at Knoxville. Just before midnight on 28 November, Confederate skirmishers captured or killed the Union soldiers in the rifle pits fronting the fortress there. Then at dawn, with only a few signal shots from the artillery, McLaw's Division along with Bryan's and Wofford's brigades charged across the frozen ground toward the fortress. Upon reaching the parapet, the Confederate infantrymen found they could not scale the slippery walls. "For fully twenty minutes, the men stood around the ditch unable to get at their adversaries, but unwilling to retreat." Two Georgia officers managed to get inside. Adjutant T. W. Cumming of the 16th Georgia was captured; Lt. Munger of the 9th Georgia emptied his revolver at the gunners and escaped.[30]

With growing daylight, the Rebels "sulkily withdrew," but Jenkin's Division then rushed to the attack even though they had been instructed to charge only if the first attack met with success. Jenkins men met the same fate on the slippery walls, and nearly 200 were lost. Longstreet had failed, but it was a failure "…made memorable by the desperate gallantry of the charge with the bayonet by three brigades of Georgians and Mississippians of General Lafayette McLaws' division, in a hopeless attempt to capture Fort Sanders, the northwestern anchor of the Union position."[31]

Union Gen. Orlando Poe later wrote of the combat at Knoxville, "No one is more ready and willing than the writer to admit the excellence of the troops that fought us at Knoxville. They had few equals, and I believe no superiors." Poe then went on to rank the "valor and persistency" of his men as the equal of the Confederates, while attributing their success to the effectiveness of their fortifications.[32]

Even as Longstreet contemplated his next move, he began to learn the details of Bragg's failure at Missionary Ridge, and the approach of Union relief columns. The IV Army Corps under Gen. Gordon Granger, some 20,000 men, and Sherman with his entire command were marching on Knoxville from North Georgia. In addition, a force under Gen. John G. Foster was marching from Kentucky through the Cumberland Gap, and two brigades of cavalry under Gen. Washington Elliott were marching from Alexandria, Tennessee. Longstreet had little choice but to withdraw from Knoxville, and the 2nd Georgia was again involved in the risky business of covering a retreat.

At dusk on 4 December, the Georgia cavalrymen moved to provide a rear guard for Longstreet's Corps as he pulled out of Knoxville. Morgan's men covered the rear of McLaw's Division on the south side of the Holston River.[33] The pickets for the Georgia Cavalry Brigade were instructed to hold their positions until after dark, and then catch up with their regiments. This they did, except for one picket post of four or five men who tarried too long and were captured by Union soldiers out of Kingston.[34]

As the Georgians passed by Knoxville in the darkness, they were cautioned to make as little noise as possible, for the Union trenches were less than half a mile distant. Long after the war, one member of the Brigade remembered that "The night was as yet very dark, and they could not see what was passing almost within easy rifle range, and we felt relieved when we again started forward. Had they but known, or even guessed, they could have cut us off and forced us to make a wide detour to reach the crossroads."[35] While there was no general engagement with the enemy, at least one member of the 2nd Georgia was seriously wounded this day. Twenty-year old Pvt. Henry Burr of E Company, a hero at Murfreesboro and Bardstown, was reportedly disabled by his wounds.[36] Pvt. Burr may have been on picket duty when wounded.

The fifty-three mile ride toward Blaines Crossroads became more arduous as the night turned brutally cold. With the dawn, the cavalrymen could see bloody footprints on the frozen ground, left there by barefoot infantrymen in Longstreet's Corps.[37]

From Blaine's Crossroads, Martin took the cavalry southeast. Thursday, 10 December was marked by freezing rain and snow—and for the ill-clad Georgia cavalrymen, it was marked also by a fight at Russellville. Gen. Martin reported, "…a brigade of the enemy's cavalry attacked General Morgan's division at Russellville, while the greater portion of it was foraging. The enemy was handsomely repulsed by one third of its number, leaving dead, wounded and prisoners in our hands." Martin's report gave special mention to the "skill and bravery" of Col. Crews, and the "gallantry" of the 1st and 6th Georgia and the 3rd Alabama.[38] This likely means that the regiments not mentioned, including the 2nd Georgia, were among those absent and foraging.

Four days later, Longstreet turned on the pursuing bluecoats and attacked them at Bean's Station, with Martin's Cavalry turning south to operate in the rear of the Union columns. White's and Wiggins' batteries of Morgan's Division inflicted some sixty casualties as they "dislodged" a Union cavalry brigade guarding May's Ford, allowing Martin to cross the Holston. The next morning the batteries enfiladed the enemy's breastworks, as the Confederate cavalrymen drove in the Union pickets and gained high ground on the Knoxville Road. Under cover of the artillery, the 2nd Georgia and the rest of Morgan's Division made a dismounted attack on the enemy's flank. Martin later complained that the Confederate infantry did not at this time attack the Union center, and thus allowed the Federals to reinforce their flanks against the dismounted cavalry attack. "With concert of action great damage could have been done the enemy on this day," wrote Martin.[39] Three men of the 2nd Georgia's H Company—Sgt. John Evans, Cpl. A. M. Yancey, and Pvt. Perry Gray—were captured this day.[40]

On 16-19 December, the 2nd Georgia was engaged in a series of skirmishes around Blaines Crossroads, Cheek's Crossroads, and at Morristown.[41] Pvt. J. W. Speer of F Company was apparently mortally wounded in one of these encounters.[42]

For several days, Crews' First Brigade, Georgia Cavalry was stationed at Kimbrough's Crossroads with little action. It is probably during this brief respite that Gen. Martin reported "A very large proportion of my men, and even officers, are ragged and barefooted, without blankets or overcoats." Martin added that the quartermaster of Wheeler's Cavalry had "left my command in great need of clothing. We have drawn none for fall or winter. A very large number of my horses are unshod. The men have received no pay for six months."[43]

If Martin's Division received any winter clothing, it was apparently not enough to supply the 2nd Georgia. On 21 January, Gen. Longstreet himself wrote to Quartermaster General Ira Foster in Atlanta, "There are five Georgia brigades in this army—Wofford's, G.T. Anderson's, Bryan's, Benning's and Crews' cavalry brigade. They are all alike in excessive need of shoes, clothing of all kinds, and blankets. All that you can send will be thankfully received."[44]

On 22 December, members of Crews' Brigade were picketing half-way between Morristown and Dandridge, with Russell's Brigade four miles east of Dandridge and Armstrong at Talbott's Depot. Then, early on Thursday, Christmas Eve, Union cavalry launched simultaneous attacks on Russell and Armstrong. Col. Crews with his little brigade of some 600 men (the 4th Georgia was detached at Kingston) was ordered to take four regiments toward Dandridge "to get in the rear" of the 2,000 men under Col. Campbell who were attacking Russell's Alabamians. Campbell had left Dandridge to attack Russell's Brigade, which like Crews' Brigade, was part of Morgan's Division.[45]

Campbell met and engaged Russell at Mays Ferry a few miles above Dandridge. Russell's men fell back in some confusion but rallied and formed a defensive line. Campbell, apparently content he had done enough, turned for Dandridge through the woods toward the Chucky Road. Upon reaching the road, Campbell found the 2nd Georgia and the other three regiments with Crews blocking his return to Dandridge. To avoid this blockade, Campbell turned through North's Farm. Crews then sent the 6th Georgia's G Company on a charge, capturing an artillery piece at the road crossing. One of the Union regiments countercharged this company, driving them away, and recapturing the canon.[46]

While this was going on, one of Campbell's regiments hastily built a rail breastworks on the North Farm, hoping to delay the Confederates while the rest of the brigade escaped. The 6th Georgia charged the breastwork and was repulsed with loss, including popular Maj. Alfred Bale, shot in the head "ten paces" from the union barricade.[47]

Now dismounted, the 2nd Georgia and the rest of Crews' Brigade swung left in pursuit of Campbell, who was "doing his best" to save his two remaining artillery pieces. The Federals frequently halted and countercharged to check the pursuit, but "always giving ground." The men of the 2nd Michigan dismounted and used their Colt revolving rifles to slow the Confederate pursuit.[48]

Crews sent couriers in search of Col. Russell in the hope that Campbell could be trapped, but the Alabama Regiment could not be found. The Georgians continued the pursuit across the Morristown Road, but darkness eventually forced him to give up the chase. Casualties for the 2nd Georgia were light, but the 6th Georgia lost thirteen men captured and another seven killed in the attack against the rail breastworks. The men of the 6th Georgia felt badly used this Christmas Eve, as they never received the promised support when one of their companies captured the artillery piece, and they regarded mounted assaults against any breastwork as folly.[49]

Martin reported, "I have never witnessed greater gallantry than was displayed by Colonel Crews and the officers and men of the First, Second, Third and Sixth Georgia Cavalry." (The 4th Georgia was on detached service at Kingston during this engagement.) Added the general, "The enemy, mounted, three times charged our dismounted men in open field, and were as often repulsed, but not until, mingling in our ranks, some of his men were brought to the ground by clubbed guns." The Federals in these charges were from the 9th Pennsylvania, the 2nd Michigan, and the 1st Tennessee.[50]

Five days later, the 2nd Georgia was among the 2,000 cavalrymen that Gen. Martin sent against strong Union positions at Mossy Creek. Martin complained that he had wanted to make this attack on 27 December, but Gen. Morgan had "...without orders moved his command, dismounted, from the position I had assigned to him, and made it thus impossible to effect my object."[51] Morgan's reason for changing his position on the 27th is unclear, but there apparently was some action this day. Pvt. Jasper Screws of the 2nd Georgia's C Company was wounded on the 27th. He would be killed in some unrecorded action during 1864.[52]

On the 29th, the 2,000 Confederate horseman crossed Mossy Creek and attacked a brigade of infantry and another of cavalry, driving them back until checked by artillery. Fighting continued into the afternoon, but Union reinforcements eventually made it an uneven contest.

One of Crews' men described the action in his diary. "Friday 29th— fought Yanks at Mossy Creek Crews' brigade Charged up & fought one Div. Of Yankee infantry until forced away by a firce (sic) charge Dibbrell's Brig of Tenn Cav came up to Support us we rallied fired again a few rounds—when the Yanks fell back—and began to fortify We remained in line some two hours—-when we began to fall back to our old position after carrying off our wounded & dead."[53]

Martin's report of the fighting at Mossy Creek is more descriptive, and better punctuated:

> The fighting occurred on both sides of the railroad leading from Mossy Creek to Morristown, and commenced one-quarter of a mile west of Talbott's Station, and ended near the same place at dark. General Morgan's division was dismounted and formed on the left of the railroad, General Armstrong on the right. The country from this station to Mossy Creek is composed of open, rolling fields, that had been tilled during the past year, flanked by high woodland on each side. I could not maneuver the artillery except near the railroad. Armstrong's division, with the artillery, was moved rapidly upon the enemy to engage his attention, while I hoped to flank him with Morgan's division on his right. His rapid retreat enabled him to avoid this, and both divisions finally were moved at double-quick, and drove the enemy rapidly and in confusion back to Mossy Creek. Up to this time the force opposing us was not greater than 4,000 men, with two batteries. Owing to the nature of the ground, Crews' brigade had been thrown to the right of the railroad, and General Armstrong, with Crews' brigade, was ordered to move up his artillery to within cannister range, and to charge some woods in his front and that of Colonel Crews.
>
> Colonel Russell's brigade had its right resting on the railroad and its left on the woods. Immediately in his front the enemy had occupied some barns and outhouses. I ordered him to dislodge him. The whole line moved forward. The enemy was driven from his position on our left, but by a charge of cavalry on our right and of a brigade of infantry upon Crews' brigade and Armstrong's left, we were compelled to yield the ground. The enemy fixed bayonets and moved some 200 yards in his front. Perceiving this, I wheeled the Seventh Alabama Regiment to the right and moved it into a cut of the railroad, securing a good position within fifty yards of the flank of the advancing infantry. The fire from this regiment and a countercharge by the Georgians soon drove the enemy into and through the woods, with heavy loss in killed and wounded.[54]

Despite this apparent success, Martin soon found that the larger Union force overlapped both of his flanks. Moreover, he could see a fresh blue brigade of cavalry and an infantry reserve arrive on the field. His division commanders were reporting an average of only five rounds of ammunition remaining per man, and his artillery ordnance was exhausted except for cannister. Martin then ordered a withdrawal, which

> …was effected in perfect order, the regiments falling back in succession to advantageous points, and then fighting until, having checked the enemy sufficiently, they could gain another point of vantage.
>
> While the officers and men deserve great credit for their gallantry in the advance, their conduct during this difficult and hazardous movement to the rear entitle them to the highest praise. The enemy's bugles often sounded the charge. At first the charge was made, but not a second one. At dusk, after nine hours of severe fighting and marching, the command was halted and formed and the enemy finally repulsed. There was not then an average of one round of ammunition to the man.[55]

Col. Crews was again cited for gallantry by Gen. Martin, but the common soldiers felt "ill-used" in this conflict.[56]

In January the 2nd Georgia was involved in operations between Dandridge and Sevierville, including a sharp "action" at Dandridge on the 17th. The 1st Cavalry Division, Army of the Ohio, under Col. F. Wolford had been sent to feel-out the enemy, while the 1st Division of Cavalry, Army of the Cumberland, commanded by Col. A.P. Campbell, had been sent on the Morristown Road to "flank the enemy." Col. Thomas Jordan of the 9th Pennsylvannia reported "…it became evident from the firing that the enemy was fast driving Colonel Wolford back toward Dandridge." Jordan moved his brigade up to offer support, but soon found "…Colonel Wolford's division in full retreat, galloping away from the enemy, leaving my flank entirely exposed." With his artillery well positioned on high ground, and with help from the 2nd Indiana, Jordan reported that he was able to check the pursuit of the Confederates.[57]

> Longstreet's report of this action reads a little differently.
> On the 16th, he made an effort to throw his cavalry in rear of ours, but the cavalry came in contact with these divisions of infantry and was driven back in some confusion. On the 17th, a part of Hood's division was moved down to the enemy's immediate front. The sharpshooters of this division were ordered to advance against the enemy's left flank, and Martin's cavalry (dismounted) were ordered to follow this move,

advancing in the enemy's front. The battalions of sharpshooters were closely supported by the main force of the division, the immediate object being to gain a favorable position for future operations. The flank movement was handsomely executed, and it was handsomely followed by the dismounted cavalry….During the night the enemy retired to New Market and to Strawberry Plains, leaving his dead upon the field. The retreat seems to have been made somewhat hastily and not in very good order. Our infantry was not in condition to pursue, half of our men being without shoes. Our cavalry is almost as badly off for want of clothing, and the horses are without shoes, or nearly half of them. It was sent forward, however, with orders to make the effort to distress the enemy, and if possible to drive him from this side of the river. The enemy is much demoralized, and seems to have been in our power again, had it been possible for us to avail ourselves of this opportunity. The weather has been very severe for the past three weeks, and we are now having a snow storm. Our men suffer a great deal for want of clothing even in their huts, and some few have been severely frosted.[58]

If the Union soldiers were demoralized, the events of ten days later must have greatly restored their morale. Late on the afternoon of 26 January, the 2nd Georgia and the rest of Morgan's Division joined with Armstrong's Division in attacking Wolford's Division at Fair Garden, driving the Federals some two miles toward Sevierville. As night fell, the two Rebel cavalry divisions became separated.

A break in the bitter cold of the previous weeks brought a thick fog with the dawn of 27 January. Out of the fog, McCook's Division counterattacked Morgan's cavalry. Campbell's brigade struck the Confederates first, forcing them to fall back to the McNutt House and set a defensive position. In changing their position, Morgan's men, including the 2nd Georgia, drove the 2nd Michigan from the field, which "necessitated the withdrawal of the entire brigade" back across the Middle Fork of Pigeon River. But Gen. McCook then sent Col. Oscar LaGrange's regiment on Morgan's right flank, and now both LaGrange and Campbell were pressing in under very effective artillery fire from a battery commanded by Capt. Eli Lilly, the future pharmaceutical entrepreneur. The Confederates fell back to McNutt's Bridge where they put up "stubborn resistance."

The fighting wore on into the afternoon as Morgan's men fell back to successive positions until they reached Fair Garden. To this point the fighting had all been by dismounted cavalry, but now LaGrange sent the 2nd and 4th Indiana regiments on a mounted charge against the Confederate battery, where according to McCook, they succeeded in reaching the guns and "sabering" the crews just before dark.[59] Capt. Lilly's report indicates, however, that it was his artillery which silenced the Rebel guns, as he brought his own battery "into position at the gallop to within 500 yards of the rebel battery and opened furiously. They fired a few shots and left the field...." [60]Attempts by Morgan's men to retake the guns were repelled. Just as the Rebel artillery fell silent, LaGrange's dismounted men achieved a "flank fire" on the Confederates engaged with Campbell. Lilly also reported shelling the "columns" of retreating Confederates, an account that does not square with McCook's report that Morgan's Division was "disgracefully routed." If McCook overstated the case, it was nevertheless a resounding victory for the Federals. [61]

Longstreet blamed the defeat on the growing numbers of Union cavalrymen, and implicitly at least, on Gen. Martin. His report to the adjutant inspector general closed with a terse line. "Do send me a chief of cavalry." [62]

Longstreet reported a "loss of 200 killed, wounded and missing and 2 pieces of artillery," numbers quite close to those reported by McCook.

At least thirty-two of these losses occurred in the 2nd Georgia and included two company commanders—Capt. Peter Twitty of C Company who was captured, and Capt. Robert Mitchell of D Company who was wounded and captured. Pvt. Milsey Strickland, whose loss of a finger the year before had not excused him from service, was one of at least eight members of F Company captured at Fair Garden. In D Company, three members of the Bennett family were captured. Known losses for the 2nd Georgia are shown below.[63]

Edward Fagan	pvt., A Company	wounded in thigh & captured
William Patrick Gormley	pvt., A Company	captured
Peter Twitty	capt., C Company	captured
Joseph Salter	pvt., C Company	captured
Robert Mitchell	capt., D Company	wounded & captured
Thomas Camp	2nd lt., D Company	captured
John Bennett	pvt., D Company	captured
Mason Bennett	pvt., D Company	captured
Nathan Bennett	pvt., D Company	captured

Joseph Brown	pvt., D Company	captured
Virgil Freeman	pvt., D Company	captured
William Michael	pvt., D Company	captured, apparently wounded
Egbert Smith	pvt., D Company	captured
John Bridges	pvt., E Company	captured
James Ivey	pvt., E Compnay	captured
Charles Travis	pvt., E Company	captured
John F. Smith	pvt., F Company	captured
Henry Johnson	sgt., F Company	captured
David Hartsfield	pvt., F Company	captured
Joseph Morris	pvt., F Company	captured
Seaborne Smith	pvt., F Company	captured
Freeman Speer	pvt., F Company	captured
Milsey Strickland	pvt., F Company	captured
Haywood Thornton	pvt., F Company	captured
Jesse Ward	pvt., F Company	captured
Napolean Chesire	pvt., H Company	captured
Buford Gant	pvt., H Company	wounded
Ellison Hope	pvt., H Company	wounded
John Kilgore	pvt., H Company	captured
John Smith	sgt., H Company	captured
Owen Cochran	2nd Lt. I Company	wounded & captured
William Fain	pvt., K Company	killed

It was one of the worst days of the War for the 2nd Georgia and the entire Georgia Brigade. It was also a particularly tragic day for the Fain family in Decatur County. James and Edward Fain had been captured the previous September during the skirmishing prior to Chickamauga. James apparently was wounded, for he died within days. Edward died as a POW at Camp Chase on 23 December, barely a month before William, the last of the Fains in K Company, was killed at Fair Garden.

Over in the 6th Georgia, there was some consolation for Capt. Jack Lay. Lt. Col. Leslie of the 4th Indiana was killed in the mounted charge on the battery and his horse recovered by Capt. Lay, who found that it was his own. Lay had been knocked from this horse at Mays Ferry the previous Christmas Eve. While Lay had escaped capture, the horse had not. Having recovered his mount, "Captain Jack then rode him to the end of the war, without further mishap, and surrendered with Johnston's army."[64]

Fighting continued throughout the 28th, with skirmishes at Indian Creek and Swann's Island.

Those actions were apparently the last conflicts of this bitterly cold winter for the Georgia cavalrymen. Still ill-clothed and poorly equipped, their horses "jaded," the respite came in the nick of time.

The 2nd Georgia had seen heavy fighting in the East Tennessee Campaign, and one of its own, Col. Charles Crews, had repeatedly distinguished himself as a brigade commander. Records for 31 January 1864 show Crews commanding both the Georgia Brigade and the 2nd Georgia Regiment. What happened to Ison is unclear. Surviving muster rolls indicate that in October of 1864 he was "in arrest by order of Gen'l Allen, cmdg Division."[65] Whatever the cause of his absence, he is shown as being present at the surrender, although it is not clear in what capacity. Long after the war one veteran of the Regiment, Rosemun M. Nolan who served in F Company, listed Ison as his commanding officer at the time of the surrender.[66]

The command structure for the 2nd Georgia as of 31 January 1864 is shown below.[67]

Martin's Corps
Morgan's Division
Crews' Brigade
Crews' Regiment

A Company	Capt. Fleming Crews
B Company	unknown
C Company	Capt. W. C. Hood
D Company	Capt. James Shepard
E Company	Capt. James Ellis
F Company	Capt. Hardy Chapman
G Company	Capt. Thomas Merritt
H Company	Capt. Francis Allen
I Company	Capt. George Looney
K Company	probably 1st. Lt. Jesse Barber

[1] John P. Dyer, *From Shiloh to San Juan, The Life of Fightin' Joe Wheeler* (Baton Rouge LA: Louisiana State University Press, 1941) 113.

[2] *War of the Rebellion, Official Record of the Union Confederate Armies* Series I Vol. 31 Part 1 (Washington DC: U.S. Government Printing Office, 1890) 545.

[3] Compiled Service Records, 2nd Georgia Cavalry (Atlanta GA: Georgia Department of Archives and History).

[4] J. W. Minnich, "Freezin and Fighting, Dec. 10, 1863" *Confederate Veteran Magazine,* 60.

[5] *War of the Rebellion, Official Records* Series 1 Vol. 31 Part 1, 5.

[6] W. B. Corbitt, "Diary of a Veteran of Wheeler's Corps" (Atlanta GA: Robert W. Woodruff Library, Emory University) 31.

[7] J. W. Minnich, "The Affair at Mays' Ferry, Tenn." *Confederate Veteran Magazine,* Vol. 33, 55.

[8] *War of the Rebellion, Official Records* Series I Vol. 31 Part 1, 441—442.

[9] Ibid. Vol. 32 part 2.

[10] Compiled Service Records, 2nd Georgia Cavalry.

[11] E. Porter Alexander, "Longstreet at Knoxville" in *Battles and Leaders of the Civil War, Vol. III, The Tide Shifts* (Edison NJ: Castel Books, 1995) 746.

[12] Ibid. 750.

[13] Dyer, *Shiloh to San Juan—The Life of Fightin Joe Wheeler,* 112. See also Stanley F. Horn, *The Army of Tennessee* (New York NY: Bobbs Merrill Company , 1941) 294.

[14] Stephen Z. Starr, *The Union Cavalry in the Civil War, Vol. III, The War in the West 1861-1865* (Baton Rouge LA: Louisiana State University Press, 1985) 333.

[15] J. W. Minnich, "The Cavalry at Knoxville" in *Confederate Veteran Magazine* Vol. 32, 10.

[16] Dodson, *Campaigns of Wheeler and His Cavalry,* 145.

[17] Ibid.

[18] Dyer, *From Shiloh to San Juan: The Life of Fightin Joe Wheeler,* 114.

[19] Dodson, *Campaigns of Wheeler and His Cavalry,* 146.

[20] Ibid. 145.

[21] Dyer, *From Shiloh to San Juan: The Life of Fightin' Joe Wheeler,* 144.

[22] Minnich, "The Cavalry at Knoxville" *Confederate Veteran Magazine,* Vol. 32, 10-12.

[23] Ibid.

[24] Ibid.

[25] Ibid.

[26] Ibid.

[27] Ibid.

[28] Compiled Service Records, 2nd Georgia Cavalry.

[29] Mamie Yeary, *Reminiscences of the Boys in Gray* (Dayton OH: Morningside Press, 1986).

[30] Alexander, "Longstreet at Knoxville" in *Battles and Leaders of the Civil War* Vol III, 749.

[31] Ibid.

[32] Orlando M. Poe, "The Defense of Knoxville" in *Battles and Leaders of the Civil War, Vol III,* 744.

[33] Dodson, ed., *Campaigns of Wheeler and His Cavalry,* 149.

[34] Minnich, "The Cavalry at Knoxville" in *Confederate Veteran Magazine,* Vol. 31, 10-12.

[35] Ibid.

[36] Compiled Service Records, 2nd Georgia Cavalry.

[37] Minnich, "The Cavalry at Knoxville" in *Confederate Veteran Magazine,* Vol. 31, 10-12.

[38] *War of the Rebellion, Official Records* Series I Vol. 31Part 1, 546.

[39] Ibid.

[40] Compiled Service Records, 2nd Georgia Cavalry.

[41] Minnich, "The Cavalry at Knoxville, in *Civil War Veteran Magazine,* Vol. 32, 10-12.

[42] Compiled Service Records, 2nd Georgia Cavalry.

[43] Dyer, *From Shiloh to San Juan: The Life of Fightin' Joe Wheeler,* 119.

[44] *War of the Rebellion, Official Records,* Series I Vol. 31 Part I.

[45] J. W. Minnich, "The Affair at Mays Ferry" in *Confederate Veteran Magazine* Vol. 33, 55. See also Dodson, ed. *Campaigns of Wheeler and His Cavalry,* 150.

[46] Minnich, "The Affair at Mays Ferry" in *Confederate Veteran Magazine* Vol. 33, 55. See also, Julius Dowda Diary, 3rd Georgia Cavalry, (Atlanta GA: Georgia Department of Archives and History).

[47] Ibid.

[48] Starr, *The Union Cavalry in the Civil War,* Vol III, 349.

[49] Minnich, "The Affair at Mays Ferry" in *Confederate Veteran Magazine* vol. 33, 55-57.

[50] *War of the Rebellion, Official Records* Series I Vol. 31 Part 1, 547.

[51] Ibid.

[52] Compiled Service Records, 2nd Georgia Cavalry.

[53] Dowda, diary, 548-549.

[54] *War of the Rebellion, Official Records* Series I Vol. 31 Part 1, 548-549.

[55] Ibid.

[56] Minnich, "The Affair at Mays Ferry" in *Confederate Veteran Magazine* vol. 33, 57.

[57] *War of the Rebellion, Official Records* Series I Vol. 32 Part 1, 87.

[58] Ibid, 93-94.

[59] Ibid., 139.

[60] Ibid., 146.

[61] Ibid., 140.

[62] Ibid., 150.

[63] Compiled Service Records, 2nd Georgia Cavalry.

[64] Minnich, "The Affair at Mays Ferry" in *Confederate Veteran Magazine* Vol. 33, 57.

[65] Compiled Service Records, 2nd Georgia Cavalry.

[66] Confederate Soldiers Home, register of inmates, drawer 252, box 2 (Atlanta GA: Georgia Department of Archives and History).

[67] Ibid.

The Altanta Campaign

By April of 1864, Longstreet's Corps had moved into winter quarters, and the 2nd Georgia Cavalry returned to the main body of the Army of Tennessee, now at Dalton under Gen. Joseph Johnston. At the end of February, the Georgia cavalry regiments had received a new brigade commander—Gen. Alfred Iverson replacing Crews who remained in command of the Regiment—and again became part of Martin's division in Wheeler's cavalry corps, as shown in the following command structure.[1]

Wheeler's Corps
Martin's Division
Iverson's Brigade
Crews' Regiment

A Company	Capt. Fleming Crews
B Company	unknown
C Company	Capt. W. C. Hood
D Company	Capt. James Shepard
E Company	Capt. James Fambro or Capt. James Ellis
F Company	Capt. Hardy Chapman
G Company	Capt. Thomas Merritt
H Company	Capt. Francis Allen
I Company	Capt. George Looney
K Company	Capt. J. R. Butts

Iverson, a thirty-five-year-old native of Clinton, Georgia, served in the Mexican War and fought Comanches and Kiowa in the 1850s.[2] As an infantry commander in the Army of Northern Virginia, he was wounded at Gaines Mill and fought with distinction at South Mountain, Antietam, and Fredricksburg. At Chancellorsville, however, his performance was "less than shining." Then at Gettysburg, while commanding a brigade under A. P. Hill, he "suffered a breakdown when he saw what looked like his whole brigade surrendering."[3] His availability was probably due to Lee's sudden loss of confidence.

According to one account, G Company's service as Cheatham's escort ended and the company returned to the regiment about this time. A postwar biographical sketch of Lt. James T. Newsome sets their return in this time frame and notes that the company fought under Wheeler for the remainder of the war.[4] However, a similar biographical sketch of Pvt. R. M. Fletcher, who did not join the company until 1 March 1864, says that G Company remained with Cheatham until the evacuation of Atlanta.[5] From company muster rolls, it seems clear that G Company was back with the Regiment by 10 August, although a large number of its individual members remained on detached duty with Cheatham.[6]

Although the actual date of the 2nd Georgia's arrival back in their home state is unclear, it was apparently well before their next action, a skirmish at Taylor's Ridge near Ringgold on 27 April. All of the cavalry regiments returning from Longstreet's East Tennessee campaign were very low on serviceable horses. Iverson's Brigade was reportedly camped on the Etowah River during April while the men scrambled for new mounts.[7] Many of the troopers were furloughed at this time to obtain horses.[8]

Horses were not the only equipment problem facing the cavalry. Although most had been able to replace the shotguns they brought from home with more effective weapons captured in Tennessee or Kentucky, the wide range of armament types made ammunition supply a serious problem. More and more of the men were apparently being armed with the short versions of the Enfield rifle, which became the closest thing to a standard issue for Wheeler's men. The troopers also carried a wide variety of handguns, and at this point most apparently still carried the heavy cavalry saber. As the campaign wore on and they found themselves often fighting on foot and in trenches, many cavalrymen abandoned the saber. A "surprising number" of the troopers were still unarmed.[9] Many of the men had been issued shoes and clothing in late March, too late to get them through the winter, but just in time for the hard campaigning ahead.[10]

Throughout that April, other units of Wheeler's cavalry were in daily conflict with Union forces on the Georgia -Tennessee border. On 28 April, some of Wheeler's men drove the 10th Ohio Cavalry out of Tunnel Hill, and found that the Union troopers had burned the little town and murdered thirteen Confederates captured when they seized the outpost.[11] The tone was set for bitter enmity between the opposing cavalries, more bitter perhaps than between infantry units or combatants in the eastern theater.

Gen. U.S. Grant, the commander of all Union armies, in February had assigned Sherman the objective of taking the war to the deep South and destroying the Army of Tennessee, which now numbered some 44,000 men.[12] Having made the assignment, Grant provided the tools, giving Sherman three armies totaling 98,797 combat troops including 4,460 artillery men.[13] The largest of the three forces, the Army of the Cumberland, was commanded by Gen. George H. Thomas. The Army of the Tennessee was led by Gen. James B. McPherson and the Army of Ohio by Gen. John M. Schofield. They would soon be reinforced by the 17th Infantry Corps and four divisions and two brigades of cavalry, bringing the total force of infantry and artillery to over 100,000, and the cavalry to 18,000.[14] Not only were Union soldiers plentiful, they were as tough and determined as their enemy.

On 1 May, this mighty force began the grand offensive which would be known as the Atlanta Campaign. Confederate cavalry stubbornly delayed the advance for six days, prompting a northern correspondent to write, "The rebel cavalry, under Wheeler, fought our advance with an abandon and desperation worthy of a better cause."[15] Nevertheless, by 7 May, Sherman had penetrated the mountains around Dalton.

Sherman's next objective was to interject the bulk of the Union force between Johnston and Atlanta. To achieve this purpose, he planned an attack at Resaca, where a railroad span across the Oostanaula River was a tempting pinch point on the Confederate supply line.

Johnston recognized that Sherman would likely attempt to cut him off from Atlanta, but he could not know where the Union army would strike. His cavalry was, therefore, spread in a wide arc across North Georgia to watch Union movements. When Wheeler's scouts on 5 May found one of McPherson's divisions on the road to LaFayette, Johnston apparently became convinced that Sherman would strike his left flank at

Rome and the railroad. Johnston ordered Martin's Division, which included the 2nd Georgia and the rest of Iverson's Georgia Brigade, to move to Rome. Johnston then sent word to Polk in Alabama to hurry his corps to Rome.[16]

McPherson arrived at Resaca on 7 May with 25,000 men, having marched his force eastward from Lafayette through Snake Creek Gap. Only Cantey's Brigade of 4,000 men was here to receive McPherson, and he had just arrived and was not well entrenched. A sharp clash between these Confederates and the leading elements of The Army of the Tennessee convinced McPherson to retire until reinforcements arrived. McPherson did not even cut the rail line.[17] By 11 May, McPherson's men were joined by Kilpatrick's cavalry and two more infantry divisions. But McPherson, apparently worried that Hood's army would fall on his rear, still did not attack. This failure allowed Johnston to reinforce Resaca, and forced Sherman to temporarily abandon his plan to cut Johnston off from Atlanta. Sherman's next option was to intercept Johnston's divisions and destroy them before they could reach Resaca. On the 13th, however, the 2nd Georgia was apparently involved in Wheeler's "skillful rearguard action" which so slowed the advance of Howard, McCook, and Stoneman, that three Confederate divisions—Bate's, Stewart's, and Hindman's—were in Resaca's defensive line before Sherman could mass his forces there.[18]

By the morning of 14 May, most of Sherman's force faced the Confederates at Resaca. According to some sources, "the cavalry was placed in the trenches, a part on the right under Hood, a part on the left under Polk, and a part in the center under Hardee."[19] While some cavalrymen may have been in trenches, most of Wheeler's men were probably guarding the flanks of the Confederate line. The 2nd Georgia was almost certainly with the rest of Martin's Division on the Confederate left, watching the Oostanaula River. In fact, it was Martin's message to Johnston late on the 15th that two Federal corps had crossed the river which convinced Johnston to end the battle and withdraw.[20]

About noon on the 14th, Palmer's 14th Corps of the Army of the Cumberland along with Judah's Division struck Hindman's Division just to the right of the Confederate center. The attack failed, and some 1,300 Union soldiers were killed or wounded. The artillery barrage that then hit the Confederate positions has been described by some veterans as among the most intense shellings of the war.[21]

That afternoon, part of Hood's Corps, massed in column, counter-attacked the Union left. Three brigades of Stevenson's Division broke the Union line, sending Cruft's and Whitaker's brigades into pell mell retreat. As they paused at the evacuated Federal position, the Confederates were suddenly swept by devastating cannister fire from a six gun battery. The gray soldiers retreated, only to re-form and come again at the battery. This time it appeared they would reach the battery, but the XX Army Corps under General Hooker, 7,000 strong, arrived on the field and pushed the Confederates back to their entrenchments.[22]

Early on the afternoon of the 15th, three brigades under General Howard attacked Hindman's Division on the Confederate left, and were quickly driven off, with considerable loss. About the same time, Hooker's XX Corps attacked the Rebel center and momentarily captured a four-gun battery in advance of Brown's Tennessee brigade. Using three-man firing squads—two loaders feeding one marksman—Brown's brigade drove off Hooker's attack and inflicted some 1,200 casualties, almost as many as the number of men in the Tennessee brigade. Shortly after this, Stewart's thrust on the Federal left was beaten back, with about 1,000 casualties.[23]

During the day, Pvt. W. West of the 2nd Georgia's A Company was captured. He later took the pledge of allegiance and joined the U.S. Navy to escape the perils of the prison camp.[24]

Later that night, Johnston heard from Martin that the Federals had "effected a crossing of the Oostanaula several miles to his left and rear."[25] Johnston immediately called off a planned renewal of the battle and withdrew to behind the Oostanaula River. It was the first of many strategic withdrawals for Johnston. For his part, Sherman was roundly criticized in the north for failing to achieve victory at Resaca, where he outnumbered Johnston more than two to one. Federal casualties at Resaca totaled about 4,000, Confederate casualties about 3,000.[26]

As the Confederate infantry faded away, the 2nd Georgia Cavalry participated in Wheeler's "skillful" coverage of Johnston's withdrawal from Resaca. On the 15th, Stoneman's cavalry attacked the hospital tents of Hindman's Division, but Wheeler sent a brigade back and they drove the Federals away, taking thirty prisoners. Much as they had done in Kentucky, brigades or regiments of Wheeler's men fought short hold-ing actions from behind hastily erected barricades, while other brigades or regiments would be preparing another barricade a mile or so down the road. In this manner, the 2nd Georgia and other Confederate cavalry units contested the advance of the Federal IV Corps, which did not reach Calhoun until 6:00 P.M.

On the 18th, a detachment of the 2nd Georgia skirmished with Union forces at Pine Log Church as they approached Johnston's army near Cassville. Nearer the town, the entire Regiment was in action on the 18th and 19th. At Cartersville, the Regiment was part of Wheeler's force which crossed the Etowah River and set the bridge afire, thwarting Schofield's crossing. On the 24th Wheeler's men captured some seventy wagons and destroyed many others, then beat back attempts by Union cavalry to recapture the train, taking more than 100 prisoners.

In the battle at Pickett's Mill on 27 May, cavalrymen again found themselves in the trenches, with the 2nd Georgia and the rest of Martin's Division on the Confederate left. Kelly's and Humes' brigades played a particularly important role here, holding their thin line against vastly superior numbers until infantry reinforcements arrived. Pickett's Mill was a lop-sided victory, with over 1600 Federal casualties compared with 448 for the Confederates.[27]

At New Hope Church, Pickett's Mill, Pumpkin Vine Creek, Dallas, and Allatoona Hills, the 2nd Georgia and other cavalry regiments alternately served as infantry in the trenches and as a cavalry screen during movements. In none of these, however, was the 2nd Georgia heavily engaged. The sounds of the Confederate victory at New Hope Church were the first sounds of battle heard by the residents in Atlanta[28]

Late in May it began to rain, and it did not let up appreciably for almost a month. Swollen streams and deep mud complicated troop movements for Johnston and Sherman, and made life miserable for the common soldier.

On 10 June, Maj. James W. Mayo, who had apparently been serving as a regimental or brigade staff officer, replaced Crews as commander of the 2nd Georgia. Crews apparently became a staff officer at this time, as Iverson was still commanding the Georgia Brigade.[29]

On the same day that Maj. Mayo got a vote of confidence from his superiors, Gen. Kenner Garrard got just the opposite from Sherman. The Union commander had been frustrated with his top cavalry officers since Resaca, constantly urging them to be more aggressive and move faster. His dispatch to Garrard on the 10th referred to Wheeler's sorties against his supply line and said, "Surely if [Wheeler's] cavalry can make such marches ours should do something." Sherman wanted Garrard to circle the Confederate right and threaten the railroad near the

Chattahoochee River, but a week later Garrard was still on the north bank of Noonday Creek, just a few miles from Sherman's headquarters at Big Shanty. Sherman then became even more pointed with Garrard. "The enemy has detached a great part of his cavalry back to our line of railroad where they are doing mischief. Now if they can cross the Etowah, the Oostenaula, and the Connesauga—large streams—it does seem that you can cross the little Noonday. I therefore order you to cross and advance against the enemy's cavalry and drive it back and interpose betweeen the enemy and their detached infantry."[30] Garrard replied the next day he had repeatedly tried to cross the stream, but Wheeler's Cavalry—not the swollen condition of the stream—had prevented him from doing so.[31]

Indeed during this month, Wheeler's cavalry had skirmished with Garrard's cavalry division almost daily on Bell's Ferry Road and around Noonday Creek. Sgt. James Pyle of the 2nd Georgia's A Company was killed in some nameless conflict on 2 June.[32] On 5 June, Wheeler's mounted charge drove Garrard back past Big Shanty, where many members of the 2nd Georgia had trained and where the Great Locomotive Chase began two years before. Sixty-five of the retreating Yankees were captured. For the following three days there was "warm skirmishing" along Wheeler's line. On 9 June, two brigades of infantry and three brigades of cavalry advanced with artillery support against Wheeler's positions. Two charges failed, and the Federals retired, leaving their dead on the field. Skirmishing resumed the following day as Sherman shifted toward the railroad. That night the Federals retired, but their line overlapped Wheeler's right, and he moved his cavalry to a position between the Bell's Ferry and Canton roads, probably on the south side of rain-swollen Noonday Creek.[33]

On 11 June, the Confederate cavalrymen ended a long day of "uninterrupted skirmishing" when they "...checked a force which attempted to attack General Hood's right."[34] Iverson's Georgia Brigade engaged the 3rd Ohio Cavalry under Col. C. B. Seidel north of Noonday Creek and quickly drove them back, killing two and wounding twelve of the outnumbered Federals.[35] Cpl. James Davis of the 2nd Georgia's A Company was killed in this fighting.[36]

Over the next four days the skirmishing remained almost constant along Wheeler's line, now almost three miles long in the open and gently rolling farm country. By 14 June word had spread all along the line that Lt. Gen. Leonidas Polk had been killed on the 13th, struck in the chest by a twenty pound Parrot solid shot which "mangled his body horribly."[37] On 15 June, a division of cavalry attacked Wheeler's right at Noonday Creek and was repulsed. Wheeler countercharged "flank and rear," capturing forty-three of the enemy. The next day was marked by especially heavy rain and punctuated by an exchange of artillery fire.[38]

On 17 June, the Federals "turned" Wheeler's works on Noonday Creek, forcing his men into the woods. There the dismounted Southerners engaged Federal infantry and captured sixty-five, who reported heavy losses among their comrades. The next day there was "close and brisk" fighting on Bell's Ferry Road, and Wheeler's men were driven from their temporary works. It appears that Wheeler retired southward a short distance down Bell's Ferry Road, short of the crossroads (currently Piedmont Road) at Dr. Robert McAffee's house.

General Johnston's main line along Brushy Mountain and Mud Creek was being similarly hard-pressed by Sherman. On the night of 18 June, after a day of heavy skirmishing and heavier rain, the Army of Tennesee retreated through ankle-deep mud to a new line centered on Kennesaw Mountain. Exhausted, hungry, wet, and plastered with mud, the Confederates at daylight began the hard work of digging trenches and felling trees.[39]

Johnston's new line was now some six miles long, the right extending south of the current site of Town Center Mall to the area between Canton and Bell's Ferry roads, already occupied by Wheeler's Cavalry Corps. The men of the 2nd Georgia and the rest of Wheeler's Corps were on this extreme right of the Confederate line.[40]

The 2nd Georgia was immediately engaged on 19 June when Federals "vigorously" attacked Wheeler's positions below Noonday Creek near McAfee's farm. After a two-hour fight, much of it at close range, the Federals were driven off with heavy losses, "leaving their dead and some wounded on the field."[41]

On the 20th, another wet and soggy day, Wheeler's troopers checked a Union advance on the Canton Road.[42] Then Garrard's First Brigade under Col. Robert H. Minty attacked down Bell's Ferry Road. Apparently Wheeler himself then took Iverson's Georgia Brigade, and Allen's Brigade, on a mounted charge into the Federal right flank, "...forcing Garrard to fall back on Col. Miller's three regiments which had formed on the hills around the bridge over Noonday Creek." Wheeler reported, "...defeating the enemy, killing fifty, and capturing one hundred and twenty prisoners, two stands of colors, one hundred and fifty horses, besides arms and equipments. Wheeler's loss, fifteen killed, fifty wounded." Minty reported that he withdrew across Noonday Creek under cover of his artillery and that "My loss was heavy, being in the Fourth Michigan and Seventh Pennsylvania…and Third Brigade."[43] The fighting between Noonday Creek and the McAfee farmhouse was "…an old fashioned cavalry engagement, complete with charging steeds, swinging sabers, cuts, thrusts, and parries."[44]

Brisk skirmishing continued for the next two days, as the rain that had plagued both armies for almost a month gave way to a hot Georgia sun. In the fighting of 22 June, Pvt. Wiley Miner of the 2nd Georgia's I Company was killed.[45]

On the 23rd, Wheeler attacked Union defensive positions on Bell's Ferry Road to create a diversion while General Pillow's infantry was moving out of their works. Wheeler's dismounted charge carried the first line of works, and yielded "a number of prisoners." The Federals advanced in force but retired when attacked on the flank near McAfee's farm.[46] The fighting remained "brisk" for the next three days on Wheeler's line near the Rice house.[47]

The McAfee's house, witness to conflicts between Wheeler and Garrard for much of June 1864, still stands at the intersection of Bell's Ferry and Piedmont Roads, now surrounded by shopping centers and an elementary school.

Fighting on the Confederate right remained brisk on 24 and 25 June, with Wheeler's men taking thirty prisoners on the 25th. Brisk fighting commenced again the following morning, and Wheeler reported taking a few prisoners. Apparently the fighting tapered off during the day, creating a lull before the storm that would come on the morrow.

Since their mounted charge of the 20th at McAfee's farm, most of the Confederate cavalrymen had been dismounted and fighting from trenches. They had been placed there to extend the infantry line and protect the Confederate right flank. Wheeler's men were "so thin in the trenches" that General Winfield Scott Featherston, acting commander of Loring's Division on their immediate left, did not think they could hold against a strong attack."[48] Fortunately, they were not the target of the main Federal attack, which came 27 June at the Confederate center around what is now Cheatham Hill. Nevertheless, the Union feint would be convincing enough to end the lives of a number of young men in blue and gray.

The men of the 2nd Georgia and their comrades on the Confederate right were greeted on the morning of the 27th with heavy Union shelling, which killed several men near Wheeler's headquarters. A charge against the entrenched Southern cavalrymen left Union dead all along Wheeler's line, including twenty-six in one small area.[49] The Federals retreated only to their original skirmish lines, where they kept up a steady fire with artillery and small arms. In the ranks of the 2nd Georgia, Pvt. James O. Davis of A Company and Pvt. F.H. Wilkinson of F Company were wounded this day.[50]

The following day there was more of the same—an artillery barrage followed by an infantry attack. The attack lasted until nightfall, and again failed to dislodge the thin line of cavalrymen. Thirty-five of the attackers were captured by the Confederates.[51]

The morning of 29 June brought more skirmishing, but the fighting apparently played out as the day wore on. That evening Gen. Johnston visited Wheeler's lines. No doubt the commander passed on word of the victories of the Confederate center at Cheatham's Hill and Pigeon Hill on the 27th. The courageous Union charge against the strong Confederate center had resulted in some 3,000 Union casualties, compared with 630 for the Confederates. Johnston, as he would do on several occasions, commented on the valor of the Union troops, for they were after all, "Americans." Some in the North commented that Sherman "broke too many eggs to make an omelet."[52]

Skirmishing and artillery barrages continued for the next two days. On 1 July, Gen. Iverson's scout, Lt. Buice "...returned from the rear of the enemy on the Bells Ferry road, and reports that Garrard's division moved camp on Tuesday to the neighborhood of Robert McAfee's. Garrard's headquarters are at McAfee's house."[53] The scout quoted by Iverson is probably 2nd Lt. William Buice of the 2nd Georgia's H Company.

Late on the afternoon of 2 July, Union artillery again opened on the Confederate cavalrymen. Blue infantry then advanced on the positions, thinking them abandoned. Soon a brisk fire revealed the presence of Wheeler's troopers, and the Federals retired. That night the shelling of Wheeler's positions continued, as General Johnston's army abandoned their positions at Kennesaw Mountain.[54]

The following day found Wheeler's cavalry out of the trenches for the first time in over a week. They were covering a retreat again, fighting first at Marietta. From there they fell back to State School on the railroad where they built breastworks and put ten artillery pieces in place. The fight here lasted two hours and inflicted considerable casualties on the Union forces. That night Wheeler shifted his line to the right where he connected with the Rebel infantry line at Nickajack Creek.[55]

Arriving in Marietta shortly after Wheeler's men left there, Sherman was not pleased with Garrard's cautious pursuit of the retreating Confederates.[56]

The 4 July edition of the *Daily Intelligencer* in Atlanta reported that "The whole country around Kennesaw Mountain and over the whole extent of Noonday Valley is burrowed and ditched with an interminable net of earthworks."[57] On the fourth, Thomas' IV Corps was repulsed with heavy losses by Confederate infantry that included the 1st Alabama, and probably the same elements of Wheeler's cavalry that had been present the previous day. There was also fighting on the fourth at Nickajack Creek, around Ruff's Mill, that may have involved the 2nd Georgia Cavalry.[58] Wherever the 2nd Georgia was fighting this day, Pvt. John G. Starr of F Company was wounded in the arm. In mid August his arm would be amputated.[59]

The following day, Wheeler was presented with the difficult job of crossing the Chattahoochee River while being hard-pressed by Howard's infantry. Elements of Howard's Corps struck Wheeler's rear about a mile from their crossing point at Pace's Ferry. Fighting from behind temporary barricades, Wheeler first repulsed a Federal charge, then countercharged with his men dismounted. It was probably in this action that Pvt. James Wright of the 2nd Georgia's D Company was wounded.[60] Retiring quickly from their countercharge, the men hurried across the pontoon bridge before the Union troops could reform for another attack. Gen. Wheeler was reportedly the last man across as the pontoons were cut loose and swung to the south bank under heavy fire.[61]

In the days that followed, 2nd Georgia troopers were among the Confederates facing Union pickets across the Chattahoochee River between Pace's Ferry and Turner's Ferry. The adversaries often bathed in the river in full view of each other, and sometimes would "meet in the center of the stream at a neutral log and joke one another, making trade of coffee, tobacco, and newspapers...." The Yankees seranaded Iverson's Georgia cavalry "with national, humorous, and sentimental songs, and elicit a response in kind."[62] On 6 or 7 July, Wheeler's men burned the Chattahoochee bridge at Roswell before Garrard's Cavalry arrived at the town. Garrard was slow to ford the river, "…fearful of being pounced on by Wheeler…."[63]

Wheeler's men were involved in brisk skirmishing at Pace's and Power's ferries on 8 July. Late that afternoon, some of Sherman's soldiers crossed the river at Isham's Ford and built defensive positions on the south bank.[64] On the ninth, one regiment of Union Cavalry attempted to cross the river at Roswell. "Our cavalry pickets waited until they were half-way across, when they opened on them and drove them back in great confusion, wounding many horses."[65]

But Union cavalry was getting across the Chattahoochee. That same day, cavalry of the 2nd Division, Army of the Cumberland "were fording the river under heavy fire." By this time, many Union cavalrymen were armed with Spencer repeating carbines, and Confederate infantrymen contesting the river crossing were amazed to see the Federal horsemen— hunched low in the water with only their heads exposed—raise their carbines out of the water and fire. The Rebels were even more amazed to see individual Yankees repeat the maneuver over and over again. Wrote Pennsylvanian Joseph G. Vale, "Now the Rebels had never seen anything of this kind before, nor for that matter had we, and their astonishment knew no bounds…. Something over two hundred in number remained on the bank, not firing, and surrender as soon as we got on the south side anxious only to see the guns that could be loaded and fired under water."[66]

For the next seven days, Wheeler's troopers were constantly skirmishing with Union troops crossing the river or setting defensive lines on the south bank. On 9 July, Wheeler's men captured sixty Federals near Isham's Ford. The next day there was fighting all along Wheeler's line, and on the 11th, Confederate cavalrymen captured another forty-eight Federals. On the 12th and 14th they captured more than thirty additional men and horses.[67] By this time, however, more than two Union corps had crossed the Chattahoochee.

On 15 July, General Iverson reported to Assistant Adjutant, Maj. E. S. Buford that he was on duty in command of Martin's Division. Martin was on sick leave, and would not return until some point prior to 10 August.[68]

On 17 and 18 July, Wheeler personally took portions of Iverson's, Kelly's, Williams', and Ferguson's brigades into breastworks where they "contested the ground in front of Peachtree Creek." Thus the 2nd Georgia was among the dismounted cavalry which fought behind successive lines of breastworks in an attempt to slow Thomas' advance.[69] "We then charged enemy, breaking through their infantry line and capturing sixty."[70] By noon, however, Wheeler's badly outgunned force had been driven back across Peachtree Creek, where they destroyed several bridges. Lt. James T. Newsome of the 2nd Georgia's G Company was captured here, but soon managed to escape.[71]

On 19 July, Wheeler moved these brigades to join the rest of his command in covering the Confederate right, the eastern approaches to Atlanta. That same day, Gen. Johnston was relieved and replaced by Hood, a move that demoralized much of the Confederate Army. A lieutenant in the 4th Tennessee Cavalry probably reflected the feelings of the men of the 2nd Georgia when he wrote in his diary, "The army was shocked this mornin (sic) by the sad intelligence that they were to be separated from their beloved commander Gen Johnston he being called to Richmond. They were no less astounded at the fact that Lt Gen J B Hood had been made a full General and assigned to the Command of the army. The parting of Gen Johnston from his Staff this evening was an affecting scene. The army gives him up reluctently (sic) They feel they have—" Perhaps Lt. W. B. Corbitt thought it unwise to complete the final sentence.[72]

On 20 July, the 2nd Georgia was part of Wheeler's 3,500 man force in the trenches on the Decatur road. Before them at 1:00 P.M. were 25,000 infantrymen from McPherson's army. Fortunately, McPherson was cautious, and at first only stood off at a distance to fire on the Confederates. Some of his artillery was directed not at the works of the cavalrymen, but at the city. The 1st Illinois Light Artillery, under Captain Francis DeGress, had the honor of firing the first artillery rounds into Atlanta. One of their first rounds exploded at the corner of Ellis and Ivey (now Peachtree Center Boulevard) streets, and a small girl became the first civilian casualty. (The elegant 191 Building on Peachtree Street today backs up to that corner, its twin cupolas on the Atlanta skyline unknowingly marking the death of an innocent.) It was perhaps the first of several clear messages that Sherman meant to take the war to the populace, not just the Army of Tennessee.[73]

Fighting from successive prepared lines, Wheeler's men vigorously resisted McPherson's three corps. The Federal's repeatedly charged "...supported by six lines of battle, all of which charges were signally repulsed, with heavy losses to the enemy." At one point that afternoon, seeing the Federals "carelessly deploying" their troops and creating a weak point in his line, Wheeler charged and drove part of the Union line back toward Decatur, capturing a number of the Union soldiers. So strong did the dismounted cavalry resist, that McPherson became convinced that he would soon be attacked by Hood's infantry.[74] In fact, while McPherson was moving cautiously against Wheeler, Hood's attack was falling upon Thomas at Peachtree Creek. With a determined effort, McPherson doubtless could have pushed into the center of Atlanta and threatened Hood's rear.

Not until 8:45 that night did Sherman learn what a small force had opposed McPherson. McPherson acknowledged that he faced only cavalry, but explained that Wheeler had four pieces of artillery and his men were armed with short Enfield rifles.[75] Sherman was not impressed by the excuse.

Union Maj. Gen. Oliver O. Howard wrote of this encounter, "The battle of the 20th did not end till Gresham's Division, on McPherson's left, had gone diagonally toward Atlanta, sweeping the hostile cavalry of Wheeler before it, past the Augusta Railroad and skirmishing up against an open knob dominated by Bald Hill. General Gresham, a fine officer, was severely wounded during his brisk movement." Added Howard, "Wheeler had made a desperate and successful stand here, and soon after, in the evening, the division (Cleburne's) which was taken from Newton's sorely handled front was brought hither and put in the trenches in order to make secure the right of Hood's line."[76]

As daylight faded on the 20th, Cleburne's Division arrived to relieve Wheeler's men. No doubt the arrival of Cleburne's vaunted fighters was a great relief to the cavalrymen, but it forced Hood to abandon plans to renew his attack at Peachtree Creek.

During the night, after being relieved by Cleburne's infantry, Wheeler shifted to the Decatur Railroad and Bald Hill. Daylight on 21 July found the 2nd Georgia Cavalry and the rest of Iverson's Georgia Brigade positioned just north of the Bald Hill on the right flank of Cleburne's Texas brigade. To Iverson's right was Ferguson's Cavalry Brigade on the Bald Hill, which dominated the field.

Accounts of the action this day differ, and the 2nd Georgia's performance on 21 July is a matter of some conjecture. According to one account, General Giles Smith's infantry division encountered little resistance as it drove Iverson's Georgia cavalry brigade from its position north of Bald Hill. The flight of the cavalry exposed the right flank of the Texas Brigade in Cleburne's Division, and a retreating cavalry colonel warned the Texans to "leave here or you will all be captured." According to this account, only the Texas infantry counterattacked, and drove back Smith's division.[77] Smith's losses have been estimated at 250 killed and wounded.[78]

Information provided by Wheeler tells a very different story. Early on the 21st, according to that source, McPherson "again advanced and made a determined charge upon Wheeler's works. The enemy was repulsed at every point during the first charges, but finally, by turning our right flank, our right gave way."[79] This post-war account compiled by Wheeler's officers refers first to Ferguson being driven from Bald Hill, and the subsequent retreat of the Georgia Brigade. According to this account, "...Wheeler rallied his men, charged the victorious enemy, who were upon our fortifications, and drove them off in confusion, retaking our works, with thirty prisoners. In this engagement, the enemy admitted a loss of eight hundred killed and wounded. The position thus gallantly regained was held by Wheeler until the following day, when he was relieved by infantry."[80]

While some accounts make no mention of cavalry involvement in the counterattack, Wheeler's account makes no mention of infantry involvement. The statement that Wheeler held the position until the following day is contradicted even in subsequent paragraphs of the same account, which show Wheeler moving on the enemy's flank on the night of the 21st.[81]

A history compiled by Confederate veterans is perhaps the most illuminating. *Confederate Military History* notes "On the right General Ferguson gave way in some confusion, exposing the right of Allen's brigade, which, with the Georgia brigade, nevertheless fought brilliantly, repulsing a desperate assault by hand-to-hand fighting. On the enemy's second assault, both the Georgia and Alabama brigades, with the right brigade of Cleburne's Division, were forced back, but rallying they charged the enemy and retook the works, with over twenty prisoners." Gen. Wheeler said of this action, "This was a most brilliant feat, and the Georgia brigade deserves great credit for its conduct on that day."[82] General Cleburne, a highly regarded commander of a tough, veteran infantry division, described the fighting here as the "bitterest" of his life.[83] Cleburne was not critical of the cavalry's role here, where the Union loss was reported as 728 men.[84]

This account is consistent with surviving service records which show the 2nd Georgia suffered at least nine casualties this day, including its commander, Maj. James Mayo, who was severely wounded. Company A lost two of its sergeants, L. Davis killed in action, and John Reid Smarr wounded. Another A Company casualty was Pvt. Joseph Hillman Astin, wounded just two months after leaving his job as a musician for the Georgia Provost Guards to join the cavalry. Other known losses for the regiment on the 21st, doubtless incomplete, are:

2nd Lt. Wyatt Rayle,	Company E	killed in action
Pvt. Jacob Calloway,	Company F	wounded and captured
Pvt. Wesley Hawkins	Company H	captured
Cpl. John Carlton	Company I	captured
Pvt. Solomon Harris	Company K	captured [85]

That night and into the following day, Wheeler joined Hardee in an unsuccessful effort to outflank the Union forces after the Battle of Peachtree Creek. Some historians contend that, had it succeeded, Hood's strategy here would have ranked with Lee and Jackson's brilliant movement at Chancellorsville.[86] But darkness, rugged terrain, and thick vegetation made it impossible for the flanking move to be carried out in a timely manner. The attacks were vigorous and resulted in the capture of 2,000 prisoners, eight cannon, and thirteen stands of colors, but coordination was poor, and the Union flank was not turned.[87]

The cavalry's first role in Hardee's flanking movement was to attack McPherson's supply wagons, parked at Decatur and guarded by Col. John W. Sprague's strongly entrenched infantry brigade. In this fight, the 2nd Georgia and the rest of Wheeler's men were again on foot. Two Union regiments advanced to meet the dismounted cavalry, but they were outnumbered and soon driven back to their works. "Here supported by artillery, Sprague's men pour a galling fire into the lines of the dismounted cavalrymen."[88] Wheeler countered with a coordinated frontal and flank attack that routed the Union infantry. Most of the wagon train had already fled in a virtual stampede. After two hours of fighting, Wheeler's men occupied the town, captured 225 prisoners, one artillery piece, six wagons, and a quantity of small arms. Wheeler's pursuit had barely begun when his cavalry was ordered back to support Hardee, which he did at a gallop.[89]

The 2nd Georgia casualties at Decatur this day included First Sgt Jake Little of A Company who was mortally wounded. Two men from

F Company, privates Elijah Lasseter and Samuel Lee Jones, were captured.[90]

One trooper in the 2nd Georgia's C Company later described the fighting of the past two days. "The Company was engaged in two desperate fights on the 21 & 22 July 1864. On the 21st one man was captured and one horse killed. On the 22nd the Co. acted gallantly around Atlanta."[91]

Sherman now was apparently concerned that he was in for a prolonged siege if he could not cut Hood's supply line from the South. The prospect of Confederate reinforcements arriving from Virginia has also been reported as a concern in Sherman's command.[92]

Sherman devised a plan to cut Hood's supply line. He would send the Army of the Tennessee against the railroad at East Point, and, at the same time, send his cavalry south to destroy the Macon and Atlanta Railroad above Macon, and to capture Macon itself. (East Point, so named because it was at the opposite end of the railroad from West Point, is located on the southwest side of Atlanta.) Toward this end he divided his cavalry into three commands, one under Stoneman to capture Macon, another under McCook to cut rail lines south of Atlanta, and a third under Garrard to keep Wheeler's Cavalry occupied. On 27 June, he set the plan in motion.

At 4:00 A.M., Maj. Gen. George Stoneman, Sherman's chief of cavalry, started south through Decatur toward Macon, a major rail terminal and the site of an arsenal, a cannon foundry, and numerous warehouses. In addition to capturing and destroying Confederate supplies in Macon, he hoped to free Union prisoners held in Macon and Andersonville. While Sherman refused to exchange for the POWs, the idea of freeing prisoners without the necessity of an exchange was appealing.

Stoneman, a native New Yorker who had been Stonewall Jackson's roommate at West Point, was leading a command that included the 5th and 6th Indiana cavalry regiments in Col. James Biddle's brigade, the 14th Illinois and 8th Michigan cavalry regiments and the 1st Ohio squadron in Col. Horace Capron's brigade, the 1st and 11th Kentucky regiments in Col. Silas Adams' brigade, and the 24th Indiana Battery under Capt. Alexander Hardy.[93] In all, they totaled about 2,100 men with two pieces of artillery.

As Stoneman's command headed south that morning, Gen. Edward McCook's cavalry division moved west toward the Chattahoochee River, where they turned south and attacked the railroad below Atlanta. This division included the 8ᵗʰ Iowa Cavalry, the 4ᵗʰ Kentucky Mounted Infantry, and the 1ˢᵗ Tennessee (Federal) Cavalry in a brigade under Col. John T. Croxton, the 2ⁿᵈ and 4ᵗʰ Indiana Cavalry regiments along with the 1ˢᵗ Wisconsin in another brigade under Lt. Col. William Torrey, and Col. T. J. Harrison's brigade of the 8ᵗʰ Indiana, 2ⁿᵈ Kentucky, 5ᵗʰ Iowa, 9ᵗʰ Ohio, and 4ᵗʰ Tennessee (Federal) cavalry regiments. A portion of the 18ᵗʰ Indiana battery was also attached to McCook's command. In all, McCook's command included about 4,000 men.[94]

Wheeler's cavalrymen arrived in the trenches east of Atlanta at 3:00 A.M. to relieve Hardee's Corps which had been facing three Union corps now under Gen. Black Jack Logan after the death of McPherson. At daylight, Wheeler tested the Federal resistance and found it soft. Pushing the Federals out of their works, he was able to extend his line to a point "about a hundred yards north of the Georgia Railroad."[95] From this action, Wheeler learned that the Army of The Tennessee had pulled out of its works. (The Union infantry was moving to the south of Atlanta where they would repulse the attacks of Gen. S. D. Lee's Corps in the Battle of Ezra Church.) From his scouts, Wheeler also learned that a large Union cavalry force was moving eastward from Decatur along the Georgia Railroad.

After notifying Hood of the Union movement and receiving the commander's permission, Wheeler set out in pursuit of Stoneman. Apparently still unaware of McCook's westward march, Wheeler surmised that Stoneman would strike the Macon and Western Railroad at Lovejoy Station or at Jonesboro. Wheeler knew that he would have to cross the South River to head west toward the railroad, and he knew that the most likely crossing point would be at Flat Shoals.

Anticipating Wheeler's next move, Stoneman left Gen. Kenner Garrard's cavalry at Flat Shoals to engage and hold Wheeler. Wheeler sent Gen. John H. Kelley with George Dibrell's and Robert Anderson's brigades down the west side of South River, while he moved down the east side. Near Tucker's cabin, Kelley encountered the 4ᵗʰ Michigan Cavalry behind barricades. During the early morning hours of 28 July, Wheeler struck Garrard's flank, and at daybreak, he renewed the attack on Garrard's 4,000 cavalrymen who had occupied high ground between Flat Shoals and Snapfinger Creek. Garrard soon began a rapid retreat toward Lithonia, with Wheeler in pursuit. In several small actions, the Confederates captured horses, arms, and wagons as well as prisoners.[96]

It was apparently in these actions that privates. George W. Chandler and John A. Ellison of the 2nd Georgia's H Company, Samuel James Lee of F Company, and John Estes of B Company were captured.[97] From the Union prisoners and some of his own men who had been captured and then recaptured, Wheeler learned of the Federal plan.

While Wheeler was thus employed, Stoneman paused at Covington on the 28th, with no more apparent purpose than harassing the staff and patients at the Confederate hospital there. While Wheeler was defeating Garrard at Flat Shoals and Snap-Finger Creek, Stoneman's men were eating the breakfast prepared for hospital patients at Covington.[98] Some of them were also getting drunk on the large supply of whiskey they found in the town, and making sport of the Confederates in the hospital.[99] "Grandma" Smith, a nurse at the Covington Hospital, said that…. "some four or five dirty drunken scamps dashed up, almost in the door (of the hospital), saying, 'Oh you d—Rebels, come out of there and march on the square, where General Stoneman is. We will show you how to fight against the Union." After rousting many of the patients and their doctors, Stoneman released them to return to the hospital, proclaiming, "You can go to hell for all I care, I have no use for you now."[100]

One of those rousted by the Federals was former 2nd Georgia sergeant from G Company, John A. Freeman. Freeman, whose health apparently was not up to the rigors of cavalry life, had been serving as a clerk at the hospital since the previous February.[101] The momentary prisoners could see that Stoneman was in a hurry. Said one, "I guess General Wheeler and his men are too close on his heels for his good health…."[102]

[1] Compiled Service Records, 2nd Georgia Cavalry (Atlanta GA: Georgia Department of Archives and History).

[2] Robert S. Bridgers, ed., *Confederate Military History* Vol. VII (Wilmington NC: Broadfoot Publishing Company, 1897) 267.

[3] Stewart Sifikis, *Who Was Who in the Confederacy* (New York NY: Facts on File, Inc., 1988) 141.

[4] Bridgers, ed., *Confederate Military History* Vol. VII, 889.

[5] Ibid. 665.

[6] Compiled Service Records, 2nd Georgia Cavalry.

[7] Thomas L. Connelly, *Autumn of Glory—The Army of Tennessee 1862—1865* (Baton Rouge LA: Louisiana State University Press, 1967) 330.

[8] Albert Castel, *Decision in the West—The Atlanta Campaign of 1864* (Lawrence KS: University Press of Kansas, 1992) 140.

[9] Ibid., 112.

[10] Compiled Service Records, 2nd Georgia Cavalry.

[11] Castel, *Decision in the West,* 119.

[12] Stanley F. Horn, *The Army of Tennessee* (New York NY: The Bobbs-Merrill Company, 1941) 319.

[13] W. C. Dodson, ed., *Campaigns of Wheeler and His Cavalry* (Jackson TN: The Guild Bindery Press).

[14] Theo F. Rodenbough, ed., *The Photographic History of the Civil War, Vol. II, The Decisive Battles of the Cavalry.* (Secaucus NJ: The Blue & Gray Press, 1987) 104.

[15] Dodson, *Campaigns of Wheeler and His Cavalry,* 175.

[16] Castel, *Decision in the West,* 128, 130.

[17] Horn, *The Army of Tennessee,* 323.

[18] Joseph E. Johnston, "Opposing Sherman's Advance to Atlanta"in *Battles and Leaders of the Civil War, Vol. IV, Retreat With Honor* (Secaucus NJ: Castle Books) 263.

[19] Dyer, *From Shiloh to San Juan Hill—The Life of Fightin' Joe Wheeler,* 129. See also Dodson, ed. *Campaigns of Wheeler and His Cavalry,* 179.

[20] Castel, *Decision in the West,* 168.

[21] Ibid., 156.

[22] Ibid., 166.

[23] Ibid., 177.

[24] Compiled Service Records, 2nd Georgia Cavalry.

[25] Horn, *The Army of Tennessee,* 325.

[26] Ibid.

[27] Castel, *Decision in the West,* 237, 241.

[28] Ibid.

[29] Compiled Service Records, 2nd Georgia Cavalry.

[30] *War of the Rebellion, Official Records,* Vo. 33 Part 4, 450.

[31] Ibid, Part 5, 76.

[32] Compiled Service Records, 2nd Georgia Cavalry.

[33] Dodson, ed. *Campaigns of Wheeler and His Cavalry,* 190.

[34] Ibid.

[35] *War of the Rebellion, Official Records,* Vol. 33 Part 2.

[36] Compiled Service Records, 2nd Georgia Cavalry.

[37] W. B. Corbitt, Diary (Atlanta GA: The Robert W. Woodruff Library, Emory University).

[38] Dodson, ed., Campaigns of Wheeler and His Cavalry, 191.

[39] Dennis Kelly, *Kennesaw Mountain and the Atlanta Campaign,* (Marietta GA: Kennesaw Mountain Historical Association, Inc., 1990) 23.

[40] Ibid.

[41] Dodson, ed., *Campaigns of Wheeler and His Cavalry,* 191, 192.

[42] Ibid.

[43] *War of the Rebellion, Official Records,* Series I Vol. 38 Part 4, 849-850.

[44] Kelly, *Kennesaw Mountain,* 24.

[45] Compiled Service Records, 2nd Georgia Cavalry.

[46] Dodson, ed., *Campaigns of Wheeler and His Cavalry,* 193.

[47] Ibid.

[48] Castel, *Decision in the West,* 301.

[49] Dodson. ed. *Campaigns of Wheeler and His Cavalry,* 193.

[50] Compiled Service Records, 2nd Georgia Cavalry.

[51] Dodson, ed., *Campaigns of Wheeler and His Cavalry,* 193.

[52] Horn, *The Army of Tennessee,* 337.

[53] *War of the Rebellion, Official Records,* Series I Vol. 38 Part 5, 858.

[54] Dodson, ed., *Campaigns of Wheeler and His Cavalry,* 194.

[55] Ibid.

[56] Stephen Z. Starr, *The Union Cavalry in the Civil War, Vol. III, The War in the West 1861-1865* (Baton Rouge LA: Louisiana State University Press, 1985) 461.

[57] *Atlanta Daily Intelligencer,* 4 July 1864, (Atlanta GA: Georgia Department of Archives and History).

[58] Castel, *Decision in the West,* 330-332.

[59] Compiled Service Records, 2nd Georgia Cavalry.

[60] Ibid.

[61] Dodson, *Campaigns of Wheeler and His Cavalry,* 196.

[62] Castel, *Decision in the West,* 352.

[63] Ibid, 339.

[64] Dodson, *Campaigns of Wheeler and His Cavalry,* 197.

[65] A. A. Hoeling, *Last Train From Atlanta* (New York NY: Thomas Yoseleff Publisher, 1958) 62.

[66] Ibid, 58.

[67] Dodson, ed., *Campaigns of Wheeler and His Cavalry,* 198.

[68] *War of the Rebellion, Official Records,* Series I Vol. 38 Part 5, 881.

[69] Dyer, *From Shiloh to San Juan—The Life of Fightin' Joe Wheeler,* 137.

[70] Dodson, *Campaigns of Wheeler and His Cavalry,* 199.

[71] Robert S. Bridgers, ed., *Confederate Military History, Vol. VII* (Georgia Confederate Publishing Company, 1897) 890.

[72] Corbitt, diary.

[73] Hoeling, *Last Train From Atlanta,* 144, 147, 158, 159, 163, 167.

[74] Dodson, *Campaigns of Wheeler and His Cavalry,* 209.

[75] Castel, *Decision in the West,* 380.

[76] Oliver O. Howard, "The Struggle for Atlanta" in *Battles and Leaders of the Civil War, Vol. IV,* Johnson and Buel, editors. (Secaucus NJ: Castle Books) 314.

[77] Castel, *Decision in the West,* 384.

[78] Horn, *The Army of Tennessee,* 354.

[79] Dodson, *Campaigns of Wheeler and His Cavalry,* 209-210.

[80] Ibid.

[81] Ibid.

[82] Bridgers, ed. *Confederate Military History Vol. VII,* 326-327.

[83] Horn, *The Army of Tennessee,* 354.

[84] Bridgers, ed. *Confederate Military History Vol. VII,* 327.

[85] Compiled Service Records, 2nd Georgia Cavalry.

[86] Horn, *The Army of Tennessee,* 352.

[87] Ibid, 357.

[88] Castel, *Decision in the West,* 398.

[89] *War of the Rebellion, Official Records,* Series I Vol. 38 Part III, 506-507.

[90] Compiled Service Records, 2nd Georgia Cavalry.

[91] Bridgers, ed., *Confederate Military History Vol. VII,* 889.

[92] Byron H. Mathews, *The McCook-Stoneman Raid* (Brannon Publishing Co., 1976) 7.

[93] *War of the Rebellion, Official Records,* Series I Vol. 38 Part I, 114.

[94] Mathews, *The McCook—Stoneman Raid,* 56.

[95] Dodson, *Campaigns of Wheeler and His Cavalry,* 217.

[96] Mathews, *The McCook—Stoneman Raid,* 56.

[97] Compiled Service Records, 2nd Georgia Cavalry.

[98] Hoeling, *Last Train From Atlanta,* 127.

[99] David Evans, *Sherman's Horsemen, Union Cavalry Operations in the Atlanta Campaign* (Bloomington IN: Indiana University Press, 1996) 293.

[100] Hoeling, *Last Train From Atlanta,* 127.

[101] Compiled Service Records, 2nd Georgia Cavalry.

[102] Hoeling, *Last Train From Atlanta,* 127.

Brown's Mill and Sunshine Church

After learning the full scope of the Union raid, Wheeler divided his force, leaving Kelly to keep Garrard in check, and sending Iverson in pursuit of Stoneman. Wheeler would go after McCook.

Iverson was functioning here as a division commander in the absence of Martin, who was on sick leave. Martin would return to the division between Atlanta and Decatur on 3 or 4 August.[1] With Iverson were the Georgia Brigade, presumably under the command of Crews, and three other cavalry brigades.[2]

McCook reached Fayetteville before dawn on 29 July. One of his brigades formed up on the square of the Fayette County Courthouse, while the rest of his men rousted some 300 Confederate soldiers on quartermaster or medical duty from their slumber. Almost half of that number were officers quartered in private homes.[3]

McCook did not tarry at Fayetteville, but soon moved east toward the Macon and Western Railroad. His target was Lovejoy Station, five miles south of Jonesboro and not far from Cainey Strickland's farm. On their short march, McCook's men captured and destroyed a 500-wagon supply train, using their sabers to kill more than 1,000 mules. At Lovejoy Station, they tore up two miles of railroad track and five miles of telegraph wire. Expecting to reunite with Stoneman here, McCook lingered at Lovejoy until the afternoon. But Stoneman had changed his plans and moved on toward Macon without McCook. By now McCook was probably aware that Wheeler was moving rapidly toward Jonesboro, and that Hood had sent an infantry brigade under Gen. Joseph Lewis by train to Jonesboro.[4] When his scouts were unable to locate Stoneman, McCook turned back toward Fayetteville.

As McCook began to retrace his steps, he ran into elements of Jackson's cavalry and there were several short, sharp fights, including one particularly notable clash between the 8th Iowa and the 9th Texas. McCook was able to get most of his command across the Flint River, but in the process lost two companies of the 4th Kentucky Mounted Infantry who had been serving as rear guards. McCook reached Fayetteville after dark, and continued his flight toward Newnan.[5]

Wheeler had arrived at Jonesboro late on the afternoon of 29 July, and pressed on to Lovejoy Station only to find McCook already gone. Wheeler then moved directly toward Fayetteville and passed through the town around midnight. A short time later, his lead elements caught McCook's rear guard, and a running battle began. At Line Creek, McCook destroyed the bridge and deployed two companies of the 4th Kentucky Mounted Infantry behind strong barricades to delay Wheeler's pursuit. This they did most effectively, repulsing several charges before Wheeler flanked their position some time after 3:00 A.M. and directed an enfilading fire upon them.[6]

For the remainder of this exceedingly dark night, Wheeler's men encountered similar barricades at short intervals. Then, at dawn on the morning of the 30th, Wheeler's troopers came upon the Union main line of defense. Wheeler attacked with two mounted columns, one on the center and another on the flank. The charge broke the Federal center, "…driving them in utter rout from the field, capturing over three hundred prisoners, with their horses, arms and equipments."[7] The Federals left some forty dead on the field and continued their retreat toward Newnan. When the luckless Union troopers reached Newnan, they found not refuge, but some 600 dismounted Confederate cavalry under Gen. Phillip Roddey who had arrived there by train from West Point the night before.

Roddey and McCook were totally unaware of each other's presence until McCook's advance ordered the engineer to surrender his train. The engineer's warning whistle alerted Roddey's men who opened fire on the blue cavalry. Roddey, bareback on his horse, formed his men in a line of battle, and a sporadic fighting ensued.[8]

Apparently unaware that he greatly outnumbered the Confederate force in the town, McCook did not attack, which gave Wheeler time to regroup his men and move toward Newnan, where most of the buildings and even the courthouse lawn had become hospitals. Early that afternoon "…Wheeler's cavalry was pounding down the highway to relieve the beleaguered defenders…." around the Newnan station house. "O, how joyfully we hailed them!" said Nurse Kate Cumming. "They came galloping in by two different roads; the enemy in the meantime hearing of their approach, were retreating."[9]

Wheeler followed in hot pursuit and caught McCook at Brown's Mill. According to Nurse Cumming, the booming of cannon could be heard in Newnan for about two hours, and about 4:00 P.M."word was brought that we had killed and captured the whole lot."[10] In truth, McCook had escaped, but some 600 of his men and a like number of horses were captured. "A gentleman who was there says he counted ninety-six dead Yankees in one place."[11] According to veterans of the Brown's Mill fight, over 200 Federals were killed in the first forty minutes alone, and two brigade commanders, Cols. Harrison and Torry, were among the prisoners. The 300 Confederates captured at Fayetteville were liberated in this battle.[12]

As McCook defended Line Creek during the early morning hours of 30 July, Stoneman's command approached Clinton just north of Macon. The blue column, 2,112 men and two Rodman cannon, passed through Clinton at about 4:00 A.M. and then destroyed rails and rolling stock at Gordon and Griswoldville.[13]

Nestled across the Ocmulgee River and bristling with cannon and a determined militia, Macon, proved to be a tougher nut to crack. For several hours the Federals traded artillery rounds with Macon's defenders, but their attempt to advance was thwarted by the river and artillery fire. In mid afternoon, Federal scouts erroneously reported Rebel cavalry south of the town, and Stoneman gave the order to withdraw. Abandoning any plans of liberating the prisoners at Andersonville, Stoneman turned back north toward Clinton. Stoneman's point regiment, the 8th Michigan, ran into Iverson's pickets almost immediately, and was able to advance only three miles in four hours. Shortly after midnight, Stoneman halted his advance to feed and rest his men and animals.[14] It is not clear which Confederate units were performing this dangerous picket duty, but it is quite possible that all or part of the 2nd Georgia was involved.

As his command camped that night near Clinton, Stoneman probably did not know that he was bivouacked in the hometown of his adversary, Gen. Iverson. Indeed, he may not have known what force was before him. Iverson's command included Gen. William W. Allen's Alabama Brigade and Gen. John S. Williams' Kentucky and Tennessee Brigade, as well as the Georgia Brigade. That the seventeen regiments in these brigades amounted to only about 1,300 men illustrates the manpower problems of the Confederate cavalry in late 1864. At full strength, a single regiment would, theoretically at least, have 1,000 men. As we have seen, Confederate cavalry regiments in the Army of Tennessee rarely had more than 500 men at any one time.

In addition to the 2nd Georgia, the Georgia Brigade included the 1st Georgia under Lt. Col. James H. Strickland, the 3rd Georgia under Col. Robert Thompson, the 4th Georgia under Maj. Augustus R. Stewart, and the 6th Georgia commanded by Col. John R. Hart.[15] Some accounts show the 2nd Georgia at this time commanded by Maj. James Mayo.[16] As we have seen, however, Mayo was severely wounded a week earlier at Bald Hill and most certainly was not with the regiment at this time. Records indicate that Colonel Charles Crews returned as the regiment's commander no later than 31 July, so it is clear that he was in this familiar role at Sunshine Church, probably while also commanding the Georgia Brigade.[17]

While Stoneman camped near Iverson's hometown, Iverson's Confederates were resting at Round Oak. But Iverson knew exactly where Stoneman was, and of course, he knew this countryside. He knew the most advantageous places to post his pickets. He knew Stoneman was coming his way, and he had picked the battleground, a rugged area around Sunshine Church, ill-suited to mounted operations by anyone unfamiliar with the terrain.

Iverson centered his defensive line on a small rise in the road, with the right and left extending about a mile at 45° angles southward toward the enemy. The Union cavalry would have to march into the open end of this "V" and subject themselves to enfilading fire, or they would have to find a way to flank one wing in this rugged country.[18]

At first light on 31 July, Stoneman resumed his march north from Clinton toward Wayside, Round Oak, and Hillsboro on what is now Georgia Highway 11. With Capron's brigade on point, the Federals drove the Confederate pickets before them until they reached their main defensive line, less than two miles down the road.

Now Stoneman brought his main force up into a line of battle, with one artillery piece on a hill in the center opposite Sunshine Church, and the other held in reserve along with the 3rd Brigade. Stoneman himself led the first mounted charge, which was met by accurate fire from the short Enfields favored by the Rebels. As this fire "…quickly covered the field with dead and wounded…" the charge faltered. With their familiar Rebel yell, some of Iverson's dismounted troopers immediately charged on the Federal left and mounted Confederates charged on the right. These charges were checked, and, when the Confederates rallied, checked again. In this action the 14th Illinois played a key role in stopping the Rebel mounted countercharges.[19]

The fighting continued with charge and countercharge all morning. Shortly after noon, Stoneman sent his horses to the rear and massed his men for a dismounted charge. Only one regiment was held in reserve. This charge advanced through effective fire from the Confederates, but was met by a counter charge from dismounted Rebel troopers. The Federals began to fall back toward their mounts, and in the confusion Capron's brigade was almost surrounded. Iverson's men were close on their heels, and hand-to-hand fighting broke out over the horses. Many of the blue troopers were unable to remount, and their horses were used by Rebels to continue the pursuit.[20]

As this charge played out, Stoneman rallied his forces, and continued efforts throughout the afternoon to break the Confederate line. All of these efforts failed. Shortly after 4:00 P.M., Iverson sent the 1st and 3rd Georgia regiments on flanking movements as he concentrated heavy fire on the Union center. This he followed with a general charge which caused the Union line to fall back, and then fall back again.[21]

This Confederate attack commenced just as Stoneman's officers were returning to their units from a conference with the commander. In that conference he had given the commanders the option of attempting breakouts for their brigades if they chose, while noting that he would stay and fight. As the Federal troopers fell back in some disorder, Capron found his brigade cut off from the rest of Stoneman's command. He immediately gathered what he could of his brigade—part of the 14th Illinois, the 8th Michigan, and the 1st Ohio Squadron—and galloped to the northeast, where he had determined the Rebel line was thin. Shortly thereafter, Adams' brigade and the 6th Indiana Regiment took the same escape route toward Eatonton.[22]

Stoneman, with 700 men, resisted for several more hours, buying valuable time for the escaping Federals. Then, with darkness falling and ammunition for his two cannon running low, Stoneman surrendered with about 500 of his men. Among the captured Union officers was Maj. Miles Keogh, who would die with Custer at the Little Big Horn twelve years later, and whose horse "Comanche" would be the only survivor of that battle.

At first Stoneman demanded that Iverson himself accept his sword in surrender, but then gave the sword to Col. Crews and sat down on a log and wept.[23] Stoneman had expected this raid to make him a hero in the North. Instead, Wheeler's cavalry, at Brown's Mill and Sunshine Church, achieved one of the biggest cavalry victories of the war. Thus, the 2nd Georgia was in the thick of the action when more than two-thirds of Sherman's cavalry was destroyed.

Stoneman entered Macon that night not as a conqueror but as a prisoner of war. From there he wrote this report to Sherman on 6 August.

> General: In regard to the operation of my command from the time I left the Army up to the time I returned back from near this place, I will only say now that I feel assured, when you know what was done and why it was done you will be satisfied with the reasons and results. All I wish to say now, through the medium of a flag of truce, is solely in regard to how I and a small portion of my command became prisoners of war. Before I had completed what I desired to accomplish, I learned that a force of the enemy's cavalry was close upon my rear, and the only course for me to pursue to get out was to turn upon, and, if possible, whip this force. This, I think we might have done, had my command fought as it ought to and as I hoped it would have done. Without entering now into particulars, we were whipped, and this principally on account of the bad conduct of the Kentucky Brigade in the attack during the morning and in fact through the day. In the afternoon the enemy attacked us, when Capron's brigade gave way at once and was followed by Adams (Kentucky) brigade, leaving me with Biddle's (Indiana) brigade and a section of artillery to contend against the whole force of the enemy, and cover the retreat of the remainder of my force. A portion of the brigade I sent to hold a crossroad and keep the enemy from getting between me and the main force, pack train, etc. This also gave way and followed the rest, so that near the end of the day, I found myself with about 200 of the Fifth Indiana Cavalry and a section of artillery. This regiment had been engaged nearly the whole of the day previous. I insisted on continuing the contest and, if taken prisoners at all, upon being taken fighting, but the officers with me protested that, being

without ammunition and surrounded, our escape was next to impossible; that there was no use in fighting longer; that we had accomplished our object in covering the retreat of the rest of the command until it was well under way and that in justice to all concerned, we should surrender. To extricate the section of artillery and the men with me, it was impossible. My own horse had been shot under me, and I was scarcely able to mount a worn down one and the only one I could find to replace the one that I had lost, and our chances of escape were so small that I consented to be taken prisoners of war, and as such, our treatment has been everything that could have been expected. Our loss in killed and wounded was quite large.

I understand from captured fugitives that they were informed that I had surrendered the whole command and that the order was given for everyone to save himself. I have not heard from the Kentucky Brigade since it left. Capron's Brigade, I learned, was considerably cut up and several hundred of it captured. I feel better satisfied with myself to be a prisoner of war, much as I hate it, than to be amongst those who owe their escape to considerations of self preservation.[24]

Stoneman's comment about Capron's brigade being "cut up" was a reference to the final chapter of this story, the pursuit of the escapees from Sunshine Church.

Capron and Adams had led their men at a gallop across the rough landscape until they reached the Eatonton Road. Their retreat was in such disorder that no rear guard was in place, and some of the Federal troopers were killed or wounded by pursuing Rebels. After they had covered about eight miles, they were joined by several other escaping elements of Stoneman's command. At this point Capron was able to put out a rear guard and take a brief rest.[25]

Many of the Federals had lost their firearms during the struggle over the horses, and Capron used this respite to place those unarmed troopers in the middle of his column. With the best armed and best mounted men in the lead or in the rear, Capron's column crossed Murder Creek. From here, Adams and Capron split up, with Capron bypassing Eatonton while Adams entered the town and gathered all the food his men could find. Capron meanwhile rode on through the night toward Madison. The next morning, 1 August, Capron's exhausted troopers received a lift when they were joined by 128 men of the 14th Illinois under Major Francis M. Davidson who had been detached on the Gordon mission and were not present at Sunshine Church.[26]

Adams was also headed toward Madison, and he also received reinforcements when he was joined by detachments of the 8th Michigan and the 6th Indiana. About two in the afternoon this column reached Madison, where they burned some Confederate stores. By nightfall they had rejoined Capron at Pouder's Farm. The march continued through the night, with short rest breaks, until dawn when they entered the town of Watkinsville, about eight miles south of Athens.[27]

While their men plundered Watkinsville, Capron and Adams pondered their next move. With Atlanta still some seventy miles to their west, the Union colonels decided to enter Athens, still untouched by the War, where they could find supplies, and perhaps a haven for man and beast.[28]

As Adams advanced up the Watkinsville Road, he encountered pickets, probably local militia, and captured twenty-six of them. As Adams' column topped the hill south of the bridge, they were fired upon by artillery. On the high ground north of Barber's Creek, artillery emplacements and a "well concealed trench line" overlooked the road. Maj. Gen. Howell Cobb, whose defensive preparations had thwarted Stoneman at Macon, had in early July organized Athens' defenses.

Adams immediately pulled back and sent word to Capron of the defensive line guarding the road and bridges, and informing him that he would now move westward on the south bank of the Oconee River toward Jefferson. After hearing from Adams' courier, Capron immediately set out to join him. The rendezvous never took place, however, as Capron apparently took the wrong road. Looking for Capron all the way, Adams kept moving until midnight when he stopped to rest about sixteen miles northeast of Lawrenceville. Moving up the Hog Mountain Road toward Jug Tavern, Capron halted for about an hour to rest his exhausted men and horses. When the march resumed the column became so spread out in the darkness that Capron was compelled to stop again, this time near Mulberry Creek. Maj. Davidson's detachment from the 14th Illinois and the remnants of the 8th Michigan, being the best armed of Capron's men, were posted front and rear to protect the command. Between these pickets and the main body of Capron's command, was a large group of former slaves who had fallen in with the Union columns.[29]

After Capron and Adams made good their escape from Sunshine Church, Wheeler had sent Col. W.C.P. Breckenridge with the Kentucky Brigade, fewer than 500 men, in pursuit. Like the Federals, the gray troopers and their mounts were exhausted. As his horses began to drop in alarming numbers, Breckenridge halted the pursuit and inspected his ranks for serviceable mounts. He found only eighty-five men with horses still strong enough to continue at a fast pace. These he placed under the command of Lt. Richard Bowles and sent them forward with orders to attack the Federals wherever they could be found. The rest of the Kentucky Brigade would follow.[30]

Just before dawn on 3 August, Bowles' little command found Capron's Brigade resting at Mulberry Creek. Bowles' men bypassed the 14th Illinois and charged yelling and firing into Capron's camp. Capron later reported:

> Just before daylight, the morning of the 3-d instant, a body of the enemy cavalry came upon my rear, and as near as I can ascertain, passed around the main body of the pickets on both flanks, striking the road where the Negroes lay. The Negroes became panic stricken, and rushed into the camp of my men, who are yet asleep (we having been in camp about an hour and a half), throwing them into confusion. The enemy now charged into my camp, driving and scattering everything before them. Every effort was made by the officers to rally the men and check the enemy's charge, but it was found impossible to keep them in line, as most of them were without arms and ammunitions. Partial lines were formed, but, owing to the confusion which ensued in the darkness, they soon gave way. A stampede now took place, a portion of the men rushing for the woods and the balance running down the road and attempting to cross the bridge over the Mulberry River, in our front. The enemy still continued to charge my men, killing, wounding, and capturing a large number. In their rush to cross the bridge, it gave way, precipitating many of them into the river. The men now scattered in every direction. I became separated from my command and made my escape through the woods.[31]

It is not clear what role the men of the 14th Illinois and the 8th Michigan played in the fight at Mulberry Creek. The detachment of the 14th Illinois alone had 128 well armed men, easily outnumbering Bowles' detachment. Very likely, the darkness and confusion prevented them from offering significant resistance. Even with morning's light, however, Bowles' found little or no resistance as his men rousted the hiding Federals trapped on the banks of the Mulberry River. By the time Breckenridge came up with the rest of the brigade later than morning, Bowles' eighty-five men had taken some 300 Federals as prisoners.

The Kentucky Brigade escorted their prisoners into Athens at about 3:00 P.M. on 3 August. The prisoners were placed under guard in the quadrangle of the University of Georgia, which had been closed for the duration of the War. The Kentuckians were welcomed as heroes, and plans were laid to honor them the following day. Maj. J. P. Austin of the 9th Kentucky later wrote,

> The people of the 'Classic City' treated us with enthusiastic consideration. They supplied us with plenty of good things to eat, and gave us an ovation in the college chapel. The large auditorium was crowded to its utmost capacity with the youth and beauty of Athens. The back part of the auditorium was occupied by the soldiers, while the front was given up to the ladies. On the rostrum were seated the mayor and a few distinguished gentlemen, either too old to be in the army, or by their professions, exempted. Our soldiers were a motley looking set compared with those well dressed people. We had not seen our wagon train for a month, and were dirty as pigs.[32]

About 9:00 o'clock on the night of 3 August, Adams forded the Chattahoochee River, and at dawn the following day he reached the safety of Marietta with 490 men. Col. Capron escaped with his son and a lieutenant of the 8th Michigan. Avoiding towns and farms, they moved cautiously cross-country on horseback and then on foot. After four days they came to the Chattahoochee River where they found a dugout. They floated downstream for two days and reached the Union lines at Marietta on 10 August.[33] The Stoneman-McCook raid was over.

Although some reports have placed the 2nd Georgia in the actions at Jug Tavern and Mulberry Creek, official records show only the Kentucky Brigade engaged in these conflicts for the Confederates. The 2nd Georgia probably remained with Iverson as he returned north toward Atlanta. As we have seen, Federal dispatches of 3 and 4 August place Martin's Division between Decatur and Atlanta. Whether Martin or Iverson was actually commanding the division at this time is a matter of conjecture.

On 5 August, Pvt. Robert Beavers of the 2nd Georgia's I Company was "killed in action" in some unrecorded conflict.[34]

[1] *War of the Rebellion, Official Records of the Union and Confederate Armies* Series I Vol. 38 Part 5, (Washington DC: U.S. Government Printing Office, 1890) 347-353.

[2] W. C. Dodson, ed., *Campaigns of Wheeler and His Cavalry (Jackson TN: The Guild Bindery Press)* 220.

[3] David Evans, *Sherman's Horsemen, Union Cavalry Operations in the Atlanta Campaign*, (Bloomington IN: Indiana University Press, 1996) 296-297.

[4] Byron H. Mathews, *The McCook—Stoneman Raid* (Brannon Publishing Co., 1976) 72, 75.

[5] Ibid, 76-77.

[6] Ibid, 82.

[7] Dodson, ed., *Campaigns of Wheeler and His Cavalry,* 225.

[8] A. A. Hoeling, *Last Train From Atlanta* (New York NY: Thomas Yoseleff Publisher, 1958) 189-190.

[9] Ibid. 194.

[10] Ibid.

[11] Ibid, 198.

[12] Dodson, ed., *Campaigns of Wheeler and His Cavalry,* 227.

[13] Mathews, *The McCook—Stoneman Raid,* 117.

[14] Ibid, 119.

[15] Ibid, 122.

[16] Ibid.

[17] Compiled Service Records, 2nd Georgia Cavalry (Atlanta GA: Georgia Department of Archives and History).

[18] Mathews, *The McCook—Stoneman Raid,* 123.

[19] Ibid.

[20] *War of the Rebellion, Official Records,* Series I Vol 38 Part II, 927.

[21] Ibid, 917.

[22] Evans, *Sherman's Horsemen,* 327.

[23] Robert H. Kingman, in *Reminiscences of Confederate Soldiers, Vol. XII* (unpublished: Georgia Department of Archives and History) 210.

[24] Mathews, *The McCook—Stoneman Raid,* 126-128.

[25] Ibid, 130.

[26] Ibid, 130-131.

[27] Ibid, 131-132.

[28] Ibid, 133.

[29] Ibid, 134.

[30] Ibid, 135.

[31] Mathews, *The McCook—Stoneman Raid,* 135.

[32] Ibid, 132.

[33] *War of the Rebellion, Official Records,* Series I Vol. 38 Part 5, 347, 353.

[34] Compiled Service Records, 2nd Georgia Cavalry.

Working on the Railroad

Regarding his failed cavalry raid, Gen. Sherman said, "The loss of this cavalry is a serious one to me, but we are pushing the enemy close." Sherman called on Brig. Gen. J. D. Webster in Nashville to send "all the cavalry that can be spared," and he reorganized his remaining cavalry into three new divisions, one under Brig. Gen. Kenner Garrard, one under Brig. Gen. E. M. McCook, and another under Brig. Gen. Judson Kilpatrick.[1]

With Sherman's cavalry now in disarray, Gen. Hood decided that the best use of his own horsemen was to send them northward against the Union supply lines. Also working in support of this decision was the scarcity of grain for Wheeler's horses around Atlanta. It had been more than a month since corn had been issued for the animals, and their steadily worsening condition had become a real concern.[2]

Wrote Hood:

> The severe handling by Wheeler and Iverson of the troops under Stoneman and McCook, together with Jackson's success, induced me not to recall Wheeler's 4,500 men, who were still operating against the railroad to Nashville. I had moreover become convinced that our cavalry was able to compete successfully with double their number. Our cavalrymen were not cavalrymen proper, but were mounted riflemen trained to dismount and hold in check or delay the advance of the enemy, and who had learned by experience that they could without much difficulty defeat the Federal cavalry.[3]

If Hood overstated the case a bit for his cavalry, certainly Sunshine Church and Brown's Mill were remarkable victories. The Rebel cavalrymen were now veterans of many campaigns, and if their horses were thin, they were probably better armed than ever due to the capture of Federal weapons. Hood's description of his cavalrymen as "mounted riflemen" indicates that shotguns were largely a thing of the past for Confederate troopers.

So it was, that on 10 August, with Atlanta under siege, Wheeler left his camp at Covington and headed north with the "cream of his cavalry," Martin's, Kelly's, and Humes divisions, to attack Sherman's supply lines.[4] Now we see that Martin is back in charge of his old division, which still includes the 2nd Georgia. Iverson at this point was placed in command of another division which included Gen. Morgan's and Col. Hanson's forces. In addition, Lewis' Brigade of Hardee's Corps was ordered on 4 September to report to Iverson at Griffin for the purpose of being mounted.[5] Iverson had remained behind to provide "a rendezvous for all the cavalry absent and unable to reach their commands"[6] and to guard Hood's supply line south of Atlanta. Hood's order of 7 September gave Iverson command of all cavalry east of the railroad, and instructed him to move up to Stockbridge and extend his line eastward from the railroad.[7]

A Union dispatch casts some doubt on whether the 2nd Georgia was with the rest of the Georgia Brigade in Martin's Division on this campaign, or with Iverson south of Atlanta. The dispatch of 15 August noted only the 1st, 3rd, 4th, and 6th Georgia regiments crossing the Chattahoochee River with Martin's Division.[8]

Other evidence clearly shows, however, that the 2nd Georgia was indeed with the rest of the Georgia Brigade as they followed Wheeler on the raid into Tennessee. A post-war biographical sketch of Lt. James T. Newsome in *Confederate Military History* places the G Company officer with the 2nd Georgia on "...the raid into Tennessee during the siege of that city [Atlanta]." A similar sketch of C Company places that unit with Wheeler through this period,[9] and a deserter's account also confirms that the 2nd Georgia was with Wheeler. Moreover, numerous records show the 2nd Georgia as still part of Crews' Georgia Brigade in subsequent months.

The men of the 2nd Georgia, so close to home for the last month, found themselves riding again toward Tennessee in the late summer of 1864. What thoughts of home and loved ones must have played upon their minds? For all the men in F Company, what fears must have assaulted their senses with the news three weeks later that Hardee had been defeated in their home town of Jonesboro. While the Federal victory at Jonesboro forced the evacuation of Atlanta, the men of F Company were no doubt more concerned about their families and farms.

In G Company, a number of men were detached to Gen. Cheatham, thus avoiding the march back to Tennessee. Throughout the regiment, others avoided the march by going AWOL. Morale among Confederate soldiers, cavalry and infantry alike, had taken a major blow when Hood replaced Johnston as Commander of the Army of Tennessee. The heavy casualties at Peachtree Creek, Bald Hill and other environs of Atlanta made matters worse, as the Army had lost confidence in its commanders and in its own ability to prevail. Probably at no other time did the infantry fight with less verve than at Jonesboro, and the men of Wheeler's Cavalry headed north to Tennessee were in no better spirits than the infantry. After meeting with Wheeler 20 September, Forrest would write the following about Wheeler's command to Gen. Richard Taylor:

> His command is in a demoralized condition. He claims to have about 2,000 men with him; his adjutant-general says, however, that he will not be able to raise and carry back with him exceeding 1,000, and in all probability not over 500. One of his brigades left him and he does not know whether they are captured or have returned, or are still in Middle Tennessee. He sent Gen. Martin back in arrest, and his whole command is demoralized to such an extent that expressed himselve (sic) as disheartened, and that, having lost influence with the troops, and been unable to secure the aid and co-operation of his officers, he believes it to the interest of the service that he should be relieved from command. [10]

Forrest may have embellished the description of his old rival's troubles. Forrest's rivalry with Wheeler notwithstanding, there is little doubt that morale was low among Wheeler's men that August. The statement of Pvt. Malachi Carter, a deserter from the 2nd Georgia's A Company, is even more illuminating than Forrest's report. On 23 October 1864, Pvt. Carter wrote the following statement for the Provost Marshall, Army of the Cumberland.

I reached Atlanta yesterday. I live in DeKalb County, seven miles from Atlanta. Was conscripted in June, 1864, and kept under guard until I reached my regiment, belonging to Iverson' Brigade. About August 10 we left Covington to make a raid under Wheeler. The three consisted of William S. Robinson's [F. H. Robertson's] brigade, Humes' division, Martin's division, and all but part of our brigade. We were not all armed. We went into East Tennessee, crossed the river at Strawberry Plains, and there back through Middle Tennessee. Recrossed Tennessee River below Muscle Shoals and crossed the Coosa at Edward's Ferry, near Round Mountain Iron Works. Joined Hood's army near Cedartown; were assigned to the advance, and recrossed the Coosa on pontoons, fifteen miles below Rome, going northwest. All the army crossed, but sent back most of their wagons and beef cattle to Jacksonville and Blue Mountain. The report was that the army was going to Summerville. Opinions vary as to whether they will only cut the railroads and then come back into Alabama.

The men are discouraged, just now are very poorly fed and clothed. Many more would desert, but fear being caught and shot. I escaped at Dirt Town, Chattooga County, on the 11th instant, after the army had crossed the river. Came around through Alabama. Saw no troops but train guards. The army get their supplies by wagon from Blue Mountain, in Calhoun County, fifty or sixty miles from Summerville and five to ten miles north [of] east from Jacksonville, it is the terminus of the railroad. Wheeler has lost about half of his men by desertion since August 1. Iverson is now somewhere below Stockbridge, between Jonesborough and McDonough, with several hundred men. At Morrow's Mills, west of Jonesborough, about nine miles this side of Fayetteville, is a cavalry force of 300 or 400; don't know who commands them. Know of no other forces near Atlanta. There are some militia at Macon. I have heard, I believe, that there are many Union men hiding throughout Northeast Georgia, many of them armed. There are some such between Lawrenceville and Gainesville. These men often bushwack the rebel cavalry very pertina-ciously. I am an original Union man and was near hung for my sentiments in this city.[11]

For the men in the Georgia regiments, the lift they received from victories at Browns Mill and Sunshine Church must have evaporated with the news that they were headed back north. Whatever their thoughts as they left Atlanta, the men of the 2nd Georgia were soon too busy with manual labor in the August heat to dwell at length on their situation. Near Marietta, they helped rip up several miles of railroad track before Martin's division was detached on 13 August to strike the railroad at Tilton. Wheeler took the remainder of his force toward Adairsville and Resaca, where they destroyed more track and burned the bridge over the Etowah River.

Late in the afternoon of 14 August, Wheeler attacked the Union garrison at Dalton, driving them out of the town and back to their earthworks on a small hill. While Wheeler waited for Martin's Division to rejoin his forces, the Federals in the earthworks received a large rein-forcement of infantry and cavalry. At dawn, Martin still had not arrived, and Wheeler found that, instead of rejoining the main body as ordered, Martin had put his men into camp for the night several miles from Dalton. Wheeler promptly relieved Martin from duty, and he was even-tually transferred to Mississippi.[12] General William Wirt Allen succeed-ed him as the commander of the division which still included Crews' Brigade and the 2nd Georgia Cavalry Regiment. Allen had been serving under Martin as commander of John T. Morgan's old brigade.

As Wheeler's men moved out of Dalton on the 15th, they were attacked by a superior force of infantry under Gen. Steadman. Wheeler fell back toward Spring Place, and in the skirmishing forty Union sol-diers were killed and forty-five wounded, including Gen. Steadman. Wheeler kept his command in the vicinity of the railroad, and kept the rail line out of commission until the 19th when he left for the Ocoee and Hiawassee in search of forage for his emaciated horses. Before leav-ing the railroad, Wheeler left six thirty-man detachments to continue disrupting the line. These parties reportedly captured some twenty well-loaded trains.

Wheeler's stay in the Ocoee and Hiawassee area was brief, and his men were soon at work destroying rails between Cleveland and Loudon. At Stewart's Landing they captured sixty-nine wagons and a number of Union soldiers and horses. Wheeler then crossed the French Broad and Holston rivers "in the face of the enemy" around Knoxville. "Forces of cavalry were also sent out against us, but they were promptly attacked, dispersed and captured or driven back to the fortifications at Knoxville." Two brigades, Williams' and Anderson's, were allowed to raid the garri-son at Strawberry Plains, and never rejoined Wheeler for the rest of the campaign. This left Wheeler with only about 2,000 men and two pieces of artillery.

Raiding parties from Wheeler's command next struck garrisons at Lebanon and Smyrna, as well as railroad bridges and the blockhouses guarding the bridges. A Union force under Gen. Rousseau attacked and was repulsed, losing two stands of colors and a number of prisoners. At LaVergne, Wheeler captured a train of wagons and several more prisoners. [13]

Late on the evening of 28 August, Wheeler reached the Alabama and Tennessee Railroad below Nashville. By the end of the following day, his men had torn up miles of track and captured stores at several depots on the line. But Rousseau attacked again, and a running fight developed, with clashes at Clifton on 31 August and at Clifton and LaVergne on 1 September.

The following day, Wheeler's favorite subordinate, Gen. John H. Kelly, was shot through the head in a "minor affair" at Franklin.[14] Kelly, an Alabama orphan who somehow won an appointment to West Point, was also highly regarded by the common soldiers in his division.

But Kelly's death was just a footnote to the events of 2 September. This was the day that Atlanta fell. The defeat of Hardee at Jonesboro had allowed Sherman's infantry to cut the rail lines south of Atlanta.

The events of 2 September at Cainey Strickland's farm near Jonesboro were no doubt repeated at the homes of most troopers in F Company. Captain White, a quartermaster of the XVI Corps of the Army of the Cumberland, confiscated livestock and produce from the Strickland family farm near Jonesboro. After the war, Cainey Strickland petitioned for $480 in compensation for the loss of "one fine mare, 400 lbs. of pork, 100 bushels of corn, two horses second quality, and four pounds of honey." Although it was no doubt galling for a farmer to see a year's work taken by the enemy, the Stricklands were lucky that their house was left standing.[15]

There is no surviving record of the events for the Hutcheson family in Jonesboro that day, but they were probably similar to the experiences on the Strickland farm. For the Hutcheson's, however, the events at home were only part of their troubles. Two of their three sons and a son-in-law in the 2nd Georgia's F Company were captured on 2 September near Macon, where they had been detailed to guard cattle. Ladson Hutcheson, brother Rolin, and brother-in-law John Creel were probably pleased with their assignment, for it meant that they would not have to march back north again with the Regiment. Little did they know that they would soon be heading back north as prisoners of war. Pvt. Samuel

D. Whaley of F Company, a cousin of the Strickland brothers, also appears to have been part of this detail, for he was captured the same day. Whaley died in prison, but Creel and the Hutcheson brothers survived and returned home after the war.[16]

After Kelly's death, Wheeler crossed the Tennessee River near Florence, Alabama. A Federal dispatch of 6 September reported, "Crews rebel brigade passed Lewisburg at 1 P.M. yesterday."[17] One veteran recorded that Company C of the 2nd Georgia was "...in an engagement at Campbellsville Tenn 11 Sept 64. No losses."[18]

Other records show the 2nd Georgia involved in several skirmishes with Union forces around Florence, 9, 10, and 12, September, but Wheeler was not looking for a fight here. His men and horses were worn, and his supply of ammunition very low. Moreover, he had become encumbered by captured wagons, captured horses and mules, wagons loaded with his wounded, and a large group of unarmed recruits. His plan was to rest man and beast and re-supply his command before returning to work on Sherman's supply line.[19] However, Wheeler reluctantly had to abandon the plan when, in mid-September, he received orders to rejoin Hood in the vicinity of the Etowah.

Wheeler's efforts to destroy supply lines caused only short-term problems for the Federals. Some historians have contended that the benefits of this raid were greatly outweighed by the loss of two veteran generals, Martin and Kelly. That argument could as easily be applied to the entire war. Others have been critical of Wheeler's and the cavalry's ability to disrupt railroads. It seems unlikely, however, that any commander with any force of infantry could have kept the railroad out of commission without repeated destruction. Wheeler's recall denied him that opportunity. In his reply to Hood's order, Wheeler wrote,[20]

Lovejoys, Sept. 18, 1864

General J.B. Hood

When I left the railroads in Middle Tennessee, it was with the intention of replenishing my ammunition, resting my men and returning to continue operations before the enemy had repaired what I destroyed.

If permitted to carry out this, I feel certain I can keep Sherman's railroad communications constantly broken between Nashville and Chattanooga.

J. Wheeler, Major-General

Hood's response was unequivocal. Wheeler's Cavalry was headed back to Georgia, and the men of the 2nd Georgia were no doubt more than glad to comply with this order. Hood wanted the cavalry back because he had decided, with the fall of Atlanta, to take the Army of Tennessee north and strike in Sherman's rear. He needed the cavalry to screen his movements and protect his flanks.

The 2nd Georgia's C Company, and very likely other companies in the regiment as well, engaged in several skirmishes near Gadsden as they moved back toward Georgia.[21]

[1] Byron H. Mathews, *The McCook—Stoneman Raid* (Brannon Publishing Company, 1976) 141.

[2] W. C. Dodson, ed., *Campaigns of Wheeler and His Cavalry* (Jackson TN: The Guild Bindery Press) 248-249.

[3] John B. Hood, "The Defense of Atlanta" in *Battles and Leaders of the Civil War Vol. IV*, Johnson and Buel, editors (Secaucus NJ: Castle Books) 342.

[4] Albert Castel, *Decision in the West—The Atlanta Campaign of 1864* (Lawrence KN: University Press of Kansas, 1992) 466.

[5] *War of the Rebellion, Official Records of the Union and Confederate Armies* Series I, Vol. 38 Part 5 (Washington DC: U.S. Government Printing Office, 1890) 1020.

[6] Ibid, 964.

[7] Ibid, 1029.

[8] Ibid. 515.

[9] Robert S. Bridgers, ed., *Confederate Military History vol VII* (Georgia Confederate Publishing Co., 1897) 889.

[10] Steven Z. Starr, *The Union Cavalry in the Civil War, Vol. III The War in the West, 1861-1865.* (Baton Rouge LA: Louisiana State University Press, 1985) 529.

[11] *War of the Rebellion, Official Records,* Series I Vol. 39 Part 2.

[12] John P. Dyer, *From Shiloh to San Juan: The Life of Fightin' Joe Wheeler* (Baton Rouge LA: Louisiana State University Press, 1941) 149.

[13] Dodson, *Campaigns of Wheeler and His Cavalry,* 252-254.

[14] Ibid, 253.

[15] Confederate Claims Commission records (Atlanta GA: Georgia Department of Archives and History).

[16] Compiled Service Records, 2nd Georgia Cavalry (Atlanta GA: Georgia Department of Archives and History).

[17] *War of the Rebellion, Official Records* Series I, Vol. 38 Part 5, 816.

[18] Bridgers,ed., *Confederate Military History Vol. VII.* 889.

[19] Dodson, ed., *Campaigns of Wheeler and His Cavalry,* 254-255.

[20] Ibid, 257.

[21] Bridgers, ed., *Confederate Military History, Vol. VII* 889.

On Sherman's Flanks

Wheeler reached the Oostanaula River near Dalton on 2 October. His men destroyed two locomotives and several miles of track here. From here they also floated heavy log rafts down the swollen river, "sweeping away" the railroad trestle bridges at Resaca.[1]

On 6 October, Lt. William Buice of the 2nd Georgia's H Company was wounded in the right lung when his detail was cut off from the command.[2] Two days later, Wheeler hooked up with Hood on the Coosa River near Rome. On 9 October, Hood started north with Wheeler 's Cavalry on his flanks. At Resaca on the 13th, the Confederates found that the trestle bridges had just been rebuilt after their destruction almost two weeks previous. By-passing the Union soldiers in the formidable works at Resaca, Hood destroyed some twenty miles of track as he moved toward Dalton.[3]

Gen. Kenner Garrard reported that on 13 October he "routed" Allen's Cavalry Division, which included the 2nd Georgia, in the hills west of Rome. Garrard reported capturing two cannon and more than seventy prisoners, while killing and wounding many more.[4]

Wheeler's account is quite different, ascribing the action to Colonel Harrison with five regiments left to slow Federal advances toward Hood's wagon train at Rome. Wheeler reported the loss of the two cannon, ten killed, thirty-four wounded, and sixty captured or missing. Acknowledging that Harrison was driven back, Wheeler stated, "The enemy were, however, checked at a point ten miles from Rome, and our wagons and artillery remained unmolested."[5] There are no indications that the 2nd Georgia was with Harrison in this action.

As Hood passed Dalton on the 14th, Wheeler's assignment was to slow powerful Union forces now in rapid pursuit and attempting to turn Hood's left. The 2nd Georgia was involved in a series of skirmishes throughout the rest of the month that were probably related to this rear guard action. Those skirmishes were at:

Rome, Ga.	17 October
Ruff's Station, Ga.	19 October
Wagleville, Ala.	21 October
Round Mountain Iron Works, Ala	22 October
King's Hill near Gadsden, Ala.	23 October
Turkeytown, Ala.	23 October
Round Mountain, Ala.	25 October
Goshen, Ala.	26 October

Gen. Washington L. Elliott, Sherman's new Chief of Cavalry, reported that on the 21st, his 2nd Division and one brigade of the 1st Division attacked Wheeler near Leesburg and "drove him in disorder" from his position. The following day at King's Hill, Elliott reported only that he "...found the enemy strongly posted in a narrow part of the valley near Turkeytown...with three or more pieces of artillery...and the loss which would have occurred did not, in my opinion warrant an attack." Elliott added, "...every place susceptible of defense was held until he was forced from it by a movement on his flank."[6] Little else is known about these engagements.

Elliott's accounts of his encounters with Wheeler may have been embellished to stem Sherman's growing disenchantment with his cavalry. Sherman had written Elliott:

> I reiterate my order for all the cavalry to act boldly against Hood to-morrow, leaving all trains and artillery with the infantry. Of course I don't want them to attack infantry in position, but to strike detachments....We must not let Hood send off all his cavalry and hold ours at bay by mere squads. It does look as though our cavalry was afraid to meet an inferior force. Let them wipe out this impression. The fact that a single regiment [of infantry] went out to-day where a division of cavalry would not venture elicited universal comment. I was asked

by a hundred where our cavalry was, and why it did not reconnoiter instead of men on foot.[7]

The 26 October skirmish at Goshen would be the last time that Wheeler's cavalry would cover a retreat of the Army of Tennessee, until the final battle of the war. Sherman decided this day to quit the chase and take the Army of the Cumberland back through Georgia, leaving other Union armies to handle Hood's frail forces.

Now the mission changed for the 2nd Georgia and the rest of Wheeler's Cavalry. Wheeler's horsemen were sent, alone, to watch Sherman's mighty army, and impede his progress when they could— some 3,000 ill-equipped, dispirited cavalrymen, contending with an Army of 60,000 veterans, well-equipped, confident, and tough. For the rest of the year, the cavalry would have no infantry (except for some militia units) to protect, and no infantry to protect them.

Wheeler of course had no hope of stopping Sherman's Army. He could only harass his foragers and engage his cavalry. Sherman and other ranking officers in his command continued to have a low opinion of their own cavalry, and perhaps an unjustifiably higher opinion of the Confederate horsemen. In September Sherman had wired Grant, "I do want very much a good cavalry officer to command. My present cavalry needs guards and pickets, and it is hard to get them within 10 miles of the front...anybody with proper rank will be better than Garrard."[8] Stoneman had blundered badly at Sunshine Church, and Garrard was far too timid for Sherman's tastes as he prepared for his march to the sea. To command his cavalry division on this march, Sherman selected General Judson Kilpatrick.

Kilpatrick had been Wheeler's classmate and rival at West Point. Like Wheeler, he was small of stature, energetic, and bold. But while Wheeler's men called him "Fightin Joe," the Federal cavalrymen and infantry alike referred to Kilpatrick as "Kill-Cavalry." Major James A. Connolly of the XIV Corps referred to Kilpatrick as "the most vain, conceited egotistical little popinjay I ever saw." Connally's opinion of the Union cavalry itself was no better. He said they were "a positive nuisance; they won't fight, and whenever they are around they are always in the way of those who will fight. They are good for nothing but to run down horses and steal chickens."[9]

Connally's description of the Federal cavalry is extreme, and displays the sort of inter-service rivalry that has been common in military cultures. His opinion of Kilpatrick, however, was too widely shared by other officers to be ignored. One Federal staff officer referred to Kilpatrick as a "frothy braggart without brains," and Sherman himself called him a "a hell of a damned fool," while adding that he was nevertheless the kind of cavalry commander he needed on his march.[10]

During October, Wheeler began to develop intelligence indicating that Sherman would march for Savannah or perhaps Mobile with one or more of his three armies. On 13 November, Wheeler joined Iverson at Jonesboro, ahead of his command, to discuss Union troop movements.[11]

Two men from the 2nd Georgia's F Company were already in Jonesboro. On that same Sunday that Wheeler arrived, Pvt. Cary Strickland was getting married to Eveline Virginia Ogletree. Brother Henry was present for the wedding, and exactly one week later, he married Mary Mundy, the sister of his best friend, Pvt. Reuben Mundy. Records show that Cary was detached to drive beef during this time, and it appears that Henry simply left with him. Records also show that Cpl. Henry Perry Strickland was absent without leave in November and December of 1864. Cary was never shown as AWOL. According to Henry's affidavit in a pension application after the war, and the affidavit of Reuben Mundy, Henry returned to the regiment and was present at the surrender.[12] Accounts of Mundy descendents also have Henry Strickland returning to Jonesboro at the conclusion of the war.[13] Very likely, he and Cary rejoined the regiment the week after Christmas, before Sherman left Savannah.

Confederate cavalry units that November were scattering south, east, and west of Atlanta to try and determine whether Sherman was moving toward Macon, Augusta, or Milledgeville. On 15 November, elements of the 2nd Georgia were involved in a skirmish at East Point as heavy blue columns began marching out of Atlanta. This detachment from the 2nd Georgia was probably among Wheeler's scouts who found three Federal corps—the 15th, 17th, and 20th—on the Jonesboro and McDonough roads. Sherman's march to the sea had begun, but his destination was not clear to his adversaries.

At midnight on the 16th, Wheeler reported that he had "checked" the enemy advance at Bear Creek Station, now Hampton, Georgia.[14] The Federal report of this action read quite differently, as 2nd Brigade commander Smith D. Atkins reported that his men at mid-day made a "gallant saber charge" and then dismounted and "drove the enemy in confusion." But Atkins also reported that he camped that night near Bear Creek Station, leaving open the question of why he did not pursue with so much daylight remaining.[15] Very likely the action at Bear Creek Station was just a holding action like those Wheeler had employed since the retreat from Kentucky two years previous. Most of the men Wheeler had taken north in August had not yet rejoined their commander. Those forces at his disposal, apparently Iverson's men, Wheeler had scattered in an attempt to determine Sherman's intentions. The 2nd Georgia apparently was not part of the small force that fought at Bear Creek Station.

Wheeler the next day checked a Union advance on Griffin. On 18 and 19 November, elements of Wheeler's Cavalry clashed with a superior force of Federals near Forsyth. These engagements indicated that the Union advance was headed for Macon.[16]

Early on the 19th, Wheeler sent Crews' Georgia Brigade to Macon, with orders to report to Maj. Gen. Howell Cobb for the defense of that city. On arriving at Macon, Crews found not only Cobb, but Lt. Gen. Hardee who had assumed command. Hardee sent the Brigade to the Milledgeville Road with orders to "follow and engage any raiding party of the enemy which might move toward the railroad."[17] Pursuant to these orders, Crews moved his brigade just west of the Milledgeville Road toward Clinton, putting the Georgia troopers squarely in the path of the Union 2nd Brigade of cavalry which was marching on Macon. Crews also sent a courier to Wheeler, informing him of his movement. Although the advance of the Union brigade appears to have been a diversion, the reports of its commander, Col. Atkins, indicate that he planned to attack the city.[18]

Atkins' men encountered the Georgia Brigade about four miles east of Clinton, not far from the Sunshine Church battlefield of the previous July. Atkins sent the 92nd Illinois Mounted Infantry on a dismounted charge. Crews countercharged on horseback, but the fire of Union Spencer repeaters forced the Confederates to withdraw. According to Atkins, "…the enemy cowardly ran off, scattering through the woods." Indications are, however, that Crews simply fell back to a pre-selected position at Walnut Creek where he had artillery support, apparently from Georgia militia. Upon arriving at the Confederate position, Atkins went immediately on the attack. The 10th Ohio Volunteer Cavalry gained "momentary possession of the enemy's outer works, and several pieces of artillery, which, however, could not be brought off and the regiment retired." Atkins did not comment on why other elements of the brigade were not sent to the support of the 10th Ohio. The 92nd Illinois was dismounted in the creek bed, and the 5th and 9th Ohio Volunteer Cavalry regiments were in reserve. That night Atkins withdrew to the junction of the Clinton and Macon and Macon and Milledgeville roads, where they began barricading.[19]

When Crews' courier found Wheeler, he was on his way to Griswoldville after skirmishing with Osterhaus' Corps. Crews' message changed Wheeler's plans, sending him to fill the gap on the Milledgeville Road left by the departure of the Georgia Brigade. Upon his arrival Wheeler found the militia and Crews' Georgia Brigade had already "driven back" one charge of Federal forces. It is not clear why Atkins did not press the issue at Walnut Creek near the Milledgeville Road. The thin line of Confederate cavalry and militia probably was no match for his veteran regulars with their Spencer repeaters. Perhaps he knew that Wheeler was on the way, or perhaps he was ordered to withdraw. At any rate it would be apparent by the end of the next day that Macon was not Sherman's objective.[20]

Late on the night of the 20th, Wheeler moved out toward Griswoldville. Indications are that the 2nd Georgia and the rest of Crews' brigade were with Wheeler as he headed back. Hardee had ordered Wheeler to drive the Federals out of the town, and Wheeler reported matter-of-factly that he did so on the 21st, "...capturing a few prisoners." Wheeler arrived too late to save the town, however. During the afternoon of the 20th, Atkins had sent a 100-man detachment there to "burn public buildings and destroy the railroad." They did their job well, and the town of Griswoldville ceased to exist.[21]

The events of the 21st and 22nd are unclear. Wheeler reported no fighting on the 21st except for driving the small Federal party out of Griswoldville.[22] Atkins, however, reported that his rear guard, the 92nd Illinois Mounted Infantry was "...furiously attacked at 9 A.M.while in position behind rail barricades. The enemy charged them with one regiment dismounted and two columns mounted, at the signal of the bugle. They came on desperately close to the barricades, but the cool steady fire of the Spencer rifles broke the charge, and doubled them back with great loss." Atkins added that a captured Rebel later set the Confederate loss at 65 killed and wounded.[23]

For the 22nd, Atkins reported only that his brigade marched away at 9 A.M. toward Gordon. Wheeler, on the other hand, reported that he "...attacked and drove the enemy for some distance, capturing sixty prisoners, besides killing and wounding a large number."[24] It seems possible that one of the commanders had his dates mixed up, and Atkins' report of the 21st and Wheeler's of the 22nd describe the same action, with the usual allowance for vastly different perspectives of the contending commanders. Two factors argue for the 22nd as the actual date of this engagement. If the action had occurred on the 21st, then Wheeler would probably still have been close enough to Griswoldville to participate in the attack that would come there on the following day. Secondly, Pvt. Frank Jones of the 2nd Georgia's A Company was killed on the 22nd.[25]

So it appears that Wheeler's men moved away from the smoldering ruins at Griswoldville on the 21st, and attacked Atkins Brigade on the 22nd. That same day, Gen. Walcutt's brigade paused near Griswoldville around mid-day, behind a light defensive line of fence rails, while they ate. They were attacked there by three brigades of Georgia Militia, about 2,000 of the very young and the too old. Walcutt's 1500 veterans welcomed them with a blistering fire from their Spencer rifles. The militia men were not routed—they stayed on the field and made at least three charges through that long afternoon—but they were badly bloodied. Over 600 militia men died there, while Walcutt lost fewer than 100 men. After walking among the dead and wounded when the fighting had stopped, and seeing the nature of his enemy, one Union soldier wrote, "I hope we never have to shoot at such men again."[26]

Even as the gray-haired men and beardless boys were dying at Griswoldville, it became clear that Sherman was headed not for Macon, but Milledgeville and beyond. Hardee had little choice but to concede the Georgia Capital to Sherman, and sent Wheeler to intercept his probable line of march at Sandersville. Wheeler's Cavalry crossed the Oconee River at Dublin and Blackman's Ferry on 24 November. They reached Sandersville on the 25th and deployed on the west of the town just ahead of the approaching Federal XIV and XX Corps, which had already dispersed the local militia. Wheeler sent word to the people of Sandersville that "…the enemy would enter the town the next morning, and…advised them to send off all movable property of value." Wheeler reported that his men repulsed the first attack and then counter-charged, driving the Federals for a mile and "…capturing, killing and wounding about thirty of the enemy…." The next morning, Wheeler's Cavalry was "…slowly driven back toward and finally through the town."[27]

While the men of the 2nd Georgia were fighting at Sandersville, rations of bread, meat, and corn, as well as pistol ammuniton—7,000 rounds of Remington New Army and 5,000 rounds of Navy Colt—were sent to Millen for Wheeler's Cavalry.[28] It is not clear whether they were able to acquire these supplies, but if they did it probably didn't happen quickly.

Late on the 26th, Wheeler's scouts reported that Kilpatrick with a force of some 3,700 cavalry had left the main column and was marching on Augusta and its factories and warehouses. Leaving Iverson to watch the Union infantry, Wheeler set out in pursuit with about 1,800 exhausted men and horses on a night march to cut Kilpatrick off before he could reach the city. The 2nd Georgia was clearly with Wheeler during this march, as veterans of the regiment later indicated that they were involved in the fighting of late November.[29]

Wheeler's weary troopers followed a trail of destruction as they pursued Kilpatrick's columns. Said Pvt. J. A. Williams of the 4th Tennessee Cavalry, "We saw thousands of old men and women, bowed with age, crying and wringing their hands, saying everything they had was burned.[30]

Late on the evening of the 26th, Wheeler's scouts reported that Kilpatrick had crossed the Ogeechee River perhaps forty miles east of Milledgeville. Wheeler caught up with Kilpatrick about midnight at his camp on the main Augusta Road and immediately attacked. In the darkness, Kilpatrick retreated to the lower Augusta Road and continued toward his objective. Wheeler renewed the pursuit, frequently encountering rear-guard actions like those he had used so often himself since the long-ago days of the Kentucky campaign. Much of this rear-guard action was performed by the 92nd Illinois Mounted Infantry with their Spencer repeaters and supported by at least one rifled artillery piece. Atkins reported that Wheeler "…with dogged persistence, continued to attack our rear."

"On reaching Brier Creek Swamp," reported Wheeler, "we pressed the enemy so warmly that he turned off toward Waynesborough. During the chase the enemy set fire to all corn cribs, cotton gins, and a large number of barns and houses. We succeeded in driving him off in nearly half the instances in time to extinguish the flames, and frequently pressed him so rapidly as to prevent his firing a number of houses, thus saving a large amount of property."[31]

The pursuit by Wheeler's troopers probably saved Dr. Amos Whitehead's Ivanhoe Plantation northwest of Waynesboro from total destruction, but substantial damage had been done before the Union soldiers fled. Several outbuildings and twenty-five bales of cotton were destroyed. Catherine Whitehead, the teenage daughter of Ivanhoe's owner, described Kilpatrick's visit in her diary.

"The first detachment of the enemy behaved very well considering they were the enemy, but they were most audacious in their manner and walked about as if everything belonged to them. They not only stole all the mules and horses and all meat from the smoke house, but when Kilpatrick came up with the main body of his army, they commenced the work of destruction and committed every kind of depredation." According to Miss Whitehead, "Even Kilpatrick asked for the silver, and when the General condescends to anything of that kind you cannot expect anything more from the men." The diary also noted that, "They took everything from the Negroes, at which I was much surprised as they profess to love them so much. They stole all their clothes and money and whatever would be at all useful...."[32]

The chase had been going on all day on 26 November when Kilpatrick reached Waynesboro. His men had just torched the town and were in the process of wrecking the railroad when the pursuing Confederates arrived about 2:00 A.M. on the 27th. Wheeler's men helped extinguish the flames, and, according to Wheeler's report, only one building in the town was completely destroyed. Wheeler then disrupted Kilpatrick's work on the railroad, forcing him to form up in line of battle.

The running fight continued through the day, and at dawn on the 28th, Wheeler stormed the Union front in what Kilpatrick himself called "One of the most desperate cavalry charges I have ever witnessed," killing and capturing many Federal troops. Wheeler had all of his buglers with him at the head of his charge on the Louisville Road, and all twelve of the buglers were killed, wounded, or unhorsed. Pvt. Madison Moon of the 2nd Georgia's D Company also had his horse shot from under him in this charge, which resulted in some 100 Confederate casualties. But the charge inflicted several hundred Union casualties, broke Kilpatrick's line, and sent his men in a pell mell retreat of some two miles. Reported Wheeler, "They continued to flee, refusing to surrender, notwithstanding the demands of my men in close pursuit.

Consequently, no alternative was left but to shoot or saber them to prevent escape."[33]

In this pursuit the Confederate ranks became disorganized, and Lt. James Newsome of the 2nd Georgia's G Company was captured. As he had done at Peachtree Creek, however, Newsome soon escaped from his captors.[34]

At Buckhead Swamp, the Federals set another defensive line where they checked their now disorganized pursuers long enough to escape across Buckhead Creek, burning the bridge behind them. Here they established a more formidable defensive position across the creek from their pursuers. Soon, however, dismounted Confederates forded the creek and drove away the Federals on the opposite bank. This allowed the rest of Wheeler's men to extinguish the flames on the bridge, which they repaired with pews from the nearby Buckhead Baptist Church.[35]

After crossing Buckhead Creek, Kilpatrick retired to Reynolds' Farm, close by his infantry. Despite the proximity of the Union infantry, Wheeler attacked again. It does not appear that the 2nd Georgia crossed the creek soon enough to be engaged at Reynold's Farm. It was the 8th and 11th Texas, 3rd Arkansas, and 4th Tennessee cavalry regiments which, in a mounted charge, again routed the Union cavalry despite its superior numbers and repeating rifles.[36]

Atkins reported that "The rebels charged in splendid style, coming up in close range, when six pieces of artillery, double shotted, and our dismounted troops, opened upon them, and repulsed them handsomely, with little loss to us."[37] With darkness falling, Wheeler attacked again, this time on the weaker Union left. This charge drove the Union troopers from their works and yielded a number of prisoners, captured horses and arms, and one stand of colors.[38]

In the darkness, Kilpatrick escaped toward Louisville. Although almost captured himself and forced to fall back on his infantry, Kilpatrick claimed victory. Sherman would later claim that Kilpatrick's move toward Augusta was only a diversion, and the city had never really been a target. If indeed that were true, it seems a high compliment to Wheeler's Cavalry that the Union commander felt the need to divert their little force.

The engagements with Kilpatrick showed that Wheeler's men were still soldiers, despite great adversities which they faced. Some 250 Confederate troopers became casualties. Fighting mostly from behind barricades, the Federals apparently suffered fewer casualties—about 190 by most estimates. But Wheeler was convinced that Kilpatrick's casualties were much higher, and that his force dwindled from 5,000 to 3,700 as the fighting wore on.[39] With much of the action occurring in rapid night pursuits, it is possible that large numbers of Union troopers were separated from Kilpatrick before the final action at Reynolds' Farm.

On the first day of December, Sherman again ordered his cavalry and Gen. Jefferson Davis' XIV Corps to clear Wheeler from his path. Wheeler's main force was at Rock Spring Church, five miles west of Waynesboro, but elements of his command watched all of the Brier Creek crossings for any movement of the enemy. The 2nd Georgia Cavalry was in the vicinity of Louisville, for they skirmished there with Kilpatrick and Davis on 1 December as they set out toward Waynesboro.

The following day, the advancing blue columns ran into Wheeler's main force at Rock Spring Church. Here the Rebels received the Union so warmly "…as to compel them to turn their course, and bypassing through the fields, moved over to their main column between Thomas Station and Millen." Pvt. Dodson Bennett of the 2nd Georgia's D Company was captured this day. Three other Bennett's in D Company had been captured the previous January at Fair Garden, Tenn.[40]

Wheeler's attack on the main Union body on 3 December again halted destruction of the railroad. When the destruction resumed that night, Wheeler's artillery shelled the Union camp, inflicting a substantial number of casualties.

During the night, Wheeler scattered his force over a three-mile front two miles from Waynesboro, with the men camping by brigades to ensure adequate forage for his rapidly weakening horses. Then, at dawn on the 4th, 15,000 infantrymen of the XIV Corps under Gen. Baird and Kilpatrick's Cavalry advanced from Thomas Station driving in Wheeler's pickets. A single, unidentified regiment was quickly thrown against the advance, which they checked just long enough for Wheeler to position a brigade behind a barricade. A cavalry charge against this position was repulsed, and Wheeler placed the remainder of his troops in position to the rear. The brigade which had been initially engaged began falling back on this position, a movement which the Federals mistook for a general retreat. Federal infantry and cavalry charged and were repulsed by the dismounted Confederates. According to Dodson, Wheeler rode along his line, "Exposed to a shower of bullets," encouraging his men. Reportedly, Kilpatrick said he easily recognized his old school mate.

A second charge was also repulsed, but it was becoming clear that the presence of so many infantry on his flanks was making Wheeler's position untenable. According to veterans of Wheeler's command, the retreat was an orderly one, and was possible only because the 8th Texas and 9th Tennessee, previously held in reserve, made a bold mounted charge as the other regiments withdrew to the other side of Waynesboro. The Federals not only did not pursue, but left many of their wounded on the field.[41]

The fighting at Waynesboro had lasted from noon until about two in the afternoon. Confederate veterans claimed that their losses were "trifling" while one Union brigade alone admitted a loss of fifty killed and 147 wounded. Col. Connally, however, said the Confederates lost 300 men.

The 2nd Georgia's precise role in this fighting is not clear, but Wheeler "commended in high terms" the bravery of Colonel Crews. One C Company trooper reported that two men in the company were wounded in the "...desperate fight with the enemy at Waynesboro...."[42]

Surviving records show that at least eleven members of the 2nd Georgia became casualties this day, although none of them are recorded as killed. The wounded included:

Sgt. John B. Hill of C Company
Pvt. David Patrick of E Company
Pvt. Henry Waller of E Company
Pvt. Joseph Story of G Company
Pvt. Randolph Vaughn of I Company

Members of the regiment known to have been captured in this action were:

Pvt. Enoch Leviner of A Company
Sgt. Dickinson Sanders of C Company
Pvt. Archie Knight of E Company
Pvt. James Phipps of F Company
Pvt. H. E. Richardson of I Company
Pvt. Thomas Wiley of K Company [43]

Maj. Connally of the XIV Corps gave grudging credit to the Union cavalrymen for their actions this day, noting that "Kilpatrick's men behaved very handsomely today." He added, "But then Kilpatrick's men had the moral support of two of our brigades that were formed in line right behind them and kept moving as they moved forward, so that our cavalry all the time knew that there was no chance of their being whipped."[44]

During the next week, Wheeler continued to harass the rear guard of the XIV Corps, taking over 100 prisoners as well as horses and arms. Detachments from the 2nd Georgia were apparently in skirmishes 5 December at Statesboro and the Little Ogeechee River. On the 8th, Wheeler's men drove in the Union pickets near Ebenezer Creek and shelled the Federal works. Later in the month, his men provided a cavalry screen for Hardee during the siege of Savannah, and for his 21 December evacuation of his troops from the city.

During Sherman's march to the sea, Wheeler kept detachments on the flanks of all three Union columns. The small bands of Confederate horsemen could do little more than harass the army of 60,000 veterans, which some historians say was then the most potent military force in the world. The Confederate cavalrymen sometimes captured and killed small parties of Union foragers preying on civilians. Typical was an incident reported by one of Wheeler's men. "In the morning we found three Yanks driving off a lady's cows. We soon scattered their brains and moved on."[45]

When Sherman turned his three columns east toward Savannah that November, the huge blue army simply disappeared from public view into Georgia's interior. Sherman barred news correspondents from accompanying his force, so the events and progress of the march were a mystery to the outside world for a time. Slowly, however, the news of the devastation wrought by Sherman began to reach even the northern press. Wrote one Union corporal in a letter home, "The cruelties practiced on this campaign toward the citizens have been enough to blast a more sacred cause than ours. We hardly deserve success."[46]

According to the historian of one Federal unit, "the Army left Atlanta with twenty days' rations..but not a hardtack or a pound of sow-belly has been issued. The men were living off the produce of the land, and leaving a trail of destruction." Wrote Col. Thomas Jordan of the 9th Pennsylvania Cavalry, "We find them living in plenty, with fine horses, carriages, etc., and leave them too poor to know where their next meal will come from."[47]

Sherman himself commented about the reaction of southern women to the offenses of his men. "I doubt," he said, "if history affords a parallel to the deep and bitter enmity of the women of the South. No one who sees them and hears them but must feel the intensity of their hate."[48]

Soon, however, Wheeler's men developed a reputation for theft almost as bad as that of the Yankee soldiers. With no wagons or pack animals, Wheeler's rag-tag cavalrymen had to carry their individual provisions with them, which meant they had to live off the land. Wheeler vehemently denied that his troopers committed crimes against civilians, and blamed roving bands of armed men who claimed to be part of the cavalry, but were actually organized by Governor Joseph E. Brown. Some individuals of this description were later convicted of depredations against civilians.

While, there can be little doubt that the isolated Confederate cavalry took what they needed from civilians, there is strong evidence that the worst of the depredations against civilians were committed not by Wheeler's cavalry, but by deserters and armed militia groups organized by Governor Brown. At the time, however, there was considerable public outcry, some from leading citizens, against Wheeler's cavalry. Conversely, the cavalrymen felt that many Georgia civilians were less hospitable than the war-ravaged civilians in Tennessee. After the war, one veteran wrote of Tennessee, "…Wheeler's Cavalry was always welcome, and even in the humblest homes the doors of smoke-houses and barns were opened at our approach and food for man and beast was cheerfully furnished. In striking contrast was the reception accorded in other parts of the South, where Wheeler's men were the only soldiers the citizens had ever seen." An Inspector General's report and Gen. Hardee's own investigation largely absolved Wheeler's men of criminal activity during this time.[49]

Early in November, a large number of the 2nd Georgia's men were horseless, and were with the wagon train in Macon. These "wagon dogs" as they were called, were mobilized into an infantry battalion and placed under the command of four Tennessee officers. Their orders were to take the new battalion by way of Thomasville to Savannah, in an attempt to reach Hardee's command there before Sherman arrived. Traveling by rail and foot, the Wagon Dog Battalion reached Savannah, where it was stationed outside the city at Woodlawn. Here they were behind substantial fortifications fronted by levees and rice fields. One of the "wagon dogs" was A. S. McCollum of the 2nd Georgia's C Company, who had been captured at Stones River at the end of 1862 and exchanged.

McCollum, who had been promoted to sergeant since becoming an infantryman, said, "The wagon dogs in the fort seemed to enjoy it," when the shelling started. At one point, though, the shelling was so heavy that the men lay prone on their bellies with their feet against the rampart and their faces just above the water in the ditch behind them. The explosions threw dirt down on the backs of the prone men, who soon had another problem. "A moccasin came winding his way among the men," said McCollum, "but not an inch would they move their heads. One man cried out, 'Lord, Lord, just look at that snake.' Others said let him blow."

As Hardee began his evacuation of Savannah, a detail of the Wagon Dogs stayed behind to keep the camp fires going so that the Federals would not know of the Confederate departure. It was McCollum's turn to pull duty, but his old C Company comrade Sgt. George W. Cochran and five other men were given this dangerous assignment. McCollum appealed that the duty should be his, but his appeal was denied. McCollum then voluntarily remained behind with the detail. Said McCollum, "How can I go home and live among his people to remember that by an unfair deal George Cochran was killed or went to prison to save me that fate...." But Cochran, McCollum, and the five other Wagon Dogs were able to carry out their assignment and rejoin the command in South Carolina later that day. After a time, the Wagon Dog Battalion was disbanded, and the men sent in search of the 2nd Georgia in the Carolinas.[50]

[1] W. C. Dodson, ed., *Campaigns of Wheeler and His Cavalry* (Jackson, TN: The Guild Bindery Press) 274.

[2] Compiled Service Records, 2nd Georgia Cavalry (Atlanta GA: Georgia Department of Archives and History).

[3] Dodson, ed., *Campaigns of Wheeler and His Cavalry,* 274-275.

[4] W. L. Curry, *1st Ohio Volunteer Cavalry* (Champlin Printing Company, 1898).

[5] Dodson, ed., *Campaigns of Wheeler and His Cavalry,* 280.

[6] *War of the Rebellion, Official Records of the Union and Confederate Armies* Series 1 Vol. 39 Part 1 (Washington DC: U.S. Government Printing Office, 1890) 725.

[7] Ibid, Part 3, 107-108, 110.

[8] Stephen Z. Starr, *The Union Cavalry in the Civil War, Vol. III The War in the West, 1861-1865.* (Baton Rouge LA: Louisiana State University Press, 1985) 533.

[9] David Evans, *Sherman's Horsemen, Union Cavalry Operations in the Atlanta Campaign* (Bloomington IN: Indiana University Press, 1996) 383.

[10] Ibid. 382-383.

[11] Dodson, ed., *Campaigns of Wheeler and His Cavalry,* 284.

[12] Compiled Service Records, 2nd Georgia Cavalry.

[13] Joe Mundy, recollections of accounts by contemporaries.

[14] *War of the Rebellion,* Series 1 Vol. 44, 406.

[15] Ibid, 389.

[16] Dodson, *Campaigns of Wheeler and His Cavalry,* 287.

[17] *War of the Rebellion, Official Records,* Series 1 Vol. 44, 406.

[18] Ibid, 389.

[19] Ibid, 390.

[20] Ibid, 407.

[21] Ibid, 390.

[22] Dodson, ed. *Campaigns of Wheeler and His Cavalry,* 288.

[23] *War of the Rebellion, Official Records,* Series 1, Vol. 44, 407.

[24] Ibid, 390.

[25] Compiled Service Records, 2nd Georgia Cavalry.

[26] Lee Kennett, *Marching Through Georgia* (New York NY: HarperCollins Publishers, 1995) 254-255.

[27] *War of the Rebellion, Official Records* Series 1 Vol. 44, 391.

[28] Louella H. Bales, *Confederate Cavalry* (Jacksonville FL: 1989) 285.

[29] Robert S. Bridgers, ed., *Confederate Military History, Vol. VII* (Georgia Confederate Publishing Co., 1897) 890. See also Dodson, ed., *Campaigns of Wheeler and His Cavalry,* 289.

[30] Angela Lee, "Tangling with Kilcavalry" in *Civil War Times Illustrated* June 1998, 67.

[31] *War of the Rebellion, Official Records* Series 1 vol. 44, 391.

[32] Lee, "Tangling with Kilcavalry" in *Civil War Times,* 67.

[33] Ibid, 70.

[34] Bridgers, ed., *Confederate Military History, vol. VII,* 889.

[35] Lee, "Tangling with Kilcavalry" in *Civil War Times Illustrated,* June 1998, 70.

[36] Dodson, ed., *Campaigns of Wheeler and His Cavalry,* 291-292.

[37] *War of the Rebellion, Official Records,* Series 1 Vol. 44, 391.

[38] Dodson, ed., *Campaigns of Wheeler and His Cavalry,* 291-292.

[39] Ibid.

[40] Compiled Service Records, 2nd Georgia Cavalry.

[41] Ibid, 297-300.

[42] Bridgers, ed., *Confederate Military History, Vol. VII,* 889.

[43] Compiled Service Records, 2nd Georgia Cavalry.

[44] Starr, *The Union Cavalry in the Civil War, Vol. III*, 673.

[45] Geoffrey C. Ward, *The Civil War, An Illustrated History* (New York NY: Alfred A. Knopf, 1990) 346.

[46] Ibid.

[47] Starr, *The Union Cavalry in the Civil War, Vol. III*, 575—576.

[48] Ward, *The Civil War*, 344.

[49] Dodson, ed., *Campaigns of Wheeler and His Cavalry*, 380-406.

[50] A. S. McCollum, "The Wagon Dogs" in *Reminiscences of Confederate Soldiers, Vol. XIII* (Atlanta GA: Georgia Department of Archives and History, Sept. 15, 1932).

The Carolinas and Surrender

The 2nd Georgia began 1865 under Capt. George Looney, the last recorded commander of the Regiment. There is no record of his promotion beyond captain, but the presence of higher ranking officers on the regimental staff at the surrender in April suggests that he was promoted if he remained in command for any length of time. The regiment's command structure at this time was:[1]

Wheeler's Corps
Allen's Division
Crews' Brigade (1st, 2nd, 3rd, 4th, 6th, and 12th regiments of Georgia cavalry)
Looney's Regiment

A Company	Capt. Fleming Crews
B Company	unknown
C Company	Capt. W. C. Hood
D Company	Capt. James Shepard
E Company	Capt. James Ellis
F Company	Capt. Hardy Chapman
G Company	Capt. Thomas Merritt
H Company	probably still Capt. Francis Allen
I Company	probably 1st Lt. Thomas Dean
K Company	probably 1st Lt. Jesse Barber

According to the February inspection of Wheeler's cavalry, two companies of the 2nd Georgia were on detached duty at this time, one in Virginia and one in East Tennessee.[2] The detachment to Virginia appears earlier, and may have been longstanding. There is no record of which companies were detached, but one could reasonably speculate that the detached companies were B and H. These are the only two companies in the regiment whose muster roles reveal no casualties after November of 1864. Since the recorded casualties in the other companies indicate the presence of those companies, one might speculate that the process of elimination points to B and H as the detached companies.

The previously noted dearth of records on B Company could be explained by an extended duty in Virginia. At least one member of B Company, Abraham Dias, was captured at Cassville, in southwestern Virginia in December of 1863. The last recorded casualties for H Company were on 29 July 1864 at Stone Mountain, Georgia. Eleven days later the regiment left with Wheeler on his raid into Tennessee.

Whichever two companies were detached in early 1865, they appear to have been back with the regiment before the surrender. Surviving records show at least three members of every 2nd Georgia company as present when the regiment surrendered 26 April at Salisbury, North Carolina.[3]

Sherman used the month of January to rest and refit his command. However, at least some elements of his command crossed the Savannah River into South Carolina during January. The 2nd Georgia was engaged in skirmishes three times that January in South Carolina: on the Savannah Road 19 January, on the Combahee Road 22 January, and at Robertsville a week later.

The great blue army moved into South Carolina bent on revenge, with only Wheeler's cavalry in their path. The Confederate cavalry was assigned the task of delaying Sherman's advance until the remnants of the Army of Tennessee could be united with Hardee's command, the former defenders of Savannah and Charleston.

Over the next two months Confederate cavalry was in almost daily conflict with Union forces. Wheeler biographer John P. Dyer wrote that some of the most brutal fighting of the war occurred in small unit engagements between Wheeler's and Kilpatrick's men in the Carolinas.[4] Blue-coated foragers were pillaging every home in their path and then burning them to the ground. In retaliation, Wheeler's men were taking no prisoners when they came upon foragers.[5]

Some sources indicate that detachments of the 2nd Georgia skirmished at Barker's Mill, and Whippy Swamp on 2 February. During the following three days, detachments from the regiment are shown skirmishing at Edisto River bridges. Official records indicate, however, that the 2nd Georgia was still well south of the two branches of the Edisto as late as 6 February.

On the 6th, there was "considerable skirmishing between Crews' Brigade and the U.S. Third Brigade" at Barnwell and at Cowpen's Ferry on the Little Salkahatchie River as the Federals marched from Allendale to Barnwell Courthouse. It was probably during this action that Pvt. George Dillon of G Company was wounded. When the war ended, Dillon was trying to return to the regiment.[6] On the 7th, the 3rd Brigade commander reported that he had "routed" Hagan's Alabama Brigade, consisting of the 1st, 3rd, 5th, 9th, 12th and 51st Alabama cavalry regiments.[7]

Late on the afternoon of the 8th, Allen reported that he had established his headquarters at "Kitchen's house about a mile and a half below Pine Log Bridge." He had a regiment fortified at the bridge and inquired "whether there are any further instructions for Colonel Crews' or Colonel Hagan's brigades."[8] This inquiry may allude to the assignment of these brigades to cover the movements of various elements of the Army of Tennessee moving toward Charlotte.

On the 10th, the 2nd Georgia was in action at Orangeburg and on the 11th at Johnson's Station. The action at Johnson Station was probably part of Wheeler's attack that day on Atkins' Brigade in Aiken. Atkins was "...most furiously attacked by Wheeler's entire command" and was driven back on the rest of Kilpatrick's division which was busy destroying the railroad at Johnson's Station.[9]

Kilpatrick's cavalry, which had been blocked from reaching Augusta while the Union Army was in Georgia, was attempting to reach Augusta from South Carolina. But Wheeler's victory at Aiken, had again forced him to retreat back to his infantry, thus saving Wheeler's hometown of Augusta from destruction.

By February the charges of depredations against civilians led Gen. Beauregard to replace Wheeler as chief of cavalry with Gen. Wade Hampton, late of Gen. Lee's Army of Northern Virginia. Wheeler, though, continued to lead the cavalry as a division commander. It would have been difficult for Wheeler to control the foraging of his men even if he wanted to, and it is possible he did not want to, for he had little ability to keep them mounted and fed otherwise.

As previously noted, however, an inspector general's investigation largely cleared Wheeler's men, noting "...but one or two instances of outrage which could be proven to his corps." Added the IG, "No one who visits this corps and observes closely can fail to be impressed with the idea that these men cannot be the desperadoes they are often said to be....It can be affirmed with truth that few commands have borne more hardships uncomplainingly, and are today more zealous in their country's cause than the Cavalry Corps commanded by General Joseph Wheeler."[10]

The 5 February return of the Wagon Dogs who had been under Hardee at Savannah illustrates Wheeler's approach to the foraging problem. According to McCollum, when the Wagon Dogs reported back to the 2nd Georgia, Gen. Wheeler himself told them that they had been accused of killing civilian hogs on their march. "The Sergeant told the General the hogs tried to bite us and the men wouldn't stand for it, and they killed the hogs in self defense." General Wheeler must have suppressed a smile when he replied only that "it would be his pleasure to grant a furlough to each of us for the thirty days, who could remount himself and report to his proper place in our several companies."[11]

On 10 February, the 2nd Georgia lost its most experienced company commander, when Capt. Hardy Chapman resigned due to disability. Chapman had commanded the 2nd Georgia's F Company since the regiment mustered into Confederate service in May of 1862. It is not clear who replaced Chapman as company commander, but it was very likely former 1st Sgt. Benjamin Camp, who appears to have been the company's ranking lieutenant at this time.[12]

Wheeler needed every man he could muster to delay Sherman's advance on Columbia. On the 14th, Wheeler, "...seizing a favorable opportunity, charged through the skirmish line of the XIV Corps, captured forty prisoners and broke this main line of battle."[13] That same day, a detachment of the 2nd Georgia skirmished with Union forces at Gunter's Bridge on the North Edisto River. The following day the regiment was in action at Bates' Ferry on the Congaree River, under the direct command of Wheeler. This action also involved Alabama and Texas troopers, with Wheeler leading a flank attack on the Union right wing, temporarily stalling its advance on Columbia. Later that same day, the Regiment engaged in a skirmish at Two Leagues Crossroads near Lexington.

A 15 February message from Col. Crews informed Capt. B.A. Terrell, assistant adjutant general, that the Georgia Cavalry Brigade had been ordered by Gen. Hill to report to Gen. Cheatham at the Grantville and Bethlehem roads. A 23 February dispatch from Crews to Gen. Cheatham's adjutant shows clearly that the Georgia Cavalry Brigade was scouting for boats and fords in advance of generals Cheatham and Stewart, who were leaving Augusta and Newberry for Charlotte.[14]

A 17 March dispatch from Gen. Wade Hampton would later note that Crews' brigade "…has been with General Stewart's Corps…."[15] From this and Crews' 15 February dispatch, it appears that the 2nd Georgia and the rest of the Georgia Cavalry Brigade spent much of late February and early March providing a cavalry screen for elements of the Army of Tennessee as they marched toward a rendezvous with Hardee's command.

Wheeler's command, meanwhile, fought at Winnsboro on 17 February, Wadesboro on the 19th, Youngsville on the 20th, and Camden on the 22nd and 24th. None of these actions ever had a chance to do more than delay the inevitable sacking of Columbia. As one of Wheeler's veterans wrote about Columbia after the war, "Every gun fired in its defence [sic] was fired by Wheeler's cavalry. Every soldier who fell in its defence [sic] belonged to Wheeler's brave command."[16]

On 24 February, Joseph E. Johnston was brought out of retirement in an attempt to salvage the rapidly deteriorating situation in the Carolinas. The appointment of Johnston had been one of the first acts of Gen. Robert E. Lee upon his appointment as commander in chief of Confederate armies. Johnston's return was extremely well received by the common soldiers.

Johnston took the responsibility "…with no other hope than of contributing to obtain favorable terms of peace; the only one that a rational being could then entertain. For the result of the war was evident to the dullest." The forces available to Johnston were clearly no match for Sherman's veteran masses. Johnston must have been shocked to see that the proud Army of Tennessee which he left the previous summer had been almost destroyed during Hood's tenure as commander, and now numbered fewer than 5,000 men, the size of an infantry division. These men marched toward North Carolina under generals Stevenson, Alexander P. Stewart, and Cheatham.[17] (As we have seen, Stewart was in

Newberry on 24 February, and the Georgia Cavalry Brigade served as his advance and screen.) Not only were their numbers reduced, they had lost their best general when Cleburne fell at Franklin, Tennessee.

Early on the morning of 25 February, Allen notified Wheeler's adjutant that he crossed both prongs of Fishing Creek. Two days later he reported that his command crossed over the railroad bridge near Nation's Ford. Allen added that he "…will have to go upstream to Morrow's Station to get over the streams between there and Lancaster, as the creeks are swollen and deep. I have already lost much ammunition by swimming creeks. After crossing Sugar Creek, I shall move forward to Lancaster." At 6 P.M. Allen reported that he would move down the Lancaster Road from Morrow's Station for the purpose of rejoining the Corps.[18] Given the Georgia Brigade's assignment to serve as a screen for Stewart's infantry, the 2nd Georgia probably was not involved with the rest of Allen's Division in the movement to Lancaster.

In addition to the remnants of the Army of Tennessee, Johnston had the former Savannah and Charleston garrison troops under Gen. Hardee, Braxton Bragg's North Carolina command, and the cavalry under Hampton and Wheeler. In all, the force was only 15,400 infantry and 4,200 cavalry. They would face Sherman's command of 64,400, with another 30,000 Federals marching from the coast under generals John M. Schofield and Alfred H. Terry.

March opened with more of the same for the men of the 2nd Georgia—a skirmish at Thompson's Creek near Chesterfield on the 2nd. The next day there were two skirmishes for the regiment near Cheraw, one on Thompson's Creek and another at Juniper Creek. There was another skirmish for a detachment from the 2nd Georgia at Cheraw on the 6th, and then others that same day and the following day at Rockingham.

Some sources have placed the 2nd Georgia with the rest of Allen's Division under Wheeler when, at daylight on 10 March, the Confederate cavalry attacked Kilpatrick at Monroe's Crossroads near Fayetteville. Allen's and Humes' commands along with three brigades under Gen. Butler from Hampton's command, were arranged in five mounted columns, with Dibrell in reserve. (Hampton determined that a dismounted attack would be too dangerous in such close proximity to large bodies of Union infantry.) Perhaps because most of the men present were Wheeler's, Hampton reportedly stayed with the reserve while Wheeler led the attack on a white horse. The charge carried into the

Federal encampment where "Wheeler, himself in the midst of the melee, engaged in some dozen encounters, killing two and capturing a number with his own hand."[19]

Forced to flee the attack in his night clothes, Kilpatrick later wrote, "In less than a minute, they had driven back my people and taken possession of my headquarters, captured the artillery, and the whole command was flying before the most formidable cavalry charge I ever witnessed." Three Confederate generals, Humes, Hannon, and Hagan, Col. King of the Georgia cavalry and numerous other field grade officers were wounded, and Gen. Allen's horse was shot under him.[20] But a large part of Kilpatrick's staff and some 350 Union troopers were captured in this battle with a badly deprived and depleted Confederate cavalry. (A month before an inspector had reported that in Wheeler's cavalry there were fewer than 3,900 rifles for the 4,200 men. Brigades were no larger than regiments, and one company had only one officer and one man, while another company had only one man and no officers.)

Kilpatrick, in his night shirt, joined those troopers who had not been shot or captured in running into a swamp a few hundred yards to the rear. Here he set a new defensive line as artillery and infantry support came up behind them. Accounts vary, as to the cause, but the Confederate charge played out before it reached the new position of the Federal troopers. Some Federal accounts say that many of the Confederates had given up the chase to plunder the Yankee camp.[21] Veterans of Wheeler's Corps wrote that the attack was disjointed by the broken terrain and a boggy stream. Moreover, heavy casualties among division and brigade commanders had eroded Wheeler's command and control. With the attackers now in some disarray, Kilpatrick "opened with grape and cannister," and the Confederates slowly withdrew. The Federals did not pursue. [22]

According to Federal reports, 103 Confederates were killed and a greater number wounded in this fight of some two and half hours. Wheeler later wrote that he had engaged just 1,189 men not counting Butler's men from Hampton's command, and that his losses were twelve killed, sixty wounded, and ten missing. He also reported fifty-nine horses killed and another fifty-two wounded.[23] Casualties for Spencer's Federal brigade were listed as eighteen killed, seventy wounded and 105 missing, numbers far below Wheeler's report: Col. Way, whose brigade had borne the brunt of the first charge, did not report his casualties.[24]

The following morning, Allen's Division and Anderson's Division were involved in heavy skirmishing around Fayetteville. By noon, however, two Federal corps had entered the town, and Wheeler's cavalry withdrew across the Cape Fear River, burning the bridge behind them.[25]

Union forces began moving up the Cape Fear River on 13 March, and some records show the 2nd Georgia involved in heavy skirmishing around Fayetteville over the next two days. It appears unlikely, however, that the Regiment was engaged here.

The reader will recall that Hampton's 17 March report to Hardee noted that Crews' Brigade had been with General Stewart, who had been moving from Newberry, South Carolina to Charlotte, and then to a rendezvous with Hardee and Johnston. Hampton's report expressed concern that Kilpatrick's Cavalry might be moving up the west side of the Cape Fear River "...to strike at our trains or to reach the railroad at Raleigh." Hampton added, "Two regiments of cavalry were left on the west side of the Cape Fear River, and Crews' brigade, which has been with General Stewart's Corps, should be near enough to come between them and Raleigh, if they are moving in that direction."[26] As we have seen, Crews began scouting river crossings for Stewart as early as 23 February, and very likely remained as his vanguard until just prior to Hampton's 17 March dispatch. This seems to indicate that the 2nd Georgia was not engaged in the attack on Kilpatrick at Fayetteville or the fighting of the 16th and 17th at Averasborough or Taylor's Hole Creek.

Upon hearing the sounds of battle on the 17th, Wheeler brought his cavalry to the aid of Gen. Hardee some four miles south of Averasboro. There he found Union infantry under Gen. Slocum attacking Hardee's front, while another column was moving around his right front. Wheeler attacked the flanking column, and held it in check until dark, thus allowing Hardee to withdraw.

At Averasborough, Hardee had given Slocum's XX Corps a bloody nose, inflicting some 700 casualties, while just over 100 Confederates were killed.[27]

During this period Wheeler was promoted to lieutenant general. He had been the senior cavalry officer in Confederate service since the death of Jeb Stuart in the spring of 1864, and had been a major general for more than two years.

With his pitifully small force, Johnston made one last stand at Bentonville 19-21 March. In the early morning of 19 March, units of Wheeler's cavalry engaged the left wing of the Union Army, commanded by Gen. Henry W. Slocum, as it moved toward Goldsboro on the Fayetteville road. Slocum was moving into a trap laid by Gen. Johnston.

> The trap was sprung on the Federal left wing when…howling the still terrifying Rebel yell, the Southern right wing rushed forward. Hardee himself led the charge on horseback, jumping the federal breastworks. Observers on the field described the scene as being like a picture of old—the ragged butternut lines charging out of thick woods, red battle flags flying. Staggered momentarily by a blast of musketry, they quickly recovered and came on again. Lines closed and the shredded Rebel flags seemed closer together than ever. And, of course, they were now tight little groups of fifty and 100. It was the Confederacy's last full-field charge of the war. Stunned by the assault, the Federals recoiled and then broke. Three blue-clad divisions crumpled and fled westward.[28]

The 2nd Georgia, with other elements of Johnston's army, was engaged in conflicts at the Neuse River bridge near Goldsboro on the 19th. This bridge was strategically important, especially since Johnston had the Neuse River at his flank and back. The 2nd Georgia was just one of several cavalry units assigned to guard Johnston's eastern flank along the segment of the Averasboro—Goldsboro road that paralleled the Neuse River.[29]

The fighting raged on through the 20th, as Federal counterattacks and strong defensive positions blunted the Confederate assault. The arrival of the remainder of Sherman's Army left Johnston in an untenable position. On the 21st, in a heavy rain, a charge by 500 "shrieking cavalrymen" led by Joe Wheeler repulsed an attempted flanking movement by Maj. Gen. Joseph Mower. Mower's attack ended just 300 yards from the crucial Bentonville/Mill Creek road and would have cut off Johnston's retreat across the rain-swollen creek. On the morning of the 22nd, Wheeler's cavalry remained on the south bank and fought "a pitched battle with a Union brigade" to protect the rear of Johnston's Army as it retreated across the bridge. "Finally, wet and chastened, the Federals pulled back and Johnston's weary Army withdrew toward Smithfield without further harassment."[30]

The final major battle of the War had been, like so many others, a tactical success that could not be sustained. Shiloh, Perryville, Stones River, Chickamauga, New Hope Church, Pickett's Mill, Kennesaw

Mountain, and now Bentonville—all scenes of sacrifice and apparent victory, but all devoid of real advantage for the Confederates.

On 30 March, the Wagon Dogs of Savannah fame reported back to the regiment near Goldsboro. To their surprise they were told "…that our officers had long been holding a thirty day furlough, all fully approved, and we were relieved of duty on April 1. We were offered then and there a horse, bridle, and saddle, and revolver in exchange for a furlough, but no trade was made." Wrote A. S. McCollum after the war, "I well remember a boy from Bainbridge Ga. replied, 'I wouldn't give my privilege of dancing one night with them factory gals in Bainbridge for no horse, bridle and saddle in the army."[31]

The Wagon Dogs probably knew that they would have just a slight head start in returning home. Surrender was not far away, and the hopelessness of the situation was not lost on the common soldier. Lee would agree to Grant's terms on 9 April, and three days later the Army of Northern Virginia would formally lay down their arms.

So the Wagon Dogs started for home. McCollum's report of their journey is now in the Georgia Department of Archives.

The way of our travels to South Georgia was over the line of Sherman's march, and the outstanding observation was of his carelessness with fire and destruction of railroads. Sometimes we could ride a few miles and then march forty miles to another railroad and get another short ride.

On the march we passed many brick chimneys which marked the spot where a nice home was recently burned, and some chimneys had marble plates built into the backs, bearing the dates in which they were built. The dates ranged from around 1812. We finally reached the railroad between Augusta and Atlanta, but the water tank had been destroyed and we were told that Decatur was as near Atlanta as the train could run. Beyond Decatur, everything had been destroyed, although the track had been re-layed with burned and warped rails and was unsafe to run a train upon it.

The number of soldiers now were several hundred. We were placed on lumber cars and headed for Decatur. During the night we heard the conductor hail the engineer by the name 'Jackie,' and Jackie was soon told by the soldiers they were headed to Atlanta to catch the early morning train for Macon. And the train we were on put us in Atlanta in time to make the connection. Jackie remained silent. The train reached Decatur and Jackie disappeared, as he had allowed the fire to burn down and steam run low.

Some soldiers fired up and blew the whistle and hollered, ' All aboard for Atlanta.' Jackie reappeared and said the boiler would explode in five minutes, that we had up ninety pounds of steam and but little water in the boiler, so we rolled off the flat cars and made for the tall timbers. Some soldiers stood pat and made a treaty with Jackie under which Jackie was to run the train and soldiers were to fill the tender, when we reached a pond on the way. The cars were soon off the track so we carved fence rails to keep them on the tracks.

At the pond we formed a bucket brigade...until some said 'enough'. Of course Jackie insisted on filling the tender as promised, but we told Jackie to pull out and we reached Atlanta at daylight.

The City looked like a sea of brick chimneys and craning walls. One small frame house had escaped Sherman's fire. The smoke was rolling away from the train as it was pulling out. We ran to get on board calling, 'Goodbye, Jackie,' and Jackie replied, 'Goodbye, Goodbye, God knows I do hope l never lay my eyes on -e of you men again."[32]

Dawn on 10 April found Sherman's mighty army on the march, advancing toward Smithfield, where the Army of Tennessee was breaking camp and preparing to fall back toward Raleigh. At least a portion of the 2nd Georgia was engaged this day with Union cavalry at Nahunta Station.

Johnston learned of Lee's surrender early on the afternoon of 11 April as his army continued its retreat toward Raleigh. By the evening of the 12th, Johnston's infantry was positioned on a line from Pope's Station, eight miles west of Raleigh, to Durham Station, twenty-six miles west of the City. Wheeler's cavalry, including the 2nd Georgia, entered the Capital, clashing with Union cavalry on their way.

When informed that Governor Zebulon Vance and Mayor William H. Harrison planned to formally surrender the Capital to Sherman, Wheeler agreed to withdraw.[33] As they evacuated Raleigh on 13 April, the 2nd Georgia, and other elements of Wheeler's command, again fought Kilpatrick's cavalry. The following day, twelve miles east of Raleigh at Morrisville, the 2nd Georgia was part of a holding action that allowed supply wagons and a train of wounded men to escape. Here the Rebel cavalrymen were severely pounded by the 23rd New York Battery.[34]

The Regiment's final action of the War came in a conflict near Chapel Hill on 15 April, the day after Lincoln's assassination.

On 26 April, 1865, the same day that John Wilkes Booth was shot to death in Virginia, the Army of Tennessee surrendered at Durham Station. When surrender came, the 2nd Georgia Cavalry was at Salisbury. According to some accounts, only eighteen enlisted men were left in the regiment at the surrender.[35] Those accounts are clearly wrong, however, as compiled service records reveal more than 100 men of the 2nd Georgia present at the surrender.[36] The men surrendering at Salisbury were paroled on 3 May at Charlotte.

In addition to the 2nd Georgia troopers recorded as present at the surrender, about fifty others, perhaps fearing execution or imprisonment, turned for home without the benefit of formal surrender and parole. The murder of Lincoln had created a thirst for revenge, and cavalrymen had reason to fear that actions against Union foragers would lead their captors to treat them harshly.

One who did not hang around to be paroled was Cpl. Littleton Spinks of Marion County and G Company. After the War Spinks wrote, "The 5th day of May I rode up to my father's gate the happiest ragged boy on earth, and have not surrendered yet. With nothing but a pony, a ragged suit of clothes, and an old white hat…, I started life anew."[37]

Wheeler himself was among those who did not surrender, as the General volunteered to help Confederate President Jefferson Davis escape to the "Trans-Mississippi." Davis had journeyed to Charlotte after the fall of Richmond, and it was in Charlotte that he learned of Lincoln's assassination.

Wheeler and Hampton met with Davis at Charlotte and then returned to Greensboro to gather an escort of cavalry volunteers for Davis. Wheeler's command was camped at Company's Shops, a small town just east of Greensboro. He explained the plan to his men and asked for volunteers. Some 600 men stepped forward.[38] Some of these were probably from the 2nd Georgia.

Hampton's men were less responsive, only about thirty volunteering. Even these left Hampton as they marched toward South Carolina, and the General simply returned home to Cokesboro to await arrest.

Wheeler's plan was to link up with President Davis at Washington, Georgia. It soon became apparent, however, that he could not move hundreds of cavalrymen without attracting great attention from the Union forces which seemed to be everywhere. Wheeler split his force into small groups which were to move toward Washington by various routes.[39]

Wheeler arrived at Washington some time after 5 May only to find that Davis had already left for Florida, as the presence of so many Union troops made Washington unsafe. The Union troops also prevented most of Wheeler's scattered troopers from reaching Washington. Thirty-five 2nd Georgia troopers captured on 8 May near Athens, Georgia, may have been part of this group. About ten others were captured during this period near Augusta.[40]

Hotly pursued by Union cavalry, Wheeler and his small band eluded capture for a few days before they woke from an exhausted sleep near Conyers to find themselves surrounded. Wheeler later wrote of the capture, "One evening toward dark, we were suddenly overtaken by a force of about forty Federal soldiers, who galloped down the road, firing upon us as they approached. I stopped at the first favorable point, and with a gallant private soldier, M.A. Whaley, fired upon and checked the advancing Federals. It was soon dark, and we turned off the road and sought the cover of a thick pine undergrowth. The Federals knew we were in the woods, and halted in the main road directly opposite us." Wheeler and two scouts crept close enough to hear one of the Yankees say, "They had fine equipments and bouncing horses; it must be Davis and his men." Eluding capture here, Wheeler and his exhausted men rode all night, stopping to sleep about daylight. They awoke to find themselves under the guns of the Union cavalrymen.[41]

From there Wheeler was taken to Athens, where he joined Davis and his family, as well as Confederate Vice President Alexander H. Stephens and other distinguished prisoners. Davis had been captured near Irwinsville on 10 May. From Athens they were taken through Wheeler's hometown of Augusta and on to Savannah where they were put upon a prison boat for transport to Washington and Fort Delaware.[42]

On 31 December 1864, Wheeler had written the following letter to his troopers.

My brave Soldiers:

The close of the year terminates a campaign of eight months, during which you have engaged in continuous and successful fighting.

From Dalton to Atlanta you held the right of our army. Opposed almost continuously by a force of infantry ten times your number, you repulsed every assault, inflicting upon the enemy a loss in killed and wounded numerically greater than your entire strength. Every attempt on the part of the enemy to turn or strike our right flank was met and repulsed by your valor and determined courage. It should be a proud reflection to you all, that during the entire campaign, the Army of Tennessee never lost a position by having the flank turned which it was your duty to protect.

During every movement of our lines, you have been between our infantry and the enemy, hurling back his exulting advance, and holding his entire army at bay until our troops had quietly prepared to receive and repulse his gigantic assaults. Having failed by other means to drive our army from the position in front of Atlanta, he now sends three heavy columns of cavalry to destroy our communications, to release prisoners of war, and march in triumph with them through our country. You promptly strike one column and drive it back discomfited; then quickly assailing the two others, you defeat them and complete their destruction and capture. This alone cost the enemy more than five thousand men, horses, arms and equipment, besides material, colors, and cannon. This was due to your valor, and is without parallel in the history of this war.

Having been detached and sent to the rear of the enemy you captured his garrison, destroyed his stores and broke his communications more effectually and for a a larger period than any other cavalry force, however large, has done.

During Sherman's march through Georgia, you retarded his advance and defeated his cavalry daily, preventing his spreading over and devastating the country.

During the last five months you have traveled nearly three thousand miles, fighting nearly every day, and always with success. You must have been victorious in more than fifty pitched battles, and a hundred minor affairs placing a number of the enemy hors du combat fully four times the greatest number you ever carried into action.

I desire, my brave soldiers, to thank you for your gallantry, devotion and good conduct. Every charge I have asked you to make, has been brilliantly executed. Every position I have asked you to hold, has been held until absolutely untenable. Your devotion to our country fills my heart with gratitude. You have done your full duty to your country and to me; and I have tried to do my full duty to you. Circumstances have forced upon you many and great deprivations. You have been deprived of the issues of clothing and many of the comforts and conveniences which other troops have enjoyed and borne all without a murmur.

Soldiers of Kentucky, Tennessee, Texas and Arkansas! You deserve special commendation for your sacrifices and fortitude. Separated from your homes and families you have nobly done all that gallant devoted men could do. Soldiers from Alabama and Georgia! Your homes have nearly all been overrun and destroyed, yet without complaint you have stood to your colors like brave and patriotic men. Your country and your God will one day reward you.

The gallant Kelly whom we all loved so well is dead. Many other brave spirits whose loss we deeply feel sleep with him. They fell—the price of victory.

Allen, Humes, Anderson, Dribbrell, Hagan, Crews, Ashby, Harrison and Breckenridge, and many other brave men whose gallantry you have so often witnessed are here still to guide and lead you in battles yet to be fought and victories yet to be won.

Another campaign will soon open in which I only ask you to fight with the same valor I have always seen you exhibit upon the many fields where your determined courage has won victory for our cause.

J. Wheeler
Major General

[1] Compiled Service Records, 2nd Georgia Cavalry (Atlanta GA: Georgia Department of Archives and History).

[2] W. C. Dodson, ed., *Campaigns of Wheeler and His Cavalry,* (Jackson TN: The Guild Bindery Press) 416.

[3] Compiled Service Records, 2nd Georgia Cavalry.

[4] John P. Dyer, *Shiloh to San Juan: The Life of Fightin' Joe Wheeler,* (Baton Rouge LA: Louisiana State University Press, 1941) 173.

[5] Stephen Z. Starr, *The Union Cavalry in the Civil War, vol. II, The War in the West, 1861-1865,* (Baton Rouge LA: Louisiana State University Press, 1985) 585.

[6] Compiled Service Records, 2nd Georgia Cavalry.

[7] *War of the Rebellion, Official Records,* Vol. 47 Part 1, 891.

[8] Ibid, Part 2, 1128.

[9] Ibid, Part 1, 891.

[10] Dodson, ed., *Campaigns of Wheeler and His Cavalry,* 429—430.

[11] A. S. McCollum, "The Wagon Dogs" in *Reminiscences of Confederate Soldiers Vol. XII,* (Atlanta GA: Georgia Department of Archives and History, 15 Sept. 1932) 2.

[12] Compiled Service Records, 2nd Georgia Cavalry.

[13] Dodson, ed., *Campaigns of Wheeler and His Cavalry,* 326.

[14] *War of the Rebellion, Official Records,* Series 1, Vol. 47 Part 2, 1200, 1261.

[15] Ibid.

[16] Dodson, ed., *Campaigns of Wheeler and His Cavalry,* 329.

[17] Nathaniel Cheairs Hughes, *Bentonville,*(Chapel Hill NC: The University of North Carolina Press, 1996) 22.

[18] *War of the Rebellion, Official Records,* Series 1 Vol. 47 Part 2, 1286.

[19] Dodson, ed., *Campaigns of Wheeler and His Cavalry,* 344-345.

[20] Ibid, 340.

[21] Starr, *The Union Cavalry in the Civil War, Vol. III,* 584.

[22] Dodson, ed., *Campaigns of Wheeler and His Cavalry,* 347.

[23] Ibid, 346.

[24] *War of the Rebellion, Official Records,* Series 1 Vol. 47 Part 1, 894, 1130.

[25] Dodson, ed., *Campaigns of Wheeler and His Cavalry,* 346.

[26] *War of the Rebellion, Official Records,* Series 1 vol. 47 Part 1, 1415.

[27] Hughes, *Bentonville,* 15.

[28] George Beronious, "Joe Johnston's Last Charge" in *Civil War Times Illustrated,* May 1996, 44—53.

[29] Hughes, *Bentonville,* 49.

[30] Beronious, "Joe Johnston's Last Charge" in *Civil War Times Illustrated.*

[31] McCollum, "The Wagon Dogs" in *Reminiscences of Confederate Soldiers.*

[32] Ibid.

[33] Mark Bradley, "The Road to Bennett Place" in *Blue & Gray Magazine,* Columbus OH: 1999, 45.

[34] Ibid, 46.

[35] Joseph H. Crute, *Units of the Confederate States Armies* (Gaithersburg MD: Old Soldier Books, 1987) 82.

[36] Compiled Service Records, 2nd Georgia Cavalry.

[37] Mamie Yeary, *Reminiscences of Boys in Gray* (Dayton OH: Morningside Press, 1986).

[38] Dyer, *From Shiloh to San Juan—The Life of Fightin' Joe Wheeler,* 179-180.

[39] Ibid, 181-182.

[40] Compiled Service Records, 2nd Georgia Cavalry.

[41] Dodson, ed., *Campaigns of Wheeler and His Cavalry,* 368-369.

[42] Dyer, *From Shiloh to San Juan—The Life of Fightin' Joe Wheeler,* 183.

Warriors No More

They had been the last of the old and first of the new, and fought a war on horseback entirely of their own making. No other cavalry service, anywhere in any war to come would be quite like theirs. The cavalrymen took home a sense of pride after the War. Indeed, men North & South would look back upon their days in the saddle as the best of their lives, forgetting in time the hardship, the heat, dust, and hunger.

–Fighting Men of the Civil War

The Civil War was undoubtedly the central event in the lives of the men who fought it, and the men of the 2nd Georgia Cavalry were no exception. Service in the cavalry was certainly dangerous, but it apparently did not carry all the horrors associated with the infantry, where massed charges against fortified positions wasted so many young lives.

In 1898, a veteran who served under Wheeler wrote, "The hardships Wheeler's men endured would have seemed to a civilian or modern soldier simply appalling, yet ask almost any grizzled old veteran who 'galloped with the old gang' and he will tell you that he had more fun than he ever had before or has had since."[1] This comment brings to mind the officer who spoke of having "an immense amount of fun" on Wheeler's 1863 raid around Rosecrans' Army. Lifelong friends Henry Strickland and Reuben Mundy also talked after the War of all the "fun" they had in those years. It might even be said that Henry prospered from the War, as a Mundy descendant remembers hearing that he left with one horse and returned three years later riding one horse and leading another.[2]

The men of the 2nd Georgia, like all Confederate veterans, returned to a homeland forever changed. Farms that were prosperous before the War now barely produced a living. Most would not recover from Reconstruction before the Great Depression came in 1929. For those associated with the 2nd Georgia Cavalry Regiment, peace brought many different experiences.

Capt. Francis Marion Allen, who assumed command of H Company in November of 1863, returned to Atlanta after the War and, with his brother Elisha, opened E.T. and F. M. Allen Family Grocery on Whitehall Street. He and his wife Milly A. Allen had a son in 1867. The 1870 Atlanta City Directory shows that an A. J. Pierce had joined the brothers in the grocery business at 52 Whitehall Street. Capt. Allen died 4 March 1872, in Atlanta, and was buried in the Stone Mountain Cemetery.[3]

Elisha T. Allen is not shown in the Compiled Service Record, but his obituary in a September 1884 issue of the *Atlanta Constitution* reported that he served in the Confederate Army for four years and was a member of the 2nd Georgia Cavalry. By 1871, Elisha was running the grocery business he had started with his brother alone, and was now located on Capitol Avenue. He was a Mason and served as an Atlanta City Councilman during the 1887-1889 term. Elisha had been married before the War and had a son. In 1867 he married Anna A. Parks and they had several children. Elisha is buried in Oakland Cemetery in Atlanta, not far from where he fought at Bald Hill and Decatur during July of 1864.[4]

Gen. William Wirt Allen, last division commander over the 2nd Georgia, was wounded both at Perryville and at Stones River. After the war he returned to Alabama where he resumed farming and dabbled in railroading. He also served as state adjutant general and as a U.S. marshal. Allen died in 1894 at age 59.[5]

Pvt. John L. Atcherson of I Company returned to his farm in Paulding County, where he had left his wife and two sons. A daughter was born into the family around 1866, and a third son in 1875. Atcherson, who had been born in Newberry County, South Carolina in 1834, moved to Paulding County in 1855. He may have joined Campbell County's I Company out of a preference for cavalry service.

Atcherson sold his farm when his health began to fail, and he died in April of 1909, almost exactly 44 years after the surrender.[6]

Pvt. Henry Clay Burr of E Company, one of the four men who braved the Federal fire to enter the Courthouse at Murfreesboro on 13 July 1862, and who participated in Wharton's breakout at Bardstown, returned to Griffin to become a banker and a city alderman. He married Lucilla Nelms and they had one son.[7]

Capt. W. Hardy Chapman, returned to Clayton County after resigning his commission in February of 1865. He appears to have been the most enduring of the Regiment's company commanders, serving as the leader of F Company from the mustering into Confederate service in May of 1862 until illness forced his resignation in the closing weeks of the war.[8] It is possible, however, that he commanded the Regiment for a brief time at the end of 1864. Records show W. H. Chapman operated a restaurant, complete with billiard table and liquor license, until at least 1877. Chapman died 20 March 1895. He is buried next to his wife, Mrs. E. P. Chapman at the Chapman-Morrow cemetery, also known as the Watterson cemetery, in Clayton County.[9]

Col. Charles Constantine Crews, reportedly was promoted to brigadier general while disabled by wounds in the closing days of the War. Although there is no official record of this promotion, veterans of the regiment addressed him by that title after the war, lending credence to the claim that the promotion actually occurred. Crews returned to his native Cuthbert after the war where he became a druggist.[10] Within five years, however, he had left Georgia and headed West, eventually settling in Hillsboro, New Mexico, where he apparently continued to practice pharmacy. The *Cuthbert Liberal Enterprise* reported in November of 1887 that Crews had died on the fourteenth of that month in Hillsboro, leaving his wife and several children. His death had been reported by the *Headlight,* published at Deming, New Mexico, and picked up by the Cuthbert paper.[11]

Capt. James E. DeVaughn of F Company, who with twenty men had made the "handsome fight" with a Union regiment at Mt. Washington in the Kentucky Campaign, by some accounts became the commander of F Company.[12] This seems doubtful, however, as Hardy Chapman apparently served in that capacity until February of 1865, and DeVaughn was captured in October of 1863. DeVaughn "…experienced the miseries of two winters…" as a POW at Johnson's Island, Lake Erie, "…insufficiently housed and clad, in that inhospitable climate."

Although surviving muster rolls do not show him as a Captain, he was addressed as such after the war. It is possible that he commanded B Company, K Company, or I Company for a brief period. In 1866 he returned to Montezuma where he became one of the most successful merchants in Macon County. DeVaughn served on the town council and on the local school board. He married Sarah V. McLendon and they had three sons and two daughters. After Sarah's death, he married Mary E. Porter. DeVaughn died on 13 July 1908, the 46th anniversary of the regiment's first fight at Murfreesboro.[13]

Pvt. R. M. Fletcher enlisted 1 March 1864 in G Company, then commanded by his uncle, Captain Thomas Merritt. After the war he returned to his native Butts County and married Hattie McKibben. They had three sons and a daughter.[14]

Maj. Gen. Nathan Bedford Forrest, certainly one of the most striking figures of the War, was expected by many to flee westward after the surrender and attempt to carry on the struggle. But Forrest decided against such a course, and advised his officers and men to lay down their arms. The fortune Forrest had amassed before the war was gone, so he started over in farming and railroading. He was one of the early leaders of the Ku Klux Klan, but later distanced himself from the organization and called for improved race relations. He died in 1877.

Brig. Gen. Alfred Iverson, although still a division commander, was at home in Georgia when the surrender came and was paroled there in May of 1865. The son of Senator Alfred Iverson and Caroline Goode Holt Iverson, he was born in Clinton, Georgia, but spent much of his childhood in Washington City and in Columbus. Iverson was married to Harriet Harris Hutchins, the daughter of Gwinnett County Judge N. L. Hutchins. After the War, he went into business in Macon, and then in 1877 he moved to Orange County, Florida where he became a citrus farmer. In 1898 he was living in Kissimmee with his second wife, Adele Branham. He died in 1911 at age 82.[15]

Dr. John T. Lamar began the study of medicine in 1855, attending a course of lectures in New York and graduating from Atlanta Medical College in 1858. Two years later he married Sarah Lawhon. He apparently joined G company as a private soldier in April of 1862. Although he served much of 1863 as assistant surgeon for the Regiment, it appears he served most of the War in the ranks of G Company. After the War, he returned to his medical practice in Sumter County. He and Sarah later moved to a plantation in Terrell County where they raised a large family. Later in life, they moved to Parrott, where Dr. Lamar served as mayor for a time. A devout Methodist, "he was a man of strong personality, unimpeachable integrity, generous, noble, and true." He died in 1901 and is buried in a family plot at Cedar Hill Cemetery in Dawson.[16]

Gen. William Thompson Martin served in the Army of Northern Virginia early in the war and participated in Stuart's ride around McClellan. After Wheeler dismissed him as division commander over the 2nd Georgia in 1864, Martin served as a district commander in Mississippi. A lawyer, he served several terms in the Kentucky legislature after the war, and was also involved in railroading and education. He died in 1910 at age 83.[17]

Pvt. Joseph A. McConnell of F Company, wounded at Murfreesboro and discharged in Tennessee during 1863, was a retail liquor dealer in Jonesboro in 1870. He served as a Judge on the Clayton County "court of ordinary" from 1872 to 1880. Married to Malissa Ann Starr, he died 4 July 1914 in Cullman, Alabama.[18]

Pvt. A. S. McCollum of C Company and the "wagon dogs" survived the War, and his writings now in the Georgia Department of Archives, are among the few original sources detailing events in the Regiment.[19]

Pvt. John James McDonald, who joined A Company at age sixteen, became aide-de-camp to his future business partner, Col. Charles Crews. For five years after the war, he and Crews were druggists in Cuthbert. McDonald later organized the Bank of Cuthbert and invested heavily in farmland. He served as a Cuthbert city councilman and as a member of the Georgia General Assembly. In 1866 he married Eudora Harris, and they had one daughter.[20]

Capt. Thomas Mickleberry Merritt, an 1857 graduate of the University of Georgia and commander of G Company, returned to his wife Anna Hamlin Lewis Merritt and settled in Marion County. He later bought a plantation in Sumter County and subsequently moved into the town of Americus. He died in 1892 and is buried in Oak Grove Cemetery there. His grandson, Capt. George Norman Munroe, U.S. Army Regulars, was awarded the Distinguished Service Cross "for gallantry and extraordinary heroism" in the Meuse Argonne Offensive in France (World War I).[21]

Pvt. James Joseph Moses Mills, who before the War "saw the hand of God in the freeing of the slaves," returned to his wife Rebecca and three-year old son John William in Clayton County. There daughter Mary

Elizabeth, "Mamie", was born in 1867. In 1871 Mose moved his family to Shelby County, Texas, where his father was a Methodist Minister. By 1873, Mose was also an itinerant Methodist minister, riding horseback "through real dangers" to make his appointments. Six more children were born to Mose and Rebecca in Texas—Georgia Irene, Robert Owens, James Walter, Lovick Jefferson, Anna Blanche, and Alice Douglas. In 1914, his old comrades, Henry Strickland, J. L. H. Waldrop, and W. L. Watterson, witnessed his application for a soldier's pension. They noted that he never deserted his command, and added "...nor do we believe that there was any more honorable and faithful soldier in the Confederate Service...than J. M. Mills, known to us then as Mose Mills." Mose Mills died 4 January 1929, his eighty-eighth birthday, after 56 years as a frontier minister. Wrote his son-in-law, Lawrence Elrod, "He was guileless and trusted his brethen. He accepted his appointment uncomplainingly, even when he felt that a better plan could have been made. I often wonder if we today have the great faith that he had."[22]

Pvt. John Francis Moon of I Company, who escaped the sleeping Union guards on the road to Nashville in the summer of 1862, went on to fight at Perryville, Stones River, and Dover. He was captured again during the events leading up to the Battle of Chickamauga and was a POW at Camp Douglas near Chicago until 15 June 1865. Just 5'5" tall, John was the fifth of J. W. Moon's eight sons, at least four of whom were in Confederate service, three with the 2nd Georgia Cavalry. A native of Walton County, he gave his residence as Cobb County to his captors in 1863. John Moon joined I Company in May of 1862 at Camp McDonald near Big Shanty (now Kennesaw, Ga.). He was among those detailed to guard the Anderson raiders of the Great Locomotive Chase before they were hung in Atlanta in 1862.[23]

Pvt. Madison Moon of D Company, whose horse was killed in the charge at Waynesboro, was among those who fought from the Regiment's first battle at Murfreesboro on 13 July 1862 until the surrender on 26 April 1865. He was the brother of John Moon and the eighth and youngest son of J. W. Moon of Walton County. Another brother, *W. W. "Lump" Moon* was in the 2nd Georgia's I Company, and died in camp on 30 March 1863. Brother Stephen served in Company D 17th Confederate Infantry, and died of pneumonia on 30 July 1863. Apparently another of J. W. Moon's sons was Isaac, a physician who remained in Walton County and cared for wounded soldiers.

Manuscripts in the Georgia Archives also show a Joseph Moon from Walton County who had eight sons in Confederate service, none of whom appear to be Madison, Lump, or Stephen. Joseph Moon's sons are listed as William, LaFayette, DeKalb, Edom, George, Charles, Andrew, and Augustus, all of whom were in the 35th Georgia Infantry. From this record, it appears that there was a J. W. Moon and a Joseph Moon in Walton County, each with eight sons, and that at least 12 of the 16 young Moons served in the War.[24]

Pvt. William Harrison Morrow of F Company, one of the few 2nd Georgia troopers for whom there is a surviving photograph, in 1863 was detached as superintendent of a harness shop at the Atlanta Arsenal. In the last desperate months of the war he became a captain, 2nd Battalion State Guards infantry, and was sent to Columbus. The son of Radford E. and Mary Ann Strickland Morrow, he died on 23 August 1868. William's Chapel in Morrow, Georgia was named for him.[25]

Pvt. Reuben Mundy of F Company after the War moved to the Oakwood community in Hall County, along with three brothers and his best friend and brother-in-law, Henry Strickland. Two of the brothers remained in Hall County, but Henry and Reuben returned to Clayton County. Eventually there was a "Mundy's Mill" in Hall County and another in Clayton County. Reuben Mundy died 7 October 1912.[26]

Pvt. Robert Mundy returned to Clayton County where he lived for a time with a brother, Erasmus T. Mundy. He later married and became a successful farmer. His other brother and comrade in F Company, Reuben, apparently lived for a time in Hall County before returning to Clayton County. Their grand nephew, Erasmus' grandson Joe Mundy, served for many years as the clerk of court in Clayton County.[27]

Capt. James T. Newsome, who enlisted in G Company as a private, lived in Hawkinsville and worked for the Southern Railroad after the War. He had four sons. During the War he was captured three times, and each time managed to escape. He was present with the Regiment at the surrender.[28]

Cpl. Littleton Marion Spinks of G Company, who almost drowned in Stones River in 1862, served throughout the War and "…was never wounded, taken prisoner, nor promoted." He married Sarah F. Moore at Buena Vista, Georgia, about 1870 and they had many children. The family moved to Valley Spring in Llano County, Texas, around 1880. After Sarah's death in 1895, Spinks returned to Buena Vista and married

Fanny Thaggerty, and returned to Llano County. He died in 1926 and is buried in the Valley Spring cemetery.[29]

Pvt. Carey Jefferson Strickland, of F Company, who with brother Henry left the regiment in November of 1864 to get married, returned to his bride in Clayton County after the war.

Cpl. Henry Perry Strickland of F Company settled briefly in Hall County with his wife Mary Mundy Strickland. He returned to the family farm in Clayton County in the mid 1870's, probably upon the death of his father, Cainey. Henry and Mary had several children. "Uncle Henry," as he came to be known by his neighbors, was remembered for his good humor and physical strength. When he died on 7 November 1921, there was not even enough money to pay the undertaker's bill of $212.45. The bill included $20 for a suit, $0.75 for "sox," and $1.00 for a tie, collar, and buttons. He was buried in the Mundy family cemetery in Clayton County, a short distance from his farm.[30]

Pvt. Milsey Eli Strickland, one of three Strickland brothers in F Company, was wounded in the hand during 1863 and then captured at Fair Garden during the Knoxville Campaign in January of 1864. Like many others, he would not swear allegiance to the Union while the war still raged, so he remained a POW at Camp Douglas near Chicago until late June of 1865. He apparently returned to Pike County after the war.[31]

Pvt. James Henderson Waldrop of F Company, who had served as Clayton County's first sheriff before the war, died of unrecorded causes 11 March 1863 in Tennessee. He may have been wounded the week before in the fight at Dover. Waldrop, who was about 49 years old at the time of his death, left his widow Mary Simpson Waldrop a substantial tract of land on the Flint River.[32]

Pvt. William R. Ward of F Company served throughout the War, and later became a popular merchant in Jonesboro. He served in the Georgia House of Representatives in 1888 and 1889, and was a long-time Clayton County Commissioner and school board member. For many years he was a deacon and superintendent of the Sunday School at Jonesboro Baptist Church. He died 24 September 1906.[33]

Maj. Gen. John Austin Wharton, who commanded first a brigade and then a division which included the 2nd Georgia, did not live to see the peace. Wharton had been wounded at Shiloh and Murfreesboro, and in the spring of 1864, he was granted furlough for health reasons. On his way back to his Texas home, however, he took command of the cavalry in the Red River Campaign. On 6 April 1865, he was shot and killed by George W. Baylor, a subordinate disgruntled over his failure to receive a promotion. Although Wharton was unarmed, Baylor was acquitted of murder.[34]

Lt. Gen. Joe Wheeler met his future wife when the 2nd Georgia camped on her father's land in North Alabama after their escape from Tennessee in October of 1863. The recently widowed Mrs. Daniella Sherrod asked to meet the General, whom she remembered seeing in New York when he was a West Point cadet. After the war, Wheeler returned to Ella Sherrod in Alabama rather than his native Augusta, Georgia. They had four daughters and two sons. Wheeler served for many years as a member Alabama's Congressional delegation, and was a major general in command of the volunteer cavalry, including Colonel Teddy Roosevelt's Rough Riders, during the Spanish American War. He died in 1906 while visiting his sister in New York City.[35]

---

[1] W. C. Dodson, ed., *Campaigns of Wheeler and His Cavalry* (Jackson TN: The Guild Bindery Press) 112.

[2] Joe Mundy, recollections of family stories (Jonesboro GA).

[3] Bill and Pat Allen, family records (Marietta GA).

[4] Ibid.

[5] Stewart Sifikis, *Who Was Who in the Confederacy* (New York NY: Facts on File, Inc.) 2-4.

[6] Bill and Pat Allen, family records (Marietta GA).

[7] Robert S. Bridgers, ed., *Confederate Military History, Vol. VII* (Georgia Confederate Publishing Co.) 532.

[8] Compiled Service Records, 2nd Georgia Cavalry (Atlanta GA: Georgia Department of Archives and History).

[9] Joseph H. Moore, *History of Clayton County Georgia 1821—1983* (Atlanta GA: W. H. Wolfe Associates, 1983) 620.

[10] Bridgers, ed., *Confederate Military History, Vol. VII.*

[11] *Cuthbert Liberal Enterprise* 24 Nov. 1887 (Cuthbert GA: Randolph College Library).

[12] Moore, *History of Clayton County, Georgia,* 207.

[13] Compiled Service Records, 2nd Georgia Cavalry.

[14] Ibid. See also *Confederate Military History, Vol. VII.* 655.

[15] Sifikis, *Who Was Who in the Confederacy* 141.

[16] Personal papers, drawer 283, box 30 (Atlanta GA: Georgia Department of Archives and History).

[17] Ibid, 196.

[18] Moore, *History of Clayton County, Georgia,* 351.

[19] A. S. McCollum, *Reminiscences of Confederate Soldiers Vol. XII* (Atlanta GA: Georgia Department of Archives and History) 97-99.

[20] Bridgers, ed. *Confederate Military History, Vol VII.*

[21] Jennie Merritt Boon, "Reminiscences of My Father, Thomas Mickleberry Merritt" personal papers file, drawer 283, box 34 (Atlanta GA: Georgia Department of Archives and History).

[22] Mamie Mills Elrod, *Life as I Recall it, or Sunshine and Shadows on a Long Trek,* unpublished memoir, circa 1941.

[23] Willard Wight, ed., *Reminiscences of Confederate Soldiers, Vol. VII,* 97-99.

[24] Ibid.

[25] *Historical Bulleting No. I,* Clayton County Historical Society , May 1963. (Atlanta GA: Georgia Department of Archives and History).

[26] Joe Mundy, recollections.

[27] Ibid.

[28] Bridgers, ed., *Confederate Military History, Vol. VII,* 889.

[29] Mamie Yary, *Reminiscences of the Boys in Gray* (Dayton OH: Morningside Press, 1912).

[30] Bill Strickland, family records (Atlanta GA: Georgia Department of Archives and History).

[31] Compiled Service Records, 2nd Georgia Cavalry.

[32] Bridgers, ed., *Confederate Military History, Vol. VII,* 955.

[33] Moore, *History of Clayton County, Georgia,* 521.

[34] Sifikis, *Who Was Who in the Confederacy,* 301—302.

[35] John P. Dyer, *Shiloh to San Juan—The Life of Fightin' Joe Wheeler* (Baton Rouge LA: Louisiana State University Press, 1941).

Appendix

Roster of the 2nd Georgia Volunteer Cavlary Regiment

REGIMENTAL FIELD STAFF

Lawton, Winburn J., col., Resigned in the fall of 1862 during Kentucky Campaign. Previous service in the cavalry battalion of Cobb's Legion in the Army of Northern Virginia.

Eberhardt, J.B. "Bee," lt. col. Appears on roll at surrender 4-26-65 as present at Bennett's House near Durham Station, N.C. Also shown as captured at Augusta, Ga. 5-19-65.

Hood, Arthur, 1st lt., 3-4-62. Originally a 2nd lt. in A Company. Elected lt. col. 5-7-62, second in command of regiment under Lawton. Resigned 11-7-62, during Kentucky Campaign. Later served in Georgia militia.

Lawton, Richard F., lt & adj./capt. & adjutant. Issued clothing 3-27-64. Roll of 12-31-64 shows as detached with Gen. Iverson and AAI, probably acting adjutant.

Smith, T. S., adjutant. Captured 5-12-65 near Hartwell, Georgia.

Carter, Isaac, sgt. quartermaster sgt., transferred from H Co.

Hill, James, sgt.. assistant quartermaster sgt, transferred from E Co.

Westbrook, J. S., Shown as "a.q.s.", probably assistant quartermaster sgt.

Courtney, W. A. Shown as "a.q.s.", probably assistant quartermaster sgt.

Flynt, Thomas J. Shown as "a.c.s.", probably assistant commissary sgt.

Zellars, Simeon Shown as "a.c.s.", probably assistant commissary sgt. nsferred from I Company.

Heard, George B. Surgeon

Buffington, J. O. Acting Surgeon

Perryman , James L.D. A s s t . Surgeon, 7-62.

Shorpshire, James W. Asst Surgeon, 5-17-62. Originally in G Company.

Sutherland, Andrew J. Asst. Surgeon, 6-1-63. Clothing issued 3-27-64. Present at surrender 4-26-65. Paroled 5-3-65 Charlotte, N.C.

Hoyt, H. D. Chaplain

A COMPANY

Crews, Charles Constantine, capt., 3-6-62. Promoted to colonel in November 1862. At various times commanded the Regiment and Brigade in Wharton's, Martin's, Allen's Divisions under Wheeler. Cited for gallantry by Wheeler several times. Wounded in South Carolina during 1865 and may have been promoted to brigadier general.

Bridges, Bennett L., 1st lt. 5-7-62. Succeeded Crews as company commander and promoted to captain. Severely wounded in hip 2-4-63 Dover, Tenn. and captured. POW at Johnson's Isl. Exchanged 3-3-64. Resigned 7-28-64.

Crews, J. Fleming, jr 2nd lt., 3-4-62. Wounded at Fort Donelson 2-4-63. Present 12-63. Promoted to captain 10-27-64 and apparently succeeded Bridges as company commander. Present at surrender 4-26-65.

Trippe, John F., lt., 3-29-62. Prior service with 5th Ga. Infantry, discharged with disability. Present 2-63, 5-63. Discharged with disability 10-10-63, "chronic bronchitis affecting his voice so that he cannot be heard."

Little, Jacob A. "Jake", 1st sgt., 25 years old. Horse valued at $265. Captured 9-21-62, Lebanon Junction, Kentucky and exchanged. 6'1" dark hair, hazel eyes. Present 5-63, 6-63 as member of Wheeler's "elite batt." Roll of 5-63 shows "Reduced to ranks for incompetency & detailed by Gen. Wheeler." Left sick near Harrison's Landing on Tennessee River 10-1-63. Issued clothing 6-15-64. Wounded at Atlanta 7-22-64, died of wounds in 1864.

Jenks, R. D., 2nd sgt. Surrendered at Greensboro, N.C. 4-26-65.

Davis, James O., 3rd sgt. 5-7-62. Twenty-two years old. Wounded at Kennesaw Mountain 6-27-64 and in Cuthbert Hospital.

Davis, James L., cpl., 4-3-62. Killed 6-11-64.

Davis, L., 3rd sgt., 1906 Roster Commission record shows killed 7-21-64 at New Hope Church. (Probably killed at Bald Hill. Battle of New Hope Church was previous May and 2nd Georgia not engaged.)

Martin, Paul L., 4th sgt. Born 8-11-32. Present at surrender 4-26-65. Paroled at Charlotte 5-3-65.

Frith, Thomas, 3rd cpl. 5-4-62. Born in Stewart County 4-11-41. Captured at Lebanon Junction, Ky., 1862 and exchanged. POW record shows 5'9" gray eyes, lt. hair, lt complexion, twenty-one years old. Present–'63. Issued clothing 27 March 1864 and 15 June 1864. Present 12-31-64.

Abell, Detached as courier 11-64, 12-64.

Acree, Jackson, pvt. Detached to drive wagon 1862; in Atlanta hospital

Adkinson, Crof., pvt.

Allen, John Pope, pvt. Captured and paroled 5-65 near Athens, Ga. by forces under Gen. W. J. Palmer.

Astin, Joseph Hillman, pvt. 6-8-64. Born 2-19-28. Musician for Ga. Provost Guards 9-9-62. Bn. disbanded 6-64. Wounded 7-21-64 at Bald Hill. Died 2-24-81.

Atkinson, A. C., cpl. Present through 2-64; AWOL on roll of 12-64.

Ball, William D., pvt. 5-7-62. Horse valued at $250. Captured 9-21-62 Lebanon Junction, Ky. Died 10-22-62 from diarrhea as POW at Cairo, Ill.

Bamson, Robert, pvt. 5-7-62. Detached as blacksmith. Present at surrender 4-26-65, Salisbury, N.C.

Barry, Osgood A., pvt. 3-3-62. Promoted to sgt. 7-10-64. Present at surrender 4-26-65.

Benton, James W., pvt. 5-7-62. Present on all records to surrender 4-26-65. Paroled 5-3-65, Charlotte, N.C.

Bethea, James, pvt. 1862.

Black, Emanuel M., pvt. 3-4-62. Roll of 12-31-64 shows on detached duty with S.W.R.R.

Blackburn, William R., pvt. or sgt. 5-7-62. Discharged due to chronic enlargement of prostate gland.

Blackshear, James J., pvt. 5-7-62. Captured 9-21-62, Lebanon Junction, Ky. POW at Camp Chase, Ohio. Twenty-three years old, 5'10" blue eyes.

Boon, Nicholas, pvt. 5-7-62. Forty-nine years old. Horse valued at $225. "In prison at Tullahoma, Tenn." circa 2-63. Died of unknown causes during 1863.

Bray, R. T., pvt. Captured & paroled 5-8-65 at Hartwell, Ga. by forces under Gen. S. B. Brown.

Bridewell, W. P., pvt. 5-7-62. Present at surrender 4-26-65 Salisbury, N.C.

Bridges, William H. Sr., sgt. 2-4-62. Elected sgt. 7 May 62: AWOL on roll of 12-63. Shown as pvt and on detached service roll of 12-64.

Bowden, William, pvt.

Broadwater, James H., pvt. 5-5-62. Prior service with Ga. militia. Present through 12-31-64.

Brown, David S., pvt. 3-4-62. Detailed 3-28-63. 2nd Lt. Resigned 11-25-64.

Bryan, F., pvt. 8-1-64. Present at surrender 4-26-65, Salisbury, N.C.

Busbee, John, pvt., 1862. Captured 9-21-62 Lebanon Junction, Ky. POW record shows twenty-two years old, 5'8". Exchanged. Clothing issued 12-16-64.

Camp, F., pvt. 1862

Cantrell, Wiliam W., pvt. Captured at Tompkinsville, Monroe Co. Ky. POW at Camp Chase. Transferred to Ft. Delaware 7-63.

Capps, Amos, cpl.

Carter, James H. pvt. 5-7-62. Twenty-seven years old. Horse valued at $175. Detailed as waggoner 5-63, 6-63, 11-63, 12-63.

Carter, M. G., pvt. 7-8-64. Enlisted Decatur, Ga. Deserter on roll of 9-64.

Cheshire, S. T., cpl. 5-7-62. Twenty-three years old. Horse valued at $150. Present 5-63. Present at surrender 4-26-65.

Clements, C.L., pvt. Captured & paroled 5-8-65 Athens, Ga. by forces under Gen. W. J. Palmer.

Coleman, Elisha, pvt. 3-15-62

Conner, Stephen F.V., pvt. 4-5-62. Captured 9-21-62 Lebanon Junction, Ky. POW at Camp Chase, Ohio. Transferred to Cairo, Ill. for exchange. 5'7", hazel eyes, lt. hair, lt. complexion. Back with regiment—issued clothing 3-27-63.

Crawford, Samuel, pvt. Surrendered at Augusta, Ga 5-19-65.

Cunningham, C., pvt. Captured & paroled at Athens, Ga. 5-8-65.

Davison, William, pvt. Captured 9-12-63 at Morgan Co. Ky. Remark on roll, "Belongs to Morgan's Command."

Dixon, Henry, pvt. 5-/-62. Thirty years old. Horse valued at $250. Died 2-26-63 in Tenn.

Dixon, Morris, pvt. 5-7-62. Horse valued at $150 and owned by Inferior Court of Randolph County. Issued clothing 3-27-63. Detached as forager 5-63, 6-63. Present on roll of 12-31-64. Present at surrender 4-26-65 paroled at Salisbury, N. C.

Dodd, F. M., pvt. 5-27-64. Absent sick 11-64, 12-64.

Dunn, Jacob W., pvt. 5-7-64. Captured 9-21-62 Lebanon Junction, Ky: POW at Cairo, Ill. Exchanged 9-29-62.

Roll of 5-1-63 shows sick at reserve camp. 5'7", hazel eyes, dark hair, thirty-three years old.

Eberhardt, J., pvt. Captured 5-8-65 Athens, Ga. by forces under Gen. W. J. Palmer.

Fagan, Edward, pvt. 5-7-62. Horse valued at $175. Present 5-63 roll. Wounded and apparently captured 1-27-64.

Federal record shows "admitted to Div. CC with gunshot wound in thigh." Listed as "Rebel" 34 yrs old from Cuthbert, Ga.

Fleisheim, Sigmund, pvt.

Foster, James A., pvt. 4-22-62. Thirty-one years old. Horse valued at $250. Detailed to hospital 4-63. Absent at Augusta hospital 12-31-64.

Fountain, L., pvt. Substitute for Wiley Jones. Killed at Ft. Donelson (Dover) 1862.

Frith, Frank, pvt. 1862. Captured at Lebanon Junction, Ky. 1862 and exchanged. Killed in action 1862.

Fuller William H., pvt. 3-15-62. Forty-three years old. Horse valued at $200, and owned by Inferior Court of Randolph County. Present 5-63. Absent sick 12-31-63. Present 12-31-64.

Gardner, George H., pvt. 5-9-62. Absent with brigade wagons. Issued clothing 3-27-64 and 6-15-64. Roll of 12-31-64 shows in hospital in Columbus. Furloughed 2-65. Surrendered 5-10-65 Tallahassee, Fla.

Gardner, Hilsey or Hillary, pvt. 1862.

Gardner, John, pvt. 3-4-62. Twenty-eight years old. Horse owned by David Bryant. Absent sick in hospital 5-63. Absent sick through 12-31-64.

Gay, Elias, pvt. 3-15-62. Twenty-eight years old. Horse valued at $150. Present 5-63. Absent sick 12-31-63. Deserted 8-10-64.

Gormley, William Patrick. pvt. 8-1-63. Captured 1-27-64 Sevierville, Tenn. Federal record shows captured at Pigeon River, Tenn. POW at Camp Chase, Ohio & Rock Island Barracks, Ill. Eighteen years old when released 6-18-65.

Green, Alex, pvt. 1862.

Green, John A., pvt. 3-29-62. May be same as Alex Green above. Thirty-five years old. Apparently among those captured at Lebanon Junction, Ky. Records show on roll of prisoners exchanged 10-25-62 at Vicksburg. Horse valued at $185. Present 5-63. Detached 2-12-64 as tailor for regiment. Absent, sutler for regiment, 12-31-64. Present at surrender 4-26-65, paroled 5-3-65 Charlotte.

Griffin, Hezekiah H., pvt. 3-4-62. Twenty-seven years old. Horse valued at $175 and owned by Seaborne A. Smith. Absent sick in Atlanta hospital 5-63. Absent with brigade wagons 12-31-63. Issued clothing 6-15-64. Absent, at Cuthbert hospital 12-31-64.

Griffin, J. A., pvt. 4-10-64. Absent at Cuthbert hospital 12-31-64.

Griffin, Richard J., pvt. 62.

Gwinn, G. C., pvt. 5-1-64.

Hamer, James R., pvt. 3-4-62. Twenty-one years old. Horse valued at $200, and owned by Charles C. Crews. Present 5-63. Absent with brigade wagons in Ga. 2-12-64. Present at surrender 4-26-65. Paroled 5-3-65 at Charlotte, N.C.

Harden, R. L., pvt. 10-1-64. Enlisted at Gadsden, Ala. by Lt. Moody. "Absent on detached service, dismounted" 12-31-64.

Hardin, Benjamin F., pvt. 4-28-62. Thirty-two years old. Horse valued at $225. Present 5-63. Absent sick 2-64 & 12-31-64. Paroled 5-23-65 Albany, Ga.

Harper, Elias, pvt. 1862. Shown as sixty-three years old at enlistment. Horse valued at $225.

Harper, Wiliam E., pvt. 4-25-62. Died in Atlanta hospital 4-28-63. Buried Oakland Cemetery.

Hillhouse, Richard Henry, pvt. 3-4-62. Thirty-two years old. Horse valued at $200. "Absent detailed as nurse at Rome hospital" 2-12-64.

Hix, John,

Jarrett, F., pvt. Absent sick furlough 11-64, 12-64. Surrendered 5-19-65 Tallahassee, Fla. Paroled 5-23-65.

Jenks, Robert D., pvt. 3-4-62. Thirty-seven years old. Horse valued at $250. Captured 9-21-62 Lebanon Junction, Ky. Exchanged 9-29-62. Dark hair and eyes.

Jernigan, Joshua, pvt. 1862

Jernigan, John R., pvt. 3-24-62. Twenty-five years old. Horse valued at $165 and owned by Capt Charles C. Crews.

Johnson, John C., pvt. 5-3-62. Forty-six years old. Horse valued at $275. Prior service 9th Regiment Ga. militia. Present 5-63, "furnished own gun." Roll of 12-31-63 shows detached as reg. blacksmith. Clothing issued 3-27-64. AWOL 12-31-64.

Jones, Abner F., pvt. 1862. Horse valued at $250. Present 11-64, 12-64. Paroled at Charlotte 5-3-65 (indicating he was present at the surrender 4-26-65).

Jones, Frank, pvt. 1862. Killed at Griswoldville, Ga. 11-22-64.

Jones, F. C., pvt. 5-3-64. Present 12-31-64.

Jones, James M., Captured 5-8-65 near Athens, Ga. by forces under Gen. W .J. Palmer.

Jones, Wiley, pvt. 1862.

Jordan, Alex H., pvt. 1862. Seventeen years old. Horse valued at $275. Captured 9-21-62 Lebanon Junction, Ky. 6' gray eyes, lt. hair. Exchanged and present through 1863. Paroled near Columbia, S.C. 4-65.

Jordan, James J., pvt. 1862. Horse valued at $200. Present through 1863. Clothing issued 3-27-64. AWOL 12-64.

Langford, William H., pvt. Captured 11-25-63 near Missionary Ridge. POW at Rock Island Barracks.

Lessner, Drury M., pvt. 3-8-62. Fifty-three years old. Horse valued at $165 and owned by Inferior Court of Randolph Co. Born in Elbert Co. 5'8" dark hair, gray eyes. Discharged with disability 11-18-62, "incapable of performing the duties of a soldier because of hemorrhoids & age, being 54 years old."

Leveritt, Thomas J., pvt. 3-29-62. Thirty-two years old. Horse valued at $225. Bugler. Roll of 5-13-63 shows with Whites Battery Horse Artillery. Arrested for desertion 10-25-63 at Adairsville, Ga.

Leviner, Enoch J., pvt. 3-9-62. Forty-six years old. Horse valued at $212 and owned by Inferior Court of Randolph County. Absent sick 6-30 through 12-31-63. Captured 12-4-64 at Waynesboro, Ga. Exchanged 2-18-65. In Danville, Va. hospital with pneumonia 4-7-65. Buried in Greenwood Cemetery at Cuthbert, Ga.

Lewis, W. C., pvt. Captured 5-8-65 near Athens, Ga. by forces under Gen. W. J. Palmer.

Little, Joseph, pvt. 4-22-62. Twenty-three years old. 1906 Roster commission shows "Discharged with disability" in 1863. Appears on roster of soldiers surrendered by Gen. Sam Jones, CSA, 5-10-65 at Tallahassee, Fla. Paroled 5-18-65 Albany, Ga.

Lockett, Abner "Ab", pvt. 3-4-62. Twenty-two years old. Horse valued at $200. Wounded at Stones River 12-31-62. Roster commission shows "Drowned in French Broad River in 1863." Muster roll shows drowned in Holston River near Knoxville, Tenn. 11-3-63.

Mattox, J.H.F, pvt. 5-13-64. Enlisted at Decatur, Ga. Absent as scout 11-64 and 12-64.

McDonald, James J., pvt. 3-4-62. Seventeen years old. Horse valued at $200. Present 2-63, 5-63. On furlough 2-12-64. Issued clothing 3-27-64. Present at surrender 4-26-65 Salisbury, N.C. Paroled at Charlotte 5-3-65.

McGuire, W., pvt. 10-1-64. Enlisted at Gadsden, Ala. Absent, dismounted and on detailed service 12-64.

Mellen, J. M., pvt. Captured 5-8-65 near Athens, Ga. by forces under Gen. W. J. Palmer.

Melton, A. Jackson, pvt. 3-4-62. Twenty-five years old. Horse valued at $230 and owned by Inferior Court of Randolph Co. Present 2-63, 5-63. Detached to drive brigade wagon 2-12-64. Issued clothing 3-27-64. AWOL 12-64. Present at surrender 4-26-65. Paroled 5-3-65 Charlotte, N.C.

Melton, Richard, pvt. 3-4-62. Eighteen years old. Horse valued at $175. Roll of 5-1-63 shows him with Whites Battery. Present on roll of 12-31-64. Surrendered at Augusta, Ga. 5-65.

Millirons, Henry, pvt. 3-4-62. Twenty-six years old. Horse valued at $150. Captured 9-21-62 at Lebanon Junction, Ky. & exchanged 9-29-62. Present 2-63, 5-63. Absent on roll of 2-12-64 "sick in hospital" 5'10" dark hair, hazel eyes.

Millirons, Leroy, pvt. 3-4-62. Thirty years old. Horse valued at $150. Furloughed thirty days from hospital in Rome, Ga. 4-21-63. Absent sick at hospital 6 through 12-63. Issued clothing 3-27-64.

Mize, Parson L., pvt. 3-4-62. Forty-two years old. Horse valued at $225 and owned by Inferior Court of Randolph Co. Shown with White's Battery 1863. Roll of 12-31-64 shows "absent detailed in hospital."

Moody, John R., pvt. 3-15-62. Thirty years old. Horse valued at $175. Prior service with 7th Reg. Ga. militia. Roll of 5-63 shows "present at reserve camp." Roll of 2-12-64 shows absent, detailed as nurse in Atlanta hospital. Roll of 12-64 shows absent in Cuthbert hospital.

Moody, Terrell, pvt. 3-4-62. Twenty-eight years old. Horse valued at $150. Detailed as a carpenter, 5-1-63 to 6-30-63. Present 2-12-64. Clothing issued 3-27-64. Present at surrender 4-26-65. Paroled Charlotte, N.C. 5-3-65.

Moody, William G., pvt. 3-4-62. Twenty-six years old. Horse valued at $225. Present 6-63, 1st sgt. 4-30-63. In Alexander Hospital, Atlanta during 8-63, employed as nurse. Jr 2nd lt. 7-24-64. Clothing issued 3-27-64. Present at surrender 4-26-65. Paroled 5-3-65 at Charlotte.

Moore, Francis, pvt. 7-13-63. Clothing issued 6-15-64.

Moore, Frank, pvt. 1862. May be same as Francis Moore above. Captured 5-8-65 near Athens, Ga. by forces under Gen. W. J. Palmer.

Morgan, Carl, pvt. 5-5-62. Twenty-nine years old. Horse valued at $125. "Deserted" 7-25-62.

Morgan, Isaiah M., pvt. 5-5-62. Twenty-four years old. Horse valued at $200 and owned by Col. C. C. Crews. "Deserted" 7-25-62.

Murray, W. D., pvt. 6-16-64. Present at surrender 4-26-65. Paroled Charlotte 5-3-65.

Murray, William M., pvt. 5-7-62. Twenty-three years old. Horse valued at $175. Shown as "Died at Bardstown, Ky. Oct. 1862." Apparently wounded and captured but not killed at Bardstown, 10-10-62. Paroled after taking oath of allegiance. On sick furlough 12-31-63, 11-64, 12-64.

Nevison, G. H., pvt. Captured 5-8-65 near Athens, Ga. by forces under Gen. W. J. Palmer.

Pennington, James, pvt. 5-2-62. Thirty-one years old. Horse valued at $175. Roll of 5-63 shows "Deserted Jan 5, 1862. Information received since that he died Jan. 17, 1863." U.S. record shows captured at Stones River and died as POW 1-17-63, from pneumonia near Murfreesboro.

Pittman, Enoch W., pvt. 1862. Twenty-five years old. Present 2-63, 5-63, 6-63, 12-63. 2nd sgt/ 5-9-62. Clothing issued 3-27-64. Present on detached service 12-64. Surrendered 5-10-65 Tallahassee, Fla. Paroled 5-18-65 Albany, Ga.

Powel, Robert H., pvt. 5-4-62. Twenty-three years old. Horse valued at $185. Roll of 5-63 shows "Absent, detached to Gen'l Wheeler's Elite Corps." Present 6-63, 12-63. Clothing issued 3-27-64. Present at surrender 4-26-65. Paroled 5-3-65.

Pitts, A. L., pvt. 7-8-64. Present 12-64.

Pyle, James S., pvt./4th Sgt 4-21-62. Thirty-one years old. Horse valued at $200. Roll of 5-63 shows sick in hospital. Present 6-63, 12-63. Clothing issued 3-27-64. Killed in action near Marietta, Ga. 6-2-64.

Ridley, Robert, pvt. 1862.

Rine, J., pvt. Captured 5-8-65 near Athens, Ga. by forces under Gen. W. J. Palmer.

Ruff or Roff, Freeman T., pvt. 3-15-62. Forty-six years old. Horse valued at $285 and owned by Inferior Court of Randolph County.

Ryan, R. P., pvt. Roll of 2-12-64 shows "arrested in Oct. 1863 in N. Ga. by P. Guard & assigned to Lee's Army."

Savage, C. W., pvt. 6-3-64. Roll of 6-64 shows "Deserted June 3, 1864."

Sexton, H. W., pvt. 6-8-64. Roll of 11-64 shows absent as scout. Roll of 12-64 shows "Present on detached service."

Smarr, John Reid, pvt. 5-3-62. 2nd sgt. 4-20-63. Present 6-63, 12-63. Clothing issued 3-27-64. 1906 Record shows wounded 7-21-64 New Hope Church. (Probably wounded at Bald Hill. New Hope Church battle took place previous May.)

Smith, George D., pvt. 6-19-63. Paroled Charlotte, N.C. 5-3-65, indicating presence at the surrender, 4-26-65.

Smith, Tolbert, pvt. 1862.

Smith, T. J., pvt. May be same as Tolbert Smith above. Present at surrender 4-26-65. Paroled 5-3-65 Charlotte.

Taunton, G. Washington, pvt. 5-28-64. Roll of 12-64 shows absent, in hospital at Cuthbert, Ga.

Taylor, Robert B., pvt. 5-4-62. 5th sgt. 5-9-62. 3rd sgt. 1st sgt. 8-1-64. Sixteen years old at enlistment. Horse valued at $300. Present 2-63, 6-63. Absent 2-24-64. Present 11-64, 12-64. Present at surrender 4-26-65 Salisbury, N.C. Paroled 5-3-65, Charlotte, N.C.

Thorington, Henry, pvt. 1862. Discharged with disability in 1862.

Thornton, Henry J., pvt. 5-4-62. Twenty-eight years old. Horse valued at $200 and owned by Inferior Court of Randolph County. Discharged 5-6-63.

Thompson, James R., pvt. 3-4-62. Twenty-seven years old. Horse valued at $250. Discharged 3-24-63.

Thompson, William, pvt. 1862. Bugler, twenty-three years old. Horse valued at $225. "Lost at Murfreesboro in 1862."

Trippe, James M., pvt. 4-26-62. Forty-eight years old. Horse valued at $250. Substitute for Sigmund Fleisheim. Present 2-63, 5-63. Sent to hospital 5-63.

Turner, Simeon Pierce, pvt. 3-4-62. Twenty-eight years old. Horse valued at $275. Present 2-63, 5-63, 12-63. Present 11-64, 12-64. Present at surrender 4-26-65. Paroled 5-3-65 at Charlotte, N.C. Died 11-10-1920; Buried at Shellman, Ga.

Veasey, Benjamin F., pvt. 3-4-62. Thirty-nine years old. Horse valued at $150. Roll of 5-63 shows "present, at reserve camp sick." Paid 6-11-63.

Verner, H. F., pvt. 6-8-64. Present 11-64, 12-64.

Watkins, Ab, pvt. 3-4-62. Thirty-six years old. Horse valued at $250 and owned by C. C. Crews.

Watkins, James, pvt. Captured 2-1-63 near Franklin, Tenn.

West, Duvan L., pvt. 4-30-62. Thirty-two years old. Horse valued at $150. "Died of typhoid pneumonia at Shelbyville,Tenn." 4-11-63.

West, David D. L., pvt. 4-30-62. Twenty years old. Horse valued at $225. Wounded 8-11-62 White Oak Creek, Tenn. Present 2-63, 5-63. Roll of 2-18-64 shows absent, "in arrest in Ga." Clothing issued 3-27-64. Roll of 12-64 shows absent at hospital. Present at surrender 4-26-65. Paroled 5-3-65 Charlotte, N.C.

West, W., pvt. Captured 5-15-64, Resaca, Ga. U.S. record shows enlisted in U.S. Navy.

Whitman, Abram, pvt. 1862, thirty-one years old. Horse valued at $185. Present at reserve camp sick, 5-63. At hospital sick 2-12-64. Absent sick 12-64.

Willett, Peter, pvt. 4-21-62. Thirty-eight years old. Horse valued at $150. Substitute for Wiley Jones. Died 1-6-63.

Williams, Joseph W., pvt. 3-4-62. Twenty-five years old. Horse valued at $200 and owned by Inferior Court of Randolph County. Roll of 2-63 shows "Deserted" 8-7-62.

Winter, B. G., pvt. Captured 5-19-65, Augusta, Ga.

Yates, William, pvt. 6-1-64. "Deserted" 6-1-64.B Company

Lawton, W. J., capt. Elected colonel and regimental commander prior to 5-62. (See regimental staff roster)

Wright, G. J., 1st lt.

Marshall, J. F., 2nd lt.

Canfield, C. H., 2nd lt.

Parham, Robert Stith 3rd lt. Apparently from Meriwether County

Briscoe, E. B., pvt. 5-62. Surrendered 4-65 Salisbury, N.C.

Collins, Francis M., Pvt. 4-23-62. Eighteen years old. Horse valued at $120. Present 5-15-63, 6 through 12-63. Clothing issued 3-27-64 and 6-15-64. Present 11-64, 12-64. Captured 5-8-65 near Athens, Ga. by forces under Gen.

W. J. Palmer.

Davis, W. A., pvt.

Dias, Abraham, captured 12-14-63, Cassville, Va.

Drake, James G.

Estes, John H., pvt./ cpl Captured 9-1-62 Cynthiana, Ky. POW at Camp Chase, Ohio. Exchanged 8-25-62. Captured 8-2-64 Atlanta. Died 3-10-65 of diarrhea. 25 yrs old, 5'7", dark hair.

Evanson, W.J., pvt. Captured 5-8-65 Anderson, S.C.

Finlayson, J. H., pvt. 3-63. Captured & paroled 4-16-65, Macon, Ga. Died 1912, Wilcox County.

Fowler, F. A., pvt. Captured & paroled 5-8-65 near Athens, Ga. by forces under Gen. W. J. Palmer.

Harper, J. M., pvt. Captured 5-23-65 Greenville, S.C. Paroled at Hartwell, Ga.

Hays, Arch A., pvt. 9-64. Served until surrender. Captured 5-65 between Augusta and Athens, Ga.

Lewis, W. H., Captured Lincoln Co. Ky. (Stanford)

Loggins, T. J., pvt. 7-64.

Maxwell, H. M.

McIntyre, D. C.

Michael, J. M., pvt. 5-62. Surrendered 4-65 Salisbury, N.C. Died 1912 Walton Co., Ga.

Neely, W. D. pvt. Captured 5-8-65 near Athens, Ga. by forces under Gen. W. J. Palmer.

Nooble, J. P., pvt. Captured 5-8-65 near Athens, Ga. by forces under Gen. W. J. Palmer.

Nooble, William, pvt. Captured 5-8-65 near Athens, Ga. by forces under w. J. Palmer.

Rodgers, W. C., pvt. Captured 5-8-65 near Athens, Ga. by forces under Gen. W. J. Palmer.

Taylor, Lemiel, pvt. 3-4-62. Surrendered 5-10-65 Tallahassee. Paroled 5-19-65, Thomasville, Ga. Described as 5'10" blue eyes, light hair, dark complexion.

Wallace, W. B., pvt. Surrendered 5-18-65 Augusta, Ga.

Winter, John, pvt. U.S. record shows "Rebel deserter, came into our lines near Portsmouth."

Williams, H. D.

C COMPANY

Mayo, James E., capt. 3-4-62. maj. 4-1-63. Twenty-four years old. Horse valued at $325. Prior service 2nd lt. Co D Cobbs Legion Ga. Cavalry, 8-10-61 to 12-30-61. Promoted to regimental commander. Wounded at Atlanta 7-21-64. "Absent, wounded" 12-31-64. Paroled 5-10-65 Albany, Ga.

Twitty, Peter W., 1st. lt. 5-7-62. capt. Prior service jr. 2nd lt in 18th Ga. Infantry, 5-61 through 12-'61. Thirty-two years old. Horse valued at $225. Present 2-63, 5-63. Apparently succeeded Mayo as company commander. Captured 1-27-64 Sevierville, Tenn. Released at Fort Delaware 6-16-65. Described as 5'7" blue eyes, dark hair, light complexion.

Hood, W. C., capt. Apparently succeeded Twitty as company commander. Surrendered 5-19-65 near Augusta, Ga.

Roberts, John Thomas, 2nd lt. 3-4-62. 1st lt. Twenty-three years old. Horse valued at $200. On sick furlough 2-12-64. Clothing issued 3-27-64. Acting adjutant at surrender, 4-26-65. Paroled 5-3-65 Charlotte,N.C.

deGraffenreid, Christopher T., jr 2nd lt. 3-4-62. Horse valued at $250. Detailed as commissary 12-63. Issued clothing 3-27-64. Paroled 5-3-65 Charlotte.

Heath, James M., 1st sgt. 3-4-62. Twenty-six years old. Horse valued at $225. Present 5-63. Died in Tenn. in 1863.

Hill, John B., 2nd sgt. 1st sgt. Twenty-two years old. Horse valued at $165. Wounded in Tennessee Valley in 1862. Present 12-63. Clothing issued 3-27-64. Present 5-64. Wounded 12-4-64 Waynesboro, Ga. "In hospital wounded" on roll of 12-31-64.

Odom, Ridding or Redden J., 3rd sgt. 5-7-62. Transferred to Captain Benjamin Hall's Co., Baker Reserves, 8-13-63.

Wilson, John, 3rd sgt. 5-19-62/2nd Lt. Twenty-eight years old. Horse valued at $200. Horse killed 8-15-62. Present 2-63 through 5-63 as 2nd Lt. Present 11-63 through 12-63. Clothing issued 3-27-64.

Keaton, Burrell D., 5th sgt. 4-18-62. Thirty-three years old. Horse valued at $225. Wounded at Cumberland Gap, Tenn.

Spence, Thomas, sgt. 5-7-62. Twenty-five years old. Horse valued at $175. Present 2-63 through 5-63. Shown variously as "died" 2-12-63 or 2-18-63.

Huett , Armstead P., 2nd cpl. 4-17-62/1st cpl .Twenty-five years old. Horse valued at $225. Present 4-26-65. Sick in hospital 5-63. Present 12-63. Issued clothing 3-27-64. Present 5-64, 12-64. Present at surrender 4-26-65. Paroled 5-3-65 Charlotte, N.C.

Bryant, J. B., 3rd cpl. 3-62.

Mathis, Joel V., 4th cpl./pvt. Eighteen years old. Horse valued at $165. Present 5-63, 6 through 12-63 as pvt. Issued clothing 3-27-64. Present 5-64 through 12-64.

Odom, Joseph W. cpl. 3-4-62. Appears only on roll of 5-7-62.

Adams, J. Arch, pvt. 4-64. Surrendered 4-26-65 Greensboro, N.C.

Barrett, W. W., pvt. Enlisted Cherokee Co., Ga. Captured Craig Co.,Va. 12-15-63. POW Camp Chase, transferred to Delaware & exchanged 3-7-65. Described on POW roll as "farmer 29 yrs old, 5'9" blue eyes."

Beck, Simeon, pvt. 5-7-62. Enlisted in Mitchell Co. Ga. Discharged prior to 5-15-63.

Beckman, Charles, pvt. Substitute for J. G. Montgomery. Deserted prior to 5-15-63.

Bennett, Thomas J., pvt. 5-7-62. Dougherty Co. Absent on roll of 5-63, apparently with White's Battery through 12-64.

Bennett, Thomas R. or S., pvt. 4-24-62. Mitchell Co. Surrendered to Gen. McCook at Tallahassee, Fla. 5-10-65. Paroled 6-1-65 Albany, Ga.

Bentley, William, pvt. 1-5-63 Middleton, Tenn. Substitute for William Dennard. Present 12-31-64. Present at surrender 4-26-65.

Blaylock, Samuel H., pvt. Captured 6-27-63 at Manchester, Tenn. POW at Camp Chase, Ohio. Transferred to Camp Douglas, Chicago, Ill. Died 1-1-65 from smallpox.

Borland, John P. H., pvt. 5-7-62. Baker Co. Sick in Atlanta hospital 2-12-64.

Brimberry, Benjamin F., pvt. 4-23-62. Present through 12-63. Roll of 12-64 shows detailed at Macon, Ga. Furloughed 30 days 1-7-63 on approval of "surgeon of the post." Surrendered 5-10-65 Tallahassee, Fla. Paroled Albany, Ga. 5-22-65.

Brimberry, Marion F., pvt/ 4-23-62. Detailed to quartermaster depot at Macon, Ga 8-10-62 according to roll of 12-31-64.

Bryan, William G., pvt. 2-15-62. Dougherty Co. Detailed to assist commissary on roll of 5-15-63 since 2-21-63. Present at surrender 4-26-65 Salisbury, N. C. Surrendered and paroled 5-19-65 at Augusta, Ga.

Busbee, William Jasper, pvt. 4-18-62/ 2nd cpl. Wounded 12-29-62. Wounded and in hospital on roll of 12-31-64.

Butler, Daniel K., pvt. 4-26-62. Also shown as serving in K Company. Horse valued at $2000. In hospital with pneumonia 1 & 2—63. Shown present through '63 and '64, but also appears on POW roll 5-26-63. Place of capture shown variously as Middleton, Willsborough, Millenburg, Middletown, Tenn. Apparently exchanged. Present at surrender and paroled 5-3-65 Charlotte, N. C.

Buford, Homer, pvt. 5-7-62. Thirty years old. Horse valued at $160.

Butler, Jackson, pvt. 3-4-62, Baker Co. In hospital with pneumonia 1-63, 2-63. With brigade wagons 2-12-64. Detailed with battery 11-64, 12-64.

Chambers, William M., pvt. Cherokee Co., Ga. Captured 12-15-63 Craig Co. Va. POW Camp Chase, Ohio. Transferred to Fort Delaware & exchanged 3-7-65.

Cochran, Edward D., pvt. 3-4-62. Horse valued at $250. Issued clothing 5-5-63 and 8-19-63. Roll of 12-31-63 shows him "on extra daily duty" and "Died in Tenn. during the war."

Cochran, George W. pvt./sgt 4-21-62. Horse valued at $235. Present 2 through 5—63. Present as pvt 5-64. Issued clothing as pvt 6-15-64. Shown as AWOL 12-64, but also shown as sgt on detached duty during this time. Surrendered 5-10-65. Tallahassee, Fla. Paroled 5-16-65 Albany, Ga.

Cochran, John L., pvt. 4-21-62. Dougherty Co. Present 2 through 5-63. Absent sick 12-63. Issued clothing 3-27-64. AWOL 8 through 10-64. Surrendered 5-10-65 Tallahassee, Fla. Paroled 5-15-65 Albany, Ga.

Coker, John H., pvt. 6-15-63. Substitute for Jos. Odum. Present 2-5-63.

Coker, John, pvt. 1-5-62 or 63. Enlisted in Middleton, Tenn. Issued clothing 3-27-64. Present 5-64. Present at surrender 4-26-65. Paroled 5-3-65 Charlotte, N.C. May be same as John Coker above.

Collins, Daniel, pvt. Captured 6-27-63, Manchester, Tenn. U.S. record shows captured at Shelbyville 6-30-63.

Cumbie, Barnabas, pvt. 5-7-62. Twenty-eight years old. Horse valued at $200.

Cumbie, James B., pvt. 5-7-62. Thirty-four years old. Horse valued at $215.

Dasher, Horace C., pvt. 4-24-62. Horse valued at $150. Absent sick 6 through 12 -63. Appointed hospital steward. Discharged by special order #286 12-2-64. Elected Ordinary of Mitchell Co.

Dennard, J. William, pvt. 3-8-62. Discharged, furnished William Bentley as substitute.

Dixon, Marshall Thomas, pvt. 4-21-62. Mitchell Co. Twenty-four years old. Horse valued at $175. Present 5-15-63.

Dixon, Morris, pvt. 3-4-62. Twenty-five years old. Horse valued at $150 and owned by Inferior Court of Randolph County. Present through 5-63. On detached service 6-30-63 through 12-31-63, as forage agent. Issued clothing 3-27-64. Present 12-31-64. Present at surrender 4-26-65. Paroled 5-3-65 Charlotte, N.C.

Dowse, John, pvt. 3-4-62. Forty-three yrs old. Died in 1865.

Duke, J. L., pvt. Captured 5-8-65 Athens, Ga.

Ellison, William, pvt. May have served in 2nd Bn Georgia Infantry.

Engles, William G., 1st cpl. /pvt 5-7-62. Twenty-five years old. Horse valued at $225. Reduced to pvt, 12-31-63, extra duty. Issued clothing 3-11-64, 3-27-64. On roll of 12-31-64, absent sick in hospital since 10-10-64.

Faircloth, Adam B., sgt. 7-21-62. Prior service 51st Ga. Infantry. Present through '63. Present 12-31-64. Present 4-26-65 at surrender. Paroled 5-3-65.

Faircloth, George Washington, pvt. 7-21-62. Born 1844. Prior service 51st Ga. Infantry. Surrendered 5-10-65 Tallahassee, Fla. Paroled 5-20-65 Bainbridge.

Faircloth, Green B., pvt. 4-18-62. Thirty-four years old. Horse valued at $225. Absent sick 5-15-63. Present 6-30 through 12-31-63. Issued clothing 3-27-64. Surrendered 5-10-65 Tallahassee, paroled 5-20-65 Bainbridge, Ga.

Faircloth, Redding or Redden, pvt. 4-18-62.   Fifteen years old. Horse valued at $175. Present through 12-31-63. Issued clothing 3-27-64 & 6-15-64. Present 12-31-64.   Surrendered   5-10-65 Tallahassee, paroled 5-20-65.

Gist, pvt. 1862, Bainbridge, Ga.

Gray, Reden, pvt. 4-62.

Gray, Thomas S., pvt. 3-4-62. Thirty-four years old. Horse valued at $25. Present through 12-63. Issued clothing 3-27-64. Present 12-31-64. Present at surrender 4-26-65. Paroled 5-3-65, Charlotte.

Green, Wilson D., pvt. 5-1-62. Twenty-three years old. Horse valued at $225. Captured 12-27-62 Nolensville, Tenn. and apparently exchanged. Absent 5-63. Detailed with White's Battery 12-31-63. Surrendered 5-10-65 Tallahassee, Fla. Paroled 5-17-65 at Albany, Ga.

Hall, Charles M., pvt. 3-4-62. Eighteen years old. Absent with brigade wagons in Ga. 12-31-63. Issued clothing 3-27-64. Present 5-64. Issued clothing 6-15-64. Present at surrender 4-26-65. Paroled 5-3-65 Charlotte, N.C.

Hall, Holcombe Henry, pvt. 4-20-62. Thirty-three years old. Horse valued at $200. Present 5-63. Pension record shows wounded in Ky. in 1863 (probably should be 1862). Present 12-63. Issued clothing 3-27-64, 6-15-64. Present 12-31-64. On furlough at end of war. Surrendered 5-10-65, Tallahassee, Fla. Paroled 5-15-65 Albany, Ga.

Hall, John H., pvt. 4-19-62. Thirty-three years old. Last on roll 5-15-63.

Hall, Samuel C., pvt. 4-21-62. Twenty-five years old. Horse valued at $200.

Hatcher, Leonard J., pvt./cpl. 1864. Surrendered 5-10-65. Paroled 5-22-65 Albany, Ga.

Holt, James R., pvt. 3-18-62. Twenty-nine years old. Horse valued at $175. Present 5-63, 12-63, 5-64. Admitted to hospital sick 11-27-64. Present at surrender 4-26-65. Paroled 5-3-65, Charlotte, N.C.

Hughes, Edward, pvt. 3-18-62. Thirty-three years old. Horse valued at $150. Present 5-63, 12-63. Issued clothing 3-27-64. Present 5-64, 12-64.   Surrendered   5-10-65   at Tallahassee.   Paroled   5-20-65, Bainbridge, Ga.

Hughes, James R., pvt.

Hughes, Joseph R., pvt. Captured 6-27-63 Manchester, Tenn. POW at Camp Chase, Ohio. Transferred to Ft. Delaware. Federal record shows "Joined the US Service" 2-1-64.

Hunt, D. C., cpl. Captured 5-18-65, Hartwell, Ga. by forces under Gen. S. B. Brown.

Johnson, George R., pvt. Twenty-three years old. Captured 12-15-63 Craig Co., Va. POW at Camp Chase, Ohio. Transferred 3-17-64 to Ft. Delaware. Paroled 2-65. Received at Boulware & Cox Wharves, James River, Va. 3-10-65. POW record shows 5'6" gray eyes, brown hair.

Johnson, James D., pvt. 3-4-62. Horse valued at $225. Detailed with White's Battery from 12-15-62 to 12-15-63. AWOL on roll of 12-31-64.

Johnson, Richard E., pvt. 3-4-62. Thirty-two years old. Horse valued at $180. Captured 12-31-62 at Battle of Stones River and exchanged. Roll of 12-31-63 shows absent with brigade wagons. Issued clothing 3-27-64. Roll of 5-64 shows absent detached service. Present 12-31-64.

Jones, Willis, 4-20-62.

Keaton, Benjamin B., pvt. 3-4-62. Thirty-four years old. Horse valued at $250. Absent sick 12-31-63. Present 5-64. Issued clothing 6-15-64. "Captured in field," no date.

Keaton, John D., pvt. 3-4-62. Twenty-seven years old. Horse valued at $250. Transferred to White's Battery 12-24-62. Absent with White's Battery 12-31-63. Dropped from roll prior to 3-10-64.

Lanier, R. H., 4-21-62.

Laven, J. D. W., Captured 5-8-65 near Athens, Ga. by forces under Gen. W. J. Palmer.

Law, E. B., pvt. 3-4-62.

Lawton, Benjamin H., pvt. 3-4-62/ Sgt. Issued clothing 3-27-64. Present on "extra duty" 5-64. Issued clothing 6-15-64. Present 4-26-65 at surrender as Sgt.

Lawton, John, pvt. 4-22-62. Issued clothing 3-27-64 & 6-15-64. Absent, detached with Gen. Iverson since 5-20-64. Report of 1-6-65 shows as AAAG with Iverson's Division. IG Report of 2-10-65 says "he is properly a private in C Company" of 2nd Ga.

Lawton, Winborn T., pvt. 4-12-62. Nineteen years old. Horse valued at $200. Absent sick in hospital 5-63. Present 12-63. Clothing issued 3-27-64. AWOL 5-64. On furlough 11 & 12-64. Present at surrender 4-26-65. Paroled 5-3-65 Charlotte, N.C.

Lippett, Francis or Franklin B., pvt. 4-21-62. Worth Co. farmer, 5'8" dark hair. Discharged 8-16-64 at Athens, Tenn.

Long, Crawford S., pvt. 12-1-62. Baker Co. Present 2-63, 5-63. Absent on detached service 5-64. Present 12-64. Apparently present at surrender. Paroled 5-3-65 Charlotte, N.C.

Love, Duncan S., pvt. 4-12-62. Twenty-nine years old. Horse valued at $175.

Martin, James W., pvt. 4-25-62/4th cpl. Twenty-seven years old. Present 2-63, 5-63. Absent, sick 12-63. Issued clothing 3-27-64. Captured 7-21-64 Atlanta. Died 10-28-64 as POW at Camp Chase from diarrhea. Grave #377 Camp Chase, Ohio.

McCollum, Alexander S., pvt. 3-4-62. Nineteen years old. Horse valued at $150. Captured 12-29-62 Stones River & exchanged. Detached service since 11-29-64 on roll of 12-31-64. At home on furlough at close of war. Surrendered 5-10-65 with Gen. Sam Jones at Tallahassee, Fla. Paroled 5-16-65 at Albany.

McCollum, Moses W., pvt. 4-21-63. Twenty-one years old. Horse valued at $150. Appointed bugler. Died of pneumonia Yorktown, Va. 1863. Prior service in Cobbs Legion.

McMurray, B. F., pvt. 4-22-62. "Wounded severely in body" at Donelsonville (Dover) 2-3-63. Died 2-4-63.

McMurray, David, pvt. 4-22-62. Forty-five years old. Horse valued at $225.

McRochelle George W., pvt. 3-4-62. Thirty-three years old. Horse valued at $185. Discharged 1863. Died Fairfield, Tenn. 1863.

McVay, Peter, pvt. 3-4-62. Twenty-five years old. Discharged at Camp Ector 5-62.

Mentz, Thomas, pvt. 4-21-62.

Miner, W. L., Appears on list of soldiers included in the surrender who did not appear on company rolls.

Montgomery, John S., pvt. 3-22-62. Thirty-seven years old. Horse valued at $225.

Morgan, John C., pvt. 3-4-62. Thirty-one years old. Horse valued at $225. Wounded 1862 Fort Donelson (Dover). Died of wounds 12-1-62 in Ga.

Moye, John L., pvt. 3-22-62. Thirty-five years old. Horse valued at $150. Discharged prior to 5-15-63.

Murray, W. D., pvt. 6-16-64. Roll of 12-64 shows absent on detached service. Present at surrender 4-26-65. Paroled 5-3-65.

Murray, William M., pvt. 3-4-62. Twenty-three years old. Horse valued at $175 and owned by Col. C. C. Crews. Roll of 5-63 shows "Died Bardstown, Ky" 10-2-62 , but was apparently wounded and captured 11-10-62. POW at Camp Butler, Ill. Apparently exchanged, admitted to Cuthbert, Ga. hospital 3-30-65. Kicked in leg by horse. Leg "ulcerated and never healed...presenting unhealthy appearance."

Newsom, Joel, pvt. 12-62. Substitute for E. B. Laws. AWOL 2-12-64. Present 5-64. Clothing issued 6-15-64.

Nix, D. A., pvt. Captured 5-8-65 near Athens, Ga. by forces under Gen. W. J. Palmer.

Odum, Purd L., pvt. 3-4-62/sgt. Twenty-one years old. Horse valued at $225. Appointed 4th sgt. prior to 5-63. Clothing issued 3-27-64. Present 12-31-64.

Outz, William B., pvt. 3-4-62. Twenty-eight years old. Horse valued at $200. Last on roll 5-7-62. Surrendered 5-10-65 Tallahassee, Fla. Paroled 5-25-65 at Albany, Ga.

Parker, Jeremiah M., pvt. 4-1-62/ 4th sgt. Twenty-nine years old. Horse valued at $185. Present 2-63, 5-63 as pvt. AWOL 2-12-64 as 5th Sgt. Absent, wounded 5-10-64. Absent on furlough 6 through 12-64. Surrendered 5-10-65 Tallahassee, Fla. Paroled at Thomasville, Ga.

Parmenter, William H., pvt. Captured 6-27-63 near Manchester, Tenn. U.S. record shows captured near Shelbyville 6-30-63 or 7-4 or 7-5-63. POW at Camp Chase, Ohio. Transferred to Camp Douglas. U.S. record shows "inducted into US Navy."

Perkins, W., pvt. Substitute for Joseph Lawrence. Shown as "deserter" 12-14-63.

Pierce, John H., pvt. 3-11-62. Twenty-five years old. Horse valued at $225. Clothing issued 3-27-64. Present 5-10-64 on "extra duty." Present 12-64. Present at surrender 4-26-65. Paroled 5-3-65, Charlotte, N.C.

Pollard, E. F. "Scrap," pvt. Transferred from 1st Cav. 8-4-63: Present 1-30-64.

Porter, John, pvt. 4-18-62. Eighteen years old. Horse valued at $125. Present 5-63.

Potts, R. T., pvt. Captured 5-8-65 near Athens, Ga. by forces under Gen. W. J. Palmer.

Pullen, James H., pvt. 4-22-62. Eighteen years old. Horse valued at $200. Present 5-63. On sick furlough 12-63. Clothing issued 3-27-64. Present 12-31-64.

Pullen, Henry, pvt. 4-27-62, Twenty years old. Horse valued at $175. Wounded at Chattanooga ca. 9-24-63. Absent wounded through 12-64.

Pullen, Thomas H., pvt. 3-4-62. Present 5-15-63.

Rhodes, Robert M., pvt. 3-4-62. Twenty-five years old. Horse valued at $250. Captured at "Blackwater" 8-29-63. Exchanged 3-17-64. Issued clothing 3-27-64, 6-15-64. Present at surrender 4-26-65. Paroled 5-3-65 Charlotte, N.C. Born in Ga. 12-5-35. Died Baker Co. Nov. 1919.

Sailler, W. S., pvt. Captured 5-8-65 near Athens, Ga. by forces under Gen. W. J. Palmer.

Salter, Joseph S., pvt. 3-4-62. Twenty-three years old. Horse valued at $150. Present 2-63, 5-63. Captured 1-27-64, Sevierville, Tenn. U.S. record shows captured 1-27-64 Pigeon River, Tenn. Died as POW 3-5-64 at Rock Island Barracks, Ill. Grave #736 "south of barracks."

Sanders, Dickinson Haliday, pvt. 4-22-62/ ord. sgt/ 7-20-63. Thirty-two years old, born 9-6-30. Horse valued at $225. Clothing issued 3-27-64 & 6-15-64. Captured near Waynesboro, Ga.

Sapp, Richard, pvt. 3-4-62. Twenty-four years old. Horse valued at $225. Present 2-63, 5-63. Absent with brigade wagons 2-12-64. Present 5-64. Sick in hospital 11 & 12-64. Surrendered 5-10-65, Tallahassee, Fla. Paroled 5-26-65, Albany, Ga.

Sauls, Henry, pvt. 4-10-62. Twenty-seven years old. Horse valued at $200.

Shellon, J., pvt. 7-24-62.

Screws, Jasper, pvt. 4-19-62. Twenty-six years old. Horse valued at $200. Wounded 12-27-63. Killed in 1864.

Screws, Newton, pvt. 5-7-62. Thirty-four years old. Prior service Ga. militia 11-28-61. Present 2-63, 5-63. Died 9-13-63.

Screws, William, pvt/ 4-24-64. Born 4-25-45. In hospital sick, 10-64. Surrendered 5-10-65, Tallahassee, Fla. Paroled Albany, Ga. 5-22-65.

Settle, John F. C., pvt. 3-24-62. Forty years old. Horse valued at $150. Discharged prior to 5-15-63. Surrendered 5-10-65 Tallahassee.

Simms, Thomas L., pvt/ 11-1-62. Absent sick 5-63. Roll of 12-31-64 shows detailed with battery.

Smith, M. H., pvt. Captured 5-8-65 near Athens, Ga. by forces under Gen. W. J. Palmer.

Snipes, Doctor, pvt. 4-62. May be same man as Madison Snipes below.

Snipes, Madison W., pvt. 4-24-62. Thirty-two years old. Horse valued at $175. Present 2-63, 5-63. Shown AWOL 2-12-64, but captured 12-3-63 near Knoxville, Tenn. POW at Rock Island Barracks. Released 6-21-65. POW record shows 5'10" hazel eyes, "fresh" complexion.

Sutton, Blount, pvt. 5-7-62. Twenty-six years old. Wounded in both thighs and captured at Fort Donelson (Dover) 2-3-63. Exchanged 4-28-63. Captured 1-27-64 Sevierville, Tenn.. POW Rock Island Barracks, released 6-17-65.

Swindle, George W., pvt. 4-24-62. Thirty years old. Horse valued at $175. Absent, sick 2-12-64. Clothing issued 3-27-64. Present 5-64, 11 and 12-64. Present at surrender 4-26-65. Paroled 5-3-65 Charlotte, N. C.

Tiner, Lewis H., pvt. 4-24-64. Clothing issued 6-15-64. Present 11 & 12-64. Present at surrender 4-26-65. Paroled 5-3-65 Charlotte, N. C.

Tripp, Richard H., pvt. Captured 12-15-63 Craig Co., Va. POW at Camp Chase Ohio. Transferred to Ft. Delaware. Exchanged 3-7-65. Received at Wayside Hospital in Richmond, Va. 3-10-65. Described as 30 years old, 6'1" gray eyes, black hair, dark complexion.

Twitty, Andrew Jackson, pvt. 4-18-62/ 5th sgt. Twenty-four years old. Horse valued at $225. Present 2-63. Present 5-63 as sgt. Present 5-64. Clothing issued 6-64. AWOL roll of 8-12-64: Roll of 12-64 shows "Captured in field."

Wagner, John T., pvt. 3-4-62. Twenty-five years old. Horse valued at $230. Present 5-63 as acting ordinance sgt. Absent on furlough 2-18-64. Clothing issued 3-27-64. Present 5-64, 12-64. Present at surrender 4-26-65. Paroled 5-3-65 Charlotte, N.C.

Walker, Charles W., pvt. 3-4-62. Thirty-one years old. Horse valued at $175. Discharged with disability 8-31-62 at Chattanooga. Described as 5'6" blue eyes, light hair.

Webb, John, pvt. 3-4-62/ 3rd sgt/ 2nd lt. 3-63. Twenty-five years old. Horse valued at $250. Clothing issued 3-27-64. Paroled Albany 5-10-65.

Weders, J. W., pvt. Captured 5-8-65 near Athens, Ga. By forces under Gen. W. J. Palmer.

Wilder, Edward E., pvt. 4-21-62. Twenty-nine years old. Present 2-63, 5-63. AWOL 2-12-64. Roll of 12-31-64 shows detailed as saddler for Brigade since 4-20-64.

Williams, Green B., pvt. 4-21-62. Twenty-five years old. Horse valued at $200. Present 2-63, 5-63. On detail Atlanta hospital 12-31-63. Appointed asst. surgeon 6-1-64.

Willingham, Isaac, pvt. 3-4-62. Forty-two years old. Horse valued at $285. Present 2-63, 5-63. Clothing issued 3-27-64. AWOL 5-10-64. Detailed with brigade 8-1-64: Paroled 6-1-65 Albany, Ga.

Willingham, Newton, pvt. 3-4-62. Eighteen years old. Present 2-63, 5-63. Absent, with brigade wagons 2-12-64. Present 5-64, 11 and 12-64. Present at surrender 4-26-65. Paroled 5-3-65, Charlotte, N.C.

Wilson, John, 3rd sgt. 5-19-62/ 2nd lt. Twenty-eight years old. Horse valued at $200. Horse killed 8-15-62. Present 2-63, 5-63 as 2nd lt. Present 11-63, 12-63. Clothing issued 3-27-64.

Winchester, George P., pvt. 4-21-62. Twenty-four years old. Horse valued at $285. Wounded, roll of 5-10-64 shows absent, wounded. Paroled 5-16-65, Albany, Ga.

D COMPANY

Grant, William D., capt. 5-1-62. Twenty-two years old. Horse valued at $200. Absent sick 5-63. Resigned 5-9-63 on certificate of disability.

Ammons, John W., 1st lt. 5-1-62. Moved to K Company 5-1-63: Present 1-31-64. 1906 Roster Commission record shows resigned with disability 11-15-62.

Sorrells, John B., 2nd lt. 5-1-62. Thirty years old. Horse valued at $185. Discharged, furnished substitute 3-63.

Mitchell, Robert R., 2nd lt/1st lt. 5-22-63/capt. Thirty-three years old. Horse valued at $140. Wounded and captured 1-27-64 Sevierville, Tenn.

Shepard, James M., 1st sgt./1st. lt./capt. Twenty-eight years old. Horse valued at $175. Present 2-63, 5-63. Present 12-64, present at surrender 4-26-65. Paroled Charlotte 5-3-65.

Gibbs, Joseph W., 2nd sgt. Prior service with 3rd Bn Ga. militia: Discharged 12-4-62, furnished substitute.

O'Kelly, Robert S., 3rd sgt. 5-1-62. Twenty-two years old. Horse valued at $115. Present 6-62. Discharged 9-30-63.

Preston, Francis M. 4th sgt. 5-1-62. Thirty years old. Horse valued at $225. Killed at Murfreesboro, 7-13-62.

Briscoe, William S., 5th sgt/ 5-1-62. Horse valued at $225. Shown as pvt after 5-15-63. Wagon driver 11 and 12—63. Present 12-31-64.

Camp, James Ray, cpl. 5-1-62. Prior service 2nd lt 16th Ga. infantry. Captured 9-2-64 at Atlanta.

Ivey, Warren J., cpl. 5-1-62/sgt./ 1st sgt. Twenty-four years old. Horse valued at $200. Prior service 11th Ga. infantry. Absent sick in hospital 5-63. Present 12-63. Clothing issued 3-27-64 and 6-15-64. Present 12-31-64.

Cooper, Warren J., 3rd cpl. Present 12-31-64.

Griffin, Richard P., 4th cpl. 5-1-62/pvt. Prior service 3rd Bn Ga. militia. Twenty-two years old. Absent detached with brigade escort 5-15-63. Absent, "cut off with Army of Tenn." 12-63. Issued clothing 3-27-64. On roll of 12-31-64 shown AWOL since 8-10-64.

Mayne, James R., cpl. 5-1-64. AWOL on roll of 12-31-64.

Abercrombie, James B. A., pvt. 5-1-62. Last on roll 6-62.

Adams, George A. J., pvt. 5-1-62/Sgt. 1864. Absent, sick on roll of 12-31-64.

Adams, Mathew D., pvt. 5-1-62. Discharged with disability 1863 or 64. Died 4-18-1907.

Adams, Reuben or Robert H, pvt. 5-1-62. Last on roll 6-62.

Akridge, Thaddeus P., pvt. 5-15-62. Last on roll 6-62.

Allen, S., pvt. Monroe Co. AWOL "never paid."

Arnold, Francis Marion, pvt. 8-1-63. AWOL 2-10-64. Apparently present 12-31-64.

Aycock, James A. or T., pvt. 6-1-64. Present 12-31-64.

Bannister or Bennett, J. C., pvt. 3-1-63. Absent sick in hospital 5-15-63. "Dropped from rolls and reported to conscript office."

Beardin, James T., pvt. 5-1-62. Died 7-31-62.

Bennett, Dodson, pvt. 5-1-62. Walton Co. On list of prisoners exchanged to Maj. F. W. Hundley, CSA 12-15-62, Vicksburg, Miss. Sick in hospital 5-63. Captured 12-2-64, Griswoldville, Ga.

Bennett, John, pvt. 5-7-62. Walton Co. Captured 1-27-64 Sevierville, Tenn. Released after oath of allegiance 6-17-65. POW records show thirty six years old, 5'8", blue eyes.

Bennett, Mason, pvt. Captured 1-27-64 Sevierville, Tenn. POW at Rock Island Barracks, Ill.

Bennett, Nathan, pvt. 5-7-62. Captured 1-27-64 Sevierville, Tenn. POW at Rock Island Barracks, Ill. Sent to Camp Chase 2-14-64 for exchange. POW record shows twenty six years old, 5'11" blue eyes, auburn hair.

Bennett, W. B., pvt. 8-1-64. Present 12-1-64.

Benton, Stephen, pvt. 5-1-62. Walton County. Present through 5-15-63.

Blackmore, J. D., pvt. Captured & paroled 5-8-65 Athens, Ga. by forces under Gen. Palmer.

Booth, James, pvt. Captured and exchanged 1-11-63. Sent to Atlanta as a Shoemaker in '63: "ordered back to hospital" 5-63. Absent sick 1-64. Detailed at hospital at Bulls Gap.

Braggs, Y. D., cpl. Captured and paroled 5-18-65 Hartwell, Ga. by forces under S. B. Brown.

Briscoe, Egbert B., pvt. 5-1-62. Prior service 11th Ga. Infantry. AWOL on roll of 12-31-64 since 8-10-64.

Broadnax, Samuel Houston, pvt. 8-1-64. Prior service 2nd reg. Ga. militia. Accidentally wounded while on picket duty 3-65 Goldsboro, N.C. Sent home with broken arm 4-5-65.

Broadnax, William, pvt. Prior service with 11th Ga. Inf. 7-3-61. Wounded at Malvern Hill. On furlough wounded 1-31-63. Transferred to 2nd Ga. Cav. Present 12-31-64.

Brockwell, William H., pvt. 5-1-62. Present through 1863 and 1864.

Brown, Joseph T., pvt. 5-1-62. Prior service 11th Ga. Infantry. Discharged with disability 11-20-61, Culpepper, Va. Captured 1-27-64, Sevierville, Tenn. Exchanged 3-2-65 Rock Island, Ill.

Buchanan, John D., pvt. 3-1-62. Discharged 4-14-63 Rome, Ga. due to disability. "Unfit for service due to chronic diarrhea & broncitis."

Bullock, James Sherman, pvt5-7-62./2nd lt. Thirty-three years old. Walton Co. Absent sick 5-63 as lt. Resigned 8-11-63 due to disability. Died 1863.

Burger, D. N., pvt. 5-1-62. Detached with brigade battery 2-21-63 to 5-15-63. Roll of 11-63 shows "transferred from battery to infantry."

Camp, Thomas C., pvt. 5-1-62/2nd lt. As pvt, absent sick 5-63. As lt. captured 1-27-64 Sevierville, Tenn. POW at Camp Chase, Ohio. Transferred to Fort Delaware 3-25-64. Released 6-6-65. POW record shows 5'10", light hair, blue eyes.

Carter, J., pvt. 8-1-64. Social Circle, Ga. AWOL after 8-10-64.

Carter, M., pvt. 9-9-62. Social Circle, Ga. Paid 11-1-63.

Cosby, Dawson "Doss"

Carrithers, William Griffin, pvt. 4-1-64. Paroled 5-3-65 Charlotte, N.C.

Carter, Jesse A., pvt. 5-1-62. Died prior to 8-1-62.

Carter, Willis Mathew, pvt. 9-9-62. Present 12-31-64.

Cleaton, William C., pvt. 5-1-62. Seventeen years old. Prior service 9th Ga. Infantry. Present through 5-63. Issued clothing 4-7-63 and 6-15-63. With wagon train 12-63. Roll of 12-31-64 shows absent sick since 8-10-64.

Conner, James M or W., pvt. 5-1-62. Present through 5-63. Captured 10-9-63 Sugar Creek, Tenn. U.S. record shows captured 10-7-63 Huntsville, Ala. Received for exchange at Boulware & Cox Wharves, James River, Va. 3-10 or 12-65.

Conner, T. Y., pvt. 5-1-62. Present through 5-63. Detached with brigade battery 11-12 -63. Captured 9-21-62 Lebanon Junction, Ky. Received 11-1-62 at Vicksburg for exchange. Transferred to Capt. White's Battery horse artillery. Present 12-31-64.

Cooper, Francis M., pvt. 5-1-62. Walton Co. Last on roll 6-62. Name appears on list of deceased soldiers. Survivor filed claim for pay 9-63.

Cooper, V. A., cpl. 5-1-62/sgt. Horse valued at $235. Present through 12-63. Clothing issued 3-27-64.

Dany, George W., Coweta Co. On list of POWs at Wheeling, Va. Atheneum Prison, 12-31-63. Captured Craig Co., Va. 12-4-63 and sent to Camp Chase. POW record shows twenty years old, 6' tall, dark complexion, blue eyes.

Dickinson, John Nick, pvt. 5-1-62. Detailed with brigade battery 5-15-63. AWOL 2-10-64. Issued clothing 3-27-64 and 7-15-64. Present 12-31-64. Paroled at Augusta 5-20-65.

Dillard, Moses, pvt. 8-1-63. Issued clothing 3-27-63. Roll of 12-31-64 shows AWOL since 12-10-64.

Draughn, John Craton, pvt. 3-1-64. Issued clothing 3-27-64 and 6-15-64. Present 12-31-64. Paroled 5-3-65 Charlotte, N. C.

Eckles or Echols, John T., pvt. 5-1-62. Walton Co. Prior service as sgt 11th Ga. Infantry. Discharged from infantry with disability 1-27-62, Centreville, Va. Horse valued at $80. Absent sick 5-63. Paid 8-63. Paroled 5-20-65, Augusta, Ga.

Edwards, L. B., pvt. 5-7-62. Walton Co. Twenty-six years old. Discharged with disability, 1862.

Eland, Marrion R., pvt. Transferred from H Company where he had been a cpl.

Felker, Stephen Boone, pvt. 8-1-63. Issued clothing 3-27-64. Roll of 12-31-64 shows AWOL since 8-10-64.

Freeman, Virgil C., pvt. 5-1-62. Roll of 5-63 shows detached with brigade scouts. Captured 1-27-64, Sevierville, Tenn. Died 3-20-64 as POW at Rock Island Barracks of "measles and variola."

Fuller, F. Martin, pvt. 5-1-62. Absent, sick at hospital 12-31-63. Issued clothing 3-27-64, 6-15-64. Present 12-31-64.

Gaughee or Guaghey, W.C., pvt. Captured 4-21-63 McMinnville, Tenn. POW at Louisville 5-2-63.

Goodson, William H., pvt. 5-1-62. Killed or captured 10-1-62, Perryville, Ky. Also shown as "lost at Perryville, Ky Oct-8-1862."

Hamilton, Charles L., pvt. 3-1-64. Issued clothing 3-27-64 and 6-15-64. Roll of 12-31-64 shows AWOL since 8-10-64.

Harrison, S., pvt. 4-1-64. AWOL 12-31-64.

Hawkins, T., pvt. Captured 5-8-65 near Athens, Ga. by forces under Gen. Palmer.

Head, H. C., pvt. 5-1-62. Twenty-five years old. Horse valued at $140. Present 2-63, 5-63. AWOL 3-63. Clothing issued 3-27-64. Present 11-64, 12-64.

Hutson, J., pvt. Roll of 12-31-64 shows AWOL since 9-10-64.

Hogan, Francis M., pvt. 5-1-62. Thirty-two years old. Horse valued at $175. Died 10-24-62. Farmer, blue eyes, lt. hair.

Hogan, Judge J., pvt. 5-1-62. Killed or captured 10-15-62, Crab Orchard, Ky.

Ivey, D. H., pvt. 5-1-62. Twenty-six years old. Horse valued at $160. Present 5-63. Absent, detailed with wagons 12-63. Present 12-64.

Ivey, Elisha H., pvt. 5-1-62. Twenty-seven years old. Horse valued at $110. Prior service 3rd Bn Ga. militia. Died 1863 on sick furlough at home in Walton Co., Ga.

Kilgore, Charles, pvt. 9-1-62. Last on roll 12-63, sick in hospital.

Kinery, J. T., pvt. Captured 2-1-63 Williamson Co., Tenn.

Lanier, George W. H., pvt. 5-1-62. Eighteen years old. Horse valued at $200. Prior service 3rd Bn Ga. militia. Present 5-63, 12-63. Clothing issued 3-27-64. Roll of 12-31-64 shows AWOL since 8-10-64.

Lanier, John R., pvt. 3-1-62. Twenty-eight years old. Horse valued at $110. "Discharged by reason of disability." No date.

Lanier, Rene L. or S. D., pvt. 5-1-62. Twenty-two years old. Prior service 3rd Bn Ga. militia. Present 5-63, 12-63. Clothing issued 3-27-64. Roll of 12-31-64 shows AWOL since 12-1-64.

Lawrence, James G., pvt. 5-1-62. Nineteen years old. Horse valued at $200. Prior service 3rd Bn Ga. militia. "Detached with Elite Corps" 5-63. "Absent, cut off with Army of Tenn." 12-63. Issued clothing 3-27-64. Present 12-31-64.

Lawrence, Joseph P., pvt. 5-1-62. Twenty-four years old. Horse valued at $160. Prior service 3rd Bn Ga. militia. Transferred to C Company 5-15-63. Discharged, furnished substitute.

Leach, James, pvt. 8-1-63. Present 12-63. Issued clothing 3-27-64, 6-15-64. Present 12-31-64.

Lowe, J. H., pvt. 5-1-62. Twenty-six years old. Horse valued at $170. Present 5-63. AWOL 2-64. Issued clothing 3-27-64. Present 12-31-64.

Lunceford, Glenn O., pvt. 5-1-62 / sgt. major/ 2nd lt. Twenty-nine years old. Wounded, captured 10-9-63 Sugar Creek, Tenn. Paroled at Fort Delaware, received at Wayside Hospital Richmond, Va. 5-10-65.

Mayfield, Isaac W., pvt. 8-1-64. Present 12-31-64. Pension records show he was near Charlotte waiting for remount at close of war. Died 1-17-1920 in Walton Co., Ga.

Maxwell, J. W., pvt. 8-1-64. Enlisted at Monroe, Ga. Present 11 & 12-64.

McComby, Joshua, captured 7-10-63 near Windsor, Va.

McGaughey, Howard H., pvt. 5-1-62/cpl. Twenty-eight years old. Horse valued at $90. Captured 10-6-63. Sugar Creek Tenn. Paroled at Camp Morton, Ind., forwarded to City Point, Va. for exchange 3-4-65. Received 3-10 or 12-65 at Boulware & Cox Wharves.

McGaughey, Warren, pvt. 5-1-62. Twenty-three years old. Horse valued at $115. Present 2-63, 5-63. Issued clothing 7-20-63. Roll of 12-63 shows "present, in arrest." Issued clothing 3-27-64 and 6-23-64. Absent, sick on roll of 12-31-64.

McGaughey, William W., pvt. 5-1-62. Sixteen years old. Horse valued at $170. Captured 4-21-63, McMinnville, Tenn. Paroled at Fort McHenry, Baltimore, Md. 5-10-63. Received at City Point, Va. 5-14-63. Shown AWOL 11 and 12-63, 11 and 12-64. Detailed for garrison guard at Marietta, Ga. 9-63 through 2-64.

Michael, John M., pvt. 5-1-62. Twenty-one years old. Horse valued at $90. Present 2-63, 5-63. Roll of 12-63 shows "Absent, cut off with Army of Tenn." Present 12-31-64.

Michael, William L., pvt. 5-1-62. Thirty years old. Horse valued at $250. Present 2-63, 5-63. Captured 1-27-64 near Knoxville, Tenn. (Probably Sevierville) and sent to hospital 1-29-64.

Miller, John G., pvt. 5-1-62. Thirty-three years old. Horse valued at $150. Rejected by surgeon prior to 5-16-62.

Mitchell, Francis William, pvt. 4-1-63. Issued clothing 3-27-64. Present 12-31-64.

Mize, F. M., pvt. 5-1-62. Thirty years old. Horse valued at $150. Present 6-62.

Mize, Nathan T., pvt. 5-1-62. Died 10-62.

Moore, Andrew L., pvt. 3-1-63. Present 12-31-64.

Moore, Benjamin S., pvt. 5-1-62. Discharged with disability 3-6-63 Fairfield, Tenn.

Moore, David M., pvt. 5-1-62. Prior service 3rd Bn Ga. militia. Twenty years old. Horse valued at $120. Present 2-63, 5-63. Detailed as "provo guard" 11-63, 12-63. Roll of 12-31-64 shows detached on courier line in Ala. since 11-1-64.

Moore, R. S., pvt. 5-1-62. Twenty-five years old. Horse valued at $130. May be same man as Benjamin Moore above.

Moore, Thomas, J., pvt. 5-10-62. Present 2-63, 5-63. Clothing issued 3-27-64 & 6-15-64. Roll of 12-31-64 shows AWOL since 12-20-64.

Moore, William James, pvt. 5-1-62. Nineteen years old. Horse valued at $90. Appears last on roll 5-15-63. "Relieved by furnishing Jas Booth as substitute."

Moore, William Y., pvt. 5-1-62. Thirty-three years old. Horse valued at $150. Detached as teamster 11 and 12-63. Clothing issued 3-27-64. Present 12-64. Present at surrender 4-26-65. Paroled 5-3-65, Charlotte, N. C.

O'Kelly, James W., pvt. 5-1-62. Twenty-five years old. Horse valued at $170. Died prior to 12-15-62. Described as a farmer, 5'8" blue eyes, light hair.

O'Kelly, Jacob M., pvt. 5-1-62. Twenty-two years old. Horse valued at $120. Roll of 5-63 in hospital sick. Paid 6-63, 7-63, 9-63. Roll of 12-64 shows "absent, with dismounted men. Returned from desertion" 7-1-64.

Reeves, C. H., pvt. 5-1-62. Twenty-seven years old. Horse valued at $125. Present 2-63, 5-63. Wounded 12-15-63 and sent to hospital.

Reeves or Reaves, J. F., pvt. 5-1-62, Twenty-two years old. Horse valued at $120.

Reaves, Thompson, pvt. Twenty-three years old. Horse valued at $140.

Richardson, Henry W., pvt. 5-1-62. "Substitute for R. F. Ser——"

Richardson, H. F., pvt. 12-1-62. Present at surrender 4-26-65. Paroled 5-3-65, Charlotte, N. C.

Robinson, T. L., pvt. 8-1-63. Clothing issued 3-27-64. Present 12-64.

Rutledge, Henry M., pvt. 5-1-62. Twenty years old. Horse valued at $100. Died 7-26-62.

Seffins, E. B., pvt. Captured 5-8-65 near Athens, Ga. by forces under Gen. W. J. Palmer.

Shacklett, D. pvt. Captured 5-8-65 near Athens, Ga. by forces under Gen. W. J. Palmer.

Skeen, P. A., pvt. Clothing issued 9-21-63.

Smith, Calvin L., pvt. 5-1-62. Prior service with 11th Ga. Infantry. Discharged 9-16, Richmond on account of disability. Nineteen years old. Horse valued at $130. Present 2-63, 5-63. Roll of 11 & 12-63 shows "Absent detailed on courier line in Ala." Captured 2-1-64 Wills Valley, Ala. POW at Rock Island Barracks, Ill. Released 6-21-65.

Smith, Egbert, pvt. 5-1-62/cpl.10-1-62. Thirty-one years old. Horse valued at $160. Captured 12-31-62 at Stones River. POW at Camp Chase, apparently exchanged. Captured 1-27-64 at Sevierville, Tenn. POW at Rock Island Barracks, Ill.

Smith, J. H., pvt. "Died 1-28-63 near Wartrace."

Smith, W. G or S., pvt. 5-1-62. Twenty-nine years old. Horse valued at $140. Died prior to 5-7-63 in "Pikerville, Tenn."

Snow, R. T., pvt. 5-1-62. Present 2-63 and 5-63.

Sorrells, C. B., pvt. 5-1-62. Nineteen years old. Horse valued at $120. Present 2-63, 5-63. Detached on courier line in Ala. 11 and 12-63, 11 and 12-64. Present at surrender 4-26-65. Paroled 5-3-65, Charlotte, N. C.

Sorrells, H. B., pvt. 7-1-64. Roll of 12-31-64 shows AWOL since 12-20-64. Paroled 5-3-65 at Charlotte, indicating he was present at surrender 4-26-65.

Sorrells, T., pvt. 8-1-64. Roll of 12-64 shows AWOL since 8-10-64.

Sorrells, W. C., pvt. 5-1-62. Twenty-three years old. Horse valued at $120. Died 7-26-62. Described as 5'11" blue eyes, light hair, light complexion. (Could be same man as W.G. Sorrells below, but records indicate that W. C. Sorrells did not die in hospital.)

Sorrells, W. G. pvt. 5-1-62. Twenty-two years old. Horse valued at $150. Died in Chattanooga hospital. "Date not known."

Starke, John B., pvt. 5-1-62. Thirty-three years old. Horse valued at $180. Present 2-63, 5-63, 11 and 12-63. Clothing issued 3-27-64. Roll of 12-31-64 shows AWOL since 12-1-64.

Stephens, J., pvt. 6-1-64. Roll of 12-31-64 shows AWOL since 12-20-64.

Stephens, S., pvt. 8-1-64. Roll of 12-31-64 shows AWOL since 8-10-64.

Stephens, T. pvt. 8-1-64. Roll of 12-31-64 shows AWOL since 8-10-64.

Stewart, W. H., pvt. 5-1-62. Twenty-six years old. Horse valued at $135. Present throughout 1863.

Strange, J., pvt. 8-1-64. "Died in Ala." 10-64.

Summerour, Berry, pvt. 5-1-62. Thirty-three years old. Horse valued at $130. Admitted to Dalton Hospital 9-10-62. "Deserted" 11-17-62. Present 2-63, 5-63. Clothing issued 3-27-64. Roll of 12-64 shows AWOL since 11-1-64.

Swords, A. J., pvt. 5-1-62/sgt. Twenty-three years old. Horse valued at $100. Detailed with brigade battery but returned to regiment prior to 5-63. Absent, with wagon train 11 and 12-63. Clothing issued 6-15-64. Present 11 and 12-64.

Swords, J. H., pvt. 8-1-64. Present 11 & 12-64.

Swords, Thomas H., pvt. 8-1-63, Present 11 and 12-63. Roll of 12-64 shows "absent with dismounted cavalry." Tanner, James, pvt. 5-1-62. Thirty-four years old. Horse valued at $175. Present 2-63, 5-63. "Absent, forge driver" 11 and 12-63. Clothing issued 3-27-64 and 6-15-64. Present 11 and 12-64. Present at surrender 4-26-65. Paroled 5-3-65 Charlotte, N.C.

Tanner, John T., pvt. 5-1-62. Twenty-six years old. Horse valued at $155. Sick, at hospital 5-63. Present 11 and 12-63. Clothing issued 3-27-64. Died 7-15-64 at home in Walton County.

Tanner, N., pvt. 9-1-62. Present 2-63, 5-63. Absent, sick at hospital 11 & 12-63. Clothing issued 3-27-64 and 6-15-64. Present 12-64.

Tierney, George W., pvt. Captured 12-14-63, Craig County, Va. POW at Camp Chase, Ohio. Transferred to Ft. Delaware. POW records describe as twenty years old, 6' tall, blue eyes, brown hair, dark complexion.

Tribble, W. H., pvt. 5-1-62. Twenty years old. Horse valued at $120.

Tucker, E. F., pvt. 5-1-62. Seventeen years old. Horse valued at $125. Absent, sick at hospital 5-63.

Tucker, W. P., pvt. 5-1-62. Twenty-one years old. Horse valued at $200. "Died near Shelbyville, Tenn about Ja 1 1863."

Turnbull, James H., pvt. 5-1-62. Eighteen years old. Horse valued at $140. Detached with brigade battery 5-63. Transferred to brigade battery 11-63.

Turner, James M., pvt. 5-1-62. Thirty-two years old. Horse valued at $100.

Waiter, W. B., pvt. 5-1-62/ 5th sgt Twenty-seven years old. Horse valued at $225. Present 2-63, 5-63 as sgt. Clothing issued 3-27-64 and 6-15-64. Captured 7-25-64 "near Chattahoochee." U.S. record shows captured 7-26-64 at Lawrenceville, Ga. POW at Camp Chase, Ohio. Received at Wayside Hospital Richmond, Va. 3-12-65.

Walker, W. F., pvt. 5-1-65. Twenty years old. Horse valued at $150. Present 2-63, 5-63. Clothing issued 3-27-64 and 6-15-64. Present 12-64. Present at surrender 4-26-65. Paroled 5-3-65, Charlotte, N. C.

White, A. J., pvt. 12-1-62. Present 2-63, 5-63, 11 & 12-63. Clothing issued 3-27-64 and 6-15-64. Present 11 & 12-64.

White, William W., pvt. 3-1-62. Nineteen years old. Horse valued at $150. Present 2-63, 5-63. Clothing issued 3-27-64. Present 11 & 12-64.

Whitley, W. H., pvt. 9-1-62. Present 2-63, 5-63.

Wright, James R., pvt. 5-1-62. Twenty-seven years old. Horse valued at $130. Wounded 7-5-64.

E COMPANY

Ison, Francis M., capt. 2-15-62./maj. 11-7-62/lt. col. Thirty-eight years old. Promoted to regimental commander 3-63. Field & Staff muster roll of 10-31-64 shows "in arrest by order of Gen'l Allen, cmdg Division" near Lawtinville, S.C. Present at surrender 4-26-65. Paroled 5-3-65 Charlotte, N.C.

Brooks, Thomas J.,1st lt. 2-15-62/capt. Thirty-two years old. Horse valued at $275. Apparently succeeded Ison as company commander. Resigned 3- 20-63.

Johnson, Daniel A., 2nd lt. 2-15-62. Forty-three years old. Horse valued at $225. Resigned 11-15-62.

Thompson, Robert A., 2nd lt. 2-15-62./capt. Enlisted 10-17-61 as pvt. Co B 5th Ga. Infantry and discharged 10-17-61. Elected 2nd lt. 2nd Ga. Cav. Also shown as "Thomson." Twenty-one years old. Horse valued at $275. Absent, detached service 5-63. Promoted to capt., apparently succeeding Brooks as company commander, prior to 1-29-63 when admitted to hospital. Absent sick through 12-64.

Wilson, John A., 3rd sgt. 2-15-62 / 2nd lt. Twenty-eight years old. Horse valued at $200. Promoted to 2nd lt. prior to 5-63. Clothing issued 3-27-64.

Lavender, William R., 1st cpl. 2-15-62./4th sgt/ 11-1-64. Present 12-31-64.

Rayle, Wyatt W., 2nd cpl. 3-4-62/2nd lt. 4-64. Elected 2nd lt. Twenty-four years old. Horse valued at $225. Present 2-63, 5/63. Killed 7-21-64, Atlanta, Ga.

Westbrook, John S., 5th sgt. 2-15-62/ QM sgt. 5-7-62. Thirty-five years old. Horse valued at $200. Promoted to quartermaster sgt. on regimental staff. Dropped from roll 4-11-64.

Duffee, James W., 3rd cpl. 2-20-62/5th sgt. Twenty-two years old. Paid 7-6-63, 5-11-63. Issued clothing 3-27-64. AWOL 12-31-63. Roll of 12-31-64 shows him sick since 10-3-64.

Huckaby, John, 4th cpl. 2-25-62. Twenty-four years old. Horse valued at $125. Wounded severely in hip 2-4-63, Fort Donelson (Dover). Died of wound later that year.

King, John C., 1st sgt. 2-25-62. Twenty-one years old. Horse valued at $275. Absent sick 5-63. Paid 3-63, 7-63, 11-63. Clothing issued 1-64. Present 4-64.

Adams, B. F., In state penitentiary at Milledgeville 11 and 12-64 and dropped from roll.

Adams, C. C., pvt.

Aiken or Akin, David, cpl. 5-7-62/ 2nd lt. 8-2-64. Thirty-two years old at enlistment. POW & exchanged 10-25-62. Detailed as courier 10-7-63. Horse valued at $200. Present 2-63, 5-63. Detailed as courier 10-7-63. Clothing issued 3-27-64. Present 11-64, 12-64.

Akridge, T., pvt. 5-16-62. From Walton County.

Allen, James C., pvt. 2-25-62. Absent sick 5-15-63. AWOL 2-7-64. Present 12-64.

Bailey, Charles, pvt. 3-4-62. Thirty-seven years old. Discharged 5-15-63.

Bailey, Drewry, pvt. 5-7-62. Captured 9-21-62 Lebanon Junction, Ky. Died as POW at Cairo, Ill.

Baker, F. W., cpl. Captured & paroled 5-18-65 at Hartwell, Ga. by forces under Gen. S. B. Brown.

Bamberger, Emanuel S., pvt. 5-7-62/ sgt maj. 11-15-63. Horse killed 8-15-62, Whites Creek, Tenn. Absent and in hospital 12-64 Augusta, Ga. Paroled 6-20-65 Montgomery, Ala.

Barnes, H. Turner, pvt. 5-3-64. AWOL 12-15-64.

Beeks, William M., pvt. 4-20-64. Present 12-31-64.

Berryhill, William H., pvt. Shown as AWOL 5-15-63 but was apparently on assignment as a "hide agent" and shoemaker in Atlanta Feb. to Aug. 1863. Surrendered 5-10-65 at Tallahassee, Fla. & paroled 5-16-65 Thomasville, Ga.

Bowen, John W., pvt. 5-7-62. Enlisted at Griffin, Ga.

Brady, Thomas, In state penitentiary at Milledgeville; dropped from rolls 11-12-64.

Bridges, James M., pvt. 6-19-62. Enlisted at Griffin, Ga. Last on roll 5-15-63.

Bridges, John G., pvt. 3-4-62. Twenty years old. Horse valued at $200. Captured 1-27-64 Sevierville, Tenn. Released Rock Island, Ill. 6-19-65. POW record shows 5'11", auburn hair, hazel eyes, "fresh" complexion.

Bridges, M. J., pvt. 5-13-64. Roll of 12-31-64 shows AWOL since 11-16-64.

Bridges, W. J., pvt./ 4th sgt. 5-12-64/ 2nd sgt. 11-1-64. Enlisted in Atlanta.

Brown, John, pvt. 4-14-62/cpl. 7-1-62. Terrell Co. Present through '62. Detailed 1-27-63 to take charge of government stock under Capt. Russell. Shown AWOL 12-64 but also shown on "detailed service" with Gen. Cheatham at this time, dating from   8-10-62.

Burr, Henry C., pvt. 3-4-62. Griffin, Ga. Twenty years old. Horse valued at $150. "Wounded and disabled" 12-1-63. Clothing issued 3-27-64. Roll of 12-31-64 shows as "retired."

Cabel, Jefferson, pvt. 2-1-63. Griffin, Ga.

Carriker, Jefferson, pvt. 4-15-62. Horse valued at $225. Captured 9-21-62 Lebanon Junction, Ky. POW at Cairo, Ill. Apparently exchanged. Present 5-63.

Campbell, Jesse M., pvt. 5-1-62/ 1st sgt. 5-12-64. Walton Co. Issued clothing 6-15-64. "Reduced to ranks" 11-64.

Carmichael, Andrew, pvt. 5-1-64. Enlisted at Macon, Ga. Present 12-64.

Carmichael, I. B., pvt. 11-18-64. Present 12-31-64.

Cerba, David, pvt. 12-31-62. Griffin, Ga. Substitute for M. J. Patrick.

Clements, J. C., pvt. 4-10-62. AWOL 12-1-64. Records show he was "sub-enrolling officer" of Montgomery Co. from 6-22-62 through 1864.

Conner, John A., pvt. 2-25-62. Present through 1863. Issued clothing 3-27-64. Present 12-31-64.

Crawley, James W., pvt. 2-20-62. Captured 9-21-62 Lebanon Junction, Ky. Sent from Camp Chase, Ohio to Vicksburg for exchange 11-1-62. Present through 1863. Present 12-31-64.

Darden, Augustus M., pvt. 5-7-62. Thirty years old. Horse valued at $175. Killed 7-13-62 Murfreesboro, Tenn. Widow Martha filed claim 2-6-63.

Darden, Joseph, pvt. 5-13-62. Transferred to Capt. White's Battery horse artillery. Roll of 12-31-64 shows detached to White's Battery.

Dean, Samuel H., pvt. 2-20-62/1st. sgt. 11-1-64. Eighteen years old. Horse valued at $200. Captured 9-21-62 Lebanon Junction, Ky. Sent from Camp Chase, Ohio to Vicksburg for exchange. POW record shows 5'10 1/2", dark hair, hazel eyes. Paid 4-30-63. Detached 5-63. Issued clothing 3-27-64 and 6-15-64. Present 12-31-64.

Douglas, Hugh N., pvt. 3-24-64. Issued clothing 3-27-64. Roll of 12-31-64 shows cpl., sick since 10-2-64.

Duffee, Thomas J., pvt. 5-14-62/2nd sgt. Thirty-four years old. Horse valued at $250. Issued clothing 3-27-64 and 11-22-64. Roll of 12-31-64 shows sick. Present at surrender, 4-26-65 Salisbury, N.C. Paroled 5-3-65 Charlotte, N.C.

Duffee, James W., pvt. 2-20-62. Twenty-two years old. Horse valued at $150. Absent sick 5-63. AWOL 2-9-64. Issued clothing 3-27-64. Absent, sick 10-31-64.

Ellington, J. H., pvt. 3-24-64. Roll of 12-31-64 shows absent, sick since 7-10-64. Present at surrender 4-26-65. Paroled 5-3-65, Charlotte, N. C.

Ellis, Henry E., pvt. 2-20-62/ cpl. 3-15-63. Eighteen years old, Griffin, Ga. Horse valued at $175. Detached on "special duty" 10-27-63. Issued clothing 3-27-64. Roll of 12-31-64 shows on detached service since 10-1-64.

Ellis, James Jefferson, pvt. 3-4-62/ 2nd lt/capt. Twenty-three years old. Horse valued at $225. Horse killed 8-15-62. 2nd lt prior to 5-63. Issued clothing 3-64. Present at surrender, paroled 5-3-65 Charlotte.

Ellis, John L., pvt. 3-62. Transferred to Capt White's Horse Artillery. Returned to E Company 8-28-63. Roll of 2-12-64 shows "Discharged, insanity."

Ellis, William A., pvt. 3-19-62. Eighteen years old, Griffin, Ga. In prior service wounded at Shiloh, Tenn 4-6-62. Wounded 10-7-62 Perryville, Ky. Court martialed 5-3-63. Returned to duty 5-11-63. Issued clothing 3-27-64. Wounded 7-20-64. Roll of 2-31-64 shows absent, sick. Paroled Atlanta 4-65.

English, James N., pvt. 2-20-62. Twenty-three years old, Griffin, Ga. Horse valued at $165. Horse killed 8-15-62. On detached service 5-63. Issued clothing 12-6-63. Transferred to infantry by order of Gen. Bragg.

Fambro, James F., pvt. 5-62/ capt. 6-3-63. Prior service as pvt in Co. K 1st Ga. Infantry from 3-18-61 to 3-15-62. Mustered out of infantry at Augusta, Ga. 4-2-62. Nineteen years old, enlisted as pvt in 2nd Ga. Cavalry. Horse killed 8-15-62. Captured, 9-21-62 Lebanon Junction, Ky. & exchanged. Horse killed 12-31-62 at Stones River. Elected Captain. Last on roll 12-31-63.

Findley, Emanuel A. "Bud", pvt. 5-2-62. Horse killed at Whites Creek, Tenn. Captured 9-21-62 Lebanon Junction, Ky. Transferred from Camp Chase, Ohio to Cairo, Ill. 9-29-62. Received 11-1-62 Vicksburg for exchange. Roll of 2-12-64 shows AWOL since 2-9-64. Issued clothing 3-27-64 and 6-15-64. Present 12-31-64.

Findley, John T., pvt. 3-4-65. Eighteen years old. Horse valued at $150. Captured 9-21-62 at Lebanon Junction, Ky. , transferred for exchange 9-29-62. Present 5-63. Roll of 2-12-64 shows AWOL since 2-9-64. Present 12-31-64. POW record shows 5'8" gray eyes, dark hair.

Franklin, Calloway, pvt.

Franklin, Edwin C., pvt. 3-12-62. May be same as Calloway Franklin above. Twenty-six years old. Horse valued at $200. Roll of 2-12-64 shows AWOL since 2-9-64. Issued clothing 3-27-64. Present 12-31-64. Present 4-26-65. Paroled 5-3-65 Charlotte.

Fuller, Tilman "Till," pvt. 9-1-63. Issued clothing 3-27-64. Present 12-31-64. Present at surrender 4-26-65. Paroled 5-3-65 Charlotte, N.C.

Flynt, Julius A., pvt. 3-4-62. Twenty-four years old. Prior service 2nd Bn Ga. Infantry, 4-20-61. Appointed company surgeon. Discharged from Infantry 7-12-61. Enlisted as pvt in 2nd Ga. Cavalry Co. E. Transferred to Co I 53rd Ga. Infantry 5-12-62. Died 1-24-63 of pneumonia in Richmond Hospital #1 or #9.

Gaultney, George W., pvt. 1862. "Died at home" 7-62. May be same man as George G. Gwaltney, below.

Gordon, Edward P., pvt./cpl 2-25-62.

Gordon, Ed. T., 3rd cpl. May be same as Edward P. Gordon above. Thirty-five years old. Horse valued at $175. Horse killed at Whites Creek, Tenn., 8-15-62. Discharged prior to 5-15-63.

Goodrich, William L., 2nd sgt. 3-19-62/pvt. Nineteen years old. Horse valued at $250. "Reduced to ranks 3-15-63." Present 5-63. Issued clothing 3-27-64. Roll of 12-31-64 shows absent sick since 12-16-64.

Granger, John, pvt. 2-20-62. "Died at home" 5-8-62.

Graves, J. K. C., pvt. 3-24-64. Issued clothing 6-15-64. Absent sick 11 & 12-64.

Guttenberger, Charles William, pvt. 2-20-62. Twenty-three years old. Horse valued at $175. Bugler for Col. Lawton. Last on roll 5-7-62. Other records show that on account of rheumatism he became conductor on Macon & Western RR, running from Macon to Atlanta.

Gwaltney, George G., pvt. 2-25-62. Twenty-one years old. Died in Henry County, Ga. prior to 10-15-62.

Ham, Ersmus, pvt. 3-4-62. Captured 10-9-63 Sugar Creek, Tenn. Paroled Camp Morton, Ind. & forwarded to City Point, Va. for exchange 2-20-65. Died 3-65.

Hamil, William C., pvt. 5-5-62. Twenty-one years old. Wounded at Murfreesboro. Captured 10-10-63 Sugar Creek, Tenn. Paroled 2-26-65 Camp Morton, Ind.

Hamil, Willis J., pvt. 3-1-62. Wounded. Present 5-63. Transferred 4-20-64 to Capt.White's Battery Horse Artillery. Apparently returned to company. Present 12-31-64.

Hancock, Henry U., pvt. 3-4-62/3rd sgt. 11-1-64/1st sgt. Twenty-three years old. Horse valued at $250. Present through 12-63. Issued clothing 3-27-64 and 6-15-64. Present 12-31-64.

Harris, A. W., pvt. Captured 5-8-65 Athens, Ga. by forces under Gen. Palmer.

Heflin, Shadrick James, pvt. 3-20-62. Roll of 5-15-63 shows AWOL.

Hendricks, Obe., pvt. 5-3-64. Surrendered 4-65 Raleigh, N.C.

Hicks, Dillard, pvt. 4-10-62. Deserted 7-1-64. Captured 7-64 Fayette Co., Ga. Took oath of allegiance to U.S. gov't 7-27-64 Louisville, Ky and released north of Ohio River.

Hicks, James T., pvt. 3-4-62. Killed 7-13-62 at Murfreesboro, Tenn.

Hinman, J., pvt. Captured 5-8-65, Athens, Ga. by forces under Gen. W. J. Palmer.

Holland, Francis M., pvt. 2-20-62. Deserted 2-19-63.

Holland, Mathew N., pvt. 2-20-62/sgt. On duty at Atlanta Military Prison 5-64, 6-64. Issued clothing 7-15-64.

Hutson, Jefferson H., pvt. 3-1-62. Captured 9-21-62 Lebanon Junction, Ky. Transferred from Camp Chase, Ohio to Cairo, Ill. 9-62. Received 11-1-62 near Vicksburg for exchange. Transferred to Capt. White's Battery 1-64. Surrendered 5-5-65, Horse Creek Bridge, S.C.

Hutson, James L., pvt. 3-1-62. Died of fever 5-13 or 17-62 Camp Lawton.

Ison, Emanuel I., pvt. 2-25-62/ 5th sgt. Transferred 9-4-63 Gibson's Battery Light Artillery. Apparently returned to company. Present 12-31-63.

Ison, Thomas J., pvt. 2-15-62. Paroled 5-3-65 Charlotte, N.C. indicating he was present at surrender.

Ivey, James R., pvt. 4-7-62. Twenty-one years old. Horse valued at $235. Horse killed at Whites Creek. Present 5-63. Captured 1-27-64 Sevierville, Tenn. Sent from Camp Chase, Ohio to Louisville, Ky. 1-24-64. Released 6-16-65.

Jester, Levi T., pvt. 3-7-64. Prior service 23th Ga. Infantry. Present 11 and 12-64.

Johnson, William W., pvt. 3-20-62. Eighteen years old. Present 5-63, 12-63. Clothing issued 3-27-64 and 6-15-64. On roll of patients at Ocmulgee Hospital 10-6-64 through 11-7-64. Present 12-64. Present at surrender 4-26-64. Paroled 5-3-65 Charlotte, N.C.

Jones, Hardy Amos, pvt. 5-6-62. Eighteen years old. Horse valued at $150 and owned by Capt. F. M. Ison. Transferred 5-6-63 to White's Battery. Apparently returned to company. Present 12-31-64.

Jones, James, pvt. 4-7-62. Thirty-eight years old. Horse valued at $175. Captured at Sugar Creek 10-63. U.S. record shows captured 10-11-63 near Huntsville, Ala. Died 3-10-64 of "erysipelas" while a POW at Camp Morton, Ind. Grave 832 Green Lawn Cemetery. Also shown as serving in K Co.

Jones, James M., pvt. 3-4-62/ 2nd cpl. Nineteen years old. Horse valued at $200. Captured 9-21-62 Lebanon Junction, Ky. Sent from Camp Chase, Ohio to Vicksburg for exchange 11-1-62. Exchanged 9-29-62. Transferred to White's Battery 1863. Clothing issued 5-11-63 and 3-27-64. Present 12-31-64. POW record shows 5'8" blue eyes, lt. hair.

Keeble, H. C., pvt. Captured 5-8-65 near Athens, Ga. by forces under Gen. W. J. Palmer.

Keifer, William H., pvt. 4-2-62. Twenty-five years old. Horse valued at $165. Company saddler. "Discharged, disability cause by…of femur" 6-24-62.

Kerbo, Daniel, pvt. 12-31-62. Wounded 2-4-63 Fort Donelson. Last on roll 5-13-63.

Kimble, Thomas W., pvt. 5-10-62. Eighteen years old. Captured 10-9-63 Sugar Creek, Tenn. POW at Camp Morton and sent to James River, Va. for exchange 3-65. Clothing issued 3-27-64.

Knight, Archie N., pvt. 7-1-64. Captured 12-4-64 Waynesboro, Ga. Released Point Lookout, Md. 6-28-65. POW record shows "5'10", lt. hair, blue eyes. Residence shown as Jefferson Co., Tenn.

Lasseter or Lasiter, Joshua A., pvt. 5-6-62. Twenty-four years old. Horse valued at $225. Present 5-63. On special duty 2-9-64. Clothing issued 3-27-64. Present 12-31-64.

Lavender, William R., pvt. 2-25-62/cpl./ 4th sgt.11-1-64. Thirty-five years old. Horse valued at $200. Absent sick at Atlanta 5-63. Court martial proceedings commenced 5-3-63, but subsequently promoted to sgt. Roll of 12-31-63 shows AWOL since 10-30-63. Issued clothing 3-27-64.

Leach, R. S., pvt. 5-13-64. Roll of 12-64 shows AWOL since 11-15-64.

Mathews, G. W., pvt. 5-1-64. Roll of 12-64 shows AWOL since 7-10-64.

Mathews, G. L., pvt. 5-1-64. Roll of 12-64 shows AWOL since 11-10-64.

Meremie, R. M., pvt. Captured 5-8-65 near Athens, Ga. by forces under Gen. W. J. Palmer.

Milligan, Gideon W., pvt. 4-19-64. Prior service in Co. D. 2nd Bn Ga. Infantry 4-20-61. Admitted to Floyd House & Ocmulgee Hospital, Macon, Ga. 8-24-64 with "ulcer leg with loss of muscle tissue, result, gangrene." Roll of 12-31-64 shows sick since 6-1-64.

Montique, Robert L., pvt. Captured 5-22-63 Middleton, Tenn. Sent to Baltimore as POW 5-29-63.

Moore, Alexander W., pvt. 3-19-62. Transferred 5-10-62 to Co. A 53rd Ga. Infantry. Appointed Chaplain 14th Ga. Infantry. Ordered to Holcomb's Legion, S.C. 1-16-64. Transferred to post duty, Greenville, S.C. 1-29-65.

Moore, Frank S., pvt. 2-15-62. Eighteen years old. Horse valued at $200. "Transferred to Capt. Atkins Company without pay" 5-13-62.

Norris, Burt J., pvt. 2-10-62. Substitute for O. Williams. Captured 4-21-63, McMinnville, Tenn. Admitted to Chattanooga hospital 6-18-63. Apparently exchanged. Clothing issued 3-27-64. Appears on roll of patients at Ocmulgee hospital 8-1 through 8-23-64.

Norris, Willis C., pvt. 2-15-62. Twenty-five years old. Horse valued at $200. Present 2-63, 5-63. Roll of 2-12-64 shows detailed with wagons. Clothing issued 3-27-64. Roll of 12-31-64 shows on detached service since 4-20-64.

Nunnally, James A., pvt. 3-19-62/1st sgt. 3-63. Thirty-four years old. Horse valued at $225. Roll of 12-31-64 shows sick since 8-10-64.

Parrish, John W., pvt. 3-19-62. Thirty years old. Horse valued at $200. Present 2-63, 5-63. Wounded Murfreesboro. Present at surrender 4-26-65. Paroled 5-3-65 Charlotte, N.C.

Parker, George L., pvt. 5-8-62. Twenty-eight years old. Horse valued at $180. Roll of 5-63 on detached service in Atlanta. Clothing issued 3-27-64. AWOL 12-31-64.

Patrick, David L., pvt. 2-15-62. Seventeen years old. Horse valued at $175. Detached as cpl. and courier 5-15-63. Clothing issued 3-27-64. Present 11-64. Wounded 12-4-64 Waynesboro, Ga. Roll of 12-31-64 shows absent wounded.

Patrick, Marion J., pvt. 2-15-62. Twenty-one years old. Horse valued at $200. Roll of 12-31-64 shows sick since 8-2-64.

Payne, James C., pvt. 4-9-62. Twenty-seven years old. Horse valued at $225. Horse killed 8-15-62 Whites Creek. Transferred to infantry 1863 "by order of Gen. Bragg." Took oath of allegiance to U.S. government 3-14-64, Chattanooga. POW records describe as 6'1" fair complexion, gray eyes, brown hair.

Reeves, Hughey H., pvt. 3-26-62. Twenty-four years old. Horse valued at $165. Captured 9-21-62, Lebanon Junction, Ky. Received near Vicksburg for exchange 11-1-62. Transferred to White's Battery 8-4-63. Returned to Company. Present 12-31-64.

John Reeves, pvt. 2-1-63.

Reid, John B., pvt. 4-19-64. Prior service 2nd Bn Ga Infantry. In CSA hospital Wilmington, N.C. 5-62. Roll of 12-31-64 shows sick since 6-64.

Seagraves, Thomas D., pvt. 2-20-62. Twenty-three years old. Horse valued at $250. Absent sick 5-63. Paid 5-11-63. AWOL 2-12-64. Clothing issued 3-27-64 and 6-15-64. Present 12-64. Present at surrender 4-26-65. Paroled 5-3-65 Charlotte, N.C.

Shackelford, Asmun B., pvt. 4-20-62. Twenty-eight years old. Horse valued at $250. Wounded and disabled 9-19-63 at Chickamauga.

Shannon, David H., pvt. 2-25-62/2nd cpl. Thirty-four years old. Company fairier. Present 2-63, 5-63. Present 11 and 12-63. Clothing issued 3-27-64, 6-15-64. Present 11 and 12-64. Present at surrender 4-26-65 as pvt. Paroled 5-3-65 Charlotte, N.C.

Shields, James M. pvt. Appears on U.S. list of "Rebel Deserters" taking oath of allegiance to U.S. 2-24-64.

Sloman, James F., pvt. 3-4-62. Twenty-four years old. Transferred to Co B 5th Ga. Infantry.

Smith, Henry M., pvt. 3-20-62. Prior service 2nd Bn. Ga Infantry, 4-20-61. Twenty-four years old. Horse valued at $175. Died 1863.

Swann, John A., pvt. 3-19-62. Twenty-six years old. Horse valued at $200. Absent sick 5-63. Detailed as teamster 2-12-64. Clothing issued 3-27-64. Present 12-64. Present at surrender 4-26-65. Paroled 5-3-65 Charlotte, N.C.

Thaxton, W., pvt. 4-26-64. Roll of 12-31-64 shows sick since 6-64.

Travis, Charles, pvt. 4-20-62/ sgt. 3-15-63. Twenty-seven years old. Horse valued at $250. Captured 1-27-64, Sevierville, Tenn. Died 3-5-64 Rock Island Prison, Ill.

Travis, Thomas S., pvt. 3-19-62. Eighteen years old. Horse valued at $200. Present 2-63, 5-63. AWOL 12-31-64. Unofficial records show wounded and discharged 1864.

Tusha, Eliga, Roll of 12-64 shows "conscripted and ordered to report but failed to do so. Dropped from rolls."

Waller, Charles B., pvt. 2-20-62. Twenty-seven years old. Horse valued at $190. Present 2-63, 5-63. Clothing issued 3-27-64 and 6-15-64. Present 12-31-64.

Waller, Henry A., pvt. 4-2-62. Twenty-seven years old. Horse valued at $225. Present 2-63, 5-63. Horse killed at White Oak Creek, Tenn. Forage master 8 & 9-63. Clothing issued 3-27-64, 6-15-64. Wounded 12-4-64 Waynesboro, Ga.

Wellmaker, John Henderson, pvt. 3-24-62. Twenty-seven years old. Horse valued at $175. AWOL 5-63. Wounded 10-11-63 Sugar Creek, Tenn. Clothing issued 3-27-64. Wounded and died 1864.

Westmoreland, John D. or T., pvt. 5-5-62/ 4th cpl. 3-15-63. Twenty-one years old. Horse valued at $175. Present 11 and 12-63. Clothing issued 3-27-64 and 6-15-64. Present 12-64.

Westmoreland, G., pvt. 7-20-64. Present 12-64.

Wickliff, W. C., pvt. Captured 5-8-65 Athens, Ga. by forces under Gen. W. J. Palmer.

Williams, Osburn F., pvt. 5-7-62. Bugler. Prior service Co. C 30th Ga. Infantry as sgt. major. Thirty-three years old. Horse valued at $200.

Wills, Albert G., pvt. 3-31-62. Thirty-one years old. Horse valued at $150. Absent sick 5-63. Roll of 2-12-64 shows AWOL since 2-9-64. Clothing issued 3-27-64. Present 11 and 12-64. Present at surrender 4-26-65. Paroled 5-3-65 Charlotte, N.C.

Wilson, Augustus W., pvt. 5-1-64. Roll of 12-31-64 shows sick since 6-64. F Company

Gayden, Francis Thompson, capt. 10-31-61. Retired 5-6-62, which may be the date the regiment was mustered into Confederate service. Later elected 1st lt. Co E 2nd Reg. Ga. militia

Johnson, James Franklin, 1st lt. 10-31-61. Retired, over age, 5-1-62.

Chapman, W. Hardy, 2nd lt. 10-31-61/ capt. 5-6-62. Thirty-five years old. Succeeded Gayden as company commander. Horse valued at $275. Present through 1863 and 1864. Resigned 2-10-65 due to ill health.

DeVaughn, James Elijah, jr. 2nd lt. 10-31-61/ 1st lt. 5-1-62. Twenty-two years old. Horse valued at $250. Captured 10-9-63 near Sugar Creek, Tenn (or Logan Creek). POW at Camp Chase, Ohio. Released Sandusky, 6-11-65. POW records describe as 5'11", hazel eyes, dark hair, fair complexion.

Camp, Benjamin, 1st sgt. 10-31-61/jr. 2nd lt. Twenty-four years old. Present 2-63 through 5-63. Roll of 12-31-64 shows in hospital since 10-20-64 with abscesses.

Johnson, James W., 2nd sgt. 10-31-61/ jr. 2nd lt. 5-6-62. Present 12-31-64.

Smith, William, 1st lt., Captured 10-9-63 Sugar Creek, Tenn.

Smith, John F., 3rd sgt. 10-31-61/ 2nd sgt. 5-6-62. Present 2-63, 5-63. Captured 1-24-64 Sevierville, Tenn. Released from Rock Island Prison, Ill. 6-18-65.

Waldrop, John T., 4th sgt. 10-31-61.

Johnson, Henry S., 5th sgt. 10-31-61/ 4th sgt. 5-6-62. Captured 1-27-64 Sevierville, Tenn. Transferred for exchange 3-2-65.

Strickland, Henry Perry, 2nd cpl. 10-31-61. Twenty-one years old. Horse valued at $200. Present 2-63, 5-63, 12-63. Roll of 12-64 shows AWOL since 11-64. Married 11-20-64 in Jonesboro, Ga. Pension application shows present with company at surrender, 4-26-65, in Salisbury, N.C. Died 1921. Brothers Cary and Milsey were pvts in company.

Waterson, William H or L., 3rd cpl. 10-31-61.

Briggs, William, pvt. 10-31-61/ 4th cpl. 5-6-62. Appointed orderly 3-24-62. Roll for 12-31-64 shows absent, detailed with Gen. Hood's wagon train.

Cook, James S., Musician.

Smith, Alford L., Musician 12-8-61. Discharged 4-22-62.

Allen, James M., pvt. 5-6-62. Transferred to Capt. White's Battery 12-62. Apparently returned to company. Present through 12-31-64.

Allen, John H. "Jack", pvt. 5-6-62. Wounded and captured 11-13-62 Elizabethtown, Ky. POW at Cairo, Ill. POW record describes as nineteen years old, 6'2", grey eyes, light complexion. Back on roll and present through 12-63. Captured 11-16-64 in Henry Co., Ga. POW at Point Lookout, Md. Released 6-22-65 Hilton Head Island.

Anthony, T. A., pvt. 5-7-62. In hospital during 1863. AWOL 1-64 and 2-64.

Atkinson, Burket, pvt. 5-6-62. Roll of 12-31-64 shows in hospital since 8-31-64.

Bailey, J. R., pvt. 6-6-64. Enlisted at Jonesboro.

Bailey, S. P., pvt. 2-3-64. Present 6-64.

Banks, W. C., pvt. 5-7-62; "entry cancelled."

Bankston, W. J., pvt.

Bankston, B. pvt. 5-6-62. Deserted 7-16-63.

Bell, John, pvt. 5-7-62. Horse valued at $225. In Shelbyville hospital 5-26-63. Pay records show him with regiment through 2-18-64. Appears on list of deserters to be delivered by steamer to U.S. Provost Marshall in New York. POW records describe as 5'1", blue eyes, twenty-six years old.

Bennett, Robert, pvt. 11-13-64. Enlisted in Fayetteville.

Brogdon, Colendar B. "Cole", pvt. 7-20-63. Roll of 12-63 shows captured near McMinnville. Roll of 12-64 shows captured "at Sugar Creek, Ala." Federal record shows captured at McMinnville and forwarded to Louisville for exchange 3-4-65.

Briggs, William, pvt. 5-6-62. Roll of 11-64 shows detailed with Gen. Hood's wagon train.

Byington, L. C., pvt. 3-1-63. AWOL 11-63. Present 11-63 and 12-63. Clothing issued 3-27-64.

Calloway, Jacob King, pvt. 5-6-62. Horse valued at $250. Present 6-63. "Captured in battle" 7-22-64 Atlanta. U.S. record shows captured 7-21-64. POW at Camp Chase. Transferred to City Point and exchanged. In Wayside Hospital or Hospital #9 3-11-65 Richmond, Va.

Campbell, T. G., pvt. 7-25-64. Present 12-31-64.

Campbell, William M., pvt. 5-7-62. Present 12-31-63 and 12-31-64.

Carmichael, Josephus, pvt. 5-6-62. Twenty-four years old. Discharged due to disability, "enlargement of the heart" 8-13-62.

Carter, Isaac, pvt. 5-6-62/com. sgt. 63. Twenty-five years old. Present through 12-31-64. Promoted to regimental commissary sgt. Also described as "forage agent" in 6-63.

Cates, Green B., pvt. 4-16-63. Present 12-63. AWOL 12-64.

Cates, William David, pvt. 5-6-62. Captured 10-9-63 Sugar Creek, Tenn. POW Camp Morton, Ind. Transferred for exchange 3-4-65.

Chambers, John G. pvt. 5-6-62/ 1st sgt. Nineteen years old. Horse valued at $260. In hospital 3-7-63. Issued clothing 7-17-63. Present 12-63 as pvt. On roll of prisoners captured and paroled in Ky. and "declared exchanged." Present 12-64 as 1st sgt. Present at surrender 4-26-65 Salisbury, N.C.

Chambers, Wyatt D., pvt. 5-6-62/ 5th sgt. Twenty-one years old. Horse valued at $250. Present as 5th sgt.5-63. "Died in service."

Chandler, Allen C., pvt. 7-25-64. Present 12-31-64.

Chandler, J. H., pvt. 7-25-64. Present 12-31-64. Present at surrender 4-26-65, Salisbury, N.C.

Chandler, W. P., pvt. 8-1-63. Present 12-63. Clothing issued 3-27-64.

Christian, James J. pvt. 5-6-62/ 5th sgt. Twenty-seven years old. Present as pvt 12-63. Issued clothing 3-27-64. Present as 5th sgt. 12-64. Present at surrender 4-26-65 Salisbury, N.C.

Crawford, Frank, pvt. 5-6-62. Died prior to 12-30-63.

Creel, John W., pvt. 5-6-62. Present through 1863. Roll of 12-31-64 shows detached to "drive beaves."

Davis, Lewis, pvt. 5-6-62. Horse valued at $250. Horse killed 12-29-62. Present 12-63. AWOL 12-31-64.

Denham, D. D., pvt. 6-1-63. Captured 10-9-63 Sugar Creek, Tenn. POW at Camp Morton 10-18-63. "Dide" in prison 12-19-64 from pneumonia. Grave #786 Green Lawn Cemetery.

Drewry, Joseph F., pvt. 5-7-62. Horse valued at $175. Died 4-10-63 at Rome Hospital.

Eason, Charles A., pvt. 5-7-62. Twenty-six years old. Horse valued at $175. Present 2-63 through 5-63. AWOL 1-9-64. Issued clothing 6-15-64. AWOL 12-31-64.

Eason, Elijah P., pvt. 5-6-62. Present through 12-31-64 and present at surrender, 4-26-65 Salisbury, N.C.

Eason, John, cpl. 5-7-62. Twenty years old. Horse valued at $200. Furloughed 1-13-64. Issued clothing 3-27-64. Present 12-31-64. Present at surrender 4-26-65 Salisbury, N.C.

Eason, William P., pvt. 7-1-63. AWOL 1-9-64. Issued clothing 3-27-64. Present 12-64. Present at surrender 4-26-65. Paroled 5-3-65, Charlotte, N.C.

Ellington, John C., pvt. 5-7-62. Roll of 5-63 shows on detached service with enrolling officer. To hospital 12-20-63.

Elliott, A. V., pvt. 3-1-64. AWOL 12-31-64.

Elliott, G. P., pvt. 3-1-64. AWOL 12-31-64.

Farris, F. M., pvt. 5-7-62. Twenty years old, "died at Bat. Murfreesboro" Father filed claim 9-9-62, indicating that he was killed in Forrests' 7-13-62 attack rather than the Stones River battle at the end of that year.

Farris, James P., pvt. 11-22-61/ 1st sgt. Twenty-eight years old. Horse valued at $250. Present through 12-63. AWOL 12-31-64.

Farris, John F., pvt. 1-1-62. Thirty years old. Horse valued at $250. Present 5-63. Absent with wagons 12-63. Issued clothing 3-27-64. AWOL 12-31-64.

Farmer, James, pvt. 5-6-62. Twenty-nine years old. Horse valued at $225. Discharged from Atlanta hospital 3-26-63. Captured and died as POW at Camp Morton.

Guest, Thomas, pvt. Enlisted in Henry County, Ga. POW. Released at Point Lookout 6-27-65. POW record shows 5'9" fair complexion, hazel eyes.

Hanes, W. C., pvt. 5-6-62. Twenty-nine years old. Horse valued at $250.

Hanley, J., pvt. 7-63. Present 12-31-63. Issued clothing 3-27-64. AWOL 12-31-64.

Harris, O. F., pvt. 5-7-62. Paid 10-27-62.

Harris, Seaborn, pvt./ cpl. 10-27-62. Discharged 4-1-63 or 64.

Harris, S. A., pvt. 5-7-62. Thirty-two years old. Horse valued at $125. Absent, sick at hospital 3-3-63. Present 12-63. AWOL 12-31-64.

Harris, Silas P., pvt. 10-31-62. AWOL 12-31-64.

Hartley, James J., pvt. 10-31-62

Hartsfield, David T., pvt. Captured 1-27-64 Sevierville, Tenn. Transferred for exchange 3-2-65 from Rock Island Barracks, Ill.

Henderson, Robert S. "Still.", pvt. 5-7-62. Killed at Murfreesboro, Tenn. 7-13-62.

Hine, William H., pvt.

Hudson, James F., pvt. 10-31-61.

Huey, William M., pvt. May be same as W. H. Huie below.

Huie, W. C., pvt.

Huie, W. H., pvt. Captured 10-9-63 at Sugar Creek, Tenn. (Apparently wounded) "Dide in prison" 10-28-63.

Hutcheson, C., pvt. Captured 9-1-64 while detailed to guard cattle. Place of capture shown variously as Macon or Jonesboro, Ga.

Hutcheson, Ladson, pvt. 5-6-62. Captured 9-2-64 while detailed to guard cattle. Place of capture shown variously as Macon or Jonesboro, Ga. Exchanged 9-19 or 9-22-64.

Hutchenson, M. A., pvt. 5-6-62. Present 5-63. Clothing issued 3-27-64. AWOL 12-31-64.

Johnson, Arthur, pvt. 11-18-61. Discharged with disability 2-22-62.

Johnson, John A., pvt. Home on furlough 3-65 till end of war.

Jones, Enoch G., pvt. 5-6-62. Thirty-two years old. Horse valued at $150. Roll of 5-63 shows absent, at hospital since 8-16-62. Absent, at hospital 12-31-63. Captured 9-1-64, Jonesboro, but shown as AWOL 12-31-64.

Jones, Thomas R., pvt. 10-31-61/ 3rd sgt 5-6-62. Present 5-63. AWOL 12-31-64.

Lambert, Seth H., pvt. 5-6-62. Died 2-10-63 near Fayetteville, Tenn.

Lasseter, Elijah M., pvt. 5-6-62. Horse valued at $175. Present 5-63. Detached as courier for Gen. Hardee 9-22-63. Captured 7-22-64 near Atlanta. POW at Camp Chase, Ohio.

Leach, Green, pvt.

Leach, William Alexander, pvt. 10-31-61. Nineteen years old. Horse valued at $175. Present 2-63, 5-63. Issued clothing 3-27-64. Present 12-31-64.

Lee, Samuel James, pvt 10-31-61. Twenty years old. In hospital 8-12-63. Issued clothing 3-27-64. Captured 7-22-64 Atlanta. POW at Camp Chase. Shown as member of Iverson's Brigade, Martin's Division, Wheeler's Corps. Transferred to Point Lookout, Md. for exchange 3-18-65. Received at Boulware & Cox Wharves James River, Va. 3-27-65.

Loyd, Samuel, pvt. 10-31-61, Twenty-five years old. Horse valued at $175. To Shelbyville Hospital 5-26-63. Issued clothing 3-27-64. AWOL 12-31-64.

Mallory, James, pvt.

McConnell, J. A., pvt. 5-6-62. Twenty-six years old. Horse valued at $175. Roll of 5-63 shows "Substitute by Potts."

Mills, J. J. Moses, pvt. 5-6-62. Twenty-three years old. Horse valued at $250. Present 2-63, 5-63. Detached as courier for Gen. Wheeler 10-25-63. Present 12-64

Morris, David P., pvt. 10-31-61. Twenty years old. Horse valued at $225. Wounded 7-13-62 Murfreesboro, Tenn. Roll of 5-63 shows absent, wounded since 7-13-62. Roll of 12-63 shows absent "at the wagons" since 11-22-63. Clothing issued 3-27-64. Present 12-31-64. Died in Atlanta, 1902.

Morris, James, pvt.

Morris, Pressley M., pvt. 5-6-62, Thirty-two years old. Horse valued at $165. Present 2-63, 5-63. Captured 10-9-63 Sugar Creek, Tenn. POW at Camp Morton. Transferred for exchange 2-26-65.

Morris, Richard A., pvt. 10-31-61. Twenty-three years old. Horse valued at $225.

Morris, William J., pvt. 10-31-61. May be same as James Morris above. Died 3-29-62.

Morrow, William H. H., pvt. 2-28-62. Twenty-one years old. Horse valued at $200. Roll of 5-63 shows on detached service. Roll of 12-64 shows detailed to make shoes since 10-10-63. Died 1901.

Moss, W. J., pvt. 5-6-62. Present 2-63, 5-63. Roll of 2-18-64 shows AWOL since 10-21-63. Present 11-64, 12-64.

Mundy, Reuben W., pvt. 10-31-61. Twenty-one years old. Horse valued at $225. Present 2-63, 5-63. Roll of 2-18-64 shows "absent, at wagons in Georgia" since 11-22-63. Clothing issued 3-27-64, 6-15-64. Present at surrender, 4-26-65. Paroled 5-3-65, Charlotte, N. C. Died 10-17-1912 Jonesboro, Ga.

Mundy, Robert S., pvt. 10-31-61. Nineteen years old. Horse valued at $200. Present 2-63, 5-63, 11-63, 12-63. Clothing issued 3-27-64 and 6-15-64. AWOL 12-31-64. Brother to Reuben. Died 1889.

Murphy, J. D., pvt. 5-6-62. Thirty-one years old. Horse valued at $175.

Murphy, James, pvt. May be same as J. D. Murphy above.

Murphy, Joseph H., pvt. 1-1-62. Eighteen years old. Horse valued at $185. Present 2-63, 5-63. Captured 1-27-64, Sevierville, Tenn. Transferred from Rock Island, Ill. for exchange 2-15-65. In hospital at Camp Winder, Va. 3-2-65.

Murray, Oliver, pvt.

Payne, Robert, pvt. Twenty-nine yrs old. Wounded 7-13-62 Murfreesboro, Tenn. "Shot with a rifle ball through right hip which disabled him so as to render him unable to make a living at ordinary labor. Sent home after wound. Returned to command and was again sent home."

Nolan, R. M., pvt. 5-6-62. Twenty-eight years old. Horse valued at $240. Present 2-63, 6-63, 11-63, 12-63. Paid compensation 8-11-63 for horse killed at Middleton, Tenn. 6-22-63.

Phelps, James R. pvt. 11-18-61.

Phillips, Joshua C., pvt. 11-18-61. Clothing issued 6-5-64, 6-30-64.

Phipps, James R., pvt. 5-6-62. Twenty-eight years old. Horse valued at $200. Present 2-63, 5-63. Clothing issued 6-15-64. Captured 12-4-64 at Waynesboro, Ga. POW at Hilton Head, S.C. Transferred to Point Lookout, Md. and released 6-16-65.

Phipps, Richard, pvt. 5-6-62. Roll of 6-15-63 shows absent, sick at hospital since 3-31-63.

Pollard, Elisha F., pvt. 11-18-61. Discharged with disability 12-31-61.

Pollard, James M., pvt. 11-18-61.

Pollard, William P., pvt. 11-18-61.

Potts, William F., pvt. 5-6-62. Clothing issued 3-27-64. Captured 9-30-64 near Fayette, Ga. Described as 5'6" dark hair, brown eyes.

Powell, Charles S., pvt. 11-18-61. Thirty years old. Horse valued at $200. Furlough 4-29-63. Paid 5-7-63. Absent, at hospital 11 & 12-63. Issued clothing 3-27-64. Present 12-64. Present at surrender 4-26-65. Paroled 5-3-65 Charlotte, N.C.

Powell, Simeon, "Entry canceled."

Pyron, James M., pvt. 1-1-62. Present 2-63, 5-63, 5-64.

Pyron, Marcus A., pvt. 11-18-61/ cpl. Twenty years old. Horse valued at $180. Present 2-63, 5-63, 11 and 12-63, 11 and 12-64.

Pyron, W. M., pvt. 4-1-64. AWOL on roll of 12-64.

Ranetree, Jackson, pvt. Captured 9-8-63 and sent to hospital 10-63.

Renfroe, William P., pvt. 9-1-63. Prior service as jr 2nd lt in Co F 13th Ga. Infantry 10-30-61. Resigned 2-24-63 and enlisted as pvt. in 2nd Ga. Cavalry. AWOL 1-9-64. Roll of 12-64 shows absent at hospital since 7-25-64. Present at surrender 4-26-65. Paroled 5-3-65 Charlotte, N.C.

Rowan, James M., pvt. 5-6-62. Twenty-six years old. Horse valued at $250. Present 2-63, 5-63. Clothing issued 3-27-64 and 6-15-64. AWOL 12-31-64.

Rush, E., cpl. 5-6-62. AWOL 12-64.

Slaton, Benjamin, pvt.

Smith, H. M., cpl. 5-6-62. Twenty-two years old. Horse valued at $275. Present 2-63, 5-63. Captured 10-9-63 Sugar Creek, Tenn. POW at Camp Morton. Transferred for exchange 4-18-65.

Smith, Henry M., pvt. 11-18-61. May be same as H. M. Smith above.

Smith, J. W., pvt. 5-6-62. Thirty years old. Present 2-63, 5-63, 11-63, 12-63. Clothing issued 3-27-64. AWOL 12-64.

Smith, Martin, pvt. Captured 10-9-63 at Sugar Creek, Tenn.

Smith, Seaborne S., pvt. Captured 1-24-64 Sevierville, Tenn. POW at Camp Chase. Transferred to Rock Island Barracks, Ill. Appears on roll of Jackson Hospital, Richmond, Va. 3-2-65.

Smith, Warren, pvt. May be same man as J. W. Smith above.

Speer, J. Freeman, pvt. 5-7-62. Twenty-three years old. Horse valued at $150. Present 2-63, 5-63, 11-63, 12-63. Clothing issued 3-27-64. Shown as present at surrender, but also shown as captured 1-27-64 near Knoxville, Tenn.

Speer, J. W., pvt. 5-7-62. "Transferred to Wheeler's scouts" 1-63. "Died near Morristown" 12-20-63.

Speer, W. M., pvt. 5-6-62. Twenty-eight years old. Horse valued at $180. Sent to hospital 3-63, and furloughed 3-26-63. Paid 4-63, 5-63, 8-63. Clothing issued 3-27-64. AWOL 12-64.

Starr, John G., pvt. 4-1-64. Wounded 7-4-64 in right arm near Marietta, Ga. Arm amputated 8-15-64. In hospital 12-31-64.

Strickland, C. A. pvt

Strickland, Cary Jefferson, pvt. 10-31-61. Twenty-five years old. Brother of Cpl. Henry Strickland and Pvt. Milsey Strickland. Horse valued at $225. Present 5-63, "returned from hospital." Present 11 and 12-63. Roll of 12-31-64 shows detailed to drive beef 11 and 12-64. Returned home during this time and married.

Strickland, George W. pvt. 10-31-61.

Strickland, Milsey Eli, pvt. 10-31-61. Twenty-eight years old. Horse valued at $175. Present 2-63. Wounded in hand 3-63, sent to hospital and finger amputated. Captured 1-27-64 Sevierville, Tenn. Released from Rock Island, Ill. 6-18-65. POW records show him to be resident of Flat Shoals, Pike County, Ga., 6'2" gray eyes, brown hair, "fresh" complexion. Brother of Cpl. Henry and Pvt. Cary Strickland.

Stinchcomb, George W., pvt. 10-31-61. Captured 10-9-63 Sugar Creek, Tenn. POW at Camp Morton, Ind. Transferred for exchange 3-4-65.

Stinchcomb, Victor, pvt. 11-18-61. Thirty-two years old. Horse valued at $225. Sent to hospital 3-63. Clothing issued 3-27-64. AWOL 12-64.

Tarpley, J. R., pvt. 62. Twenty-four years old. Horse valued at $140. Present 2-63, 5-63. Roll of 2-18-64 shows "absent at wagons in Georgia" since 11-22-63. Clothing issued 3-27-64, 6-15-64. AWOL 12-64.

Thames, James T., pvt. 5-6-62, Twenty-eight years old. Horse valued at $200. Died 1900.

Thornton, Haywood T., pvt. 10-1-63. Captured 1-27-64 Sevierville, Tenn. and died 10-28-64 as POW at Rock Island, Ill., from pneumonia. Grave #1587.

Toland, Asa P., pvt. 11-61 or 8-1-63. Present 2-18-64. Clothing issued 3-27-64. Present 12-64.

Tomlinson, E. S., pvt. / 2-1-62. Twenty-seven years old. Horse valued at $250. Last on roll 5-7-62. Killed 10-11-62 Fort Donelson, Tenn.

Thompson, O. C., pvt. 10-1-63. Roll of 2-18-64 shows absent with wagons in Ga. since 11-22-63. AWOL 12-64.

Travis, B. M., pvt. 5-6-62. Twenty-nine years old.

Tucker, Thomas S. or L., pvt. 10-31-61. Discharged with disability 12-18-61.

Turnipseed, George W., pvt. 5-6-62. Twenty years old. Horse valued at $225. Roll of 5-15-63 shows absent at hospital since 3-31-63. Roll of 2-18-64 shows AWOL since 7-15-63. Clothing issued 6-15-64. Present 11-64 and 12-64. Present at surrender 4-26-65. Paroled 5-3-65 Charlotte, N.C.

Vineyard, A. J., pvt. 5-6-62. Twenty-four years old. Horse valued at $150. Absent, on detached service 5-63. Roll of 2-18-64 shows "detached to make shoes" since 8-10-63.

Wade, Henry, pvt. 5-6-62. Twenty-eight years old. Horse valued at $225.

Waldrop, E. N., pvt. 4-16-63. Roll of 2-18-64 shows AWOL since 1-9-64. Clothing issued 2-27-64. AWOL 12-64.

Waldrop, James Henderson, pvt. 5-6-62. Died 3-11-63 Fairfield, Tenn.

Waldrop, John T., pvt. 5-6-62. Twenty-five years old. Horse valued at $240. Present 2-63, 5-63. Roll of 12-63 shows AWOL since 9-25-63. AWOL 12-64.

Waldrop, William, pvt. 5-6-62. Nineteen years old. Present 2-63, 5-63, 11-63, 12-63. Clothing issued 6-15-64. Present 11-64, 12-64. Present at surrender 4-26-65. Paroled 5-3-65 Charlotte, N.C.

Walker, J. M., pvt. 5-6-62. Twenty-one years old.

Ward, Jesse, pvt. 10-31-61. Twenty-two years old. Horse valued at $225. Captured 1-27-64 Sevierville, Tenn. Died as POW at Rock Island, Ill. 4-19-64. Cause of death cited as "rheumatism."

Ward, M. N., pvt. 3-1-63. Roll of 2-18-64 shows absent, at hospital since 8-63. Discharged. Died 1914 in Clayton Co., Ga.

Ward, William R., pvt. 10-31-61. Eighteen years old. Horse valued at $175. Present 2-63, 5-63, 11-63, 12-63. Clothing issued 6-15-64. Present 12-31-64. Died 1906 in Jonesboro, Ga.

Westley, Garrett L., pvt. 10-31-61.

Whaley, John F., pvt. 5-6-62. Present 2-63, 5-63, 11 & 12-63. Clothing issued 6-15-64. Present 11-64, 12-64. Present at surrender 4-26-65. Paroled 5-3-65 Charlotte, N.C.

Whaley, Samuel D., pvt. 8-1-63. Present 11-63, 12-63. Clothing issued 3-27-64. Captured 9-2-64 Jonesboro, Ga. Admitted to U.S.hospital in Chattanooga 11-2-64. Died as POW at Camp Douglas, Ill., 12-30-64, of chronic diarrhea. Block 2 Chicago Cemetery.

Wilkinson, F. H., pvt. Wounded 6-27-64 at Kennesaw Mountain.

Williams, Alexander, pvt. Captured 12-15-63 Craig Co., Va. Exchanged 3-7-65. POW records describe as twenty-four years old, 6'1" blue eyes, brown hair.

Wolf, G. W., pvt. 5-6-62. Twenty years old. Horse valued at $200.

G COMPANY

Jordan, Thomas H., capt. Company Commander 3-4-62. Thirty-two years old. Horse valued at $275. Absent, on leave 1-4-63., Killed 8-1-63.

Park, Josiah A., 1st lt. 4-24-62, Thirty-three years old. Horse valued at $235. Born 1829 Marion Co. Cashiered 12-27-62. "Court martialed under general order 31/5."

Merritt, Thomas Mickleberry, 2nd lt. 3-4-62/capt.8-63. Succeeded Jordan as Company Commander. Paroled 5-3-65 Charlotte, N.C., indicating he was present at surrender.

Hawkins, Samuel Hugh, 2nd lt. 4-19-62/1st lt. 8-63. Sumter Co. Horse valued at $300. Present 2-63, 4-63, 6-64. Roll for 12-31-64 shows detailed to AAIG. Crews Brigade. Present at surrender 4-26-65 Salisbury, N.C. Paroled 5-3-75 Charlotte.

Majors, David, 1st sgt/ 3-2-62/pvt. Thirty-one years old. Webster Co. Present as sgt. -63 through 4-63, 1 and 2-64. On furlough 3-25-64. Roll of 6-64 shows "Entitled to pay of 1st Sgt to June 6, 1864." Present 12-64. Apparently present at surrender 4-26-65. Paroled 5-3-65 Charlotte, N.C.

Collier, Erastmus L. 2nd sgt. 4-9-62. Roll of 12-31-64 shows detached with Gen. Cheatham since 8-10-64.

Cranford, Thomas, 3rd sgt. 1862. Marion Co. Died 3-6-63 in Academy Hospital, Chattanooga.

Short, William Joseph, 4th sgt. 3-24-62/3rd sgt. Twenty-seven years old. Marion Co. Horse valued at $165. Present 9-62, 10-62, 11 and 12-62. Roll for 12-31-64 shows detached with Gen. Cheatham. Forty day furlough, no horse 3-22-64. Present 5-64. Present at surrender 4-26-65. Paroled 5-3-65 Charlotte, N.C.

Hendricks, William Frank, 2nd cpl. Marion Co. Paroled 5-3-65 Charlotte, N.C.

Spinks, Littleton M., 3rd cpl. 4-14-62. Marion Co. Present 12-31-64.

Brown, John, 4th cpl. 4-19-62. Terrell Co. Roll of 12-31-64 shows detached with Gen. Cheatham.

Acree, Jackson L., pvt. 2-22-62. Dougherty Co. Present 12-31-64. Paroled 5-17-65 Albany, Ga.

Adams, Silas H., pvt. 3-4-62. Baker Co. Present through 12-63. No horse for twenty-three day period around 5-64. In Marshall Hospital 8-8-64. Roll of 12-31-64 shows AWOL since 11-23-64.

Albritton, John L., pvt. 5-2-64. Sumter Co. Born 5-9-46 Americus, Ga. Present 12-31-64. On furlough in Sumter Co. 4-3-65 to close of war.

Apple, John, pvt. Wounded and captured 12-19-64 by forces under Gen. Thomas, Livingston, Tenn. (2nd Ga. not in Tenn. this date.) Discharged from Camp Chase 7-17-65.

Avera or Avery, Thomas Jefferson, pvt. 2-12-62. Lee Co. Twenty-four years old. Horse valued at $185. Present 1-63, 2-63. Furloughed 5-2-64, no horse for forty days. Present 12-31-64.

Bailey, Duncan, pvt. 12-12-63. Henry Co. May have been from Ala. or joined in Ala. Present at surrender 4-26-65 Salisbury, N.C. Paroled 5-1-65.

Bailey, James F., pvt. 5-7-62 / sgt. Buena Vista, Ga. Present 2-64. Furloughed forty days 5-2-64 Dalton, Ga., no horse.

Bartlett, James F., pvt. 4-9-62 / sgt. Marion Co. Present 12-31-64.

Bartlett, William T., pvt. 3-17-64. Marion Co. Present 12-31-64.

Bartlett, William J., pvt/ 5-2-64. Marion Co. May be same man as above. In hospital with dysentery 6-11-64 and 7-15-64.

Beebens, William, pvt. Captured 5-23-65 Anderson, S.C. by Gen. S.B. Brown. Paroled at Hartwell, Ga.

Bell, Robert N., pvt. 2-30-61. McNary, Tenn. Detailed as orderly to Gen. Cheatham 9-13-64.

Belk, Amandus P., pvt. 3-3-62. Marion Co. Present through 4-63. Furloughed forty days to 2-19-64. Roll of 12-31-64 shows detached as courier for Gen. Cheatham. Surrendered 4-26-65 Greensboro, N.C.

Belk, Warren, pvt. 8-22-63. Marion Co. Accidentally wounded in hand 10-24-64 at Cave Spring, Ga. Roll of 12-31-64 shows in hospital. Paroled 5-17-65 Albany, Ga.

Belk, Hollis, 3rd cpl. 5-7-62. Thirty-four years old. Horse valued at $150. Present 11-62, 12-62, 1-63, 2-63, 3-63, 4-63, 1-64, 2-64. On furlough 5-64. Present 5-64, 6-64, 11-64, 12-64. Appears on roll of soldiers surrendered by Gen. Sam Jones at Tallahassee, Fla. Paroled at Albany, Ga. 5-16-65.

Black, Thomas J., pvt. 6-6-64. Sumter Co. Present 12-31-64.

Blair, William W., pvt. 4-8-62. Terrell Co. Detailed to feed stock 1-63. Detailed with Capt. Russell 5-2-64. Detailed with Maj. Young 6-64. Roll of 12-31-64 shows detached with Gen. Cheatham.

Borland, John F., pvt. 2-4-64. Henry Co. Seventeen years old. On 7-day furlough 5-2-64, no horse. Present 21-31-64.

Boyt, Uriah, pvt. 3-25-62. Marion Co. Detailed 1-27-63 "to take charge of Government stock under Capt Russell." Present 1-64, 2-64 and 5-64. No horse for 11 and 12-64. Roll of 12-31-64 shows "Absent, dismounted and sent to ditches at Savannah, Ga."

Broadaway, James P., pvt. 2-24-62. Dougherty Co. Captured and paroled in Ky. 10-62. Last on roll 4-63, "Absent at Newsome Hospital, Chattanooga, Tenn."

Brooks, Thomas H., pvt. 3-1-62. Lee Co. Thirty years old. Wounded 12-31-62 Murfreesboro (Stones River) and sent to hospital in Atlanta. Present 1-64 and 2-64 Dalton, Ga. Present 5-64. Sent to hospital 6-23-64.

Brown, Benjamin H., pvt. 4-8-62. Terrell Co. Present 1862 through 1864. Present at surrender 4-26-65 Salisbury, N.C. Paroled 5-3-65, Charlotte, N.C.

Cabaness, Benjamin F. pvt. 8-4-63. Calhoun Co. Died in Atlanta hospital 6-22-64.

Cabaness, Reb, pvt. 4-62. Calhoun Co.

Cabiness, Napoleon B., pvt. 3-2-63. Terrell Co. Substitute for J. R. Taylor. Present 2-64. Furloughed 5-64. Present 6-64. Captured 10-21-64 near Cave Spring, Ga. POW Camp Douglas, Ill. Died as POW 3-4-65 from pneumonia. U.S. record shows "claimed to be loyal was conscripted and desires to take oath of allegiance and become a loyal citizen."

Caldwell, William S. pvt. 4-8-62. Terrell Co. Wounded. Died of wounds at Murfreesboro, Tenn. 2-23-63.

Carr, David W., pvt. 2-21-62. Sumter Co. Died 4-30-62. "horse sent back home."

Carr, W. M., pvt. 4-62. Sumter Co.

Chambless, Henry, pvt. 8-2-64. Upson Co. Present 12-31-64.

Champion, Jacob, pvt. 4-20-62. Marion Co. Wounded 12-31-62. In Atlanta hospital 2-63. Present 2-64. No horse, furloughed 40 days 5-2-64. Present 6-64. Roll of 12-31-64 shows on detached duty with Gen. Cheatham since 8-10-64.

Chappell, Rufus A., pvt. 5-2-64. Twenty-four years old. Webster or Sumter Co. Present 12-31-64.

Clements, Leonidas Orb., pvt. 3-23-64. Webster Co. Present 12-31-64.

Clements, Thomas J., pvt. 3-2-62. Webster Co. Present 10-62. Detailed to guard stock under Capt. Jackson 11-22-62. Present 6-63 and 2-64. Sent to hospital 12-23-64. Surrendered by Gen. Sam Jones 5-10-65 Tallahassee, Fla. to Gen. McCook. Paroled 5-18-65 Albany, Ga.

Clements, William L., pvt. 3-2-62. Present 10-62. Detailed to guard stock under Capt. Jackson 11-22-62. Furlough without horse 30 days, 5-64. Sent to hospital 5-20-64. Present 12-31-64. Surrendered by Gen Sam Jones 5-10-65 Tallahassee, Fla. to Gen. McCook. Paroled 5-17-65 Albany, Ga. Died 1918.

Collier, Ross, pvt. Terrell Co.

Cosby, Henry F., pvt. 4-21-62. Webster Co. Present through '62. Discharged 3-19-63.

Covington, Joseph, pvt. 4-62. Muscogee Co.

Covington, James W., pvt. 3-13-64. Muscogee Co. Detached service with Gen. Cheatham through '64.

Daughtry, Andrew J., pvt. 4-1-64. Enlisted at Dalton, Ga. Present 12-31-64.

Daughtrey, Jacob E., pvt. 4-62. Captured at Carsville, Va. Paroled 6-20-63 Fort McHenry, Md. Received at City Point, Va. 1-26-63.

Davis, Addison W., pvt. 4-8-62. Marion Co. Thirty-seven years old. Horse valued at $300. Roll of 1-63 shows "Absent, sent to Atlanta, Ga., hospital, thence home on furlough." Permanently disabled by loss of limb(s)."

Davis, James O., pvt. 4-25-62. Randolph Co. Twenty-nine years old. Wounded at Kennesaw Mountain, 1864 and sent to hospital in Cuthbert, Ga.

Davis, Thomas W., pvt. 9-5-64. Present 11-64, 12-64. Present at surrender, 4-26-65 near Salisbury, N.C.

Dawson, James M., pvt. 6-6-62. Marion Co. Paroled 5-3-65 Charlotte, N.C.

Dillard, George W., pvt. 4-19-62. Webster or Sumter Co. Horse valued at $2,100. Captured 9-62 in Ky. Exchanged and present through 4-63. Furloughed 40 days, no horse, 6-27-64. Present 11 and 12-64. Wounded 2-65 in South Carolina. Returning to command when war ended. Paroled 5-16-65 Albany, Ga.

Dobson, James W., pvt. 2-21-62. Webster Co. Present through 12-31-64. Paroled 5-16-65, Albany, Ga.

Fiason, Thomas A. pvt. 4-15-62. Marion Co. Twenty-four years old. Died 7-23-62. Horse valued at $265 and apparently taken by Lt. Josiah A. Parks.

Faust, Daniel F., pvt. 4-21-62. Sumter Co. Twenty year old farmer. Present through '63. Present through 5-64. Roll for 12-31-64 shows detached with Gen. Cheatham since 6-24-64. Admitted to hospital 2-28-65, "health not good." Paroled 5-16-65, Albany, Ga.

Faust, Henry, pvt. 4-12-64. Sumter Co. "Deserted in 1864."

Faust, James, pvt. Webster Co.

Felts, William J., pvt. 4-18-62. Sumter Co. Thirty-two years old. Roll of 12-31-62 shows detailed to guard stock under Capt. Jackson. Name also appears on list of soldiers assigned at Macon, for duty of arresting deserters. Wounded at Dalton, 4-7-64 and sent to hospital. Sent to hospital 11-23-64. Paroled 5-16-65 Albany, Ga.

Fletcher, Richard M., pvt. 5-1-64.

Free, John M., pvt. 11-9-61. Dougherty Co. Captured in Ky. and exchanged 10-62. AWOL 1-63. "Died in service" 7-31-63 near Chattanooga.

Freeman, John A., 2nd sgt/ 4-8-62/pvt. Twenty-two years old. Prior service as pvt. Co I 7th Ga. militia 11-9-61. Horse valued at $250, and apparently owned by Julius Walker. Roll of 12-31-62 shows "sent to hospital in Atlanta and has not returned." Rolls of 2-63, 3-63, 4-63 show "absent, at home without authority." Furloughed 10-2-63 with chronic diarrhea. Roll of 2-64 shows detailed to Covington hospital as clerk. Roll of 12-31-64 shows absent, ordered to report to Dr. Stout at Macon hospital.

Frith, Thomas D., pvt. 5-4-62. Present 12-31-64.

Glass, Marcus S., pvt. 5-14-62. Terrell Co. Appointed Assistant Quartermaster. Roll of 12-31-64 shows "detached with Maj. Thomas' company" since 8-15-64.

Green, Berry Smith, pvt. 2-21-62. Sumter Co. Twenty-one years old. Horse valued at $180. Captured 9-62 in Kentucky and exchanged. Present, "no horse" 5-64. Present 12-31-64. Surrendered 5-10-65 in Tallahassee, Fla. Paroled 5-16-65 Albany, Ga.

Griffin, Stephen J., pvt. 2-21-62. Lee Co. Present 9-62, 10-62. Roll of 2-63 shows sent home from hospital on furlough. Present, "no horse" 5-2-64. Paroled 5-16-65 Albany, Ga.

Hale, Thomas C., pvt. 4-19-62. Twenty-six years old. Detached to guard stock under Capt. Jackson 11-22-62. Present through 8-64. Roll of 12-31-64 shows detached with Cheatham since 8-10-64.

Hamilton, Alexander, pvt. Roll of 4-63 shows "Substitute for T.A. McLarty Dec/62 but deserted in Jan/63. Since arrested and tried for desertion, but sentence not (published)—in arrest." Took oath of allegiance to U.S. 8-11-64 before Federal authorities in Nashville, Tenn. Shown as resident of Davidson, Tenn.

Haynes, Samuel S. pvt. 2-11-62. Terrell Co. Roll of 6-64 shows detached with supply train.

Hawkins, William Jack., pvt. 2-1-64. Sumter Co. Absent, in hospital 5 & 6-64. Present 12-31-64.

Hendricks, William Frank, pvt. 4-10-62. Twenty-eight years old. Horse valued at $200. Marion Co. Present 4-63,

2-64, 5-64, 6-64. Sent to hospital 11-26-64. Present at surrender 4-26-65. Paroled 5-3-65, Charlotte, N.C.

Horne, Henry W., pvt. 3-2-62. Nineteen years old. Discharged 7-31-62.

Howard, Abner H., pvt. 4-21-62. Thirty-two years old.

Jenkins, John F., pvt. 4-8-62. Terrell Co. Thirty years old. Roll of 2-64 shows dropped from roll by order of Gen. Cheatham.

Johnston, A. Simon, pvt. 3-23-64. Present 6-64. Sent to hospital 12-15-64.

Joiner, Bennett, pvt. 4-14-64. Present 6-64, 11-64, 1-64.

Jones, Nathan T., pvt. 2-22-62. Lee Co. Twenty-two years old. Horse valued at $150. Present 2-63, 3-63, 4-63. Roll of 2-64 shows detached with government stock since 5-15-63. Present, no horse 5-64. Present 6-64, 11-64, 12-64. Present at surrender 4-26-65. Paroled 5-3-65 Charlotte, N.C.

Jordan, Jesse R., pvt. 2-1-63/cpl. Lee Co. Present 4-63. Sent to hospital 1-64. Present no horse 2-64, 3-64. Present 12-31-64.

Jordan, John W., pvt. 3-6-62. Lee Co. Twenty-six years old. Horse valued at $250. Sent to hospital at Sulfur Springs 8-62. Roll of 2-64 shows AWOL since 9-15-63.

Jordan, Robert J., pvt. 12-24-64. Lee Co. Present 12-31-64.

Lamar, John Terrell, 4-19-62. Terrell Co. Thirty years old. Horse valued at $250. Detailed as asst. surgeon for regiment 1-8-63.   Returned to cav. duty 2-64. Present 12-31-64.

Lumpkin, Phillip, pvt. 3-22-62. Horse valued at $160. Stewart Co. Present 2-63, 5-63, 11-64, 12-64.

Lee, Oscar, pvt. 2-17-64. Present 1-64, 2-64. On sick furlough 5-64. Talbot Co. Roll of 12-31-64 shows on detached service with Gen. Cheatham.

Libby, Alexander B., cpl. 5-7-62. Baker Co. Horse valued at $250.

Loyless, Thomas W., pvt. 4-20-64. Terrell Co. Present 5 & 6-64. Roll of 12-31-64 detached with Gen. Cheatham since 8-10-64.

Majors, Jonathan T., pvt. 3-2-62. Twenty-seven years old. Horse valued at $275. Webster Co. Present 1 through 4-63. On forty-day furlough 2-64. Present 5 through 8-64. Roll of 12-31-64 shows on detached service with Gen. Cheatham since 8-10-64. Surrendered 5-10-65 at Tallahassee, Fla. with Gen. Sam Jones, CSA.

Majors, Marshall D., pvt. 4-62. Webster Co. Present 12-64. Present at surrender 4-26-65, Salisbury, N.C.

Majors, Newton, pvt. 5-31-64. Marion Co. Present 12-64. Present at surrender, 4-26-65, Salisbury, N.C.

Market, Zemaria, pvt. 6-6-64. Sumter Co. Paroled 5-3-65.

Mathews, James F., pvt. 6-14-64. Webster Co. Roll of 12-31-64 shows "no horse" from 11-1-64 to 12-10-64. Present at surrender 4-26-65, Salisbury, N.C.

Martin, Wesley Fletcher, pvt. 12-30-62. Whitfield Co. Present 12-31-64.

Martin, L., pvt. Whitfield Co.

Mathews, Amos, pvt. 4-12-62. Sumter Co. Thirty-three years old. Horse valued at $250 and owned by Capt. Jordan. Roll of 12-31-64 shows "absent no horse, sent from wagon train at Macon to Savannah."

Mathews, Edmund, pvt. 4-12-62. Sumter Co. Thirty-five years old. Horse valued at $250. Appointed wagon master for Regiment 7-16-62 through 10-26-62. Present 12-62. Absent, wagon master 1-28-63. Present, no horse 2-18-64. Present 5 through 12-64. Present at surrender 4-26-65 Salisbury, N.C. Paroled 5-3-65 Charlotte, N.C.

Mathews, James F., pvt. 6-14-64. Webster Co. Roll of 12-31-64 shows "no horse" from 11-1 to 12-10-64. Present at surrender 4-26-65 Salisbury, N.C.

Mathews, Joseph, pvt. 4-62. Sumter Co. Thirty years old. Present 12-62, 4-63. Roll of 12-64 shows absent, no horse. Sent from wagon train at Macon to trenches at Savannah.

McCollum, D. pvt. 4-62. Cobb Co.

McCollum, William T., pvt. 3-4-62 / cpl. 7-17-62/sgt. 2-15-63. Baker Co. Born 3-23-33, died 1-9-1927.Transferred to White's Battery: returned to co. Present 12-31-64. Paroled 5-1-65 Augusta. Apparently living in Cherokee Co in 1914.

McGarrah, Moses, pvt. 3-4-62. Sumter Co. Twenty-two years old. Horse valued at $140. Present 9-63—10-63. Killed 10-25-63 Missionary Ridge.

McLarty, Thomas A., pvt. 3-4-62. Lee Co. Twenty-six years old. Furnished substitute, A. C. Hamilton, and discharged 12-62.

Mercer, Jacob, pvt. 4-20-62. Terrell Co. Substitute for Ezekial Taylor. Present 3-63, 4-63, 1-64, 2-64. Absent, detailed with Major Young 5-64, 6-64. Present 12-31-64.

Murray, James J., pvt. 4-21-62. Sumter Co. Twenty-five years old. Present 10-62. Detailed to drive stock under Capt. Jackson in Georgia 11-17-62. Present 2-16-63. Present 5-64, 6-64. Sent to hospital 11-6-64. Surrendered 5-10-65 Tallahassee, Fla. Paroled 5-16-65 Albany, Ga.

Newsome, J. Thomas, pvt. 3-1-62/2nd lt. Lee Co. Twenty-one years old. Horse valued at $165. Elected 4-62. Present throughout '63 & '64. Sent to hospital 12-15-64. Paroled 5-10-65 Albany, Ga.

Norman, Allen J., pvt. 3-23-64. Marion Co. Present 12-31-64. In Ocmulgee Hospital 9-5-64 with diarrhea. Clothing issued 11-11-64. Paroled Albany, 5-18-65.

Norman, Daniel James, pvt. 11-19-62. Webster Co. Roll of 2-63 shows absent with stock. "Extra duty with gov't stock" 1-28-63 through 3-20-63. Present 1-64. Furloughed 36 days, no horse, 5-2-64. Present 6-64. Present at surrender 4-26-65. Paroled 5-3-65 Charlotte, N.C.

Nutt, Andrew S., pvt. 4-15-62. Marion Co. Twenty-five years old. Horse valued at $200. Present 10-62, 12-62, 4-63, 1-64, 2-64. Roll of 12-31-64 shows absent with wagon train, sent to Savannah. Surrendered 5-10-65 Tallahassee. Paroled 5-17-65, Albany, Ga.

Parker, John L., pvt. 5-14-62. Terrell Co. Prior service 7th Ga. militia 12-6-61. Mustered out 5-1-62. Present with 2nd Ga. 11-62, 12-62, 1 through 4-63, 1 through 6-64. Roll of 12-31-64 shows on detached duty with Gen. Cheatham since 8-10-64.

Perryman, James L. D., pvt. 4-19-62. Terrell Co. Detailed asst. surgeon 7-62. Relieved 12-62. Asst. surgeon 4th Ga. Reserves, Montgomery, Ala. 12-31-64.

Powell, Benjamin, pvt. 3-27-62. Marion Co. Twenty-eight years old. Horse valued at $225. Present 1-63, 2-63, 5-64, 6-64. Roll of 12-31-64 shows AWOL since 11-16-64.

Powell, Charles W., 4th sgt. 5-10-62. Prior service 7th Ga. militia 11-9-61. Mustered out 5-1-62. Roll of 12-31-64 shows on detached service with Gen. Cheatham's commissary since 6-24-64. Paroled High Point, N.C. 1865.

Powell, John A., pvt. 4-9-62. Twenty-eight years old. Horse valued at $235. Terrell Co. Present 10-62, 11-62, 12-62, 1-63, 2-63, 3-63, 4-63. Died 11-24-63.

Ragan, James, pvt. 4-12-64. Sumter Co. Present 12-31-64. Paroled 5-19-65. Albany, Ga.

Ragan, Simon F., pvt. 3-22-62. Sumter Co. Thirty years old. Horse valued at $140. Present 9 through 12-62, 1 through 4-63. Present 5 & 6-64. Furloughed no horse, 11-64. Present 12-31-64.

Randitt, James, pvt. 4-62. Sumter Co.

Randitt, Jeremiah "Jerry", pvt. 5-12-62/cpl. Sumter Co. Seventeen years old. Horse valued at $150. Present throughout '62 & '63. Furloughed 17 days, no horse 5-64. Present 12-31-64.

Ratcliff, William S. pvt. 4-12-64. Sumter Co. Sent to hospital 5-12-64. Present 11& 12-64. Paroled 5-16-65 Albany, Ga.

Richardson, E. M., pvt. 3-27-64. Enlisted at Vicksburg, Miss. by Capt. Merritt. Roll of 12-64 shows on detached service with Gen. Cheatham since 3-27-64. Residence shown as Mason Co., Ky. Surrendered at Atlanta 5-13-65.

Riviere, S. Erasmus, pvt. 3-4-64. Prior service Co K 4th Ga. Infantry 5-27-61. Discharged with disability at Camp Jackson, Richmond, Va. Roll of 12-31-64 shows on detached service as commissary for Gen. Cheatham since 6-24-64.

Rowell, Charles M., pvt. 4-21-62. Rejected by regimental surgeon.

Sanders or Saunders, James S., pvt/ 4-20-64. Terrell Co. Roll of 12-31-64 shows detached with Gen. Cheatham since 8-10-64.

Saunders, Joseph S., pvt. 3-22-62/ 2nd lt. Thirty-three years old. Horse valued at $200. Present throughout 1862-63. Present 2-64 as lt. Present throughout 1864, and present at surrender 4-26-65.

Sasser, Augustus "Gus," pvt. 4-20-64 Terrell Co. Roll of 12-31-64 shows detached with Gen. Cheatham since 8-10-64.

Sears, John W., pvt. 4-8-62. Terrell Co. Twenty-seven years old. Horse valued at $225. Present throughout 1863–64. Roll of 12-31-64 shows detached service with Gen. Cheatham since 6-24-64. Paroled at Tallahassee, Fla. 5-15-65.

Shorpshire, James W., pvt. 4-15-62. Terrell Co. Appointed asst. surgeon 5-17-62. Resigned 10-27-63 effective 7-24-62.

Sibley, Alexander B., pvt. 2-24-62. Dougherty Co. Roll of 9 & 10-62 shows in Chattanooga hospital. Subsequent rolls show detached to hospital. Roll of 12-31-64 shows AWOL since 12-15-64.

Skipper, John A., pvt. 4-8-62. Terrell Co. Forty years old. Horse valued at $25 and owned by Capt. Jordan.. Issued clothing 3-27-64. Roll of 12-31-64 shows detached with government shoe shop since 7-1-63.

Snuggs, Robert S., pvt. 4-16-62/ 1st sgt. Lee Co. Twenty-six years old. Horse valued at $200. Present as 1st sgt. throughout 1862, '63, and '64.

Solomon, J. W., pvt. 7-1-63. Enlisted in Unionville, Tenn. Absent, with brigade wagons 12-63. Hospital orderly 2-64. Detached service 12-64. On roll of soldiers surrendered by Gen. Sam Jones 5-10-65. Parolee at Albany, Ga. 5-22-65.

Spencer, Jackson, pvt. 2-22-62. Sumter Co. Paroled Albany 5-15-65.

Stanford, Jesse, pvt. 4-62. Terrell Co.

Statham, Meredith G., pvt. 4-20-62. Marion Co. Twenty-four years old. Horse valued at $175. Discharged 7-31-62. Enlisted as pvt in 29th Bn Ga Cavalry. Surrendered 5-10-65, Tallahassee, Fla.

Story, Joseph Denson, pvt. 4-7-62. Marion Co. Twenty years old. Horse valued at $75. Sent to hospital 11-62. Furloughed home 2-63. Returned to duty 4-63. Present 1 through 6-64. Wounded in arm at Waynesboro and sent to

hospital 12-5-64. Surrendered 5-10-65 Tallahassee, Fla. Paroled 5-17-65, Albany, Ga.

Story, William S., pvt. 5-7-62. Eighteen years old. Horse valued at $225. "Rejected by surgeon."

Stewart, Richard J., pvt. 4-19-62. Lee Co. Born 6-26-46. Present 12-31-64. Surrendered 5-65 Bentonville, N.C. Died 3-15-1933, Savannah, Ga.

Taylor, Ezekiel K., pvt. 4-20-62. Twenty-six years old. Horse valued at $200. Terrell Co. Discharged, furnished Jacob Mercer as substitute, 1862.

Taylor, John, pvt. Webster Co.

Taylor, Joseph B., pvt. Webster Co.

Taylor, Thomas K., pvt. 4-62. Terrell Co. Twenty-four years old. Horse valued at $175. Present 11 and 12-62, 1 and 2-63. Surrendered 5-10-65 Tallahassee, Fla. Paroled 5-18-63 Albany, Ga.

Taylor, W., pvt.

Thompson, Green B., pvt. 5-14-62 / 5th sgt. Prior service pvt. in Co I 7th Bn Ga militia 12-17-61. "Left at hospital" 10-62 Bardstown, Ky. Apparently captured and exchanged. "Absent with government stock" under Capt. Russell 1 through 4-63. Present 1 and 2-64. Present 3 and 4-64, no horse. Present 5 and 6-64. Present as Sgt 11 and 12-64. Paroled 5-5-65 Catawba Bridge.

Thrash, Fielding, pvt. 2-24-62. Dougherty Co. Twenty-six years old. Horse valued at $75. Present throughout '62. Present through 4-63. Detached 5-15-63 with Capt. Russell to tend stock at Cedartown, Ga. Present at surrender 4-26-65. Paroled 5-3-65, Charlotte, N.C.

Thrash, George A., pvt. 4-24-62. Dougherty Co. Thirty-two years old. Horse valued at $150. Present through '62. Present through 4-63. Detached with government stock in Cedartown, Ga. Returned to regiment 4-64. Detached with Gen. Cheatham 6-24-64. Present at surrender 4-26-65 Salisbury, N.C. Paroled 5-3-65 Charlotte, N.C.

Tracy, Christopher Columbus, pvt. 5-3-64. Webster Co. AWOL 12-64. Present at surrender 4-26-65. Paroled 5-3-65 Charlotte, N.C.

Tracy, John P., pvt. 5-31-64. Webster Co. Present 12-31-64. Surrendered 5-10-65 Tallahassee, Fla. Paroled 5-16-65 Albany, Ga.

Tullis, James M., pvt. 3-2-62. Marion Co. Detached and ordered to report to Gen.Wright at Macon 12-1-64. Present on roll of Co A 1st Reg. Troops & Defenses, Macon, Ga. 12-64. (Notes from 1906 roster commission indicate this man was a physician.)

Tyler, James H., pvt. 4-13-62. Marion Co. Twenty-two years old. Died 8-2-62.

Tyler, Joseph B., pvt. 3-2-62. Webster Co. Twenty-seven years old. Horse valued at $275. Present 11 and 12-62. Detached 1-63 with government stock under Capt. Russell, through at least 4-63. Present 1 through 6-64. Roll of 12-31-64 shows detached with Gen. Cheatham since 8-10-64.

Tyler, John W. pvt. 3-2-62. Webster Co. Twenty years old. Horse valued at $225. Present 11 and 12-62, 1 and 2-63, 3 and 4-63, 1 and 2-64, 5 and 6-64. Roll of 12-64 shows detached with Gen. Cheatham since 8-10-64. Surrendered 5-10-65 Tallahassee, Fla. Paroled 5-18-65 Albany, Ga.

Tyler, William T. pvt. 4-15-62. Marion Co. Rejected by surgeon 4-62.

Upton, William R., pvt. 12-19-63. Marion Co. Present 12-31-64. Surrendered 5-10-65 Tallahassee, Fla. Paroled 5-18-65 Albany, Ga.

Walker, John T., pvt. 4-15-62. Terrell Co. Thirty-three years old. Present 9 and 10-62, 11 and 12-62, 1 and 2-63, 4-63.

Wall, Nathan T., pvt. 12-24-63. Present throughout '64. Surrendered 5-10-65 Tallahassee, Fla. Paroled Albany 5-18-65.

Warren, Davidson, pvt. 4-21-62. Sumter Co. Thirty-eight years old. Horse valued at $275. Roll of 10-62 shows at hospital. Discharged 3-19-63.

Watts, William N., pvt. 3-4-64. Terrell Co. Sent to hospital 6-9-64. Present 12-31-64.

Willborn, Torris R., pvt. 4-9-62. Terrell Co. Forty-one years old. Horse valued at $175. Present 9 through 12-62, 1 through 4-63. Present through 64.

White, James R., pvt. 5-3-64. Terrell Co. Present 11 and 12-62, 5 and 6-64, 12-64.

Willis, Wiley A., pvt. 4-21-62. Spalding Co. Present 9 through 12-63. 40-day furlough. No horse 5-64. Shown AWOL 12-31-64 but sent to hospital 12-14-64.

Wilson, Henry W., pvt. 3-20-64. Present 5-64. Died 5-13-64 Fairground Hospital Number Two, Atlanta, Ga.

Woolbright, James Daniel, pvt. 6-62. Prior service 7th Reg Ga militia 11-9-61. Mustered out 5-1-62. Substitute for Willis Woolbright. Present 11 and 12-62, 3 and 4-63, 1 and 2-64, 5 and 6-64. Roll of 12-31-64 shows detached with Gen. Cheatham since 8-10-64.

Woolbright, Willis, pvt. 4-9-62. Forty-two years old. Furnished substitute, J.D. Woolbright. 6-62. Discharged.

H COMPANY

Whaley, Caleb Arthur, capt. 5-4-62 / maj. 5-7-62. Prior service as 1st sgt. in Co G Cobbs Legion. In Richmond, Va. hospital 1-62. Commander of a four-company "squadron" from the 2nd Ga. in Ky. Wounded 10-14-62 Stanford, Ky. Died of wounds 10-22 at Stanford.

Winningham, Oliver, 1st lt. 5-4-62. Thirty-two years old. Apparently succeeded Whaley as capt. Company commander. Resigned ill health, 10-25-62, heart condition and "spasmodic stricture of urethea causing retention of urine."

Allen, Francis M., 2nd lt. 5-7-62/capt. 11-1-63. Present through '62 and 11-63. Promoted to company commander 11-63. Absent sick 12-63. Present 1 through 12-64.

Mead, L. Samuel, 2nd lt. 4-15-62/1st lt./capt. Twenty-three years old. Absent 10-27-62, resignation tendered.

Graham or Grayham, Henry S. Jr., 2nd lt. 4-10-62. Resigned 6-25-62 apparently due to "drunkeness."

Graham, Robert H., pvt. 5-1-62/2nd lt. Twenty-one years old. Horse valued at $225. Absent sick on furlough 12-31-63. Issued clothing as 2nd lt. 3-27-64.

Buice, William L., sgt. 4-20-62/ 2nd lt. '62/capt '64. Roll of 12-31-63 shows absent, sick on furlough. Roll of 10-6-64 shows wounded in right lung Cobb Co., Ga. "when detail cut off from command." Elected capt. Co B 12 Bn Ga. militia cavalry in 1864. Surrendered 5-12-65.

Duren, James A. J., cpl. 4-62. Captured Sugar Creek, Tenn. 10-63. Paroled and forwarded via Baltimore to City Point, Va. for exchange 3-4-65.

Evans or Eppins, John F., 5th sgt. 4-30-62. Captured 12-15-63 Panther Springs, Tenn. Federal report shows captured 12-18 near Knoxville. Died of variola 2-15-64 Rock Island prison. Grave #496 south of barracks.

Yancey, A. M., cpl. 4-26-62. Prior service 10-8-61 pvt. 3rd Ga. militia. Mustered out 4-62. Captured 12-16-63 Knoxville. Sent to Camp Chase, Ohio 1-1-64.

Beauchamp, Newton J. L., 4th cpl. 4-25-62. Wounded 1862 necessitating amputation of hand. Discharged with disability 7-31-62 Chattanooga. (Apparently wounded at Murfressboro 7-13.)

Anglin, Joseph C., pvt. 8-4-63. Prior service 10-8-61 3rd Reg. Ga. militia. Mustered out 4-62. Roll of 12-31-63 shows "absent on courier line."

Anglin, James G., pvt. 5-62. Prior service 10-8-61 Ga. militia. Discharged 12-18-61. Enlisted as pvt. in 12 Bn cavalry Ga. militia 10-64. Surrendered 5-12-65 Kingston, Ga. Born 11-15-26 in Jackson Co., Ga.

Anglin, John W., cpl. Roll of 12-31-63 shows absent with wagons. POW paroled 2-14-64 on oath of allegiance at Chattanooga.

Anglin, William M., pvt. 4-20-62. Captured 5-15-64 Rome, Ga. Paroled 6-17-65.

Austin, William G., pvt. 5-7-62/sgt. 12/18/62. Captured 10-8 or 9-63 Sugar Creek, Tenn. POW Camp Morton. Exchanged 2-26-65. Died 3-23-65 Seabrooks Hospital.

Bailey, James W., 1st sgt. 5-7-62. Horse valued at $225.

Bearse, Jerome, 1st sgt. 5-7-62. "Detailed by the Government and sent to Atlanta" 5-3-63 Special Order #15/16 Adjutant Inspector General's office.

Blanton, John, pvt. 10-62. Sick in hospital 4-63. Died 5-1-65. Could be same man as J.J. Blunton.

Blunton, J. J., pvt. 8-4-63. Enlisted at Cumming, Ga. Captured 10-8-63 Sugar Creek, Tenn. POW at Camp Morton. Shown as transferred for exchange 4-65, but also shown on muster roll of Jackson hospital 3-16-65. Died 4-20-65.

Bradbury, J.R., pvt. 5-7-62. Horse valued at $225.

Bridewell, J., pvt. 5-7-62. Roll of 12-31-63 shows on detail by order of Col. Crews.

Bridges, John L. pvt. 5-7-62. Thirty-five years old. Horse valued at $180. Present 2-63, 5-63. Absent sick 11-63, 12-63. Clothing issued 3-27-64, 6-15-64.

Bridges, Logan, pvt. 10-62. Killed 1864 Noonday Church, Cobb Co., Ga.

Brown, Thomas M., pvt. 4-28-62. Present through 5-63. AWOL 12-31-64.

Bruce, Daniel A., pvt. 4-24-62. Present through 12-31-63. Issued clothing 3-27-64.

Bruce, William P., pvt. 3-23-62. Died 8-9-62. Described as 5'6", blue eyes, fair complexion, a farmer. His widow described as "very poor" applied for his back pay.

Buice, Joshua, pvt. 4-20-62. Absent sick 5-63. With brigade wagons 12-63. On roll of deserters released by U.S. Took oath of allegiance to U.S. government 3-8-64 at Chattanooga and released. POW records shows twenty years old, 5'8", blue eyes, fair.

Buice, Nathan, pvt. 4-20-62. Twenty-four years old. Horse valued at $225. Present through 12-63. Issued clothing 3-27-64.

Buice, Robert F., pvt. 4-20-62. Roll of 12-31-63 shows absent on detail with wagons. Enlisted in Co. H 12th Cav. Bn. Ga. militia 8-64. Surrendered 5-12-65 Kingston, Ga.

Buice, Samuel D., pvt. 3-23-62. Detailed as scout with Capt. Gordon 2 through 5-63. Captured 10-8-63 Sugar Creek, Tenn. Exchanged 3-9-65 and sent to Richmond Hospital #2.

Bulls, A. L., pvt. 5-3-62.

Camp, Abner Q., pvt. 4-15-62. Thirty-one years old, Atlanta. Horse valued at $225. Present 12-63. Issued clothing 3-27-64 and 6-15-64. Present 12-31-64.

Camp, E. F., pvt. 4-14-62. Present 12-31-64.

Camp, Marion, pvt. 4-25-62. Twenty-seven years old. Present 5-63. Roll of 12-31-63 shows "absent with wagons, in arrest."

Carter, James H., clothing issued 3-27-64.

Cawley, F. M., pvt. 5-7-62 / sgt. 27 years old. Horse valued at $200. Absent sick, 5-15-63. Present 11-63, 12-63 as 5th sgt.

Chandler, George W., pvt. Captured 7-29-64 near Stone Mountain, Ga. POW at Camp Chase. Died 2-25-65 of pneumonia.

Chatham, E. M., pvt. 2-20-62. Present 5-63 and 12-63. Issued clothing 6-15-64.

Cheshire, Napoleon H., pvt. 4-15-62. Nineteen years old. Captured 1-27-64 Sevierville, Tenn. Sent to Rock Island prison. Released 6-18-65.

Cheshire, S. J., pvt. 4-1-62/cpl. Present 5-63. Absent sick 12-63. Issued clothing 3-27-64. Present at surrender. Paroled 5-3-65, Charlotte, N.C.

Christopher, John R., pvt. 5-1-62. Present 5-63, 12-63. Issued clothing 3-27-64.

Chronic, V., pvt. 4-8-62. Present 5-63. Captured 10-8-63 Sugar Creek, Tenn. U.S. record shows captured 10-9-63 Shelbyville, Tenn. POW at Camp Morton, Ind. Transferred for exchange 3-4-65.

Coffee, Sterling T., pvt. 4-18-62. Thirty-two years old. Horse valued at $225. Present 2 through 5-63. Issued clothing 3-27-64. Present 12-31-64.

Colley, James, pvt. 5-62

Connally, Alfonzo, pvt. 5-1-62. Present through '63. Clothing issued 6-15-64.

Cunningham, J. D., pvt. 6-20-62. Apparently from Shelbyville, Tenn. Absent sick 5-63.

Crews, John, pvt. 5-7-62. Eighteen years old. Horse valued at $225. "Deserted Aug. 10/62"

Cummings, J. D., pvt. 1-20-63, Shelbyville, Tenn. Absent sick 5-63.

Duren, Thomas J., pvt. 5-1-62. Thirty years old. Horse valued at $210. Present 2 through 5-63. Roll of 12-31-63 shows with brigade wagons. Issued clothing 6-15-64.

Echols, Daniel, pvt. 7-10-62. Present 2 through 5-63. Roll of 12-31-63 shows wounded, at hospital. Issued clothing 2-27-64.

Echols, N. M., pvt. 4-62. Surrendered 5-12-65 Kingston, Ga. (May have been with Ga. militia.)Witness for L. D. Terry in Fulton Co. 1903.

Ellar, Eli, pvt. 5-7-62. "Never reported to command."

Ellison, John A., pvt. 4-16-62. Captured 7-27-64 near Stone Mountain, Ga. Sent to Camp Chase, Ohio. Paroled 3-18-65. U.S. record shows as being from Nashville, Tenn.

Fisher, John, pvt. 4-30-62. Nineteen years old. Horse valued at $175. Roll of 5-15-63 shows detached with wagons. Present 11 & 12-63. Captured 9-29-64 Warsaw Ferry, (Warrenburg) Ga. POW at Camp Douglas, Ill. Exchanged 5-23-65.

Gant or Gaunt, Blewford G., pvt. 4-27-62. Twenty-six years old. Wounded in right leg 1-27-64 Sevierville, Tenn. Leg amputated below knee.

Gash, W. G., pvt. Captured 5-8-65 near Athens, Ga. forces under Gen. Palmer.

George, F. M. pvt. Absent with brigade wagons 12-63.

Gibson, John W., pvt. 5-5-62. Thirty-four years old. Horse valued at $225. Severely wounded in groin and captured 2-2-63 at Dover, Tenn. Sent to St. Johns Hospital in Paducah, Ky. and released to Provost Marshall 6-17-63. Transferred to Ft. Delaware for exchange 2-29-65. Exchanged 3-65.

Goddard, James Baylos, pvt. 5-14-62. Discharged 5-63.

Goddard, Robert, pvt. 5-62. Transferred to Co A Carroll's Bn 11-64. Surrendered Kingston, Ga. 5-12-65.

Gray, Perry P., pvt. 4-20-62. Nineteen years old. Present 5-63. Horse killed in action 2-23-62 near Triune, Tenn. Captured 12-15-63 at Panther Springs. Federal record shows captured 1-28-64 Jamestown, Ky. POW at Rock Island Barracks, Ill..

Gully, Julius, pvt. Captured and paroled 5-19-65 near Hartwell, Ga.

Gwinn, Jacob V., pvt. 4-15-62. Twenty-three years old. Horse valued at $275. Present 5-63. AWOL 12-31-63.

Harris, Benjamin F., pvt. 4-26-62. Twenty-one years old. Horse valued at $150. Present 5-63. Wounded at Chickamauga and sent to hospital.

Harris, James B., pvt. 5-15-62. Present 5-63. Captured 10-8 or 9-63 at Sugar Creek, Tenn. POW at Camp Morton. Transferred for exchange 2-26-65. Admitted to Jackson Hospital, Richmond, Va. 3-10-65 with pneumonia.

Harris, Parker, pvt. 5-7-62/ 2nd lt. Thirty-one years old. Horse valued at $200.

Hawkins, Wesley A., pvt. Captured 7-21-64 Atlanta. POW at Camp Chase. Transferred to Point Lookout 3-26-65 and released 6-4-65.

Hinton, Joseph S. pvt. 4-27-64. AWOL 12-31-63.

Hope, Ellison, pvt. 10-62. Severely wounded in right foot at Sevierville, Tenn. 1-27-64. Admitted to hospital.

Hopkins, Henry H. pvt. 4-25-62. Twenty-three years old. Horse valued at $165. Sent to hospital 11-10-63. Clothing issued 3-27-64 & 6-15-64.

Jackson, James, pvt. 12-22-62. Enlisted at Sheltonville, Ga. by Lt. Graham. Died 5-3-63 White Co., Tenn.

J. B. Johns, bugler, 5-9-62.

Johns, G. W., pvt. 4-12-62. Bugler. Thirty-two years old. Roll of 5-15-63 shows detached with Gen. Forrest. Discharged with disability, 1863.

Johnson, H. S. pvt.

Jones, B. F., pvt. 4-1-62. Twenty-six years old. Horse valued at $200. Present 5-63, 12-63. Clothing issued 3-27-64.

Junior, A., pvt. Appears on role of POWs paroled 6-1-65 Talladega, Ala.

Kelley, William F., pvt. 4-27-62. Thirty-four years old. Horse valued at $200. Died 9-22-62.

Kimsey, James J., pvt. 4-18-62. Roll of 5-63 shows "detached with Gen'l Wheeler's Elite Corps." Captured 10-9-63 Sugar Creek, Tenn. Paroled at Camp Morton, Ind. 3-65.

Kilgore, John, pvt. 5-15-62. Twenty-nine years old. Present 5-63. Captured 1-27-64 Sevierville, Tenn. POW at Rock Island prison. Released 6-17-65. 5'7" brown hair, blue eyes, "fresh" complexion.

Leach, J. A., pvt. 8-64. Captured 5-12-65 Kingston, Ga. (May have been with Ga. militia at the time of his capture.)

Lee, W. J., pvt. 4-27-62. Twenty-eight years old. Horse valued at $175. Present 2 & 5-63. Present 12-63.

Lowe, A. C., pvt. 12-22-62. Enlisted at Sheltonville, Ga. Present 12-63. Absent, sick 5-63.

Martin, J. M., pvt. Enlisted at Stone Mountain, Ga. by Lt. Allen. Roll of 12-63 shows AWOL. Clothing issued 3-27-64.

Mathis, Daniel, pvt. 12-15-62. Enlisted at Sheltonville, Ga. by Lt. Graham. Absent, detailed with Capt. White's Battery 5-63.

Mathis, J. B., sgt. 5-7-62/pvt. Eighteen years old. Horse valued at $175. Present 10 & 11-63. Issued clothing 3-27-64, 6-15-64.

Mathis, J. Gideon, pvt. 7-64. Surrendered 5-12-65 Kingston, Ga. (May have been with militia at this time.) Died 11-14-1944 Duluth, Ga.

McCormick, William L., pvt. Wounded in chest & captured 10-13 or 14-64 near Marietta, Ga. POW at Camp Douglas. Enlisted in 5th U.S. Vol. Infantry 4-15-65.

McDuffie, Rodrick, pvt. Thirty-five years old. Horse valued at $185. Present 2-63, 5-63, 11-63, 12-63. Transferred to A Company. Clothing issued 3-27-64, 6-15-64. Present at surrender 4-26-65. Paroled 5-3-65 Charlotte, N.C.

McGinnis, Noah H., pvt. Issued clothing 6-15-64. Deserted 7-8-64 at Kennesaw Mountain, Ga. Captured Gordon Co., Ga. Took oath of allegiance to U.S. and released north of Ohio River. 5'5" dark hair, blue eyes.

McGinnis, George, pvt. 4-1-62. Twenty-one years old. Horse valued at $225. Present 2-63, 5-63. Issued clothing 5-25-64. Captured 10-26-64, Gwinnett Co., Ga. POW at Camp Douglas. Released 11-24-64 and enlisted in 6th US Vol. Infantry.

McKinney, John W., pvt. 4-25-62. Twenty-four years old. Horse valued at $200. Discharged with "rheumatis" 10-15-62.

Morrison, L. A., pvt. 4-1-62. Twenty-three years old. Horse valued at $225. Detailed with Capt. White's Battery 5-63.

Nesbit, W. J., pvt. 4-24-62. Forty-one years old. Horse valued at $200. Born in Gwinnett County. Died @ 1-19-63 in DeKalb County. POW record shows as blue eyes, dark hair.

Newsom, John H., pvt. 4-14-62. Twenty-two years old. Horse valued at $150. Present 2-63, 5-63, 12-63. Clothing issued 3-27-64 and 6-15-64. Present 12-31-64.

Newsom, Marcus Lafayette, pvt. 4-20-62. Twenty-three years old. Horse valued at $175. Present 5-63, 12-63. Clothing issued 3-27-64, 6-15-64.

Owens, A. R., pvt. 5-1-62, Twenty-five years old. Horse valued at $225. Present 2-63, 5-63. Captured 10-9-63 Sugar Creek, Tenn. Died 6-30-64 as POW at Camp Morton, Ind. from "inflammation of the brain." Buried in Green Lawn Cemetery.

Owens, Sanford D., pvt. 8-4-63. Captured 5-15-63, Rome, Ga. POW at Alton, Ill. Transferred to Rock Island Barracks, Ill. POW record shows resident of Sheltonville, Forsyth Ga. 5'5", blue eyes, brown hair, light complexion, 31 years old.

Plaster, John W., pvt. 4-1-62/ sgt. 4-15-63. Twenty-six years old. Horse valued at $200. Captured 10-9-63, Sugar Creek, Tenn. POW at Camp Morton, Ind. Released 6-12-65. Described as 6'1" light hair, blue eyes.

Plaster, Thomas W., pvt. 4-1-62/ cpl.11-1-63. Nineteen years old. Horse valued at $175. Present 2-63, 5-63. Captured 10-9-63 Sugar Creek, Tenn.

Pool, S. N., pvt. 4-27-62. "Discharged by reason of disability."

Pruitt, E. E., pvt. Roll of 12-63 shows absent, sick. Clothing issued 3-27-64, 6-15-64.

Pruitt, William H., pvt. 4-26-62. Thirty years old. Horse valued at $150. Appears on list of exchanged prisoners 1-23-63. Present 2-63 and 5-63. Furloughed 12-63. Clothing issued 3-27-64.

Rainey, William W., pvt. 4-15-62/ 4th sgt. Thirty years old. Horse valued at $175. AWOL 12-31-63. In pension application he certified he was elected capt. Co A Carroll's Bn Ga militia. Surrendered 5-12-65 Kingston, Ga. Born 6-1-33 Dekalb Co. Died 1910, Bartow, Co. Ga.

Roberts, Joseph, pvt. 5-7-62. Forty-one years old. Horse valued at $125. Detached with White's Battery 5-63.

Scott, Joseph E., pvt. 4-27-62. Twenty-five years old. Horse valued at $175. Present 2-63, 5-63, 11 and 12-63.

Shinn, Alexander, pvt. Captured 7-12-64 at Warsaw, Ga. U.S. record shows captured 7-13-64 at Marietta, Ga. by Garrard's Cavalry. POW at Camp Chase. Transferred to City Point for exchange 3-4-65.

Smith, Green B., pvt. 5-3-62. Thirty years old. Horse valued at $200. Spine injured by runaway team 7-13-62 in Tenn. Contracted chronic diarrhea 9-62. Roll of 12-31-63 shows absent, sick in hospital. Pension records show he was at home at close of war.

Smith, John W. pvt. 4-27-62/sgt. Twenty-three years old. Horse valued at $150. Present 2-63, 5-63. Captured 1-27-64, Sevierville, Tenn.. POW at Camp Chase. Transferred to Rock Island Barracks 2-15-64.

Southern, J. W., Surrendered 5-12-65 at Kingston, Ga. (May have been with militia at time of surrender.)

Spriggs, Zion, pvt. 4-23-62. Twenty-eight years old. Horse valued at $300. AWOL 10-28-62.

Stephens, Russell, pvt. 1-8-63. Enlisted at Shelbyville, Tenn. Absent, sick, 5-15-63. Paid 5-18-63, 7-6-63.

Strickland, Thomas, pvt. 4-27-62/4th sgt. 12-18-62. Twenty years old. Horse valued at $250. "Killed near

Murfreesboro, Tenn." 12-31-62. Described as "farmer" 5'8" gray eyes, fair complexion, auburn hair.

Swanson, John T., pvt. 8-1-63. Transferred to Co A Murrays Cavalry, Ga. militia 9-12-63.

Sweat, Abner, pvt. 4-17-62. Thirty-eight years old. Horse valued at $200. Present 2-63, 5-63.

Terry, Stephen, pvt. 5-4-62. Eighteen years old. Horse valued at $200. Paid 2-63, 5-63, 11 and 12-63. Detailed as scout and cutoff from command. Enlisted in 12th Cav. Bn Ga. militia. Surrendered 5-12-65 Kingston, Ga. Born 5-15-42 in Forsyth Co. Died 1907 Fulton Co.

Terry, Thomas D., pvt. 4-28-62. Nineteen years old. Horse valued at $200. Present 2-63, 5-63, 12-31-63. Clothing issued 3-27-64. Surrendered 5-12-65. Kingston, Ga. (May have been with militia.)

Turnbull, J. H., pvt. 5-1-62. Roll of 12-31-63 shows transferred to brigade battery.

Weaver, D. C. sgt. 5-7-62/ pvt. Twenty-five years old. Horse valued at $200. Present as pvt. 2-63, 5-63. "Absent with brigade wagons in arrest." 11-63, 12-63. Captured in Gwinnett County, 10-26-64. Enlisted in 5th U.S. Volunteers.

Wells, S. P., pvt. 5-1-62. Twenty-two years old. Horse valued at $180. Detached as teamster 5-63, 6-63, 9-63. Clothing issued 3-27-64. Present at surrender 4-26-65, paroled 5-3-65, Charlotte, N. C.

Whaley, J. R., pvt. 4-8-62. Roll of 5-63 shows on detached service in Atlanta. Clothing issued 3-27-64, 6-15-64.

Wiggins, Lewis, pvt. 5-7-62. Forty-nine years old. Horse valued at $175.

Wofford, William F., pvt. 10-62. Thirty years old. Horse valued at $225. Present 11 & 12-63. Clothing issued 6-15-64. Paroled 5-65 Charlotte, N.C., and apparently present at surrender 4-26-65.

Yancey, A. M., pvt. 4-25-62. Twenty-two years old. Horse valued at $225. Captured 12-15-63 Panther Springs, Tenn. POW Camp Chase.

I COMPANY

Looney, George C., capt. 4-23-62. Twenty-six years old. Horse valued at $175. Present 5-63. Left for hospital 10-63. Present 12-64. Later served as regimental commander. Present at surrender 4-26-65 as a captain.

Dean, Thomas P., 1st lt. 4-3-62. Thirty years old. Horse valued at $185. Left for hospital 5-23-63. Roll of 12-31-63 shows at home. Present 12-31-64.

Cochran, Owen H., 2nd lt. 4-23-62. Thirty-one years old, Campbell Co. Appears on list of officers disabled by wounds 12-10-62 with comment "well qualified officer, habits steady." Present 2 through 5-63. Captured 1-27-64 Sevierville, Tenn. POW at Camp Chase, transferred to Fort Delaware and released 6-16-64.

Wimberly, John T., 2nd lt. 3-10-62. 30 years old. Horse valued at $275. Resigned "permanently unfit for military duty due to injuries received at Battle of Murfreesboro."

Richardson, W. M., 1st sgt. 4-23-62/ord. sgt. Twenty-four years old. Horse valued at $125. "Died at car shed in Atlanta, Ga." 11-22-62

Zellars, Simeon, 3rd lt. 4-23-62/ bvt. 2nd lt. Thirty-three years old. Horse valued at $140. Present 2-63, 5-63. Acting regimental commissary 2-18-64. Present 11 & 12-64. Present at surrender 4-26-65, paroled 5-3-65 Charlotte, N. C. (see also regimental staff roster.)

Duke, Thomas M., 2nd sgt. 5-7-62. Thirty-four years old. Horse valued at $135. Died in Campbell Co., Ga. 7-15-62.

Ragsdale, John F.

Floyd, William W. "Will", sgt. 4-23-62. Twenty-five years old. Horse valued at $200. Present through '63.

Wilkerson, Thomas W., pvt. 4-23-62/5th sgt. Twenty-nine years old. Present as sergeant throughout '63. "Ordered to hospital" 3-64. Absent, at hospital 12-64.

Zellars, Solomon T., 3rd sgt. 4-23-62. Twenty-four years old. Horse valued at $150. "At hospital in Atlanta" and reported to be discharged" 5-63.

Brown, Madison, cpl. 3-23-62. "Sent to hospital in Atlanta" 4-10-63. Captured 10-9-63 Sugar Creek, Tenn. Federal records show captured at Pulaski 10-8-63. Transferred for exchange 2-19-65. In Wayside Hospital or Hospital #9 Richmond, Va. 3-3-65.

McLaurin, or McLain, Harrison "Bud", 3rd cpl. 4-23-62/2nd cpl. Eighteen years old. Horse valued at $190. Present 2-63, 5-63. Killed in action, 10-63 McMinnville, Tenn.

Morgan, William H., 2nd cpl. 4-23-62. "Left with wagons" 11-11-63. Present 12-64.

Ragsdale, S. B., cpl. 5-14-62. Present 2-63, 4-63. Clothing issued 3-27-64, 6-15-64. "Ordered to hospital" 12-12-64 with wound in foot.

Armor, John H., pvt. 2-3-62. Died 6-24-62 Palmetto, Ga.

Atcherson, John L., pvt. 5-14-62. Absent with wagons 12-31-63. Detailed to brigade headquarters 11 and 12-64. Present at surrender 4-65.

Bailey, John F., pvt. 5-7-62. Roll of 9-1-63 shows detailed to drive stock. Sent to hospital 11-23-64.

Bailey, S. P., pvt. 2-3-64. Clothing issued 3-27-64 and 6-15-64.

Bailey, William, pvt. 5-7-62. "Entry cancelled."

Banks, Thomas L., pvt. 5-4-62. Present 5-15-63.

Bankston, Andrew J., pvt. 7-12-61 or 62. Apparently enlisted at Big Creek Gap, Tenn.

Bearfield, Jefferson, pvt. 5-4-62. Present through 12-31-64.

Bearfield, Lewis W., pvt. 5-7-62/cpl. In Atlanta hospital 5-15-63. Discharge recommended.

Beavers, Robert O., pvt. 7-10-64. Killed in action 8-5-64.

Bennett, Robert, pvt. 11-13-64, Fayetteville, Ga.

Bond, J.B.F., pvt. 4-23-62. Present through 12-31-63.

Bond, John D., pvt. 5-4-62. Died 7-16-62.

Bond, R. R., pvt. 5-1-64. Absent sick 11-12-64.

Bond, William D., pvt. 5-7-62 Sent to Atlanta hospital 3-1-63. Detailed to drive stock 9-1-63. Present 12-31-64.

Brown, Madison, pvt. 3-23-62. Captured at Sugar Creek, Tenn. 10-9-63. Federal records show captured 10-8-63 Pulaski. Transferred for exchange 2-19-65. In Wayside Hospital or Hospital #9, Richmond, Va. 3-3-65.

Brown, Watson, pvt.

Bufford, William M., pvt.

Buffington, Joseph A., pvt. 4-23-62. Sent to hospital in Rome, Ga. 4-1-63. Appointed hospital steward 9-25-63.

Bullard, William M., pvt. 4-23-62. Sent to hospital in Rome, Ga. 4-1-63. Issued clothing 3-27-63. Furloughed 4-10-63 to 5-10-63. Left with wagons 11-63. Captured near Nashville 9-1-64. Federal records show captured near LaVergne, Tenn. 9-1-64. POW at Camp Chase. Described in Federal records as resident of Cobb Co., Ga. 28 yrs old, 5'6" brown eyes, dark hair, fair complexion.

Burney, D. L., pvt. 1-3-62. Detailed to Atlanta to drive cattle 10-64.

Byram, J. F. Present 5-62. "Entry cancelled."

Carlton, John C. C., cpl. 4-23-62/ sgt. 5-1-63/pvt. Promoted to commissary sgt. 5-1-63. On roll as pvt. when "captured in battle" 7-21-64 Atlanta. POW at Camp Chase and transferred to City Point.

Carroll, Jesse G., pvt. 4-23-62. In Rome hospital 4-1-63. Assigned with wagons 11-63. Issued clothing 3-27-64 and 6-15-64. Present 12-64.

Carter, J. T., pvt. Died of pneumonia 8-1-62 in Moore Hospital at Mannassas Junction, Va.

Clark, W. H., 3rd lt. Among troops surrendered by Gen. Sam Jones 5-10-65 Tallahassee, Fla to Gen. McCook.

Clary, John A., 6-15-62

Cochran, James, pvt. Ordered to hospital 6-6-64.

Collins, Francis M., pvt. 4-23-62. Present 2 through 6-63. Issued clothing 3-27-64 and 6-15-64. Present 12-64. Captured and paroled 5-8-65, Athens, Ga. Shown on U.S. records as member of B Company.

Collins, James A., pvt. 4-23-62. Sent to Atlanta hospital 3-20-63. Furloughed 4-10-3 to 5-10-63. Sent to hospital 4-22-64 and "recommended for retirement."

Collins, Pleasant O., pvt. 4-23-62. Present 2 through 6-63. Issued clothing 3-27-64 and 6-15-64. Present 12-64.

Collins, W. A., pvt. 8-1-64. Present 12-64.

Cousins, J. W., pvt. 4-23-62.

Crutchfield, Benjamin J., pvt. 1-27-62. Detailed as blacksmith 6-63.

Darnell, F. M., pvt. 5-13-64.

Darnell, D. E., pvt. 7-28-64. Present 12-31-64.

Dennis, A. J., pvt. 5-7-62. "Entry cancelled."

Devine, William, pvt. 7-20-64. Present 12-31-64.

Dobbins, James S., pvt. 5-7-62. Eighteen years old. "Deserted" 1-12-63. Present 2 through 5-63. Issued clothing 3-27-64 and 6-15-64. Present 12-31-64.

Dobbins, Jesse A., pvt. 5-7-62. Twenty-three years old. Sent to Rome hospital 4-1-63. Deserted 4-1-63. Issued clothing 3-27-64. Present 12-31-64.

Duke, James Frank, pvt. 5-7-62. Thirty years old. Wounded 9-23-63 at Lookout Mountain and died of wounds 9-28-63 at Germantown, Tenn.

Duke, George W., pvt. 5-7-62. Twenty-five years old. Sent to Atlanta hospital about 4-12-63. Issued clothing 3-27-63 and 6-15-63. Roll of 12-31-63 shows detailed with Division wagons. AWOL 12-31-64.

Duke, Seaborn Matt, pvt. 5-7-62. Sent to Atlanta hospital 1-25-63. Issued clothing 3-27-64. Furloughed about 5-15-64. Roll of 12-31-64 shows in Griffin hospital.

Duke, William H., pvt. 5-7-62. Died 8-19-62 in Chattanooga hospital. Widow Jane M. Duke received $119.40

Dunkin, Peter, pvt. 5-7-62. Present 12-31-64.

Eddleman, Sol P., pvt. 5-7-62. Twenty-seven years old. Horse valued at $180. Present through '63 and '64. Issued clothing 3-27-64 and 6-15-64. Present through 12-31-64.

Floyd, Wiley, pvt. 5-1-64. AWOL 12-31-64

Fowler, Captured in Ga.

Fowler, Zephaniah, pvt. 4-23-62. Twenty-eight years old. Died in camp 3-10-63 Fairfield, Tenn.

Garrison, E. C., pvt. Surrendered 5-18-65 Augusta, Ga.

Glass, F. A., pvt. 1-1-64. Present 12-31-64. Appears on list of men on special duty with headquarters of Allen's Division at the surrender, 4-26-65. Paroled 5-3-65 Charlotte, N.C. Apparently served as Division quartermaster clerk from 2-1-64 to surrender.

Green, W. S., pvt. 10-1-63/ cpl. Enlisted at Ringgold, Ga. Issued clothing 3-27-64 and 6-15-64. Present 12-31-64.

Hattaway, Emanuel, pvt. 4-23-62, Thirty-two years old. Horse valued at $155. Present 5-63. "Deserted" 2-10-64. Present 12-31-64.

Hattaway, David, pvt..

Hearn, William M., pvt. 4-23-62/ 1st sgt. Twenty-five years old. Horse valued at $200. Present 5-63 as 1st sgt. On furlough 1-3-64 to 2-17-64. Clothing issued 3-27-64. Captured 9-1-64 LaVergne, Tenn. Died as POW at Camp Chase, Ohio 12-22-64 from tonsilitis. Grave 671.

Hollis, James J., pvt. 4-23-62. Twenty-five years old. Horse valued at $100. Present 5-63. Detached with wagons 8-63. Present with regimental wagons 12-64.

Hollis, Moses, pvt. Died 7-23-62 Campbell Co., Ga.

Hood, Benjamin, pvt. 4-23-62. Twenty-five years old. Detached to "Post Forage Master" 11-1-62 through 12-63.

Hood, Bynum, pvt. 5-7-62. Twenty-five years old. Detailed as "forage master," Kingston, Tenn. 11-1-62.

Hays, Almond, pvt. 4-23-62. Twenty-eight years old, apparently from Marietta, Ga. Present 5-63. Captured 9-10-63 Summerville, Ga. POW at Camp Douglas. Released 6-15-65.

Hersey, L. H.

Hopkins, Henry H, pvt. 4-23-62. Twenty-three years old. Horse valued at $165. To hospital 11-10-63. Clothing issued 3-27-64 and 6-15-64. Present 11-64, 12-64.

Hughs, Gilfor C., pvt. 4-23-62. Twenty-eight years old. Present 5-63. Roll of 12-63 shows absent, sick. Roll of 12-64 shows "Sent to hospital 7-63 and not heard from since." Appears on roll of deserters released at Louisville 8-10-63 after taking oath. U.S. record shows arrested by Union forces at Stevensonville, Ala. 8-7-63. "Enlisted in Fed Army on or about 8-12-63."

Jackson, Robert, pvt. 7-1-64. Enlisted at Palmetto, Ga. "Never put on duty by surgeon since his connection with his company."

Johnson, Ruban S. pvt. Present 5-63. Detached as courier near Decatur, Ala. 10 through 12-63. Issued clothing 3-27-64 and 6-15-64. Present 12-31-64.

Keiser, Levi F., pvt., "Appears on list of Rebel Prisoners of War paroled by the 1st Division, 14th Army corps, Dept. of the Cumberland, Beech Fork, Ky." 10-28-62.

Kersey, Leroy H., pvt. 5-10-62. Present 5-63. Absent sick 12-31-63. Captured 8-30-64 near Red Oak, Ga. POW at Camp Douglas. Released 6-12-65.

King, William

Lanier, W. H., pvt. 4-4-64. Killed 7-31-64 at Sunshine Church, Ga.

Linley, Jonathan, pvt. 4-23-62. Palmetto, Ga. Sent to hospital 4-63.

Longino, Hugh M., pvt. 4-23-62. Eighteen years old. Horse valued at $165. Present 6-63, 12-63, 11-64, 12-64.

Longino, O.R., pvt. 5-1-64. Enlisted at Palmetto, Ga. Present 12-64.

Longino, T. D., pvt. 10-1-64. Enlisted at Palmetto, Ga.

Mapp, William, 5-7-62 "entry cancelled."

Mayfield, Tom, May be same man as Robert Mayfield below.

Mayfield, Robert, pvt. 4-23-62. Twenty-seven years old. Horse valued at $175. Detached as courier 10-27-63 near Decatur, Ala. Captured Sand Mountain, Lebanon, Ala. Paroled at Rock Island, Ill. 3-15-65 and forwarded to James River for exchange.

Maxwell, Marcus, pvt. Captured 5-20-64 Kingston, Ga. POW at Rock Island Barracks, Ill.

McElwreath, R. D., pvt. 10-1-64. Enlisted at Palmetto, Ga. Present 12-64.

McMilton, John B., pvt. 4-23-62. Died 7-25-62 at Chattanooga hospital.

Meggs, James, pvt. 4-23-62. Twenty-five years old. Present 2-63, 5-63. Captured 1-27-64, Sevierville, Tenn. POW Camp Chase, Ohio, Rock Island Barracks, Ill. Forwarded to Louisville for exchange 2-11-64.

Meggs, Joseph, pvt. 4-23-62. Eighteen years old. Horse valued at $170. Present 2-63, 5-63. Clothing issued 2-27-64, 6-15-64. Courier for Col. Crews 11 and 12-64. Present at surrender 4-26-65, Salisbury, N.C. Paroled 5-3-65, Charlotte.

Miner, Wiley, pvt. 4-23-62. Eighteen years old. Horse valued at $165. Present 2-63, 5-63, 12-63. Killed 7-22-64 near Marietta, Ga.

Mixon, James C., pvt. 4-23-62. Thirty-three years old. Horse valued at $155. Sent to Rome hospital 4-1-63. Absent at hospial 2-18-64. Absent, detailed to work in government shop 12-64.

Mobley, Eldridge C., pvt. 4-23-62. Twenty-five years old. Present 2-63, 5-63. Captured 10-24-62 Harrodsburg, Ky and exchanged. Captured 10-9-63 Sugar Creek, Tenn. US record shows captured 10-12-63 near Huntsville, Ala.

Mobley, Thomas P., pvt. 6-14-62. Clothing issued 3-27-64. Present 11 & 12-64.

Moon, John F., pvt. 4-23-62. Thirty-two years old. Present 2-63, 5-63. Captured 9-10-63 near Summerville, Ga. (Chickamauga) POW at Camp Douglas, Ill. Released 6-15-65. POW records describe as 5'5", dark hair and complexion, blue eyes.

Moon, W. W. L. "Lump," pvt. 4-23-62. Twenty-five years old. Horse valued at $180. Died in camp at Unionville, Tenn. 3-31-63.

Moss, Alfred, pvt. 4-23-62 / 5th sgt. Twenty-seven years old. Horse valued at $145. Died in Campbell County, Ga. 7-21-62.

Northcutt, Joseph H. pvt. 5-7-62, Eighteen years old. Horse valued at $160. Died in Campbell County, Ga., 7-13-62.

Parr, John A., pvt. 4-23-62. Twenty-seven years old. Horse valued at $125. Present 2-63, 5-63. Absent, left with wagons 11-63. Clothing issued 3-27-64, 6-15-64. Sent to hospital 12-5-64.

Phillips, Joshua, pvt. 4-23-62. Twenty-four years old. Horse valued at $90. Present 2-63, 5-63, 6-63, 12-63 also shown on "extra duty as teamster" 5 and 6-63. Roll of 12-64 shows AWOL since 6-10-64.

Perryman, John H., pvt. 4-23-62. Twenty-six years old. Horse valued at $120. Present 2-63, 5-63. Shown as "deserted" 1-64 but present 11 and 12-64.

Pool, E. M., sgt. Captured 5-18-65 Augusta, Ga.

Richardson, H. E., pvt. Roll of 12-64 shows AWOL since 1-10-64. Appears on U.S. roll of "Deserters from the Rebel Army" 4-27-64. Took oath of allegiance to U.S. and released north of Ohio River.

Richardson, Ira J., pvt. 11-22-63. Enlisted at Palmetto, Ga. Clothing issued 6-15-64. Captured 12-4-64 at Waynesboro, Ga. Exchanged 2-18-65.

Roberts, James, pvt. 8-20-64. Enlisted at Palmetto, Ga.

Shell, John R. H., pvt. 4-23-62. Horse valued at $120. Died 11-5-62 Kingston, Tenn. Widow Elizabeth filed death claim 4-25-64.

Shipp, John T., pvt. 5-14-62. Present 2-63, 5-63. Clothing issued 3-27-64. Roll of 11 and 12-64 shows AWOL since 6-20-64.

Stiles, John L., pvt. 4-23-62. Horse valued at $160. Present 2-63, 5-63. Present "in arrest" 2-18-64. Clothing issued 3-27-64. Present 11 and 12-64.

Stiles, Simeon, pvt. 4-23-62. Horse valued at $200. Absent, at hospital 7-62. "Discharge recommended."

Steed, William H., pvt. Twenty-four years old. Present throughout '63. Present 12-64. Present at surrender 4-26-65, paroled 5-3-65, Charlotte, N. C.

Steed, Franklyn H., pvt. 4-23-62. Eighteen years old. Horse valued at $185. Present throughout '63. Clothing issued 3-27-64. Present 6 through 12-64.

Tarrance, John W., pvt. 4-23-62. Twenty-five years old. Horse valued at $140. Sent to Atlanta hospital 3-20-63. Present 2-18-64. Clothing issued 3-27-64. Detached as teamster, 6 through 9-64.

Thropshire, Andrew J., pvt. 4-23-62. Eighteen years old.

Thropshire, John, pvt. 4-23-62. Twenty-two years old.

Turner, R. A., pvt. 5-14-62. Roll of 5-63 shows "Detached by Lt. Col J E Dunlop Mch 63, to get-up Deserters & recruits." Roll of 2-18-64 shows absent, in hospital since 11-1-63. Clothing issued 3-27-64. Roll of 12-64 shows "detached as scout for Gen. Hood" since 6-64.

Varner, Thomas H., pvt. 4-23-62. Thirty-two years old. Horse valued at $155. To hospital in Atlanta 4-10-63. Captured 9-1-64 near Nashville, Tenn. U.S. record shows captured at LaVergne. POW at Camp Chase. Released 6-11-65. Described as 5'2" blue eyes, black hair.

Vaughn, Randolph, pvt. 5-1-62. Twenty-nine years old. Horse valued at $160. Roll of 5-63 shows sent to Atlanta hospital. Present 6 through 12-63. Clothing issued 3-27-64, 6-15-64. Wounded at Waynesboro, Ga. 12-64.

Vickers, Andrew J., pvt. 4-23-62. "Left with wagons" 11-11-63. Clothing issued 3-27-64. Present 11 & 12-64 as

"forage master." Present at surrender 4-26-65, paroled 5-3-65, Charlotte, N. C.

Weaver, D. C., 5th sgt./pvt. Twenty-five years old. Horse valued at $200. Present 2 and 5-63 as private. Roll of 12-63 shows "absent with brigade wagons in arrest." Clothing issued 3-27-64. Captured 10-26-64 Gwinnett, Co., Ga. POW at Camp Douglas in Chicago, Ill. Also shown in H Company.

Westbrook, Gainey, pvt. 12-1-62/ord sgt. 5-1-63/pvt. Enlisted at Nolensville, Tenn. Promoted to brigade ord. sgt. 5-1-63. Roll of 12-63 shows detached as "forage master" as private. Clothing issued 3-27-64, 6-15-64, as private. **Whitaker, William,** pvt. 12-4-62. Substitute for W. Gibbs. Present 2-63, 5-63. Roll of 2-18-64 shows absent, sick in hospital. Clothing issued 3-27-64.

Wilkerson, William, pvt. 4-23-62. Thirty-one years old. Horse valued at $135. Present through '63. Roll of 12-64 shows absent, sick since 5-64.

Wilkins, Henry. May be same man as W. H. Wilkins below.

Wilkins, W. H., pvt. 4-23-62. Roll of 5-63 shows "detached to work in Gov Shop in Chattanooga." Roll of 12-64 shows assignment to "Favors Mill in Fayette, Ga."

Williams, A. C., pvt. 5-20-64. Present 11 and 12-64.

Williams, Thomas E., pvt. 4-23-62. Eighteen years old. Horse valued at $175. Present 2-63, 5-63. Captured 6-10-63 Unionville, Tenn. U.S. record shows captured 6-23-63 Manchester or Roverville.

Yates, Elijah E. M., pvt. 4-23-62. Twenty-three years old. Horse valued at $150. Present 2-63, 5-63. "Left with wagons" 11-63. Clothing issued 3-27-64. Present 11 and 12-64.

K COMPANY

Dunlop, James E., capt. 4-12-62/lt. col. 11-7-62. Twenty-nine years old. Two horses valued at $200 and $225. Promoted to regimental commander. On roster of Wharton's cavalry, 12-10-62 and 1-29-63, list of officers disabled by wounds, well qualified officer, habits steady," "intermittent fever". Resigned 3-19-63. Certified with rheumatic…and chronic laryngitis.

Butts, James A., 1st lt/capt. Succeeded Dunlop as company commander.Resigned 8-63.

Barber, Jesse M., 1st lt. 5-5-62. Horse valued at $1,800. AWOL 11 and 12-64. Present at surrender 4-26-65 Salisbury, N.C.

Carruthers, William, 2nd lt. 5-5-62. Thirty-five years old. Horse valued at $290. Captured 12-26-62 near Nolensville, "fight at Mossy Creek." U.S. record shows captured 12-29-62 Stones River. Died 4-21-64 of pneumonia as POW.

Wilson, Jesse, Bvt. 2nd lt. 3-10-62/1st lt. Thirty-one years old. Horses valued at $285 and $200. Captured 5-22-63 "while on a scout" near Hoovers' Gap, Tenn. POW at Ft. Delaware. Transferred to City Point, Md. for exchange, 2-24-65.

Swicord, Michael, pvt. 3-10-62/bvt. 2nd lt. 11-62. Twenty-nine years old. Horse valued at $185. Present 11 and 12-63. Clothing issued 3-27-64. Resigned 7-19-64.

Wimberly, John T., 2nd lt.

Curry, Joshua C., 1st sgt. 3-10-62. Wounded 10-14-63 near McMinnville, Tenn. Sent to hospital. Among troops surrendered by Gen. Sam Jones 5-10-65 Tallahassee, Fla. to Gen. McCook.

Neal, Thomas J., 2nd sgt. 3-15-62. Prior service as sergeant in Ramsey's Ga. Infantry. Twenty-six years old. Horse valued at $250. Present 2-63, 5-63. On "extra duty" as teamster 9-1-63 through 9-30-63. Clothing issued 3-27-64. Present 12-64.

Edwards, John G.M., sgt. 4-12-62. Thirty-three years old. Horse valued a $275. In hospital at Atlanta 12-20-62.

Belcher, Abram B., sgt. 4-12-62. In hospital 9-20-63. On "retired list" 12-64. Medical examining board certified disability from chronic "nephritis."

Connell, Rufus A., cpl. 4-26-62. Roll of 12-31-64 shows "discharged."

Knight, John W., cpl. 3-10-62. Twenty-eight years old. Horse valued at $150. Wounded 12-31-62 at Stones River. Taken prisoner and died 1-12-63.

Adams, Francis M., pvt / 5-7-62. AWOL 7-24-63. Surrendered by Gen. Sam Jones 5-10-65 Tallahassee, Fla. to Gen. McCook. Paroled 5-12-65 Albany, Ga.

Adams, John H., pvt. 5-5-62. Bugler. AWOL 12-64.

Adams, Robert A., pvt. 4-12-62. Absent sick 5-16-63 and 2-13-64.

Adams, R. E., pvt. Paid 9-62. Surrendered by Gen. Sam Jones 5-10-65 Tallahassee, Fla. to Gen. McCook. Paroled 5-12-65 Albany, Ga.

Barber, J., pvt. Twenty-two years old. Horse valued at $165. Present 2-63, 5-63. AWOL 11-64, 12-64. Surrendered with Gen. Sam Jones 5-10-65 Paroled 5-20-65 Bainbridge, Ga.

Belcher, E.S., pvt.

Belcher, David S., pvt. Twenty-five years old. Horse valued $225. Wounded severely in shoulder and captured 2-23-63 Dover, Tenn. Died at Fort Donelson 3-10-63.

Bennett, Randall F., pvt. 5-7-62.

Blount, James G., pvt. 5-7-62.

Blount, William, pvt. 4-9-62. Died 4-12-62 of pneumonia.

Bradwell Thomas M., pvt. 5-7-62. Present through 12-63. Absent 2-13-64 at wagon camp with disabled horse. Present 11 and 12-64. Present at surrender 4-26-65.

Bray, R. T., pvt. Captured 5-8-65 near Athens, Ga.

Brown, William G., pvt.

Butler, Thomas J., pvt. 4-26-62. Seventeen years old. Present through 5-63. Captured 9-13-63 near Sugar Creek, Tenn.

Chason, John, pvt. 3-10-62. Twenty-four years old. Sent to hospital in Atlanta 3-20-63. Present 12-63. Issued clothing 6-15-64. AWOL 12-10-64. Present 4-26-65 at surrender in Salisbury N. C.

Chester, James E., pvt. 5-7-62. Horse valued at $300. Died 6-18-62.

Chester, William A., pvt. 5-10-62. Twenty-six years old. Surrendered by Gen. Sam Jones 5-10-65 Tallahassee, Fla. to Gen. McCook.

Chester, William D., pvt. 3-10-62. Died 7-17-62 in Grundy Co. Tenn.

Craven, Thomas C., pvt. 3-10-64. Sent to hospital 10-30-62 in Atlanta. Sent to hospital 8-20-63 in Atlanta.

Creamer, W. A., pvt. 3-10-62. Substitute for T. J. Millirons. Present 5-63. Captured at Sugar Creek 10-13-63. Transferred for exchange 2-19-65.

Daniels, Albert W., pvt. 3-10-62. Twenty-six years old. Horse valued at $140. Sent to hospital in Atlanta 10-30-62. Absent sick 12-64. Captured 4-20-65 Macon, Ga.

Fain, Edward, pvt. 5-7-62. Horse valued at $175. Present 2 through 6-63. Captured 9-7-63 near Summerville, Ga. POW at Camp Chase. POW records show captured 9-20-63 at Chickamauga. Died 12-23-63 as POW, from inflammation of lungs. Buried in Chicago City Cemetery.

Fain, James A., pvt. 4-1-62. Twenty-one years old. Present 5-63. Captured 9-7-63 near Summerville, Ga. Also shown as captured at Chickamauga. POW at Camp Douglas, Ill. Apparently wounded, forwarded to Louisville for exchange, but died 9-19-63 before he could be exchanged. Grave 911 Chicago City Cemetery.

Fain, William E., pvt. 5-7-62. "Detached to Wheeler's Elite Corps" 5-8-63. Wounded 1-27-64 Sevierville, Tenn and died 2-1-64.

Franklin, John M., pvt. 3-10-62. Twenty-three years old. Horse valued at $150. "Killed at (Hoover) Gap, Tenn." Ellen Franklin filed a claim for back pay 11-26-63 which indicates that he died on or about 5-22-63 at Fairground Hospital No. 1, Atlanta.

Gaines, William A., pvt. 4-1-62/cpl. Eighteen years old. Captured at Stones River and exchanged. Present 12-63. Issued clothing 3-27-64. Surrendered 5-10-65 Tallahassee, Fla., and paroled 5-20-65 at Bainbridge, Ga.

Gauldins, Hiram F., 3rd sgt. 3-10-62. Twenty-six years old. Horse valued at $175.

Girtman, John W. D., pvt. 3-10-62. Twenty-one years old. Horse valued at $190. Present through 12-63. Issued clothing 3-27-64, 6-15-64. AWOL 12-31-64.

Gist, John D., pvt. Enlisted at Rocky Mount.

Godwin, John, pvt. 3-10-62. Twenty-one years old. Horse valued at $260.

Godwin, Valentine, pvt. 5-5-62/sgt. Thirty years old. Horse valued at $180. Present 5-63. Issued clothing 3-27-64. Roll of 6-1-64 shows AWOL. Promoted to sergeant 11-24-64. Surrendered 5-10-65 Tallahassee, Fla., and paroled 5-24-65.

Goodrich, V., pvt./sgt. May be same as Valentine Godwin above.

Griffin, Thomas J., pvt. 3-17-62/cpl/2nd lt. 8/1/64. Twenty-one years old. Horse valued at $225. Present 12-63. Elected 2nd lieutenant. Horse valued at $1800. Issued clothing 3-27-64. Surrendered 5-10-65 Tallahassee, Fla., and paroled 5-17-65.

Hahn, Moritz, pvt. 3-10-62. Forty years old, also shown as 47 years old. "Re-enlisted in 1st Ga. Regiment." Later captured in Tucker Co., Va.

Holloway, John W., pvt.

Harrell, Jacob, pvt. 4-12-62. Seventeen years old. Horse valued at $185. "Re-enlisted in 1st Ga. Regiment." Roll of 5-63 shows "Illegally transferred to the 5th Ga. Cavalry by Capt. J. A.Butts." AWOL on roll of 12-31-63. Captured 11-22-63 Larkinsville, Ala.

Harris, John F., pvt. 3-10-62. Thirty years old. Horse valued at $285. Died 2-2-63 or 2-28-63.

Harris, Solomon, pvt. 3-10-62. Twenty-nine years old. Horse valued at $200. Present 5-63. AWOL 11 and 12-63. Issued clothing 3-27-64. Captured 7-21-64 near Atlanta. POW at Camp Chase. Transferred to City Point for exchange 3-4-65.

Holloway, John W., pvt. 3-19-62. Twenty-eight years old. Horse valued at $200. Captured 12-26-62 at Stones River, exchanged and rejoined command. Present 5-63, 12-63. Issued clothing 3-27-64, 6-15-64. Captured 7-21-64 near Atlanta. POW at Camp Chase. Released 6-11-65.

Holsey, William G., pvt. 5-3-62. Twenty-four years old. Horse valued at $200. Sent to hospital in Atlanta 1-20-63. Absent, in hospital 12-63.

Howard, Auren, pvt. 3-10-62. Thirty-one years old. Horse valued at $275. Present 12-63. Issued clothing 3-27-64 and 6-15-64. Roll of 12-31-64 shows AWOL since 11-15-64.

Hutchinson, William J., pvt. 3-10-62. Twenty-five years old. Horse valued at $100.

Johnson, Cary, pvt. Thirty years old. Horse valued at $145. "Discharged by reason of disability" 3-10-63.

Johnson, Henry T., pvt. 4-8-62. Thirty years old. Horse valued at $180. Sent to hospital 9-26-63. Detached with regimental wagons 11 and 12-63. Issued clothing 3-27-64. Roll of 11 and 12-64 shows detached with Gen. Iverson.

Jones, Henry, pvt. 3-10-62. Thirty-one or thirty-four years old. Horse valued at $225. Died 4-13-62 of pneumonia at Camp Stephens.

Keiser, Levi F., pvt. Appears on roll of POWs paroled 10-28-62 at Beech Fork, Ky.

Knight, John M., pvt. 3-10-62. Thirty-seven years old. Horse valued at $165. AWOL 8-31-63. Present 11 and 12-64. Surrendered 5-10-65 Tallahassee, Fla., and paroled 5-18-65 Thomasville, Ga. 5'5" dark hair, blue eyes.

Knight, John W., cpl. 3-10-62. Twenty-eight years old. Horse valued at $150. Wounded 12-31-62 Stones River. Taken prisoner and died 1-12-63.

Love, Duncan S., pvt. 3-10-62. Twenty-nine years old. Horse valued at $175. Also shown in C Co. Present 5-63, 12-63, 5-64, 12-64. Surrendered 5-10-65 Tallahassee, Fla. Paroled 5-17-65 Albany, Ga.

Mann, Israel, pvt. 3-10-62. Thirty years old. Horse valued at $165. Roll of 5-63 shows absent "supposed to be taken prisoner" 4-24-63.

Mann, Thomas, pvt. 3-10-62/ord. sgt. 1-6-64. Thirty-five years old. Horse valued at $275. Present 2-63, 5-63. Present 11 and 12-64 with horse valued at $1,800.

Maxwell, Daniel, pvt. 3-10-62. Twenty-seven years old. Horse valued at $250. Captured 12-29-62 Stones River. POW record shows 5'11" dark hair, gray eyes. Exchanged and rejoined command. Roll of 2-13-64 shows absent at wagon camp without horse. Issued clothing 3-27-64, 6-15-64. Present 11 and 12-64 with horse valued at $2,000. Surrendered 5-10-65, Tallahassee with Gen. Sam Jones, CSA. Paroled 5-12-65.

Maxwell, G. W. , pvt. 3-10-62. Eighteen years old. Horse valued at $150.

Maxwell, H. M., pvt. Appears on register of Floyd House and Ocmulgee Hospitals, Macon, Ga. 12-19-64 as member of Crews' Brigade with comment: "Ball entered neck 4" below right ear and emerged to the left of cervical vertebrae, causing partial paralysis of right upper extremity."

Maxwell, M. A., pvt. 3-10-62/ 5th sgt. Present as pvt 5-63. Wounded at Mossy Creek, Tenn. 12-29-63. Absent as sgt. 2-64. "Wounded and sent to hospital Bulls Gap, Tenn." 2-4-64. Present 11 and 12-64. Surrendered 5-10-65 Tallahassee, Fla. with Gen. Sam Jones, CSA.

Maxwell, Richard M., cpl. 3-10-62/pvt. Twenty-nine years old. Horse valued at $115. Present 2 and 5-63 as pvt. Issued clothing 3-27-64. Wounded 7-21-64 at Atlanta. Surrendered 5-10-65 Tallahassee, Fla. with Gen. Sam Jones, CSA. Paroled 5-20-65 Albany, Ga.

McElvy, G.A., pvt. 3-10-62. Eighteen years old. Horse valued at $190. Substitute for H. L. McElvy. Present 2-63, 5-63. Absent, at wagons with disabled horse 2-13-64. Issued clothing 3-27-64, 6-15-64. Present 12-64. Surrendered 5-10-65, Tallahassee, Fla. with Gen. Sam Jones, CSA. Paroled 5-19-65. Federal record shows 5'10" light hair, gray eyes, light complexion.

McElvy, H. L., pvt. 4-1-63. Furnished substitute and discharged.

McFadgen, Neil D., pvt. 3-10-62. Twenty-five years old. Horse valued at $150. Died 3-29-62 of pneumonia.

Mock, Chesley, pvt. 4-28-62. Thirty-two years old. Horse valued at $150.

Mock, Harmon "Harry", pvt. 3-10-62. Twenty-six years old. Horse valued at $225. Transferred to Capt. White's Horse Artillery 12-24-62. Apparently transferred to 5th Ga. Infantry 2-21-63.

Phillips, Joseph, pvt. 4-1-62. Twenty years old. Horse valued at $225. Present 2-63, 5-63, 11 and 12-63. "Pay due as co. blacksmith" from 8-1-63 to 2-1-64. Clothing issued 3-27-64, 6-15-64. Present 11 & 12-64. Surrendered 5-10-65 Tallahassee, Fla. Paroled 5-20-65 Bainbridge, Ga.

Pierce, William W., pvt. 4-8-62 / cpl. / 5th sgt. / pvt. 12-24-64. Eighteen years old. Horse valued at $160. Present 2-63, and as cpl 5-63, 11 and 12-63. Clothing issued 3-27-64. Horse valued at $1500. "AWOL & reduced to ranks."

Porkan, J. P., pvt. Captured 5-8-65 Hartwell, Ga.

Reid, D. W., pvt. 3-10-62. Thirty-five years old. Horse valued at $275.

Robinson, John J., pvt. 4-28-62. Twenty-one years old. Horse valued at $200. Present 2-63, 5-63. Wounded 12-29-63 Mossy Creek, Tenn. and sent to hospital at Bulls Gap. Clothing issued 6-15-64. Present 12-64.

Sanders, John L., pvt. 3-10-62. Twenty-two years old. Horse valued at $165. Present 2-63, 5-63, 11-63, 12-63. Clothing issued 3-27-64. Roll of 12-64 shows absent, sick. Surrendered 5-10-65, Tallahassee, Fla.

Sanders, Thomas D., 4th sgt. 3-17-62/ pvt. Twenty-four years old. Horse valued at $100. Present 5-63 as pvt. Clothing issued 3-27-64. Roll of 12-64 shows "Detached with Gen. Iverson."

Shales, John, pvt. 3-12-62. Twenty-five years old. Horse valued at $160. Wounded 7-13-62 Murfressboro, Tenn..

Shaw, Robert, pvt. 3-10-63. Died 4-20-63 at Fairground Hospital in Atlanta, Ga.

Shuline, Moses, pvt. 3-19-62. Eighteen years old. Detached on commissary service 11-1-62. Roll of 2-13-64 shows AWOL since 9-10-63.

Smith, James T., pvt. 3-10-62. Twenty-five years old. Horse valued at $160. Detached with Engineering Corps 11-5-62. Sent to hospital in Atlanta 9-1-63. Admitted to Ocmulgee Hospital in Macon 7-31-64 with chronic rheumatism. Surrendered 5-10-65 Tallahassee, Fla.

Sparrow, John L., musician/ 3-10-62. Twenty-seven years old. Horse valued at $250.

Swicord, David, pvt. 3-10-62. Forty-three years old. Horse valued at $175.

Tait or Tate, Charles M., pvt. 3-10-62. Twenty-one years old. Horse valued at $165. Present 2-63, 5-63, 11 and 12-63. Clothing issued 3-27-64 and 6-15-64. Detached with Gen. Iverson 11 & 12-64. Horse valued at $2000. Surrendered 5-10-65 Tallahassee. Paroled 5-20-65 Bainbridge, Ga.

Thompson, John, pvt. 3-10-62. Twenty-three years old. Horse valued at $180. Died 3-1-63 near Murfreesboro, Tenn.

Thurman, Wiley A., pvt. 3-10-62. Twenty-six years old. Horse valued At $180. Present 2-63, 5-63. Roll of 2-13-64 shows AWOL since 1-14-64. Clothing issued 3-27-64. Captured 12-4 or 12-5-64 Waynesboro, Ga.

Trawick, Eugenius, pvt. 3-10-62. Seventeen years old. Horse valued at $180.

Wadwells, W. W., pvt. Captured 5-8-65 near Athens, Ga. by forces under Gen. W. J. Palmer.

Waldrop, James L. H., pvt. 6-16-62. Twenty-six years old. Shown as member of Capt. J. R. Butts' Co. Furnished substitute & discharged 12-24-62 at Nolensville, Tenn. Described as 5'7", black eyes, black hair.

Whiddon, John, pvt. 3-10-62. Thirty-three years old. Horse valued at $195. Present 2-63, 5-63. Rolls of 2-64 and 12-64 show detached to drive cattle for brigade 9-1-63. Present at surrender 4-26-65, paroled 5-3-65 Charlotte, N. C.

Whiddon, Mathew, 4th cpl/pvt. Twenty-five years old. Horse valued at $235.

Whitaker, Allen B., pvt. 3-10-62. Twenty-eight years old. Horse valued at $145. Sent to hospital in Atlanta 10-20-63. Clothing issued 6-15-64. AWOL 12-64. Present at surrender 4-26-65, paroled 5-3-65 Charlotte, N. C.

Williams, Thomas J., pvt. 3-10-62. Thirty-three years old. Horse valued at $215. Furnished substitute and discharged 6-28-63.

Williams, W. W., pvt. 3-15-62. Twenty-one years old. Horse valued at $230. "Re-enlisted in 1 Ga. Reg."

Wilson, John W., pvt. 4-28-62. Twenty-three years old. Horse valued at $130. Present 2-63, 5-63. Detached to drive cattle 9-63 through 12-63. Clothing issued 3-27-64. Present 11 and 12-64. Present at surrender 4-26-65, paroled 5-3-65 Charlotte, N. C.

Wilson, Thomas J., pvt. 3-10-62/ 4th sgt. Twenty-eight years old. Horse valued at $140. Sent to hospital 4-28-63 as sgt. .Discharged with disability 10-30-63.

Wimberly, Christopher C., 3rd cpl. Nineteen years old. Horse valued at $235. Roll of 5-63 "lost & supposed to be taken prisoner." Roll of 12-64 shows "Sent to Savannah he being dismounted by his horse being killed." Surrendered at Tallahassee, Fla. 5-10-65.

Worn, Stokley, C., pvt. 3-10-62. Nineteen years old. Horse valued at $150. Served as fairier. Sent to hospital at Chattanooga 4-28-63. "Reduced to ranks" 8-3-63 (implying rank higher than private). Absent, "on retired list" 12-64. Surrendered 5-15-65 Tallahassee, Fla.

Wright, Charles C., pvt. 3-10-62. Twenty-two years old. Horse valued at $165. Roll of 5-63 shows transferred to White's battery by order of Gen. Wharton.

Wyrick, G. W., pvt. 6-10-62. Attached to Wharton's scouts 5-63. Sent to hospital in Atlanta 8-31-63.

UNKNOWN COMPANY

Edwards, W. S., 2nd lt., Captured 5-8-65 near Athens, Ga. by forces under Gen. Palmer.

Elliot, W. A., capt. Captured 5-8-65 near Athens, Ga. by forces under Gen. Palmer.

Faircloth, S. pvt.. Surrendered 5-10-65 Tallahassee, Fla.

Freeman, Edmund J., pvt. Captured 1-20-63 near Cassville, Va.

Gordon, James J., pvt. Apparently captured at Lebanon Junction, Ky. Shown on list of POWs leaving Cairo, Ill. 10-25-62 for exchange.

Griffin or Griffins, James, Captured 1-10-63 near Windsor, Va. U.S. record shows as member of L Company, 2nd Ga. Cavalry. (No Confederate record of an L Company in 2nd Georgia)

Grimes, E.G., pvt.

Holman, William, pvt. Captured 5-8-65 near Athens, Ga. by forces under Gen. Palmer.

Hosley, H. J., pvt. Captured 5-8-65 near Athens, Ga. by forces under Gen. Palmer.

Lowell, J. H., pvt. Appears on list of soldiers surrendered 5-10-65 at Tallahassee, Fla. by Gen. Sam Jones, CSA. Paroled 5-20-65 Bainbridge, Ga.

McCall, J. B., pvt. Appears on list of soldiers surrendered 5-10-65 at Tallahassee, Fla. by Gen. Sam Jones, CSA. Paroled 5-16-65.

Newfor, P., lt. Appears on list of soldiers surrendered 5-10-65 at Tallahassee, Fla. by Gen. Sam Jones, CSA. Paroled 5-17-65.

Powell, S. J., sgt. Appears on list of soldiers surrendered 5-10-65 at Tallahassee, Fla. by Gen. Sam Jones, CSA. Paroled 5 - 1 9 - 6 5 Thomasville, Ga.

Reid, J. W., pvt. Shown on roster of POWs at Norfolk, Va. "captured 9-8-63." Died 11-9-63 of typhoid fever as POW at Point Lookout, Md. U.S. record shows as member of Company L, 2nd Ga. Cavalry. (No Confederate record of an L Company in 2nd Georgia)

Rice, Van A., 2nd lt., Captured 5-8-65 near Athens, Ga. by forces under Gen. Palmer.

Sedgwick, L. P., lt. Captured 5-8-65 near Athens, Ga. by forces under Gen. Palmer.

Triggle, B., pvt. Appears on list of soldiers surrendered 5-10-65 at Tallahassee, Fla. by Gen. Sam Jones, CSA. Paroled 5-19-65, Thomasville, Ga.

White, H. C., 1st lt., Captured 5-8-65 near Athens, Ga. by forces under Gen. Palmer.

Yates, H. M. C., pvt. Appears on list of soldiers surrendered 5-10-65 at Tallahassee, Fla. by Gen. Sam Jones, CSA. Paroled 5-20-65, Albany, Ga.

Bibliography

Alexander, Gen. E. Porter, "Longstreet at Knoxville" in *Battles and Leaders of the Civil War, Vol. III, The Tide Shifts.* Edison NJ: Castel Books, 1995.

Bales, Louella H. *Confederate Cavalry,* Jacksonville FL: 1989.

Beronious, George "Joe Johnston's Last Charge" in *Civil War Times Illustrated,* May 1996.

Blackburn, J. K. P. "Reminiscences of the Terry Texas Rangers" in *Terry Texas Ranger Trilogy.* Austin TX: State House Press, 1996.

Boon, Jennie Merritt *Reminiscences of My Father, Thomas Mickleberry Merritt.* Personal papers file, drawer 283, box 34. Atlanta GA: Georgia Department of Archives and History.

Bradley, Mark, "The Road to Bennett Place" in *Blue & Gray Magazine,* Columbus OH: 1999, Vol. XVII Issue 1.

Bridgers, Robert S. editor, *Confederate Military History* Vol. VII. Wilmington NC: Broadfoot Publishing Company, 1897.

Bunting, Chaplain B. F., memoirs, manuscript MSS#25-0567. Galveston TX: Rosenberg Library, 1862 -64.

Castel, Albert. *Decision in the West—The Atlanta Campaign of 1864.* Lawrence KS: University Press of Kansas, 1992.

Clayton County Historical Society. *Historical Bulletin #1 May 1963.* Atlanta GA: Georgia Department of Archives and History.

Clayton County tax and census records. Atlanta GA: Georgia Department of Archives and History.

Compiled Service Records of Confederate Soldiers Who Served in Organizations from the State of Georgia

Second Regiment Georgia Cavalry. Atlanta GA: Georgia Department of Archives and History, 1959. Drawer 253, boxes 82—85.

Confederate Claims Commission records. Atlanta GA: Georgia Department of Archives and History.

Confederate Soldiers Home, register of inmates, drawer 252, box 2. Atlanta GA: Georgia Department of Archives and History.

Connelly, Thomas L. *Autumn of Glory—The Army of Tennessee 1862—1865.* Baton Rouge LA: Louisiana State University Press, 1971.

Connelly, Thomas L., *Army of the Heartland.* Baton Rouge LA: Louisiana State University Press, 1971.

Corbitt, Lt. W. B. unpublished diary. Atlanta GA: The Robert W. Woodruff Library, Emory University.

Crute, Joseph H. Jr. *Units of the Confederate States Armies.* Gaithersburg MD: Old Soldier Books, reprinted 1987.

Curry, W. L. *1st Ohio Volunteer Cavalry.* Champlin Printing Company, 1898.

Davis, William C. *The Fighting Men of the Civil War.* New York NY: Gallery Books, 1989.
DeLeon, T. C. *Joseph Wheeler, the Man, the Statesman, the Soldier.* Atlanta GA: Byrd Printing Company, 1899.

DeVaughn, James E. *Reminiscences of Confederate Soldiers, Vol XIII.* Unpublished compilation. Atlanta GA: Georgia Department of Archives and History.

Dodson, W. C., editor. *The Campaigns of Wheeler and His Cavalry.* Jackson TN: The Guild Bindery Press.

Dowda, Pvt. Julius. Unpublished diary. Atlanta GA: Georgia Department of Archives and History.

Dyer, John P. *From Shiloh to San Juan—The Life of Fightin' Joe Wheeler.* Baton Rouge LA: Louisiana State University Press, 1941.

Elrod, Mamie. *Life as I Recall It, or Sunshine and Shadows on a Long Trek.* Unpublished memoir, @ 1941.

Evans, Clement, ed. *Confederate Military History,* Vol. III. Wilmington NC: Georgia Confederate Publishing Co., 1897.

Evans, David *Sherman's Horsemen, Union Cavalry Operations in the Atlanta Campaign.* Bloomington IN: Indiana University Press, 1996.

Georgia Roster Commission of 1903. Atlanta GA: Georgia Department of Archives and History. Box 79, Location 3297-13.

Gilbert, Gen. Charles C. "On the Field of Perryville" in *Battles and Leaders of the Civil War, Vol III.* Edison NJ: Castle Books, 1995.

Hafendorfer, Kenneth A. *They Died by Twos and Tens—The Confederate Cavalry in the Kentucky Campaign of 1862.* Louisville KY: KH Press, 1995.

Henry, Robert Selph *Nathan Bedford Forrest—First with the Most.* New York NY: Bobbs-Merrill Company, 1941.

Hill, Daniel H. "Chickamauga—The Great Battle of the West" in *Battles and Leaders of the Civil War, Vol. III.* Johnson and Buel, editors. Edison NJ: Castle Books, 1995.

Hoeling, A. A. *Last Train From Atlanta* New York NY: Thomas Yoseleff Publisher, 1958.

Hood, John B. "The Defense of Atlanta" in *Battles and Leaders of the Civil War, Vol. IV,* Johnson and Buel, editors. Secaucus NJ: Castle Books.

Horn, Stanley F. *The Army of Tennessee.* New York NY: The Bobbs Merrill Company, 1941.

Howard, Gen. Oliver O. "The Struggle for Atlanta" in *Battles and Leaders of the Civil War, vol. IV, Retreat with Honor,* Johnson and Buel, editors. Secaucus NJ: Castle Books.

Hughes, Nathaniel Cheairs *Bentonville.* Chapel Hill NC: The University of North Carolina Press, 1996.

Hurst, Jack *Nathan Bedford Forrest.* New York NY: Vintage Books, 1994.

Johnson, Robert and Buel, Clarence, eds. *Battles and Leaders of the Civil War, Vols. III and IV.* Johnson and Buel, editors. Edison NJ: Castle Books, 1995.

Johnston, Gen. Joseph E., "Opposing Sherman's Advance to Atlanta" in *Battles and Leaders of the Civil War, Vol. IV, Retreat with Honor.* Johnson and Buel, editors. Secaucus NJ: Castle Books.

Kelly, Dennis *Kennesaw Mountain and the Atlanta Campaign.* Marietta GA: Kennesaw Mountain Historical Association, Inc., 1990.

Kennett, Lee *Marching Through Georgia* New York NY: HarperCollins Publishers, 1995.

King, William H. "Forrest's Attack on Murfreesboro" in *Confederate Veteran Magazine* Vol. 32.

Kingman, Robert H. in *Reminiscences of Confederate Soldiers, Vol. XII.* Atlanta GA: Georgia Department of Archives and History. Unpublished compilation.

Kniffin, LT. Col. G. C. "The Battle of Stones River" in *Battles and Leaders of the Civil War, Vol. III.* Edison NJ: Castle Books, 1995.

Lee, Angela "Tangling with Kilcavalry" in *Civil War Times Illustrated.* June 1998.

Longino, Hugh M. Letter to Miss Lillian Henderson, 10 April 1926. Atlanta GA: Georgia Department of Archives and History. Georgia Roster Commission File.

Maberry, Robert. *Handbook of Texas.* Galveston TX: Rosenberg Library.

Mathews, Byron H. *The McCook-Stoneman Raid.* Brannon Publishing Company, 1976.

McCollum, Pvt. Alexander S. "A True Story of the War" in *Reminiscences of Confederate Soldiers, Vol. XIII vol. 47 Part 1.* Atlanta GA: Georgia Department of Archives and History, 1932. Unpublished compilation.

McCollum, Pvt. Alexander S. "The Wagon Dogs" in *Reminiscences of Confederate Soldiers, Vol. XII.* Atlanta GA: Georgia Department of Archives and History, 1932. Unpublished compilation.

Minnich, J. W. "The Affair at Mays' Ferry, Tenn." in *Confederate Veteran Magazine,* Vol. 33.

Minnich, J. W. "The Cavalry at Knoxville" in *Confederate Veteran Magazine,* Vol. 32.

Minnich, J. W. "Freezing and Fighting" *Confederate Veteran Magazine, [Volume # ?]*

Moon, Pvt. John F. "Cavalry War Service" in *Reminiscences of Confederate Soldiers,* Vol. XIII. Atlanta GA: Georgia Department of Archives and History, 1932. Unpublished compilation.

Moore, Joseph H. H. *History of Clayton County, Georgia 1821—1983.* W. H. Wolf Associates, 1983.

O'Shea, Richard. *Battle Maps of the Civil War.* New York NY: SMITHMARK Publishers, 1992.

Personal Papers file. Drawer 253, box 30. Atlanta GA: Georgia Department of Archives and History.

Poe, Orlando M., "The Defense of Knoxville" in *Battles and Leaders of the Civil War, Vol. III, The Tide Shifts.*
(Edison NJ: Castle Books, 1995).

Pohanka, Brian C. *Don Troiani's Civil War.* Mechanicsburg PA: Stackpole Books, 1995.

Rodenbaugh, Theo F. *The Photographic History of the Civil War, Vol 2 The Cavalry.* Secaucus NJ: The Blue and Gray Press, 1987.

Ruhanen, Richard. "A Fighting Carpenter" in *Civil War Times Illustrated.* Ann Arbor MI: February 1996.

Sifikis, Stewart C. *Who Was Who in the Confederacy.* New York NY: Facts on File, 1988.

Starr, Stephen Z. *The Union Cavalry in the Civil War, Vol III.* Baton Rouge LA: Louisiana State University Press, 1985.

Smedlund, William. *Campfires of Georgia Troops 1861—1865.* Sharpsburg GA: 1994.

Tucker, Glenn. *Chickamauga—Bloody Battle of the West.* New York NY: Bobbs Merrill Company, Inc., 1961.

War of the Rebellion, Official Records of the Union and Confederate Armies. Washington DC: U.S Government Printing Office, 1898. Series I Vol. 4: Vol. 16 Part 1, Vol. 20, Vol. 23 Part 1 Part 2, Vol. 26 Part 1, Vol. 30 Part 1, Vol. 31 Part 1, Vol. 32 Part 1, Vol. 33 Part 2 Part 4, Vol. 38, Vol. 39 Part 1 Part 2, Vol. 44, Vol. 47, Series II Vol. 16 Part 2: Series IV Vol. 1, Vol. 17 : [pg. #]

Ward, Geoffrey C. *The Civil War, an Illustrated History.* New York NY: Alfred A. Knopf, 1990.

Welsh, Douglas. *The Complete History of the Civil War.* Greenwich CT: Brompton Books Corp., 1990..

Wheeler, Gen. Joseph. "Bragg's Invasion of Kentucky" in *Battles and Leaders of the Civil War, Vol. III.* Edison NJ: Castle Books, 1995.

White, N. C. "Through the Woods with Joe Wheeler" in *Reminiscences of Confederate Soldiers* Vol. XII. Unpublished compilation. Atlanta GA: Georgia Department of Archives and History.

Wight, Willard, editor *Reminiscences of Confederate Soldiers, Vol. VII.* Atlanta GA: Georgia Department of Archives and History, 1932. Unpublished compilation.

Wyeth, John Allen. *That Devil Forrest.* Baton Rouge LA: Louisiana State University Press, 1959.

Yeary, Mamie. *Reminiscences of the Boys in Gray.* Dayton OH: Morningside Press, 1986.

Index

D

Dallas, Ga., 122
Dalton, Ga., 117, 155, 159, 160, 189
Dandridge, Tenn., 106, 109
Darden, Pvt. Gus, 23, 26
Davidson, Maj. Francis M., 145-146
Davidson, Gen. Henry B., 90-92
Davis, Pvt. Addison, 37
Davis, Cpl. James I., 123,
Davis, Gen. Jefferson, 169
Davis, Pvt. James O., 126
Davis, President Jefferson, 188-189
Davis, Sgt. L., 132
Davis, Pvt. Lewis, 58
Dawson, Ga. 197
Dean, Lt. Thomas P., 8, 177
Decatur County, 9, 112
Decatur, Ga. 129, 130, 132, 134,
    139, 148, 186, 194
DeGress, Capt. Francis, 129
Denham, Pvt. D. D., 93
DeKalb County, 8, 154
DeVaughn, Lt. James E., 7, 9, 39, 40,
    92, 93, 195-196
Dias, Abraham, 178
Dibrell, Gen. George, 134, 182, 191
Dillon, Pvt. George, 179
Dirttown, Ga., 86, 154
Dixon, Pvt. Morris, 78
Dougherty County, 6, 7, 8
Dougherty Hussars, 5, 6
Dover Battle, 6, 75-77, 198, 200
Dover, Tenn., 75
Dowda, Pvt. Julius, 78
Dry Valley, 87
Dublin, Ga., 165
Duck River, 80-81, 91, 92
Duffield, Col. William, 19, 21, 25
Duke, Gen. Basil W., 45
Duke, Pvt. J. Francis, 88
Duke, Sgt. Thomas, 22, 26
Duke, Pvt. William, 31

Dunlop, Capt./Lt. Col. James E., 9,
    13, 14, 24, 53, 55, 77
Duren, Pvt. James, 93
Duren, Pvt. J.A.J., 93
Durham Station, N.C., 187, 188

E

E Company, 6, 7, 18, 23, 26, 31, 37,
    38, 39, 40, 42, 53, 74, 76, 78, 87,
    93, 98, 111, 117, 132, 170, 177,
    195
East Point, Ga., 133, 162
Eatonton, Ga., 145
Eberhardt, Lt. Col. J. B., 6, 13, 14
Ebenezer Creek, 171
Edisto River, 179,180
Edwards Ferry, 154
Elk River Bridge, 81, 82
Elliott, Gen. Washington, 104, 160
Ellis, Capt. James, 7, 113, 117, 177
Ellis, Pvt. William, 42
Ellison, Pvt. John A., 135
Elizabethtown, Ky. 35-37
Estes, Pvt. John, 135
Etowah River, 118, 122, 123, 154,
    157
Evans, Sgt. John, 105
Ezra Church Battle, 134

F

Fagan, Pvt. Edward, 111
Fain, Pvt Edward, 86
Fain, Pvt. James, 86
Fain, Pvt. William, 86, 112
Fairfield, Tenn. 78
Fair Garden Battle, 110-112, 200
Fambro, James F., 7, 39, 99
Farmington Battle, 91-92
Fayette County, 1
Fayetteville, Ga., 139, 140
Fayetteville, N.C., 182, 184
Farris, Pvt. F.M., 22, 26

I

Acknowledgements

A great many people provided help and encouragement to the author during the more than six years of research and writing this book. While some of these have faded from memory, I gratefully acknowledge the following:

- Bill and Pat Allen of Marietta, Georgia, for family historical information.
- Karen Berryman, Andrew College Library, Cuthbert, Georgia, for information on Col. Charles Crews.
- Peter Bonner of Jonesboro, Georgia for information on Clayton County history.
- Arthur, "Skin" Edge of Newnan, Georgia for information related to the Stoneman Raid.
- Staff at the Georgia Department of Archives and History for their courteous assistance.
- A. H. Hurd, III, of Marietta, for guidance on sources and research.
- Jim Minter, for identifying potential sources of information.
- Joe Mundy of Jonesboro, for recollections of Clayton County and family history.
- Sara Jane Overall, for indentifying sources.
- Gail Pitt, for family historical information.
- Sara Strickland Poole of Watkinsville, Georgia, for family historical information.
- Susan Poole, for proof reading and encouragement.
- Edna Simpson of Kennesaw, Georgia, for family historical information.
- Bill Smedlund, for guidance on research.
- Bill Strickland, for family historical information.
- Charles Strickland of East Point, Georgia for family historical information.
- Dr. Emory Thomas of the University of Georgia, for guidance and encouragement.
- Doris Strickland Wilcox of Franklin County, Georgia, for family historical information.

JRP